American Poetry 1946 to 1965

THE CRITICAL COSMOS SERIES

American Poetry 1946 to 1965

Edited and with an introduction
by *HAROLD BLOOM*
Sterling Professor of the Humanities
Yale University

CHELSEA HOUSE PUBLISHERS ◇ 1987
New York ◇ New Haven ◇ Philadelphia

Library of Congress Cataloging-in-Publication Data
American poetry 1946 to 1965.
   (The Critical cosmos)
   Includes index.
   Summary: Critical essays on the works of some twenty-
five poets, written after World War II. Includes poetry of
Louise Bogan, Stanley Kunitz, Elizabeth Bishop, Robert
Hayden, Sylvia Plath, and others.
   1. American poetry—20th century—History and
criticism. [1. American poetry—20th century—
History and criticism] I. Bloom, Harold.
   PS324.A42   1987   811'.54'09   87-5185
   ISBN 0-87754-953-2 (alk. paper)

R
811.5409
Blo

Contents

Contents *vii*

Editor's Note

This book brings together the best critical essays so far published upon the representative poets of the two decades 1946–1965, immediately following the conclusion of the Second World War. The essays are arranged here, as far as is possible, in the order of the dates of the poets' births. I am grateful to Daniel Duffy and Frank Menchaca for their aid in editing this volume.

In the Critical Cosmos series, this book follows *American Poetry 1915 to 1945* and precedes *American Poetry 1966 to 1986*, in which volume essays will appear upon the work of our poet laureate, Robert Penn Warren. Though Warren was born in 1905, and published his first book of poems in 1935, his best and most characteristic poetry began to be written in 1966, and was published from *Incarnations: Poems 1966–1968* onwards.

The chronological arrangement of these three Critical Cosmos volumes has the advantage of illuminating the dilemma of the American poets who achieved their prime in the two decades 1946–1965. They had the dark fortune of coming after the strongest grouping of poets in our literary history: E. A. Robinson, Robert Frost, Wallace Stevens, William Carlos Williams, Ezra Pound, Marianne Moore, T. S. Eliot, and Hart Crane. Even a secondary grouping from the same years remains formidable: H. D., Robinson Jeffers, John Crowe Ransom, Conrad Aiken, E. E. Cummings, John Brooks Wheelwright, Allen Tate, and the leading poets of the Harlem Renaissance, Langston Hughes and Countee Cullen. It seems clear that the poetic generation of Elizabeth Bishop, Theodore Roethke, Charles Olson, Robert Lowell, John Berryman, and their friends confronted an enormous anxiety of influence, an anxiety that only Bishop, in my judgment, had the full capacity to transform into a strength entirely her own. I would relate Warren's late emergence into his full strength to the same factor.

It is certain that the American poets of 1946 through 1965 were one of those unhappy generations we learn to call "transitional," with consequences that were frequently unfortunate, both human and to some degree imaginative. Despite the gifts of so many among them, I myself would place only Elizabeth Bishop in the high company of Robinson, Frost, Stevens, W. C. Williams, Pound, Marianne Moore, Eliot, and Hart Crane before her, and of Warren, John Ashbery, James Merrill, A. R. Ammons, and some others after her. Perhaps the generation of Roethke, Lowell, Berryman, Delmore Schwartz, Randall Jarrell, Weldon Kees, Anne Sexton, and others will seem some day like that other doomed generation that came between the High Romantics and the major Victorians: John Clare, Thomas Lovell Beddoes, George Darley, Thomas Hood, Thomas Wade, Hartley Coleridge—another dark, transitional grouping.

My introduction to this volume is confined to three of the poets: Elizabeth Bishop, the somewhat undervalued Louise Bogan, and the rather problematic (in my judgment) but widely esteemed Robert Lowell. Bogan's characteristic mode is explored also by Sandra Cookson, who finds that the poet was accurate in her insight that "the repressed becomes the poem."

The black poet Melvin B. Tolson was born in 1898, the year before Hart Crane, and wrote his principal poems in the late 1930s, but he is covered in this volume because most of his work did not appear until the 1950s. He is studied here by Robert M. Farnsworth, who emphasizes his relation as poet to Langston Hughes, and the common origin of their work in the blues tradition.

Yvor Winters, more renowned as dogmatic critic than as neoclassical poet, receives a just estimate from Robert Hass. Another poet better known for his other writing, the dance critic Edwin Denby, is given a brief, personal appreciation as a lyric poet of Manhattan by Lincoln Kirstein. A third figure certainly more renowned as critic than as poet, R. P. Blackmur, is surveyed by his biographer Russell Fraser, who provides a fairly generous view of Blackmur's rather limited accomplishment.

Richard Eberhart, who seems to me quite uneven but also undervalued, is briefly considered by Richard K. Cross, who emphasizes Eberhart's achievement as a war poet. In his essay on Louis Zukofsky's long poem, *A*, William Harmon portrays Zukofsky's *persona* in the poem as being that of the classic *eiron*: artful, objective, and wry. Stanley Kunitz is praised by Robert Weisberg as being a visionary nihilist in the mode of Yeats, yet somehow keeping to "the stubborn middle way" also.

Theodore Roethke, another inheritor of Yeats but also of Whitman, Stevens, and Eliot, is studied here in two essays, an overview by Charles Molesworth that attempts to defend him from the judgment that he was too derivative, and a subtler reading, by the poet James Applewhite, that relates him to Romantic tradition.

Sherman Paul and Calvin Bedient present complementary essays on Charles Olson, the first summing him up as a late inheritor of Thoreau, and the second finding his occasional strength to be lyrical, in defiance of his own overt poetics.

Elizabeth Bishop, the crown of this volume, is admirably analyzed in the essays of Bonnie Costello and David Bromwich, with Costello centering upon visionary landscapes and seascapes, and Bromwich on dream houses, those ramshackle structures that rise so precariously and so joyously throughout Bishop's most characteristic poems.

In an essay upon the epigrammatic J. V. Cunningham, Jack Hill reads that American ironist as a kind of Horace mixed with Martial, or a Roman born out of his own time. The very different Brother Antoninus (William Everson), a partisan of Robinson Jeffers, is praised by Paul A. Lacey for his intense sincerity, but nevertheless is rejected for his espousal of doctrine over poetry.

Robert Hayden, one of our most distinguished black poets, is studied by Wilburn Williams, Jr., as an admirable amalgam of Romantic symbolism and realistic history. The poignant David Schubert is appreciated by Irvin Ehrenpreis for his wit and pathos, while the more famous Delmore Schwartz receives the accolade from R. K. Meiners for having had the courage to disapprove of his own equation of consciousness with suffering.

John Berryman's *Dream Songs* are examined by Edward Mendelson, who finds in them intricate strategies for both presenting and defending a personal pathology. Diane Ackerman, in a broader overview of Berryman, regards him as a poet of metaphysical desolation.

A passionate defense of Randall Jarrell's poetic originality is made by Mary Kinzie, who goes so far as to assert that Jarrell was also a great psychologist. Weldon Kees, a poet I myself find more persuasive than Berryman or Jarrell precisely because he is a more original psychologist, is analyzed by Charles Baxter as a kind of ethnographer of the void. Anthony Hecht and Alfred Corn, accomplished poets of two later generations, contribute studies of Robert Lowell that are very much at variance with my introduction. Both of them commend his poetic career as exemplary, without quite specifying what it is in his actual work that will grant it an inevitable entry into the canon.

The early death by accident of Frank O'Hara places him in this volume, rather than where we all would wish him to be, in *American Poetry 1966 to 1986*, with his friend John Ashbery. O'Hara's verse is seen here by Thomas Meyer as a lyric precursor of much that was to come.

This book ends with two essays by the urbane and learned Richard Howard, poet and critic and one of the leading translators of our age. Anne Sexton and Sylvia Plath, victims and heroines of the confessional Muse, are presented by Howard with loving respect and consummate grace. Whether their poems will continue to hold the interest of generations to come seems to me problematical, but Howard makes the best case for them that I have encountered.

Introduction

The principal poets of Elizabeth Bishop's generation included Roethke, Lowell, Berryman, Jarrell, and, in a different mode, Olson. Whether any of these articulated an individual rhetorical stance with a skill as sure as hers may be questioned. Her way of writing was closer to that of Stevens and Marianne Moore, in the generation just beyond, than to any of her exact contemporaries. Despite the differences in scale, her best poems rival the Stevens of the shorter works, rather than the perhaps stronger Stevens of the sequences.

Bishop stands, then, securely in a tradition of American poetry that began with Emerson, Very, and Dickinson, and culminated in aspects of Frost as well as of Stevens and Moore. This tradition is marked by firm rhetorical control, overt moral authority, and sometimes by a fairly strict economy of means. The closing lines in *Geography III* epitomize the tradition's self-recognition:

> He and the bird know everything is answered,
> all taken care of,
> no need to ask again.
> —Yesterday brought to today so lightly!
> (A yesterday I find almost impossible to lift.)

These poignant lines have more overt pathos than the poet ever allowed herself elsewhere. But there is a paradox always in the contrast between a poetry of deep subjectivity, like Wordsworth's or Stevens's or Bishop's, and a confessional poetry, like Coleridge's or that of Bishop's principal contemporaries. When I read, say, "The Poems of Our Climate" by Stevens, or "The End of March" by Bishop, I encounter eventually the overwhelming self-revelation of a profoundly subjective consciousness. When I read, say, "Skunk Hour" by Lowell, or one of Berryman's sonnets, I confront finally an opacity, for that is all the confessional mode can yield. It is the strength of Bishop's tradition that its clarity is more than a surface phenomenon. Such strength is cognitive, even analytical, and surpasses philosophy and psychoanalysis in its power to expose human truth.

There are grander poems by Bishop than the relatively early "The Unbeliever," but I center upon it here because I love it best of all her poems. It does not compare in scope and power to "The Monument," "Roosters," "The Fish," "The Bight," "At the Fishhouses," "Brazil, January 1, 1502," "First Death in Nova Scotia," or the extraordinary late triad of "Crusoe in England," "The Moose," and "The End of March." Those ten poems have an authority and a possible wisdom that transcend "The Unbeliever." But I walk around, certain days, chanting "The Unbeliever" to myself, it being one of those rare poems you never evade again, once you know it (and it knows you). Its five stanzas essentially are variations upon its epigraph, from Bunyan: "He sleeps on the top of a mast." Bunyan's trope concerns the condition of unbelief; Bishop's does not. Think of the personae of Bishop's poem as exemplifying three rhetorical stances, and so as being three kinds of poet, or even three poets: cloud, gull, unbeliever. The cloud is Wordsworth or Stevens. The gull is Shelley or Hart Crane. The unbeliever is Dickinson or Bishop. None of them has the advantage; the spangled sea wants to destroy them all. The cloud, powerful in introspection, regards not the sea but his own subjectivity. The gull, more visionary still, beholds neither sea nor air but his own aspiration. The unbeliever observes nothing, but the sea is truly observed in his dream:

> which was, "I must not fall.
> The spangled sea below wants me to fall.
> It is hard as diamonds; it wants to destroy us all."

I think that is the reality of Bishop's famous eye. Like Dickinson's, its truest precursor, it confronts the truth, which is that what is most worth seeing is impossible to see, at least with open eyes. A poetry informed by this mode of observation will station itself at the edge where what is most worth saying is all but impossible to say. I will conclude here by contrasting Bishop's wonderful trope of the lion, in "The End of March," to Stevens's incessant use of the same figure. In Stevens, the lion tends to represent poetry as a destructive force, as the imposition of the poet's will-to-power over reality. This image culminates in "An Ordinary Evening in New Haven":

> Say of each lion of the spirit

> It is a cat of a sleek transparency
> That shines with a nocturnal shine alone.
> The great cat must stand potent in the sun.

Against that destructive night in which all cats are black, even the transparent ones, Stevens sets himself as a possible lion, potent in the light of the idea-of-ideas. Here, I take it, is Bishop's affectionate riposte:

> They could have been teasing the lion sun,
> except that now he was behind them
> —a sun who'd walked the beach the last low tide,
> making those big, majestic paw-prints,
> who perhaps had batted a kite out of the sky to play with.

A somewhat Stevensian lion sun, clearly, but with something better to do than standing potent in itself. The path away from poetry as a destructive force can only be through play, the play of trope. Within her tradition so securely, Bishop profoundly plays at trope. Dickinson, Moore, and Bishop resemble Emerson, Frost, and Stevens in that tradition, with a difference due not to mere nature or mere ideology but to superb art.

II

Louise Bogan is usually categorized as a poet in the metaphysical tradition or meditative mode, following Donne, Emily Dickinson, and older contemporaries like Eliot and Ransom. Yet, like so many modern poets, she is a Romantic in her rhetoric and attitudes, and her procedure at least tends towards the visionary mode, in the tradition of Blake and Yeats. Her best and most characteristic poems establish their structure by a conflict of contraries, akin to Blake's clashes of Reason and Energy and Yeats's dialogues between Self and Soul. As in Blake and Yeats, there is no transcendence of this strife in Miss Bogan's poems; it is not resolved in the traditional consolations of religious belief, or in the expectation of any permanent abiding place for the human spirit. The frequent fierceness of Miss Bogan's rhetoric proceeds from a bitterness born of the unresolved contraries, the demands of reason and energy, of limiting form and the exuberance of desire, for Miss Bogan is purely a lyrical poet, and lacks the support of the personal systems of Blake and Yeats, by which those poets were able more serenely to contemplate division in the psyche. Miss Bogan is neither a personal myth-maker in the full Romantic tradition, like her near-contemporary Hart Crane, nor an ironist in the manner of Tate, to cite another poet of her generation. The honesty and passion of her best work has about it, in consequence, a vulnerable directness.

The poems in this essay largely follow the sequence of Miss Bogan's *Collected Poems*, for the sequence hints at a kind of ordering, in which the unresolved contraries of the poet's world move towards a delicate and tentative balance. "Medusa" makes an effective introduction to the landscape of Miss Bogan's poetry. What is conveyed here is a sense of unreality pervading a desolation. The scene has a frozen-fast quality pointing towards the inner significance of the Medusa myth. The poem is altogether oblique in its presentation. What is offered is an image of the memory itself turned to stone, a hint of the theme of the rejection of nostalgia to be developed in the later poems.

"Men Loved Wholly Beyond Wisdom" is a gnomic parable, with overtones of the Blake of "Ah Sunflower!" and the Yeats of "Never give all the heart." The poem is a miniature dialectic, with the contrary statement rising from the sixth line onwards. The final figure of the cricket is a striking emblem akin to those of Blake's state of Experience. Lighter and still more laconic is the subtle lyric, "The Crossed Apple," with its flavor of New England speech. Here, in a poem "about" the co-existent contraries of the freedom and necessity of choice one can observe reminders of the archetypal apple-tasting in Eden, but we recognize a humanistic emphasis:

> This apple's from a tree yet unbeholden,
> Where two kinds meet.

The preceding poems are preparations for Miss Bogan's most ambitious poem, "Summer Wish," which marks the crisis and midpoint of her work. Here the influence of Yeats is explicit and acknowledged, with the poem's epigraph being the opening of the pastoral lament for Robert Gregory, "Shepherd and Goatherd." Two voices speak in alternation in "Summer Wish," with the passionate soul expressing its longings, and the observant self describing the phenomena of its mutable world moving slowly towards summer, the season desired by the soul. The two voices fail consistently to heed the other, in an extended ironic vision of the divided psyche.

The first voice begins by crying out for full rebirth, rejecting the spring as a false hope. The second voice counters by calmly describing the very end of winter, the first touches of spring. The first voice reminds itself that experience denies the reality of its full, earlier yearning forwards, and categorizes love as fantasy. The second voice moves on to detail the early growth of the signs of renewal. The first voice, reproving itself yet more harshly, rejects the saving grace of memory. The second voice describes early April, and the movement towards summer. The first voice increases in bitterness, expounding the contraries of passion. The second voice, as if almost in response, describes the meeting of two figures with a gradual revelation of the man of the pair. Half in response, the first voice rejects the self-comfort to be found by the pride of one's own solitariness. The second voice now ceases to be as purely neutral in its descriptiveness, and emphasizes the sensuous beauty still to be found in the fading of the day. The first voice, again turning from refuges, rejects the mind as comfort. The second voice describes the spring planting, with a new note of purposefulness. The first voice, in its final outcry, acknowledges that earth's year begins, and responds to it, defying itself and the past with wish and laughter, and finding in rock a symbol of ultimate desperation and yet a mode of heroic consolation. The second voice completes the poem with the Yeatsian figure of the hawk's flight as an image both of acceptance and of the effort to hold oneself open to experience:

> See now
> Open above the field, stilled in wing-stiffened flight,
> The stretched hawk fly.

"Summer Wish" is Miss Bogan's "Resolution and Independence." Her later poems either celebrate the consequences of having cast out remorse, or return to a fiercer, more impatient preoccupation with the self.

"Henceforth, from the Mind" is an exultant Romantic lyric, chanting in Yeatsian accents the greater sweetness that has flowed into the remorseless breast, and yet acknowledging with regret (as in the second stanza) the necessity for resignation to some permanent sense of loss. The Wordsworthian image of the sea-shell betokens a darker music of mature imagination, similar to the "sober-coloring" of the close of the Intimations Ode.

"The Sleeping Fury" renews the Medusa image in an address to the self as the soul's dark double, "my scourge, my sister," and ends in the deliverance of a fuller awareness of both self and soul. "Putting to Sea" praises the enterprise of entering the abyss of the self, the dangerous exploration of our darkness. "The Dream" is Miss Bogan's most dramatic and convincing portrayal of the split in the self, with its renewal of the ancient myth of the appeased fury. "Song for the Last Act" is a graceful parting poem, being both a love song and a ritual of acceptance. Read at the end, it serves to round off the record of a life of humanistic craftsmanship.

III

Robert Lowell's final volume, *Day by Day* (1977), has about it the particular poignance that attends a last performance, a display of things in their farewell. The book's most ambitious poem, "Ulysses and Circe," seeks to elevate heroic wryness into a kind of sublimity, as when Ulysses-Lowell observes of himself: "He dislikes everything / in his impoverished life of myth." But the poetic impoverishment becomes more the burden, throughout the volume, than does the overt sorrow of personal mythology. A curious flatness or deadness of tone, indubitably achieved by considerable artistry, works against the expressive strength of the poet's struggle with tradition. The best poems in the book, upon rereading, seem to me the last four, where the pathos dares to become overwhelming, turning as it does upon the poet's reading of his life's losses as being the consequences of his mother's rejection. Yet I am left uncertain as to whether I am not being moved by a record of human suffering, rather than by a making of any kind. Lowell prays for "the grace of accuracy" and comes to rest upon the poetically self-defeating question: "Yet why not say what happened?"

From *Life Studies* (1959) on, Lowell took up his own revisionary version of William Carlos Williams's rhetorical stance as a defense against his own precursors, T. S. Eliot and Allen Tate. This stance, which is in Williams a fiction of nakedness, becomes in Lowell the trope of vulnerability. The trope, once influential and fashionable, has become the mark of a school of poets who now seem writers of period pieces: the "Confessional" school of Anne Sexton, Sylvia Plath, the earlier work of W. D. Snodgrass, the later work of John Berryman. "Confessional" verse, intended to be revelatory, soon seemed opaque. One read a poem even by Lowell or Berryman and concluded that both poet and reader knew less about poet and reader than they did before the poem was written and read. By a profound paradox, it became clear that a guarded, reticent meditation like Stevens's "The Poems of Our Climate" could yield endless knowledge of both the poet and oneself, whereas Lowell's overtly candid "Waking in the Blue" or "Man and Wife" simply impoverished all knowing whatsoever.

Time therefore seems to have darkened Lowell's aura in the decade since his death. Elizabeth Bishop is now firmly established as the enduring artist of Lowell's generation, since the canonical sequence of our poetry seems to many among us, myself included, to move from Stevens through Bishop on to James Merrill and John Ashbery, whose extraordinary works of the last decade are a range beyond anything in Lowell or Berryman. Lowell's legacy continues in the verse of poets as diverse as Adrienne Rich and Allen Grossman, but counts perhaps for rather less than seemed likely a decade ago.

Lowell's early poems, in *Land of Unlikeness* (1944) and *Lord Weary's Castle* (1946), would appear to be the most authentic expressions of his characteristic sensibility. The "fierce Latinity" of Allen Tate reverberates in these Eliotic poems, written and published in the heyday of the New Criticism, the Eliot-inspired, neo-Christian, ironic formalism of Tate, Cleanth Brooks, Robert Penn Warren, R. P. Blackmur, and the other mandarins of an anti-Romantic polemical sect. The early Lowell is the most considerable of the poets schooled by the New Critics into a verse tense with impasse, deploring the present and celebrating an imaginative past that excluded Wordsworth and Whitman, the actual founders of modern Anglo-American poetry. Setting the remote figure of John Donne over the perpetual immediacy of William Wordsworth, echoing the diction and cadences of the self-baffled Gerard Manley Hopkins rather than the prophetic rhetoric of Walt Whitman, Lowell arrived at a mode queerly similar, as David Bromwich has observed, to the American metaphysical verse of the Puritan Edward Taylor, whose courageous attempt to accommodate a baroque sensibility to the American wilderness finds a late, plangent echo in the Boston apocalypses of *Lord Weary's Castle*.

I remember once remarking to Lowell that my favorite among his earlier poems was "The Drunken Fisherman," an observation that did not please him, but forty years after first reading it, a return to the piece still finds it an eloquent and adequate reflection of the Jacobean temper of Webster and Tourneur as mediated by the revisionary ironies of Eliot and Tate:

> A calendar to tell the day;
> A handkerchief to wave away
> The gnats; a couch unstuffed with storm
> Pouching a bottle in one arm;
> A whiskey bottle full of worms;
> And bedroom slacks: are these fit terms
> To mete the worm whose molten rage
> Boils in the belly of old age?

All the benign charms of Eliot's visions of Sweeney or of Tate's "Æneas at Washington" are condensed into this New Critical performance piece. We have a portrait of St. Peter as Webster's Bosola and Flamineo or Tourneur's Vindice might have seen him:

> Is there no way to cast my hook
> Out of this dynamited brook?
> The Fisher's sons must cast about
> When shallow waters peter out.
> I will catch Christ with a greased worm,
> And when the Prince of Darkness stalks
> My bloodstream to its Stygian term . . .
> On water the Man-Fisher walks.

I think sometimes that my favorite couplet of and about the Eliotic school and its dilemmas must be this, from that pungent stanza:

> The Fisher's sons must cast about
> When shallow waters peter out.

The pun in "peter out" may stand as a representative instance of this school of wit.

The most ambitious poems in *Lord Weary's Castle* are the seven-part elegy, "The Quaker Graveyard in Nantucket," and "Where the Rainbow Ends," a vision of the Last Things. Rereading "The Quaker Graveyard" just now, on Martha's Vineyard, two hours by ferry from Nantucket, on a stormy day, I have conceived an esteem for the poem in excess of my previous judgment. Perhaps Lowell attempted too much in writing his own "Lycidas," so to speak, a little too early, and the excessive number of overt references to *Moby-Dick* insistently invite comparisons that do not make Melville shrink. But Lowell at least found fit matter for his baroque rhetoric:

> When the whale's viscera go and the roll
> Of its corruption overruns this world
> Beyond tree-swept Nantucket and Wood's Hole
> And Martha's Vineyard, Sailor, will your sword
> Whistle and fall and sink into the fat?
> In the great ash-pit of Jehoshaphat
> The bones cry for the blood of the white whale,

The fat flukes arch and whack about its ears,
The death-lance churns into the sanctuary, tears
The gun-blue swingle, heaving like a flail,
And hacks the coiling life out: it works and drags
And rips the sperm-whale's midriff into rags,
Gobbets of blubber spill to wind and weather,
Sailor, and gulls go round the stoven timbers
Where the morning stars sing out together
And thunder shakes the white surf and dismembers
The red flag hammered in the mast-head. Hide,
Our steel, Jonas Messias, in Thy side.

The last line, with its suggestion that the Eliotic school favored Jonah, more even as Messiah than as fleeing prophet, is not inaccurate, though the appropriation of Job's great trope of the morning stars singing out together is rather too bold. Lowell's early diction, rarely subdued, may be said to have attained its apotheosis in "Where the Rainbow Ends," not so much perhaps one of the poems of our climate as it is redolent of Eliot's ideological waste land:

I saw the sky descending, black and white,
Not blue, on Boston where the winters wore
The skulls to jack-o'-lanterns on the slates,
And Hunger's skin-and-bone retrievers tore
The chickadee and shrike. The thorn tree waits
Its victim and tonight
The worms will eat the deadwood to the foot
Of Ararat: the scythers, Time and Death,
Helmed locusts, move upon the tree of breath;
The wild ingrafted olive and the root.

As an instance of what must, I suppose, be called the poetry of belief, this is by no means wasted, since it does mark one of the limits of Modernist rhetoric in our time. If Eliot is, as I would suspect, the Abraham Cowley of our age, and Ezra Pound its John Cleveland or Edmund Waller, then the early Lowell may justly dispute with Allen Tate the position of our William Mason, once renowned for the vigor and flamboyance of his Pindaricks.

"The Repressed Becomes the Poem": Landscape and Quest in Two Poems by Louise Bogan

Sandra Cookson

Louise Bogan was an intensely personal poet whose poems were made from the most intimate material of her life: love, death, the mysteries of the unconscious, the terrors of mental illness, the ponderings of a subtle and analytical mind on the nature of life and art. But she was a personal poet who rejected direct autobiographical statement in her poems, except rarely and in the earlier work, and employed instead the obliquity of image used as symbol; who relied upon a symbolic language and the combined power of sound and rhythm and rhyme—form, in short—to convey meaning and emotion.

Although her poems are formal and symbolic structures, they cannot be separated from the most intimate psychological events of her life. For instance, in her poems that explore the unconscious in dream or vision and in her poems about sexual passion, images of a ravaged or hellish landscape symbolize the devastation of the psyche from assaults upon it by violently disruptive feelings which Bogan identifies as rooted deeply in her childhood. Archetypal images of the Medusa and the Furies, as well as a small gallery of more private myth figures, personify the poet's deepest fears and impulses. Thus, contrary to what one might expect from a poet who relies upon generalizing images such as these archetypal ones, and upon formal and traditional poetic structures, the urge toward the personal is always powerfully felt in Bogan's work. Her own brief remarks from a journal entry written late in life are of interest as the poet's view of the uses she made of her experience: "The poet represses the outright narrative of his life. He absorbs it, along with life itself. The repressed becomes the poem. Actually, I have written down my experience in the closest detail. But the

From *Critical Essays on Louise Bogan,* edited by Martha Collins. © 1984 by Martha Collins. G. K. Hall, 1984.

rough and vulgar facts of it are not there." The poet's conviction of absolute fidelity to her experience, although she has transformed "the rough and vulgar facts" of it, is a traditional aesthetic position, with moral overtones, of formalist lyric poets. Bogan's notion that "the repressed becomes the poem" is a kind of twentieth-century commentary on Wordsworth's idea of the poem as experience "recollected in tranquility."

The remark further illuminates the unique power of Bogan's poetry by providing an insight into her belief that the repressed material of her life was her true poetic raw material, that therefore true poetry comes from the unconscious, a belief she stated many times in reference to her poems. Bogan spent many years of her life in psychotherapy, but her greatest poems bear out the implication that her true access to "repressed" material remained largely a mystery of the poetic process.

Bogan's life and her poems are marked by two obsessions. The first is her preoccupation with a childhood full of half-remembered scenes of violence between her parents, which she focuses upon her mother. The second is her marriage to the poet and novelist Raymond Holden. Bogan left Holden in 1934 and divorced him in 1937, but his presence persisted in her poems. Both the poems and journal entires written late in life suggest that while Bogan probably succeeded in freeing herself from the Holden obsession, the terrors of her childhood remained with her to her death.

From her earliest poems to her latest, Bogan's landscapes and seascapes represent the poet's mental universe. Often they are the settings for journeys into the darkest regions of the self, undertaken in order to achieve peace through understanding. Understanding, Bogan hoped, would allow her to exorcise her personal demons, which she identified as hatred and sexual jealousy. Two of Bogan's most distinguished poems, "Putting to Sea" (1936) and "Psychiatrist's Song" (1967), complement each other as poems of quest and reconciliation. "Putting to Sea" concerns liberation from the violence of sexual jealousy and the rage which were exacerbated by the last years of the Holden relationship. "Psychiatrist's Song," looking back on that struggle from a distance of thirty years, celebrates the achievement of psychic equilibrium. Yet it still contains the haunting image of the damaged child, the victim of experiences too painful ever to fully come to light.

The sea voyage is the mode of these psychological and spiritual journeys, and Bogan signaled its importance in her work when she chose "A Tale" (1921) as the opening poem in her collected poems, *The Blue Estuaries* (1968). "A Tale," though it is not chronologically the book's earliest, is Bogan's prototypical voyage poem. In it, a "youth" prepares to relinquish the everyday world of time and flux ("the break / Of waters in a land of change") in search of something enduring, "a light that waits / Still as a lamp upon a shelf." The ideal country which he seeks will be an austere place "where no sea leaps upon itself."

The poet, however, tells us that the youth's journey will not bring him wisdom attended by peace and steadiness of spirit. If, indeed, he does journey far enough to find the truth, it will be just the opposite of what he has hoped for:

> But he will find that nothing dares
> To be enduring, save where, south
> Of hidden deserts, torn fire glares
> On beauty with a rusted mouth,—
>
> Where something dreadful and another
> Look quietly upon each other.

At the center of his universe, the youthful voyager will find nameless terror, corrupted love, and presences monstrous beyond his comprehension. This hellish landscape, populated by demons, will recur throughout Bogan's poetry as the terrain of the unconscious.

In "Medusa," written at about the same time as "A Tale," the speaker, paralyzed by the monster's gaze, finds herself suspended in a vast surreal landscape where she is condemned for eternity to watch "the yellow dust" rising in the wind. Another version of this hell is depicted in "M., Singing," written about fifteen years later, in which the song of a young girl releases the demons of the unconscious, "Those beings without heart or name," permitting them to "Leave the long harvest which they reap / In the sunk land of dust and flame."

Bogan was remarkably consistent in her use of a particular landscape with its cluster of images to signify an emotion or state of feeling. In the poems of her first book, *Body of This Death* (1923), passion is the "breeze of flame" ("Ad Castitatem") that consumes the field set afire and burned back to stubble after harvest. The image may originate in the agricultural practice of slash-and-burn, common in some tropical countries. The youthful Bogan lived in Panama for about a year with her first husband, and must have seen on many occasions whole fields set alight, the flames racing over the dry stalks. "Feuernacht" (1927) is a remarkably faithful depiction of such an event, while at the same time it clearly suggests the all-consuming power of sexual passion.

The blackened stubble which remains after the fire has burned itself out is a recurring image in these early poems, and signifies the woman's sexuality depleted by the fires of passion. The image belongs to Bogan's youth, and it disappears from her poems after the beautiful lyric of 1930, entitled "Song," in which the speaker attempts to renounce an impulse to sexual passion, claiming that she has long since paid her dues to it.

> Years back I paid my tithe
> And earned my salt in kind,
> And watched the long slow scythe
> Move where the grain is lined,
> And saw the stubble burn
> Under the darker sheaves.

Though it appears to have been Bogan's unhappy first marriage that gave expression to the pain of passion, the image of the young woman's sexuality as a "ravaged country" ("Ad Castitatem") carries over into the Holden years, where it is transformed into another tortured sexual landscape, the obscene and sterile tropical country of "Putting to Sea." Thirty years later in "Psychiatrist's Song," the same landscape recurs, but it is merely a dim shape on the horizon to the voyager now freed of the torments which it represents in the earlier poem.

In "Putting to Sea," the sea-voyage metaphor symbolizes the undertaking of a journey into the deepest self ("the gulf, the vast, the deep"), with the specific purpose of freeing the voyager from the obscenity of hatred. To accomplish this, she must confront it, and reject its temptations, which take shape in the poem's unnatural tropical landscape. "With so much hated still so close behind / The sterile shores before us must be faced."

The voyager, first of the poem's two speakers, is the conscious self and controls the narrative. "Who, in the dark, has cast the harbor chain?" she asks, as if the journey were compelled by a force beyond her will. The land she is leaving is the everyday world described in natural, cyclical images, which connect it to sensual experience, as these lines suggest: "Sodden with summer, stupid with its loves, / The country which we leave." Its counterpart in the unconscious is the tropical land, described by the poem's second speaker, the voice of the treacherous unconscious. The voyager, shunning all inducements toward the tropical shore, must journey into an awesome moral proving ground, the "bare circle of ocean," which is deep as heaven's height and "barren with despair." Later in the poem, the landscape of the quotidian, the sea, and the tropical shore will be joined by a fourth psychological country, which suggests the tender promise of childhood left unfulfilled.

The voyager understands that the second speaker's tantalizing descriptions of a gaudy and exotically flamboyant artificial land where "love fountains from its deeps" are meant to seduce her with false promises of love and fulfillment. The sly tone of this voice is supposed to conceal from her the true hideousness of the landscape:

> "O, but you should rejoice! The course we steer
> Points to a beach bright to the rocks with love,
> Where, in hot calms, blades clatter on the ear;
>
> And spiny fruits up through the earth are fed
> With fire; the palm trees clatter; the wave leaps.
>
> Fleeing a shore where heart-loathed love lies dead
> We point lands where love fountains from its deeps.
>
> Through every season the coarse fruits are set
> In earth not fed by streams."

The voyager is not taken in. She knows that this is really the landscape of madness. It is fiend's country, far more dangerous than the everyday world she has fled "where heart-loathed love lies dead." Bogan's specific reference is to the failure of her second marriage, to Raymond Holden, for which she was later to blame herself as a "demon of jealousy." In 1936, she wrote her friend and editor at Scribner's, John Hall Wheelock, that this poem would "sum up the Holden suffering, endured so long, but now, at last, completely over."

With the resumption of the narrative by the first speaker, following the passage just quoted, a new landscape enters the poem.

> Soft into time
> Once broke the flower: pear and violet,
> The cinquefoil. The tall elm tree and the lime
>
> Once held out fruitless boughs, and fluid green
> Once rained about us, pulse of earth indeed.

The "birth" of flowers, emblematic for Bogan of New England where she was born and raised, suggests her own "early time." These limpid and tender lines also contrast with the harshness of the preceding images. Moreover, "fluid green" and "pulse of earth" suggest a primordial condition that is full of promise, teeming with life, but unformed.

The potential of this tender land is not to be realized, however. With the contrasting landscapes as her psychological terrain, the first speaker traces the seeds of her destructive impulses back to her childhood: "There, out of metal, and to light obscene, / The flamy blooms burn backward to their seed." Childhood is a land of promise, but within its tender depths anything can take root. In her view, the compulsion from which the voyager now seeks catharsis stems from this time of unformed life, from her childhood.

The poet-voyager has set herself a hard task. Lacking even the celestial guides of the mariner, she wonders at the necessity of this dark and perilous journey:

> The Way should mark our course within the night,
> The streaming System, turned without a sound.
> What choice is this—profundity and flight—
> Great Sea? Our lives through we have trod the ground.
>
> Motion beneath us, fixity above.

"Putting to Sea" derives its power from the depiction of this moral/psychological deep. The descriptions of the great mythic sea and the stars have a silent and formidable grandeur, evoked equally by the bare, grand simplicity of the adjectives and the vibrations of a long tradition they set in motion. A line like "The streaming System, turned without a sound" is so suggestive that, while it is describing the absence of stars in the heavens, it evokes their presence by the infusion of light "streaming" produces. At the same time, the void and utter silence of these disturbed heavens must recall, in "turned without a sound," the ancient music of the spheres, so out of place in this poem where the heavens themselves conspire in the voyager's bafflement.

In the same letter to Wheelock, Bogan remarks on the poem's provenance. "I know what it's about, with my upper reason, just a little; it came from pretty far down, thank God." Bogan's comment states her conviction of the poem's origin in her subconscious, but it also suggests why "Putting to Sea" has such power; for in it resound echoes of the great mythic voyages which preceded it. The most reverberant of all is the quest of Odysseus. Dante provided Tennyson with the model for his Ulysses, and the opening lines of Bogan's last stanza suggest the spirit and tone of Tennyson's version of Ulysses' speech to his mariners:

> There lies the port; the vessel puffs her sail:
> There gloom the dark broad seas. My mariners,
> Souls that have toil'd, and wrought, and thought with me.

Bogan addresses her "mariners" with similar gravity: "Bend to the chart in the extinguished night / Mariners! Make way slowly; stay from sleep."

Bogan may also be indebted to Baudelaire, if not for the actual sea-voyage metaphor, at least for certain aspects of its treatment in "Putting to Sea." Bogan's voyager has a specific moral purpose for her journey into the unknown, while Baudelaire's persona is a restless seeker after experience. Yet both poets share the belief that truth may be found in the search for the self. Bogan's final line, "And learn, with joy, the gulf, the vast, the deep," is almost an imitation of the last two lines of Baudelaire's "Le voyage": "Plonger au fond du gouffre, Enfer ou Ciel, qu'importe? / Au fond de l'Inconnu pour trouver du *nouveau!*" While Baudelaire exhorts his voyager to experience for its own sake, Bogan urges the striving for understanding. Her final line reaffirms her conviction that suffering can be surmounted as well as endured.

The most contemporary voyage which "Putting to Sea" recalls is the brief echo of "Sailing to Byzantium" heard in the second line. The voyager wonders at the extraordinary journey she is about to undertake. "This is no journey to a land we know," she says, echoing Yeats, who also rejects the everyday world, remarking of it, "That is no country for old men." Each of these poems partakes of the common impulse to represent the human journey as a sea voyage. In "Putting to Sea," Bogan both epitomizes that tradition and creates a poem uniquely her own.

Early in 1967, thirty years after the publication of "Putting to Sea" and just three years before her death, Bogan sent three "songs" to *New Yorker* poetry editor Howard Moss, with the note that they "seem to go together . . . [as poems] of dream and aberration." A way to read the shifting and merging voices in "Psychiatrist's Song" is in the light of dream logic, in which identities are often fluid and interchangeable. Moreover, in the course of the long journey which psychotherapy was for Bogan, perhaps psychiatrist and patient each take on attributes of the other.

In a typescript of the poem, the only draft extant, the title reads "Psychiatrist's Recitative and Aria." The published version retains the same stanzaic divisions. In the poem's opening section, which would be the recitative, the psychiatrist begins his monologue, musing in a general way upon the persons who have played crucial roles in the lives of his patients, but of whom "they" (the patients) cannot speak directly: "Those / Concerning whom they have never spoken and thought never to speak." In spite of the psychiatrist's hint that patients deliberately conceal things, we may infer that the reason they do not have access to the whole narrative of their lives is that much of what is crucial has been repressed, and remains hidden in the unconscious:

> That place
> Hidden, preserved,
> That even the exquisite eye of the soul
> Cannot completely see.

From that generalized and somewhat rambling diagnostic beginning, the psychiatrist's attention soon settles upon particulars, and we realize that he must now be thinking of one patient:

> But they are there:
> Those people, and that house, and that evening, seen
> Newly above the dividing window sash.

At this point the narrative intensifies. Another voice enters, and from this moment to the end of the poem, the voice of the psychiatrist contains the voice of the patient. The sudden shift from generalities to particular details—"that house . . . that evening . . . the dividing window sash"— and the personal cry of anguish in the lines that follow, indicate that the point of view has shifted to that of the patient; yet there is no break in the narrative:

> The young will broken
> And all time to endure.
>
> Those hours when murderous wounds are made,
> Often in joy.

The images of the damaged child and the treacheries of passion recall major themes in Bogan's poems. As the recitative, providing exposition or background for the rest of the poem, this opening section, with its merging voices of psychiatrist and patient, is a poetic statement of the psychological traumas for which the journey of the next section was undertaken.

The second section, the aria of the typescript, begins with the line "I hear." The merging voices of psychiatrist and patient acknowledge the warning contained in the last line of the preceding section about the treachery of passion. The narration of the journey is taken over by the patient, whose voice dominates from now on, though the guiding presence of the psychiatrist is felt in the poem until the final stanzas. Since the patient is also the poet-voyager of "Putting to Sea," thirty years after, this "I" stands for the several selves of the poet. That she has absorbed the psychiatrist persona completely by the end of the poem suggests, perhaps, the health of the psyche achieved.

Although the old temptations to the evils of fiend's country are recalled in the opening lines, this tropical landscape is "far away" and no longer threatens the voyager. The old motif of sexual jealousy echoes mockingly in the three repetitions of "man"-words, probably a play on the free-associative technique often used in psychotherapy: "the *man*go trees (the *man*grove swamps, the *man*drake root . . .)." The reminder of the "clattering" palms from "Putting to Sea" fixes the identity of this receding landscape, hazy now, having lost its clear sense of evil. The voyager "watches" the thicket of palms—not even sure anymore that they are palm trees, "as though at the edge of sleep." Indeed, the narration of this section has the dream character of a perfectly sequential and straightforward presentation of fantastic events.

The voyager has now achieved such control and certainty that she can journey toward the once disastrous landscape represented by the palms "in a boat without oars, / Trusting to rudder and sail." The idea that the voyager is in control of the journey contrasts with the formidable voyage of "Putting to Sea." Moreover, the whole landscape has been scaled down from the enormous and overpowering sea and sky of the earlier poem to a size more manageably human. She now leaves the boat and walks "fearlessly" to shore. Previously, even the ripples of the shallows might have been full of peril, for the sea has, until now, been an awesome and uncharted place. The lines that suggest control over a sea which will bring the speaker to a place of repose are reminiscent of Eliot's "*Damyata:* The Boat responded / Gaily, to the hand expert with sail and oar," from part 5 of *The Waste Land*, in which the rain brings with it the possibility of the renewal of life and hope.

The dangerous landscapes of ocean and palm trees recede, and the voyager finds herself "on firm dry land," with the solidity of earth all around her. The last stanza banishes the old terrors of "flesh and of ocean" that were given full expression in "Putting to Sea." If the last stanzas also evoke death in images of imminence, darkening, and silence, it is death welcomed, celebrated even, as the final healing. We need not be troubled by the implication that the cure for human suffering is death. Bogan was sixty-nine years old and in failing health when she wrote "Psychiatrist's Song." It is nearly her last poem, and marks the very last time she would use the voyage metaphor to set down in a poem that long struggle with her private demons. The true between them was always, at best, a "troubled peace."

Bogan places a great deal of the burden for making the poem intelligible upon the reader. In "Putting to Sea" the poem's two voices were clearly separated. The voice out of fiend's country spoke a different language from that of the voyager or conscious self in the poem, and her speeches were set off from the voyager's narration by quotation marks. Bogan's decision to remove the recitative and aria directions form "Psychiatrist's Song" suggests a lightening of the poet's hand, a willingness to let the narrative take its own way.

Bogan takes more chances with language and form than she has done previously, and can risk beginning the poem with the halting awkwardness of a slightly pedantic and visually ungainly line. The play on "man" in "mango," "mangrove," and "mandrake," and the many irregularities in the free-verse line indicate greater flexibility and the freedom to experiment with the line and with the rhythms of common speech. The third line of the second section, with its truncated thought, "And the thickets of—are they palms?" is an illustration. And in the simple but strung-together statements of the line, "Coming to the shore, I step out of the boat; I leave it to its anchor," Bogan risks a kind of austere prosiness. In addition to its echoes of *The Waste Land*, "Psychiatrist's Song" is reminiscent throughout of Eliot's later poems of the 1930s, in particular "Marina" and "Coriolan."

The classical and formal Bogan still dominates in "Psychiatrist's Song," but her willingness to chance being prosaic places in relief the more poetically gorgeous phrases, such as "the exquisite eye of the soul," and the line with which she bridges the poem's two major sections, "Those hours when murderous wounds are made, / Often in joy." The elevated simplicity of the penultimate stanza is due in part to the extreme economy of the spare, predominantly one-syllable words. The luminosity of another late major poem, "After the Persian" (1951–53), glows for a moment in the final stanza. In the hortatory tone that is reminiscent of part 5, the "farewell" section of that poem, Bogan sounds again the note of sage or prophet, which is the final expression of her lifelong consciousness of herself as poet. Like "Putting to Sea," "Psychiatrist's Song" closes with an exhortation. But Bogan lowers the tone, and the moving prayer to earth, "Heal and receive me," ends the poem in an affecting combination of dignity and vulnerability.

The Literary Journey
of Melvin B. Tolson

Robert M. Farnsworth

Melvin B. Tolson's birth date, February 6, 1898, is not far from the birth date of the twentieth century. As a social activist, teacher, scholar, and poet Tolson was intensely self-conscious about positioning himself in the flux of history. Retrospectively it is clear that Tolson just missed some of the major fashions in cultural history. Born of the same generation of many of the writers of the Harlem Renaissance, he did not begin to publish until the 1930s. Later, absorbing the difficult theses of modernism of T. S. Eliot and the New Criticism, but very conscious of racial and cultural ironies, that distanced him from them, he worked out an extraordinarily complex style of his own, assimilating modernist techniques to the needs of black American experience, just as Eliot and the New Criticism began to wane as dominant forces in literary fashion. Such changes may have left him momentarily out of step, but Tolson's true place in literary history, the accuracy and penetration of his vision and the richness and technical mastery of his achievement, has by no means yet been carefully and thoroughly assessed.

Melvin B. Tolson's literary reputation depends principally upon his last published book-length poem, *The Harlem Gallery, Book I: The Curator*. In his introduction to *Harlem Gallery*, Karl Shapiro claims with much justice, "A great poet has been living in our midst for decades and is almost totally unknown, even by the literati, even by poets" Roy. P. Basler, writing eight years later, asks a rhetorical question, "What American poet will symbolize and represent our milieu to readers in the future, as Shakespeare represents the Elizabethan, Milton the Puritan, or, to come closer, Whitman the Civil War era?" He answers as follows:

From *A Gallery of Harlem Portraits by Melvin B. Tolson*, edited by Robert M. Farnsworth. © 1979 by the Curators of the University of Missouri. The University of Missouri Press, 1979.

It is not *The Waste Land* or *Four Quartets*, I think, which limn the present or light the future with the past so well that scholars salvaging libraries of this era may someday guess what manner of men were we. Nor is it even Sandburg's *The People, Yes*, nor William Carlos Williams' *Paterson*, but Tolson's *The Harlem Gallery*, rather, where the heart of blackness with the heart of whiteness lies revealed. Man, what do you think you are is not the white man's question but the black man's rhetorical answer to the white man's question. No poet in the English language, I think, has brought larger scope of mind to greater depth of heart than Melvin Tolson in his unfinished song to the soul of humanity.

These are extravagant claims, yet because Melvin Tolson's achievement is too little known and understood, their extravagance has not been, and perhaps at present cannot be, accurately measured. Critics and readers have been ducking the challenge of his work for years except for a few who have been willing to let loose some critical haymakers. Extravagant, perhaps. Yet these haymakers may well be right on the mark.

Harlem Gallery is an extraordinary poem that has not been adequately critically examined and evaluated in print. There have been several appreciative comments. And some useful attempts at explication. Among the most useful are Joy Flasch's chapter in her book-length study of Tolson and the unpublished critical edition of *Harlem Gallery* that Robert J. Huot prepared for his doctoral dissertation ("Melvin B. Tolson's *Harlem Gallery*," Ph.D. dissertation, University of Utah, 1971). Extensive critical scholarship will be necessary to fill in the lacuna between the modest critical efforts at explication and the extravagant possibilities that able critics and poets have sensed in the poem. Such criticism needs to be based on an understanding of the entire range of Tolson's writing, which covers a long period of literary and biographical history and which consistently challenges deeply ingrained but often unwitting racial and cultural biases of the American literary establishment.

The publication . . . of *A Gallery of Harlem Portraits*, Tolson's first book-length manuscript of poems, should significantly help scholar-critics to an understanding and accurate critical appraisal of Tolson's poetic achievement. This manuscript, probably completed about 1935, is Tolson's first attempt to put the life of Harlem into ambitious poetic form. It is a long but significant journey of intellectual and poetic development from this manuscript to *Harlem Gallery*, published in 1965. The latter is elaborately urbane and filled with esoteric wit, both learned and folk. The former is relatively crude, but often strong and immediate in its impact. *Harlem Gallery* is intricately organized. *A Gallery of Harlem Portraits* is loose and sprawling. *Harlem Gallery* probes with mockingly penetrating humor and irony into questions about the essential nature of man and the significance in his life of the concepts of race and art. *A Gallery of Harlem Portraits* presents brief dramatic portraits of life in Harlem much more simply and directly, without the elaborately reflective dialogues of characters such as the Curator and Doctor Nkomo. In *Harlem Gallery* Doctor Nkomo observes that "life and art beget incestuously." He and the Curator, the protagonist of the poem, like Ishmael and an African Socrates, lament and probe the cultural dilemmas posed by the aspirations and responsibilities of art complicated by the provocative absurdities and opportunities of being both African and American. Their dialogue is stimulated and pointed by the poems within the poem produced by the characters, John Laugart and Hideho Heights. In *A Gallery* the art of the poet is meant to be unobtrusive, only a facilitating agent for rendering the life of Harlem with dramatic intensity. *A Gallery* is much less cerebral, must less artistically self-conscious. It gives pleasure more simply and appeals more readily to a sense of social justice.

In 1930 Tolson began work on a master's degree at Columbia University. The stock-market crash of 1929 and the ensuing bitter economic depression were bringing down a fast curtain on the Harlem Renaissance. Much of the exotic glitter of Harlem as a fashionable playground for wealthy and sophisticated whites and as a promise of a quick and glamorous entry into the American Dream for blacks was wiped away. Harlem awoke with a proletarian morning-after headache. Harlem awoke with the blues. But the vividness of the good times and the promise of the twenties were not completely obliterated. They were too real, too close, to be forgotten. Harlem was still vital and full of ironies to be explored. In his master's thesis Tolson pays tribute to the writers of the Renaissance with whom he had become personally acquainted and who were in age his contemporaries. Claude McKay was nine years older; Rudolph Fisher, three; Eric Walrond, two. Sterling Brown and Zora Neale Hurston were one year younger; Langston Hughes and Wallace Thurman, two; and Countee Cullen, three. Harlem had embraced them all.

Portentous economic events had changed Harlem, but Harlem would always be the cultural capital of black America for Tolson. Hard times ironically brought Harlem closer to Tolson. Tolson maintained a teaching position at Wiley College throughout the depression, but his pay was always minimal. Sometime in the thirties, he actively organized sharecroppers, both white and black, in southeastern Texas. He protected his wife and family from the details of his activities, but they knew he was involved. His experiences with economic hardship and exploitation made him a Marxist. He read *New Masses* regularly, and he formed a close personal and professional friendship at Wiley with Oliver Cromwell Cox, who in his introduction to *Caste, Class, and Race* expressed his gratitude particularly to his colleagues: "Professors Melvin B. Tolson, Andrew P. Watson, V. E. Daniel, and Alonzo J. Davis." Probably just after completing *A Gallery of Harlem Portraits*, Tolson formed another close personal and professional friendship with V. F. Calverton, the radically iconoclastic editor of *Modern Quarterly* who published several poems from *A Gallery*.

Tolson himself has left a vivid literary description of the inception of
A Gallery of Harlem Portraits:

In 1932 [sic] I was a Negro poet writing Anglo-Saxon sonnets as
a graduate student in an Eastern University. I moved in a world
of twilight haunted by the ghosts of a dead classicism. My best
friend there was a German-American who'd sold stories to the
magazines. We read each other's manuscripts and discussed art,
science and literature instead of cramming for the examinations.
My ignorance of contemporary writers was abysmal.

One cold wet afternoon the German-American read my sonnet
Harlem cleared his throat, and said: "It's good, damned good,
but—"

The word "but" suspended me in space. I could hear the clock
on the desk; its tick-tock, tick-tock, swelled into the pounding of
a sledgehammer on an iron plate. The brutal words knifed into
my consciousness: "You're like the professors. You think the only
good poet is a *dead* one. Why don't you read Sandberg, Masters,
Frost, Robinson? Harlem is too big, too lusty, for a sonnet. Say,
we've never had a Negro epic in America. Damn it, you ought to
stop piddling!"

I placed the sonnet at the beginning of my thesis on the Harlem
Renaissance. Under the painstaking supervision of Dr. Arthur
Christy I had learned the beauty of the inevitable word.

At the end of four years and 20,000 miles of traveling and the
wasting of 5,000 sheets of paper, I had finished the epic *A Gallery
of Harlem Portraits.*

The sonnet Tolson refers to is not now included in the copy of his
master's thesis retained at Columbia University; however, there is not much
doubt that the Harlem of *A Gallery of Harlem Portraits* is bigger and lustier
than that described in the lost sonnet. It may be pretentious to refer to it
as an epic, as Tolson does above, but epic is what Tolson believed Harlem
deserved and *A Gallery* is unquestionably a significant step toward the
uncompleted epic that he ultimately projected almost thirty years later in
Harlem Gallery. Regrettably Tolson was able to complete only *Book I: The
Curator* before his death. Book 2 was to be titled *Egypt Land*; book 3, *The
Red Sea*; book 4, *The Wilderness*; and book 5, *The Promised Land*. After presenting the contemporary picture of Harlem in book 1, Tolson intended to
use the biblical metaphors claimed by black Americans for generations as
a narrative pattern to describe the hegira of blacks through the experience
of cultural dislocation and racial slavery to the promise of freedom and
cultural self-realization. The achievement of book 1 suggests that it would
have been an extraordinary epic indeed. Remarking on book 1, Tolson
indicates something of the larger schema he had in mind: "A poet, consciously or unconsciously etches the differentiae of his time. *The Gallery* is

an attempt to picture the Negro in America before he becomes the great auk of the melting-pot in the dawn of the twenty-second century."

Harlem was a seed that grew and flourished in Tolson's literary imagination. To indicate and clarify the stages of that development and the literary influences and insights that nurtured it with completeness is too ambitious a task for this afterword. But the importance of *A Gallery of Harlem Portraits* as a stage in this development can at least be indicated.

The seed's germination is evident in Tolson's thesis on Renaissance writers:

> Harlem is the unique product of New York City as the meeting-place of races and cultures in the Western Hemisphere. Sociologists and fictionists have made intensive and extensive studies of the metropolis within a metropolis which have revealed, to eyes familiar only with ante-bellum and post-bellum stereotypes, an El Dorado of racial dissimilarities, varying from the low life characters of the rebel Jamaican's naturalistic *Home to Harlem* to the dark intelligentsia of *Portraits in Color*.

The cultural and ethnic diversity of Harlem fascinated Tolson for both personal and cultural reasons. In "The Odyssey of a Manuscript" Tolson indicated that he felt particularly close to his mother. She told him tales of black heroes, poets, and artists. She encouraged his aspirations and even made him feel obligated to write as a fulfillment of her own dreams, or at least this is as Tolson remembers it. This "little walnut-hued woman was fiercely proud of being an American Negro, although in her veins flowed Irish, French, Indian, and African blood." As her son, Tolson too was fiercely proud of his black heritage, but he was also keenly aware of the diversity of his own ethnic and racial heritage. Harlem, "the meeting place of races and cultures in the Western Hemisphere," was always a cultural home in Tolson's imagination.

Cultural fusion of race and class continued to fascinate and preoccupy Tolson throughout his life. The character of the Curator, the protagonist of *Harlem Gallery* suggests the continued importance of this theme for Tolson:

> The Curator is of Afroirishjewish ancestry. He is an octoroon, who is a Negro in New York and a white man in Mississippi. Like Walter White, the late executive of the N.A.A.C.P., and the author of *A Man Called White*, the Curator is a "voluntary" Negro. Hundreds of thousands of Octoroons like him have vanished in the Caucasian race—never to return. This is a great joke among Negroes. So Negroes ask the rhetorical question, "What man is white?" We never know the real name of the Curator. The Curator is both physiologically and psychologically "The Invisible Man." He as well as his darker brothers, think in Negro. Book One is his

autobiography. He is a cosmopolite, a humanist, a connoisseur of fine arts, with catholicity of taste and interest. He knows intimately lowbrows and middlebrows and highbrows.

In his master's thesis Tolson saw the Harlem Renaissance primarily as the cultural expression of the New Negro as Alain Locke described him, but he also noted the fascination of the Negro for white writers and publishers. Thus Tolson, along with such Renaissance writers as Langston Hughes and Jean Toomer, was encouraged to see the Negro with all his cultural diversity, not just as a new development in the exclusive racial history of black Americans but as both test and promise of the American Dream. The New Negro held the promise of being a New American.

Chester Himes expressed the persistence of this promise [in *The Quality of Hurt: The Autobiography of Chester Himes Volume I* (New York: Doubleday, 1972)] with a scorn for the patronizing "primitive" stereotype, a scorn that Tolson would have found congenial, even though he probably would have differed on other expressions of personal taste:

> Obviously and unavoidably, the American black man is the most neurotic, complicated, schizophrenic, unanalyzed, anthropologically advanced speciman of mankind in the history of the world. The American black is a new race of man to come into being in modern time. And for those hackneyed, diehard, outdated, slavery time racists to keep thinking of him as a primitive is an insult to the intelligence. In fact, intelligence isn't required to know the black is a new man—complex, intriguing, and not particularly likable. I find it very difficult to like American blacks myself; but I know there's nothing primitive about us.

A Gallery of Harlem Portraits reveals Tolson's early fascination with Harlem's "El Dorado of racial dissimilarities." He does not generalize ambitiously about the significance of this cultural diversity as he will later in *Harlem Gallery, Book I*. At this point, he makes no great claims explicitly, but there is implicit pride in his fascination. He dramatizes the lives of Harlem people very directly and immediately so that the reader experiences the joys and pains, the frustrations and intensity, the impoverishment and the ingenuity, in short the style of Harlem life.

Tolson frequently used the public world of the Harlem Renaissance in drawing his portraits, but he usually deliberately altered names and specific biographical information so that his portraits became generalized or "type" figures rather than incisive comments on particular personalities. The portrait of "Madame Alpha Devine," for example, is almost certainly based on the life of Madame C. J. Walker, whose success in the cosmetics business made her both famous and rich, although specific biographical details are deliberately altered. "Abraham Dumas" is a fictionalized picture of Alain Locke. There are numerous veiled literary references as well. I suspect that

"Simon Southorn" is a disguised comment on Jean Toomer's *Cane*. It is perhaps relevant to note that Tolson surprisingly ignores Toomer in his master's thesis. "Willie Byrd" seems a character cut from the same cloth as McKay's Banjo. While trying out an exaggeratedly poetic style in "Percy Longfellow" Tolson may have attempted to parody the poetic elegance of Countee Cullen. Several other portraits—"Miss Felicia Babcock," "Grand Chancellor Knapp Sackville," "Napoleon Hannibal Speare," "Elbert Hartman," "Ray Rosenfield," "Xavier van Loon," "Winged Feet Cooper," and others—teasingly suggest real historical prototypes. "The Reverend Isaiah Cloud" is almost certainly an idealized fantasy self-projection. The preaching tradition is strong in Tolson's family. He always saw himself as a penetrating truth seeker, one who saw through the pretentions of wealth and position. He assimilated something of the twenties' free-spirited artistic scorn of the vulgar middle class as well as the thirties' more indignant sense of the injustice of the distribution of wealth. And he saw both snobbery and economic exploitation as deeply infused with racism. He also was neither surprised nor discouraged when the world never seemed to want to hear about the truth that he saw.

The typescript of *A Gallery of Harlem Portraits* suggests that the opening poem, "Harlem," may well have been written later than the other portraits in an attempt to give the entire book focus and some coherence. It only partially succeeds, but the effort indicates the direction in which Tolson's imagination is later to develop *Harlem Gallery, Book I*. In "Harlem," Vergil Ragsdale, consumptive poet working as a dishwasher, has written an epic poem, "An African Tragedy." Acknowledging his own rapidly approaching death, he sketches roughly the historical transformation of Harlem that he will not live to observe. This editorial gnomic observation follows:

> The Curator has hung the likenesses of all
> In *A Gallery of Harlem Portraits.*

The character of the Curator is not developed in this poem or anywhere else in this manuscript. There *is* a later poem-portrait of Vergil Ragsdale. Ragsdale's role in this manuscript suggests the roles to be played in the later *Harlem Gallery* by Mister Starks, the suicide musician poet, author of *Harlem Vignettes*, and Hideho Heights who gives the bravura public tributes to John Henry and Louis ("Satchmo") Armstrong, but whose more ambitious and private poem, *E. & O. E.* so moves and disturbs the Curator— the latter reference is an oblique advertisement for Tolson's own critically neglected poem by the same name.

In *A Gallery*, probably under the influence of *Spoon River Anthology*, the concept of a series of poetic portraits is kept relatively simple and the formal implications of the relation between poetry and painting are left relatively unexamined. In *Harlem Gallery*, Hideho Heights challengingly declares that in the beginning was the word, but the Curator, an ex-professor of art, along with the trenchant African, Doctor Nkomo, persist in trying to reconcile the claims of painter, poet, and musician, as artists who clarify and give meaning to the profusion and confusion of human experience in any historical time.

The story of Big Sadie's role in destroying Ragsdale's manuscripts after his death seems a probable source for the later version of Big Mama's role in preserving Mister Starks's *Harlem Vignettes* for the Curator's guardianship. But again we see an elaborate structure develop from a simple pathetic incident. Prince Banmurji is also a possible prototype of the later and more richly developed Doctor Obi Nkomo.

Two poems from *A Gallery* were revised and combined to appear in *Voices* in 1950. The two poems, "African China" and "Wu Shang," are combined under the title of the former. Wu Shang, a Chinese laundryman in Harlem, is a man of quick perception and enigmatic eloquence. He and Dixie Dixon of the revised poem, or Mabel of the earlier version, marry and have a son named African China. This revision is additional evidence that Harlem continued very much in Tolson's mind, "the unique product of New York City as the meeting-place of races and cultures in the Western Hemisphere."

Tolson has recalled some of the early literary influences that give impetus and form to his first book of poems:

> The first finished manuscript of the Harlem Gallery [*A Gallery of Harlem Portraits*] was written in free verse. That was the fashion introduced by the imagists. It contained 340 pages. *The Spoon River Anthology* of Edgar Lee Masters was my model. Browning's psychology in characterization stimulated me. I had deserted the great Romantics and Victorians. Walt Whitman's exuberance was in the marrow of my bones.

If the influence of Masters, Browning, and Whitman are all readily apparent in *A Gallery*, there is yet another, and probably even more important, unacknowledged influence.

The blues is such an implicit part of Tolson's experience and writing that at the time of making the above statement, it apparently did not warrant his conscious recognition. However, in his master's thesis he identifies the particular poetic achievement of Langston Hughes, who in "The Weary Blues" "catches the undercurrent of philosophy that pulses through the soul of the Blues singer and brings the Blues rhythms into American versification." The reader by means of the blues form can "experience the utter physical and mental fatigue of the Negro after the cruel sleeplessness of the night-hours, facing the desolate flatness of another day." This use of the blues indicates to Tolson that Hughes "understands the tragedy of the dark masses whose laughter is a dark laughter." The profound racial message of the blues carries for Tolson, as it did for Hughes, significant proletarian overtones. The dark laughter of the blues permeates *A Gallery of Harlem Portraits* as well.

In *Blues People* Le Roi Jones calls his reader's attention to:

the beginning of blues as one beginning of American Negroes.
Or, let me say, the reaction and subsequent relation of the Negro's
experience in this country in *his* English is one beginning of the
Negro's *conscious* appearance on the American scene. . . . There
were no formal stories about the Negro's existence in America
passed down in any pure African tongue. The stories, myths,
moral examples, etc., given in African were about Africa. When
America became important enough to the African to be passed on,
in those *formal* renditions, to the young, those renditions were in
some kind of Afro-American language. And finally, when a man
looked up in some anonymous field and shouted, "Oh Ahm tired
a dis mess, / Oh, yes, Ahm so tired a dis mess," you can be sure
he was an American.

Jones describes the "classic blues" that became prominent during the
Harlem Renaissance as, "the first Negro music that appeared in a formal
context as entertainment, though it still contained the harsh, uncompro-
mising reality of the earlier blues forms. It was, in effect, the perfect balance
between the two worlds, and as such, it represented a clearly definable
step by the Negro back into the mainstream of American society." By
affirming the Negro's sense of being a part of a particular society, the blues
also afforded him an opportunity to express racial or ethnic experiences
that paradoxically held the promise of universality: "Perhaps what is so
apparent in classic blues is the sense for the first time that the Negro felt
he was a part of that superstructure of American society at all. The lyrics
of classic blues became concerned with situations and ideas that are recognizable as having issued from one area of a much larger concern. . . .
Classic blues attempts a universality that earlier blues could not even
envision."

The introductory poem of *A Gallery of Harlem Portraits* looks forward
to the later *Harlem Gallery* by emphasizing the universality of the Harlem
experience:

> Dusky Bards,
> Heirs of eons of Comedy and Tragedy,
> Pass along the streets and alleys of Harlem
> Singing ballads of the dark world.

Then Tolson switches directly into a blues lyric:

> *When a man has lost his taste for you,*
> *Jest leave dat man alone.*
> *Says I . . . a dawg won't eat a bone*
> *If he don't want de bone.*
> *I likes de Eyetalian . . . I likes de Jew . . .*
> *I likes de Chinaman, but I don't like you.*
> *Happy days are here again.*
> *Dat's sho' one great big lie.*

Ain't had a beefsteak in so long
My belly wants to cry.

Preacher called to bless my home
An' keep it free from strife
Preacher called to bless my home
An' keep it free from strife.
Now I's got a peaceful home
An' de preacher's got my wife.

White cops sho' will beat you up, littlest thing you do.
Black cops make Black Boy feel proud, but dey'll beat you too.

Rather be a hobo, Lawd,
Wid a stinkin' breath
Dan live in de Big House
Workin' folks to death.

My two-timin' Mama says to me:
Daddy, did I let you down?
Gonna break dat woman's gawddamn neck
Befo' I leaves dis town.

Black Boy, sing an' clown an' dance,
        Strutt yo' low-down nigger stuff.
White Folks sho' will tip you big
        If you flatters 'em enough.

The poem then closes with a brief and incomplete list of blues experiences that are the subjects of later poems in the manuscript.

Years later in the opening section of *Harlem Gallery* Tolson will again invoke the blues experience:

As a Hambletonian gathers his legs for a leap,
        dead wool and fleece wool
    I have mustered up from hands
        now warm or cold: a full
        rich Indies' cargo;
but often I hear a dry husk-of-locust blues
descend the tone ladder of a laughing goose,
        syncopating between
    the faggot and the noose:
    "Black Boy, O Black Boy,
    is the port worth the cruise?"

The blues, however, in the later poem are incorporated into a more symphonic idiom and structure. The stories of John Laugart and Mister Starks are blues stories, but they are not given in the more readily recognizable blues idiom so frequently used in *A Gallery of Harlem Portraits.*

The blues root Tolson's poetry in the experience of black America, and they provide a literary means of expressing some of his most deeply felt social contradictions. He is fascinated with cultural fusion, and he sees in the Harlem experience a cultural pluralism and sophistication of extraordinary promise. But the dark laughter is always there, a sometimes bitter but strangely tonic laughter that keeps the painful but fortifying awareness of the history of the black American ever present even in the most optimistic and imaginative speculations on his future.

A few of the poems in *A Gallery* may also surprise Tolson readers with their blatant political propaganda. Tolson described himself throughout his life as a Marxist, yet placed against the background of such poems as *The Libretto* and *Harlem Gallery* such a self-definition seems almost idiosyncratic. Tolson never joined any of the Communist or Socialist parties. As mayor of Langston in the fifties, and probably much earlier in his life, he was an active Democrat. He always prized and protected his independence as a writer. He was deeply suspicious of submitting his talents to the discipline of any group or party. Yet he had personally experienced gross class and racial injustice. "The Ballad of a Rattlesnake" in *Rendezvous with America* is a powerful reminder of Tolson's experiences organizing sharecroppers. Two poems in this manuscript, "Zip Lightner" and "Uncle Gropper," are products of these same experiences. And "Lionel Bushman," "Big Jim Casey," "Edna Borland," "Freemon Hawthorne," "Ted Carson," and the closing poem "The Underdog," underscore Tolson's deep social concern.

During the forties, and certainly by the fifties, Marxism became for Tolson more a set of intellectual assumptions about the nature of history than a particular political discipline. His position in the early sixties is vividly indicated in a letter to Benjamin F. Bell, Jr., December 28, 1961:

> Ideas sift down, Marx and Lenin and Castro were not of the masses but *for* the masses. What does a Cuban peon know about *Das Kapital?* If you gave him a copy, he'd wipe his behind with it! Well, a peon has to use *some* kind of paper. What's better than that you can't read. There is not a greater strategist on the Left than Old Man Du Bois. He always catches the Wall Street Boys with their pants down and their backs bent at the proper angle. I admire the Toe Groza of the Cleveland Browns. Who is better place-kicker? Only Old Man Du Bois. Joined the Party at 93! Now mind you, he's in Africa writing a Negro encyclopedia! *Jet* says he's the most popular Negro in Africa! Lawd, Lawd, Lawd!

Some of the poems in *A Gallery* suggest that Tolson was not so certain in the thirties as he was in the sixties of the relation between art and politics. A poem as propagandistically banal as "Hilmar Enick" can hardly be defended on any grounds, but scattered through the latter portion of the manuscript there are a few tired poems, and not all of them are concerned with political sermonizing. "Harold Lincoln," for example, is also deadly flat. Fortunately, these poems are few and far between.

During the late thirties and early forties ethnic references were apt to be more blatant caricatures than we find comfortable today. Calverton, for example, when he published the final poem of *A Gallery*, which Tolson titled, "The Underdog," changed the title to a brassy, "Kikes, Bohunks, Crackers, Dagos, Niggers." This maybe a matter of particular sensitivity since we live in a time when the full horror of the Holocaust has been documented and revealed. Tolson's stereotypic portraits of Jews include anti-Semitic biases that were then so common that they could be projected with considerable personal innocence. It should be noted that by 1939 Tolson had finished a novel, *The Lion and the Jackal*, which showed that he was very sensitive to the threat that Hitler and fascism posed, and he saw clearly the links between the murderous treatment of Jews and of blacks.

One cannot help but be struck by the variety of topical references in *A Gallery of Harlem Portraits*. The thirties were a period of intellectual stretching and testing for Tolson, but he was also acutely interested in the changes that were occurring in the American social fabric. At Wiley College he was a phenomenally successful debate coach, drilling his students relentlessly on all the possible arguments related to some of the major issues of the day. He was in great demand as a public speaker, and the topics ranged far beyond the literary. From November 20, 1937, to May 15, 1943, Tolson published a weekly column in the Washington, D.C., *Tribune* titled "Caviar and Cabbage." In it he spoke out freely and forcefully on a great miscellany of social issues. *A Gallery* reflects the commitment of a passionately engaged, if often whimsically ironic imagination. But it is characteristic of Tolson's political position that when Calverton was attacked by *New Masses*, it never troubled their friendship. Tolson's political beliefs hung loosely around his strong personal loyalties.

Melvin Tolson taught all of his adult life in black schools—Wiley College, Langston and Tuskegee universities. He always lived within black communities. He seldom felt the need consciously to proclaim his blackness. Instead he feared and struggled against provincialism. Some of his public statements, by emphasizing the importance of what was happening in the literary world at large, have misled some of his critics into thinking that he was so fascinated with white writers and their achievement that he lost touch with black people. For instance, impressed by T. S. Eliot's winning the Nobel Prize in 1948, Tolson prepared a commencement address which announced a program for a "New Negro Poetry for the New Negro":

> The standard of poetry has changed completely. Negroes must become aware of this. This is the age of T. S. Eliot who just won the Nobel Prize in Literature. If you know Shakespeare from A to

Z, it does not mean you can read one line of T. S. Eliot! . . .
Imitation must be in technique only. We have a rich heritage of
folk lore and history. We are a part of America. We are a part of
the world. Our native symbols must be lifted into the universal.
Yes, we must study the techniques of Robert Lowell, Dylan
Thomas, Carlos Williams, Ezra Pound, Karl Shapiro, W. H. Auden. The greatest revolution has not been in science, but in poetry.
We must study such magazines as *Partisan Review*, the *Sewanee
Review*, *Accent* and the *Virginia Quarterly*. We must read such critics
as Crowe Ransom, Allen Tate, Stephen Spender, George Dillon
and Kenneth Burke.

Underneath the rather conventional academic admonitions is the sly
smile of the conjure poet: "Imitation must be in technique only. We have
a rich heritage of folk lore and history. We are a part of America. We are
a part of the world. Our native symbols must be lifted into the universal."
In his journal Tolson noted:

> At one time Mr. Eliot was the nigger of poetry; so he had to walk
> hard and talk loud. See essay on Milton—the first; then the last.
> Look how Pound attacked Shakespeare's "multitudinous seas
> incarnadine."
>   Eliot antithesizes in order to synthesize—that is the root of think-
> ing—which is establishing a definite relation between ideas or
> groups of ideas. . . .
>   I shall visit a land unvisited by Mr. Eliot.
>   I admire Mr. Eliot's honesty. He is a Christian: an open confes-
> sion is good for the soul—and also society. For thousands of years
> poets have been thieves. Shakespeare admitted his guilt. Mr. Eliot
> not only admitted his but in the notes told us exactly where we
> could find the stolen goods.

Joy Flasch quotes from a letter Tolson wrote to a friend in 1961: "My work
is certainly difficult in metaphors, symbols, and juxtaposed ideas. There
the similarity between Eliot and me separates . . . when you look at my
ideas and Eliot's, we're as far apart as hell and heaven." There is perhaps
a slight hint of the dark laughter of the blues in the humor with which
place is identified with author.

   Tolson saw himself as leading black poetry into a modern period that
was being shaped by nonracial historical forces, and he was both jealous
and confident about it. There is a revealing self-descriptive note among his
manuscripts at the Library of Congress, which reads as if it were intended
as PR information for *Harlem Gallery:*

> M. B. Tolson dips into varied experiences beginning in Harlem,
> as a college student in [the] 20's & 30's, his Columbia University
> study of the Harlem Renaissance later, and from them emerges

this graphic picture of the Curator of the Harlem Gallery and the inimitable Zulu Club Wits. Against a background of artists, poets, singer[s], blues, jazz, and the Negro avant-grade, Tolson, *the Father of Negro poetry in the modern idiom*, spreads before us a panorama of Negro life to be found nowhere else in American literature [italics added].

It is this image of Tolson as the crusading modernist poet that has obscured the strength and intricacy of his roots in the Harlem Renaissance.

The relationship between universality and ethnicity in Tolson's work lends itself to much sophisticated now you see it, now you don't. Allen Tate in his introduction to Tolson's *Libretto for the Republic of Liberia* comments:

> It seems to me only common sense to assume that the main thing is the poetry, if one is a poet, whatever one's color may be. I think that Mr. Tolson assumed this; and the assumption, I gather, has made him no less but more intensely Negro in his apprehension of the world than any of his contemporaries, or any that I have read. But by becoming more intensely Negro he seems to me to dismiss the entire problem, so far as poetry is concerned, by putting it in its properly subordinate place. In the end I found that I was reading *Libretto for the Republic of Liberia* not because Mr. Tolson is a Negro but because he is a poet, not because the poem has a "Negro subject" but because it is about the world of men. And this subject is not merely asserted; it is embodied in a rich and complex language, and realized in terms of the poetic imagination.

Yet Dan McCall in his review of the *Libretto* [in "The Quicksilver Sparrow of M. B. Tolson," *American Quarterly* 17, no. 4 (Fall 1966)] sees Tolson's achievement in revolutionary terms. He applies Jean-Paul Sartre's observations on the African poet in "Black Orpheus" to Tolson:

> "It is when he seems suffocated by the serpents of our culture that he shows himself the most revolutionary, for he then undertakes to ruin systematically the European acquisition, and the demolition in spirit symbolizes the great, future taking up of arms by which the Negroes will break their chains." Tolson breaks his chains with bolts of laughter. There is in the *Libretto* an exuberant spirit proper to the occasion of mastering the white man's power and turning it back on him: see how I master the master. At times Tolson seems to be running wild in the white castle of learning. You have made me, he is saying, a black thief in the night; I am a Negro and have made my meals on what I hooked from your white kitchens and now that I have made my way into your study—see here—I walked off with your library. . . .

But to get simply the outrageous comic effect is not to get

enough, for the outrage is in the service of a revolutionary possibility. Tolson is not just turning back on the white culture its own methods; he does it in the name of a new culture.

Karl Shapiro uses Tolson's work as a principal argument in his quarrel with Tate and Eliot [in "Decolonization of American Literature," *Wilson Library Bulletin* (June 1965)]:

The falsification I speak of is that of trying to assimilate Tolson into the tradition when he was doing the opposite. The fact that Tolson's *Libretto* is unknown by white traditionalists gives the lie to the critic's assertion that Tolson has risen above Negro experience to become an "artist." The facts are that Tolson is a dedicated revolutionist who revolutionizes modern poetry in a language of American negritude. The forms of the *Libretto* and of *Harlem Gallery*, far from being "traditional," are the Negro satire upon the poetic tradition of the Eliots and Tates. The tradition cannot stand being satirized and lampooned and so tries to kick an authentic poet upstairs into the oblivion of acceptance. But the Negro artist won't stay in the attic anymore than he stayed in the cellar.

Nathan Huggins, in his study of the Harlem Renaissance [in *Harlem Renaissance* (New York: Oxford, 1971)], gives only passing reference to Tolson, but his comment seems intended as high praise, although ironically its logic seems very close to that of Allen Tate's:

There is no quarrel that great literature is generated by ethos. Immigrants in the United states, as well as blacks, found their special condition a natural source of literature. Immigrants however, seemed to feel more free than blacks to write about themselves. Judging by Mary Astin, Abraham Cahan, and Michael Gold, Americanization was really the American story. Blacks, on the other hand, were plagued by a sense of being anomalous. The artistic question remained whether a work of art was a window opening onto an ethnic province—peculiar and curious—or whether through it the viewer could be drawn into a geography of his own humanity regardless of ethos. Recent writers—Bellow, Ellison, Malamud, Tolson—exemplify the possibilities. Through their works, the reader is taken through the "province" into the world at large. Also, art as craft defies parochialism. For there is pure pleasure in the discovery of a brilliant artistic conception, well constructed so that it holds together and works. Melvin Tolson's *Harlem Gallery* gives us such delight, independent of its ethnic center. The jazzmen of the 1920's seemed to understand all of this perfectly well. But for the contemporary black writer to do the same, he would have to lose the self-consciousness that made him a black man who wrote poems and novels (the same could be said for the Hoosier, the Yankee, the Jew, the Southerner, the woman, or what have you). One had to lose that self-consciousness, or rather, transform it into the very instrument that could slice through the boundaries that defined it.

Melvin Tolson frequently asserted an "I-ness" that could not be encompassed by his "Negro-ness," but he never needed to think of himself as white, and he was proud of the ability of his people to survive and achieve. He knew that it took wit, courage, and sophistication, and he believed that the world was wide open for him to learn from, or if it was not wide open he was going to do his damnedest to make it so for him and those to follow. He wrote a speech that he planned to give on the one hundredth anniversary of the Emancipation Proclamation. Some of his phrases correspond suggestively to the titles of the four books he projected for his final *Harlem Gallery:*

> Between the Egypt Land of the antebellum South and the Promised Land of the Great Emancipator stretched a labyrinth in which the black man discovered no cloud by day and no pillar of fire by night. Yet, let us remember at this hour the apocalyptic words of Abe Lincoln: "If you don't know where you came from you don't know where you're going." That's the imperative reason why we must study Negro history, Negro art, Negro music. True, we have not yet reached the sublime heights of twenty-one major civilizations pictured by the great Toynbee in his ten giant volumes. Yet, we must remember what the heroic Frederick Douglass said to the slave masters: "Don't judge me by the height I have reached, but by the depth from which I come." Douglass said these words again and again, from pulpits, from auction blocks, from tombstones in graveyards.

Tolson concluded this speech by quoting from Paul Laurence Dunbar's "Ode to Ethiopia":

> Go on and up! Our souls and eyes
> Shall follow thy continuous rise;
>   Our ears shall list thy story
> From bards who from thy roots shall spring,
> And proudly tune their lyres to sing
>   Of Ethiopia's glory.

Tolson's literary career suggests that this admonition constantly sounded in his own mind. He traveled on and up an extraordinary distance. Did he wander from the true path by listening to the Siren strains of Eliot and the New Critics, or did he break through to an advanced level of achievement and artistic sophistication with which the literary world has not yet caught up? It is too soon to answer that question with final authority and confidence. Those who have appreciated and understood how far he traveled have been too few, but they have often been persons of discernment and literary authority. We need to walk the roads Tolson actually did travel with greater attention to his signposts and his destination. It is to be hoped that the publication of his early book of poems about Harlem will help in establishing some of the markers and the principal directions of Melvin B. Tolson's literary journey. In addition to these important scholarly-critical goals, it is to be confidently expected that these poems will provide a rich and vibrant pleasure of their own.

Yvor Winters: What He Did

Robert Hass

When Yvor Winters received the Bollingen Award for Poetry in 1955, the editor of one of the small magazines that had sprung up about that time remarked in print: "Winters is not a poet; he's a policeman." As a critic, brilliant, maddening, draconian, he terrorized American letters in the 1930s and 1940s. His books, *Primitivism and Decadence* (1937), *Maule's Curse* (1938) and *The Anatomy of Nonsense* (1943), were a frontal assault on romanticism, American transcendentalism and modernism—in fact, on much of what had been written and admired in English in the nineteenth and twentieth centuries. The books are still readable. His prose style is clear, obdurate, scathing, completely self-assured. In a time when the criticism of poetry was a passionately serious matter, no one wrote about poems with more seriousness or passion. . . .

Yet the Winters we first meet in the poems is not the fierce old curmudgeon of Palo Alto, he is a tubercular boy, just beginning to read the moderns (neither Wallace Stevens nor Marianne Moore had published a book yet) in a New Mexico sanitarium. He had matriculated at the University of Chicago in 1917 at the age of sixteen and became ill after completing a year of school. He had also met Harriet Monroe, the editor of *Poetry*, and through her begun a correspondence with Marianne Moore. During the three years of his treatment and the following two, when he taught school in the parched, dusty mining towns of New Mexico, he read the magazines sent to him by Monroe and books from the New York Public Library that were loaned to him (illegally) by Moore.

The fascination of his early poems has very little to do with critical theory and much to do with watching what he read take root in the young man, his head full of Keats and Mallarmé, who looked out on the desert

From *Twentieth Century Pleasures: Prose on Poetry.* © 1984 by Robert Hass. Ecco Press, 1984.

of the Southwest in 1919 and 1920 through the eyes of symbolist and imagist poetry. One of the earliest poems is a debate—a sort of verbal harlequinade in the symbolist manner—between a black puppet and a white puppet. You can already hear Stevens in it:

WHITE PUPPET

My life is green water seen
Through a white rose leaf.
It has a sheen.

BLACK PUPPET

A dry leaf on the ground
Is much like me.
It turns around
And then lies still.

The poem also borrows from native American mythology. Winters wrote the first pioneering essay on the early translators of American Indian songs in 1928. Here, Coyote, the trickster who will show up again in the poetry and fiction of the 1960s as a figure for the quick, untrappable impulse of life, first appears:

WHITE PUPPET

You have seen Coyote
Who flows like gold,
The runner in the night
With eartips like the air.

BLACK PUPPET

Coyote is green eyes
On dust whirl of yellow hair—
My passion is untold.

WHITE PUPPET

Coyote is an ether
That is shaken in the air.
He hovers about me
When the day is white.
He passes swifter
Than the runner in the night.

BLACK PUPPET

My passion is untold.

Imagist clarity and fastidiousness of diction have already begun to discipline this adolescent melancholy, and if "The Pines Are Shadows" is a wonderfully peculiar congeries of voices and modes, what follows is more wonderful still. In 1922 Winters published a book of one-line poems, got out of imagism, Japanese haiku and Ojibway song:

THE HUNTER

Run! In the magpie's shadow.

SPRING RAIN

My doorframe smells of leaves.

HIGH VALLEYS

In sleep I filled these lands.

THE ASPEN'S SONG

The summer holds me here.

He had, by this time, begun to publish reviews that would seem comic if they were not so startlingly prescient. The voice that solemnly declares Wallace Stevens's "Sunday Morning" to be one of the great poems written in English in the twentieth century belongs to a young man of twenty-two, and he is speaking of a poem that has not yet appeared in a book. In the work of his late twenties, however, when the desert landscape takes hold of him, William Carlos Williams has become Winters's model, and some of the poems in *The Bare Hills* (1927) are very good indeed. For instance, "Jose's Country":

A pale horse,
Mane of flowery dust,
Runs too far
For a sound
To cross the river.

Afternoon,
Swept by far hooves
That gleam
Like slow fruit
Falling
In the haze
Of pondered vision.

It is nothing.
Afternoon
Beyond a child's thought,
Where a falling stone
Would raise pale earth,
A fern ascending.

Poems like this are anything but what I expected when I first came to Winters's work, imagining that it would be a cross between Malvolio and John Foster Dulles. The poems are less supple than Williams's, less playful than Stevens's, but many of them are brilliantly hard and clear:

> October
> Comes and goes
> And in the moonlight
> I wait for winter.
>
> The silence
> Is like moonlight
> In one thing:
> That it hides nothing.

The appearance of *nothing* is perhaps a clue to the dramatic change in Winters's poetic style that occurred around 1930 and gave birth to the notorious critic. He had, following the dicta of the imagists, cleaned the windows of perception. There is, in many of these poems, nothing but a tense clear perception of the world and, in their music and movement, the feeling that emerges from that perception. He had, with admirably fidelity and discipline, taken the imagist poem to one of its limits: and, an American with Calvinist roots, he found the world that he rendered, the world that was not an idea of the world or an interpretation of the world or the world as a mysterious symbol of something other than itself, insupportable.

Alone is another word that shows up many times. Williams and Stevens, Eliot and Pound, H. D. had also come, each in his or her own way, to the imagist cul-de-sac, and each of them invented a way out. Williams decided (quite easily) that there were no ideas *but* in things. Stevens discoursed for another twenty-five years about the idea that there were no ideas. Winters, in the intense loneliness of provincial places—Cerillos, New Mexico; Boulder, Colorado; Moscow, Idaho—decided that imagism was a bad, dangerous method, that it could render experience but not judge experience, and that constantly calling up feelings that you couldn't understand made people crazy. "I stood unseen," he says, movingly, at the end of one of his poems of 1928. "The rough soil / is without depth, shadow, distance; and he / lies in harshcolored air, breathing, alone," he says at the end of another.

It is possible to imagine that, in different circumstances, he might have pushed through, that the loneliness, terror, even the hysteria that haunt some of his last free-verse poems might have found a different resolution. As it happens, he arrived at Stanford University to begin studies for a doctorate in English literature. In the desert he had discovered that the black puppet was right. There is the world, and there is man; and man should not confuse himself with the world, because he is going to die. He was drawn to the poets of the sixteenth and seventeenth century who held close to this fact: and, to the end of his own life, he always praised most highly those poems that look directly and without flinching at the loneliness of human death.

The poems that come after this conversion are the ones that most readers who know his poetry at all are apt to be familiar with. They are, in style and tone, amazingly unlike his early work:

> Death. Nothing is simpler. One is dead.
> The set face now will fade out; the bare fact,
> Related movement, regular, intact,
> Is reabsorbed, the clay is on the bed.
> The soul is mortal, nothing: the dim head
> On the dim pillow, less.

He abandoned free verse and turned to meter and rhyme because he had decided that a poet could exercise more control over his materials when he composed in meter. Control was a crucial word for most of the New Critics, who tended to write about emotion the way the older Scott Fitzgerald wrote about alcohol. It is as if the inventions of modern American poetry, of Pound and Moore, Williams and H. D., had opened more psychic territory than the younger generation was prepared to explore. They wanted to go slow, to absorb the techniques and to understand what they implied. It is probably also the case that during a Depression and a world war they didn't want a medium so slippery, so full of inner agitations.

It was in this context that Winters became a figure. Where others were respectful, quizzical, imitating the excellent manners of T. S. Eliot's prose, Winters came out fighting, took the extreme positions that no one else was quite prepared to take. It was he who said that Emerson sold Hart Crane the Brooklyn Bridge, that Yeats with his Blavatsky and his gyres and Anglo-Irish country houses was an old bluff and a fascist, that Eliot's moral exhaustion was morally exhausting. This must have been very heady stuff to a younger generation who were writing in the shadow of elders who had not only done work of unprecedented brillance but who also showed every sign of going on forever.

It was, nevertheless, a holding action. There was nothing wrong with Winters's return to metrical forms. He handles them with great power. Nor was there anything wrong with his choice of models. The poets he claimed or rediscovered—Wyatt, Gascoigne, Raleigh, Greville, Jonson, Hardy, Robinson—were great poets. He has written about them stunningly in his last critical book, *Forms of Discovery*; and his classroom lectures—I had a chance to hear some of them in the years just before his death—were high drama. What is damaging about the later work is that, in addition to adopting the forms and themes of the English poets, he adopted their diction. He never solved for himself the problem of getting from image to discourse in the language of his time, and instead borrowed the solution of another age.

Just how damaging this is it is very hard to say and will probably have to be left to another generation to judge. Some of the writing is unbelievably bad. This, from a poem to his infant daughter:

> Ah, could you now with thinking tongue
> Discover what involvëd lies
> In flesh and thought obscurely young,
> What earth and age can worst devise!

But there are also poems, "Time and the Garden," "A Summer Commentary," "To the Holy Spirit," "At San Francisco Airport," of sustained power, that carry the weight of his terror and his deep sense that his own way of being in the world was limiting and took courage. Sometimes, in moments of calm, he was able to render—and to civilize—that sense of the steadiness of the earth he experienced early in New Mexico, as in "By the Road to the Airbase":

> The calloused grass lies hard
> Against the cracking plain:
> Life is a grayish stain;
> The salt marsh hems my yard.
>
> Dry dikes rise hill on hill:
> In sloughs of tidal slime
> Shell fish deposit lime,
> Wild sea-fowl creep at will.
>
> The highway, like a beach,
> Turns, whiter, shadowy, dry:
> Loud, pale against the sky,
> The bombing planes hold speech.
>
> Yet fruit grows on the trees;
> Here scholars pause to speak:
> Through gardens bare and Greek,
> I hear my neighbor's bees.

His generation of poets, which includes Kenneth Rexroth, George Oppen, Louis Zukofsky, Charles Reznikoff, Louise Bogan, Allen Tate, among others, wrote in an odd obscurity. The glamour of the first generation of modern poets seems to have passed directly from them to their explainers, and neither ordinary readers nor university English departments have really begun yet to absorb the work of the second generation. Winters is particularly a victim of this situation. He saw himself as a poet and wrote criticism to explain what had happened to him as a poet, but the more interesting explanation is in the poems themselves. His own final judgment of his work is disarmingly modest and accurate; it appears in the last poem he wrote before his death: "What I did was small but good."

On Edwin Denby

Lincoln Kirstein

Edwin Denby is well-known as a dance critic. By the time he was sixty, the two volumes of his collected notices from the forties and fifties [*Looking at the Dance* and *Dancers, Buildings and People in the Streets*] were taken as basic theatrical history. Although his particular attention referred to performances no longer visible, moral and aesthetic judgment illuminated current parallels. His analyses were superbly constructed, usually constructive, and warmly glowing with an absolute love of the art. They also had a scalpel's delicate, sanitary edge when detecting a spot as false. His prose was didactic, schooling those in the audience willing to be more than lightly amused. He taught three generations to see more than they had first suspected, and inspired more than one young English literature major to think with care about writing on dancing.

Edwin was a great dance critic primarily because he was a fine poet. His poems while collected and well presented in 1975 [*Collected Poems*], through the enthusiasm of close friends, are available today for readers who prize good verse as much as good dancing. He is not anthologized. Modern literature courses don't take much account of him, nor is he treated as an important lyricist by many beyond a band of admirers, too often discounted as a coterie. But some poets, now far more fully published, appreciate such poetry; this was the only fame he liked. He accepted the nomination of journalist, but craft and insight lifted him to the level of professional artist. In his elegy, "Snoring in New York," he presents himself:

> Summer New York, friends tonight at cottages
> I lie motionless, a single retired man

From *The Complete Poems of Edwin Denby*, edited by Ron Padgett. © 1983 by Lincoln Kirstein. Random House, 1986.

White-haired, ferrety, feminine, religious
I look like a priest, a detective, a con
Nervously I step among the city crowd
My private life of no interest and allowed

Brutality or invisibility
We have for one another and to ourselves
Gossamer-like lifts the transparent city
Its levitating and ephemeral shelves
So shining, so bridged, so demolished a woof
Towers and holes we sit in that gales put to proof.

It is hardly by chance that the most thorough writers concerned with dance were prime poets—Théophile Gautier, Stéphane Mallarmé, Paul Valéry. Other verse makers who observed dancing with some attention, but rarely read for it, are Federico García Lorca and Hart Crane. It is to these master choreographers of words that Denby is most akin.

When his verse is read with the care it deserves and commands, he may be recognized as the clearest lyric voice of Manhattan since Crane's epopoeia of the Brooklyn Bridge. He shares Crane's quirkiness in implosive short circuits of dense, awkwardly precise rhetoric, odd broken rhymes, reckless rhythm, sharpness of physical imagery and incandescent metaphor. There is a sense of place, of American loneliness similar to that in some of Edward Hopper's paintings. Crane was a hysteric, his hysteria increasing tragically from self-inflamed euphoria. Compulsive self-indulgence did him in early on. Denby was a survivor, who put an end to himself only when old, when he could no longer manage his body. This he accomplished, with much good work behind him, large in instruction and influence. He endured unspoken pain and took a stoic exit, disdaining to burden further his friends or himself. This is a matter more for celebration than for sadness.

His poetry concerns cities in history, past and present, European and American, detailed with domestic intimacy, an experienced tourist's familiarity. Rudy Burckhardt, his lifelong friend and illuminator, provided a visual gloss on specific sites. Controlled accident in snapshots is always present in Edwin's imagery. He had a "photographic" eye and a powerful visual memory. The atmosphere, societies, and qualities of many cities, Mediterranean and American, form an album of superpostcards, more real than any nostalgic material souvenir.

I stroll on Madison in expensive clothes, sour.
Ostrich-legg'd or sweet-chested, the loping clerks
Slide me a glance nude as oh in a tiled shower
And lope on dead-pan, large male and female jerks.

Later from the open meadow in the Park
I watch a bulging pea-soup storm lie midtown;

Here the high air is clear, there buildings are murked,
Manhattan absorbs the cloud like a sage-brush plain.

In the grass sleepers sprawl without attraction:
Some large men who turned sideways, old ones on papers,
A soldier, face handkerchiefed, an erection
In his pants—only men, the women don't nap here.

Can these wide spaces suit a particular man?
They can suit whomever man's intestines can.

García Lorca, in exile at Columbia University, was miserable in Manhattan. Nevertheless, out of misery, he composed his memorable portrait of Walt Whitman, another psalmist of cities. Whitman's voice resounds in García Lorca, Crane, and Denby, not only for their "love of comrades" and "sleepers," but in their substantial miniatures of cityscapes, their crowds, corner bars, shops which frame fierce and tender lives. There is a short-breathed sonnet by Denby, "On the Home Front—1942,"encapsulating a moment in our national story, as every famous wartime photograph does, and its final couplet makes a generalization which is also the portrait of its poet:

The small survivor has a difficult task
Answering the questions great historians ask.

Edwin's presence was that of a dancer. Forty years ago he looked like a boy retired from ballet. His trimness and courtesy never left him. Quiet elegance solidified in a firm aura while his handsome head turned gray to white. His presence at performances of the New York City Ballet was steady reassurance to the company; while his fair opinion was always hoped for, his silent authority made any casual gossip superfluous.

His essay on Stravinsky and Balanchine's *Agon* (1957) is the most telling and comprehensive technical appreciation of a dance work that has been written. To be able to make visible in words what was, and is, difficult to grasp by eyes alone, treating steps lacking any narrative pretext, is in itself a tour de force, more exhausting than any thirty-two *fouettés en tournant*. Denby's degree of penetration touching the irreducible skeleton of a masterpiece was equivalent in quality to the matters in question.

Many attached to classic academic ballet read his particulars of performance as sturdy correctives. He loved every tribe of dancer, traditional, ethnic, experimental, popular. He had no preconceived prejudice and was not the keeper of any personal, possessive flame. He tended to lean eagerly toward pioneers, not only giving newcomers benefit of doubt for their daring, but because he delighted in and was amused by any effort to budge human bodies in alternatives to habit.

Balanchine talked little and thought less about journalism covering dance events. Actually, he read everything he laid his hands on relative to his own company, while steadfastly denying this. However, it amounted to the same thing, since he was so secure in his own opinion that he disqualified columns he found irrelevant as nonexistent. After all, dance critics, like cobblers, had to earn their living. But after reading Edwin's extraordinary essay on *Agon* he sent it to Stravinsky.

When Balanchine read Denby's criticism of *Concerto Barocco*, he told Richard Buckle, "If you must write, try writing like that." Buckle replied sadly: *"But I'm not a dancer."* Edwin was trained as a dancer: he knew in his own bone, mind and muscle how dancers feel about how they step. Gautier, Mallarmé, Valéry, were not dancers, but their gifts as lyric poets fulfilled the discrepancy. Edwin was both dancer and poet. His prose is textbook information, chapter *and* verse.

Some of us believe in the beauty and scope of his songs (written for Aaron Copland's operas), his sonnets, his elegiac praise of towns, his strong sense of the inhalation and exhalation of peoples, day and night, in their mass, in their individuality. Here is scent and sense not to be found in any other "modern" American versifier. This, a second stanza from "Groups and Series":

> In enterprise, in sleep, how well men wear
> the shifting illuminations of the air:
> watching a sleeper we will come to trust
> the body anchored in its breathing's thrust;
> loosened in sleep, his weight lies there as such,
> rounded in all this moonlight, cool to touch.
> Beside you, broken by the lamp's short beams,
> he shows you shadows black as parts of dreams.

Blackmur at Poetry

Russell Fraser

R. P. Blackmur at nineteen saw himself as the Great Poet—the capital letters are his—whose role was to annihilate the "sickening 'transition' under which the last centuries have writhed." He knew that so far he filled this role "but barely and only remotely." Still he said, "it's worth working for— even a lifetime?" The question is poignant now that the life has been lived.

He wrote in the diary he kept as a boy: "All these last few days enormous rhythms have swept my chest; rhythms more powerful than those of any poem I can find." He tried to get these rhythms on paper. Throughout one summer he wrote a poem a day. A notebook crammed with this poetry ends with the notation: 230 poems, 52 good. For years he poured it out. "I only want to write a long poem," he said to Allen Tate in his twenties. He was in his thirties when he wrote to his cousin, George Anthony Palmer: "I have yet to learn to write slowly enough." Then the outpouring slowed to a trickle. "There was a wellspring in me bubbled and even brimmed for so long, so many years"—when he entered these remarks in his journal, he was just into his thirties—"a cold utter boiling, source of all fire, drawn, filtered, purified from upland miles, the second or permanent water-table. This dried up." Afterwards his poetry was surface water drawn from runnels and ditches, "fertile but foul, coming in excess but intermittently." He wondered, though, if in the excess of drought the bottom ledge might crack or be tapped in a new place, "and the sweet hard water flow again." It didn't flow again.

To his public but not to himself, he recited excuses. He said he had to go to work, so stopped writing. This anecdote, from one of his Princeton students, is radical oversimplifying but gets at a piece of the truth. Poetry for Blackmur was everything or nothing, not something you did in your

From *Salmagundi*, nos. 44–45 (Spring/Summer 1979). © 1979 by Skidmore College.

closet. Lack of money—the wherewithal of writing—obsessed him. "I'm horribly hard up," he told Harriet Monroe, begging poetry reviews. "I grow poorer with days and need all the pennies I can garner." Small sums remain miracles. He wasn't Wallace Stevens. In the fifties, Stevens came down to Princeton for a visit. He was severe on Blackmur (who told the story on himself) for giving up poetry and settling for criticism and teaching. "Stevens, of course, was staying at the Waldorf."

When Blackmur was very young, he did without money and literally he went without food. He was the poet as hero. He read the little magazines like *Broom*, *The Double Dealer*, *Secession*—they were his schoolhouse—and he kept a record of their addresses. "Bring your *Dials* previous to September," he instructed his cousin. "I have finished October and November." He was like Delmore Schwartz, ten years his junior, reading Joyce to pieces while his contemporaries were reading *Anthony Adverse*. At seventeen he was submitting his poems to *The Dial*. The editors didn't think these poems were successful. He disapproved strongly of *The Dial*'s taste. "I, personally, think them entirely 'successful.' "

His conviction that he was meant for greatness kept him going. But he knew he was a provincial, so looked for correction beyond his own country. He read to tried to read *La Ronda* and *Der Sturm* and *La Nouvelle Revue Française*. He, who never got to college, studied Verlaine and Laforgue. Nobody told him what was approved. He made his own hierarchies of value. Rilke wasn't up to Thomas Mann. "But on its own plane," Rilke's *Journal of My Other Self* "stands equally alone." Later he read Baudelaire. At last, he wrote Rob Darrell, "I . . . have him inside me in his own tongue which is the way he should be." He knew no one today could use Baudelaire directly. But he saw how to use him as a "parallel way of feeling—a discipline." Blackmur the young man was "the only prisoner in a world set free"—quoting from an early poem of his. Through discipline he found his way to freedom.

In his twenty-first year he began corresponding with Harriet Monroe, who played tutor to his still untrammeled, hence unliberated youth. Her death, eleven years later, brought him, he told Morton Zabel, "a dreadful sense of age, and worse, of pause." At first Miss Monroe rejected the poems he sent her for *Poetry*, feeling in them an overstressing of method. Some of the poems were taken, though. "Alma Venus," after Lucretius, was the first. Blackmur was twenty-one. After a while his presence in *Poetry* was being bid for. Other journals published him, too—like his friend Sherry Mangan's little magazine, *larus*, printed by Mangan on his own Press of the Lone Gull. Who cares about Mangan or *larus*? Everyone ought to. In Blackmur's young manhood, the little magazine was the access point for talent—better to ask, Who cares about *Harper's* or the *Atlantic?*—and not little at all in the talent it enlisted. Virgil Thompson served *larus* as European editor. He got Gertrude Stein to contribute, and Robert McAlmon, Mary Butts, others. Blackmur isn't on the periphery in writing for *larus*. A poem of his in the second issue precedes a poem by Hart Crane.

Within a few years, his right to call himself poet was pretty generally conceded. Lincoln Kirstein was negotiating with financial backers, hoping to find the money to publish a small volume of his verse. In 1935, the *New Republic* commissioned him to make an anthology of "Eight New England Poets." He was the best of the lot. John Wheelwright, whom Blackmur included in his anthology, thought so. He said Blackmur at epigrams was better than Savage Landor, "that supposed unsurpassable master of the epigram." He quoted:

> Pride is the thing outside
> pride is the itching hide:
> the proud man out of doors
> goes naked in his sores.
> Forgive him that he shrinks inside.

J. V. Cunningham, saluting Blackmur as among "the foremost 'younger' critics," added his opinion that "your poetry at its best is flawless. I am thinking of the epigrams and *Phasellus Ille*, in the *Magazine*, and of the *Sea Miscellany* in the *Hound & Horn*." Winters agreed. He designated Blackmur one of the five best poets of his generation. He liked the short poems for their "solidity and power." The "bundle of sea-poems" sent him by *Hound & Horn* was "very beautiful stuff."

Blackmur's major work in poetry during these years was the long poem, more precisely the reticule of short poems, to which he gave the exotic title, "From Jordan's Delight." The tidal waters and islands of the Maine coast are the fabric of this poem and represented for Blackmur what Aran meant for John Millington Synge. In his love affair with Maine, he shed himself and discovered an identity. This doesn't mean he was untrammeled. He rebelled against himself in a created self, he subjected himself to his material. "The letting go method," he write later to a poet who had sought his opinion, "only works . . . in the cry, the lyric, etc.; but you were writing a long poem, which cannot (to the audience) be a series of cries." The better way is to "find yourself an objective means which you modify only so far as necessary to get yourself into it." He had found his means and now he waited anxiously on his cousin's "minute and scarifying opinion."

His anxiety was deep in part because the poem was for him his most " 'important,' " in part because of the torpor—more than run-of-the-mine laziness—that vexed him all his life. To excuse this vexing condition, he pleaded the pressure of time. "I worked a few hours the other day on my foulness next to god ballad," he wrote to Rob Darrell shortly after joining the faculty at Princeton, "but there were other foulnesses in the shapes of freshman and sophomores who trooped in"—and that was that. "Because for so many years I wrote so regularly for *Poetry*," he said to Henry Rago, who was editing that magazine in 1958, "I wish I could let you lure me into doing so again." But he hasn't the time. The life of Henry Adams was going to be his great achievement in prose, and when he died this work remained unfinished. There were plenty of reasons and he offered them endlessly. The chief reason he defined in his essay on *Madame Bovary*. "Ennui is the ignoble form in which we exercise our instincts for martyrdom: in which we cannot sit still but are aimless in motion looking for a motive." He couldn't find a motive for action, unless the action was to fill the void of silence he dreaded. Always he felt himself "trembling into stone." He wrote, in his "Scarabs for the Living":

> Smugness is the first reward
> befalls impatient certainty
> . . . the last is being bored.

He wasn't smug nor certain. But he lapsed in boredom even so, and his inspiration flagged. He wrote to Harriet Monroe, for whom he intended "From Jordan's Delight": "It is the only poem I have been able to finish for a long time."

His poem didn't appear in *Poetry*. Robert Penn Warren, who found "much beautiful verse" in "From Jordan's Delight," brought it out a year later in the *Southern Review*, concurrent with the publication, by Arrow Editions, of Blackmur's first volume of poems. Here and there the title poem seemed obscure to Warren. Brooks agreed. Blackmur didn't agree. He had sweated the poem, going over it "syllable by syllable with both Horace Gregory and Jack Wheelwright," and felt he "could hardly do better except, as always, in the intimate structure of the verse."

The impinging of felt experience on the verse is obvious and vivid—

> this island has a loom
> Never to be forgotten from the west—

but the experience is most vivid when Blackmur apprehends it at a remove, the definition and usefulness of objective means. Blackmur in his failed poetry comes straight from the shoulder, so makes you put up your hands in self-defense. Delmore Schwartz saw the remedy: "let your poems grow as you rightly said Stevens' did in the mind . . . and as the scab about the what happened once in the monarch darkness grows in my mind." He is remembering Blackmur's "Scarabs for the Living." He wants Blackmur to draw on "the unseen drama in these very scabs, which gives them tension and depth, but not a living action." The living action is unmediated experience, not yet pounded in the churn. Only

> the unprayable flowing,
> the vast sluiceage of sleep,
> sets the great churn going.

But more than sleep is requisite, guile is requisite. Blackmur in his criticism didn't have to be told. To Ransom, who taught Emily Dickinson's erotic poems constituted her tragic mask, he responded: "I think of her almost as a maskless person." That wasn't a virtue. In his poem, he practiced guile.

"Jordan's Delight is an island," he wrote to Zabel, "off the mouths of Naraguagus and Pigeon Hills Bays, eastern Maine." This literal place the "poem describes, populates, and identifies," but the identification is only partly verisimilar. There is the real island rock populated by a simple, bearded fisherman, full of "small-boat intimate pieties." Right up against it is Baudelaire's *Cythère* The fisherman, rehearsing his piety, speaks or sings rather in Blackmur's voice. But he employs the refrain of an old ballad as the seed of Blackmur's refrain. What you see as you approach the island are the flowers and colors of Jordan's Delight—

> Such is the red stonecrop
> The purpling pink sea-pea
> The blue legume with bluest bell
> And blue harebell—

but filtered through the eye of St. Francis in his Canticle of the Sun, and I think through the ear of Milton in *Lycidas*. In section 10, "All Siren's Seine," you meet Blackmur proclaiming his eddying faith that is part "inevitable denial and earned despair," also you meet Odysseus abiding this denial—but "always, I hope, in sensual terms of the sea."

The adverbial phrase, invoking the real sea and "its recurrent overwhelming encroachment," establishes, so lets Blackmur negotiate—what would otherwise be the mere purlieus of thought—"that fundamental disorder and disequilibrium for which any profound conception of order must first of all make room." How shall we know, he inquired later, "what, and in what measure, to accept as living poetry and what to dismiss as merely occasional, or personal, or vain before the possibility?" He answered, look for "the conceiving imagination and for the twist and shape of idiom." Blackmur's poetry gains assent as he hides himself among the stuff: he is a poet of the conceiving imagination; it reaches what he called "the dignity of fate" as it reaches the condition of idiom. He loses himself to find himself—so far, what you can call his persona. But what he finds is persuasive only so far as his words verge on flesh—

> Look at the tide's bare hand
> then at the flotsam trove
> it scatters in this cove,
> a melting jellyfish
> a sailor's wooden dish
> and an old galley stove
> content on the bare sand.

"Content" is not so good, a little clamant maybe. What goes before is better. The element Blackmur lives in is matter-of-fact.

Blackmur in his poetry likes to raise big questions. He does best when he leaves them alone or when he answers sparely, the answer being in the detail.

> East of the eastern ledge a hundred yards
> the haddock feed on rising tides.

I call that perfect poetry. Then the lachrymose thing we generally call poetry supervenes:

> The tide of hours comes to its full, and I
> wonder why men abuse their flesh with mermaids,
> image sea-nymphs and such like fictive things.

The conceiving imagination is a casualty of these fictive things. They are only imaginary.

Towards the end of his life, Blackmur got a letter from two college students who wanted to know about the genesis of his poem, "Mirage." He said: "you all have your own rights to give my mirage any meaning that suits you." He went on to repudiate the high a priori road: "It was not for me an ideal or a way of life or much of anything except a mirage." Many readers of the poem seemed to have thought differently. In fact "my mirage was an actual mirage on a very hot, quiet day on an island in the Gulf of Maine." No doubt "you might say we felt within a rather dangerous land of the lotus-eaters." But on the whole, the real mirage "made its own meaning." Blackmur concluded, inconsequently and rightly, "I hope you both can try sailing enough to find out for yourselves." The poems of *From Jordan's Delight* make their own meaning. Tate, who saluted publicly their "capacity and range," wrote Blackmur "to say that the book is the best American poetry of this decade." Forty years or so later, this doesn't seem a preposterous judgment.

The poetry that followed *From Jordan's Delight* is, to my taste, mostly personal. I mean it is no one's business but the author's and not least when it is occasional poetry. Blackmur had a wonderful passage-at-arms with his friend Richard Eberhart, whose poems he reviewed in 1938. The review made Eberhart angry: "You erect craft at the expense of the vital impulses that make a poem. . . . you think of art only as artifice; you eschew the deeper issues, you skip any relation of poetry to the times," the familiar guff, like Gorton to Jake Barnes in the bar of the Paris *Herald Tribune*. The short of it is: "Nothing but the deepest sincerity will do." Blackmur had written: "I do not charge Mr. Eberhart with insincerity; it would be nearer home to charge him with insufficient insincerity—for the best of poetry is Jesuit's trade, once the end is in view." That is immaculate criticism. But the casuistical temper, the source of much great poetry, doesn't show enough in Blackmur after *From Jordan's Delight*.

The drift in the later poetry is from the particular to the general. Intellectual apprehension does duty for the thing itself. Dudley Fitts, reviewing *The Second World* in 1942, wished for his friend Blackmur "a third world where the Empsons cease from troubling and the Richards are at rest." Weldon Kees, in a sympathetic account five years later of *The Good European*, remarked the almost unrelenting "dependence upon abstraction"—that was Tate's perception, too—also the "presumption that ideas can carry the burdens of poetry." Blackmur at his characteristic best knew this presumption for a heresy. As he got older he embraced the heresy with the zeal of the middle-aged convert and not only in poetry. It is the trademark, said Kees, "stamped on every paragraph of Mr. Blackmur's more accessible works of criticism."

Denis Donoghue, in his introduction to the Princeton edition of Blackmur's poems, tells us how "in the later criticism he spoke of ideas and attitudes directly, whether they transpired in the poetry or not." He turned from poetry to writing about European novels and he compromised the occasion by dealing with his novels in translation. "Purity of texture in the fiction is already a lost cause." He took a further license. He treated the constituents of the fiction expansively, you could almost say he made it a vehicle for writing prose poems. The movement from verse to fiction has its parallel in the edging away from the personal themes of Blackmur's first book of poetry to the public and social themes of *The Second World* and *The Good European*. I have been putting down the merely personal and don't mean to sow confusion. Personal means here all that transpires—

> the odour of pennyroyal, where your fingers
> frittered and bruised the fresh leaves—

and public and social all that remains inert.

Blackmur's imagination went to seed but his desire persisted. Robert Penn Warren, who met him first in 1939, remembers chiefly how excited he was at having to read his poetry in public. Poetry, Warren thought, was what he cared about most. Just before he went to Princeton he was writing again—I assume a long hiatus—and is hard put to express "how much of a personal kick" this gave him. Friendly competition with Wheelwright spurred him on. "This Ancient Bards were meeting Wednesday at Jack's, and it was so annoying to me that Jack was the only one with fresh poems that amounted to anything, that I set about writing a few myself." Through the winter of 1940, he wrote hard. The poems he wrote don't cash as poetry. Idiom dies when your hear the ax grinding.

Blackmur's reputation as a poet remained alive. In the spring of 1941 he was invited to read his "verses to the Cooper Unions." He said he dreaded the event. His letters belie this. "You can have no idea," he wrote to Lee Anderson, "how pleasant and reassuring it is to have anyone . . . seem actually to get something out of my verse. . . . Criticism is a chore except when, occasionally, I can write it as if it were a poem"—a sentence that speaks profoundly to the best and worst of his critical prose. Robert Lowell in an interview caught this best and worst, and so succinctly that it makes you despair of the labor of biography. Blackmur, who "was more of New England than anyone," had a particular genius, Lowell said. "In his prose, every sentence struggles to be poetry, form ringing on rock. He was a good poet, weird, tortured, derivative, original—and more a poet in his criticism. A side of him wanted to write novels, because he remembered everything and felt things most critics can't—people. He was more industrious than other stylist critics, wrote heavily and yet with a grace; had anarchy and discipline—perhaps he overcherished both." The cherishing of anarchy in discipline declares the poet. He found his greatest satisfaction in subjugating the anarchic impulse to the discipline of verse, at the same time giving it rein. This wasn't free rein but permitted, hence controlled.

Blackmur met his own satisfaction in the response of friends. "I think your Churn is excellent," said John Walcott, the friend from Harrington days who died in Italy during the war and whom Blackmur memorialized in "Three Poems from a Text of Isaiah." The poem—Walcott means "Missa Vocis"—"strikes me as hard without a single thing to soothe." Delmore Schwartz wrote to Blackmur in 1942: "It was pleasant to open *Time* this morning and see you described as a remote and excellent poet." But the title poem of Blackmur's volume appearing in this year—maybe the best poem in a slim and uneven collection—first appeared four years earlier in *Twentieth Century Verse*. Looking back, *The Second World* seems a posthumous event.

Delmore in the forties, as poetry editor of *Partisan Review*, used this job to cherish his friend. Blackmur sent him a long poem and he responded loyally: "you are right in thinking this is one of your best pieces." To Delmore in a letter of 1946, Blackmur confided his intentions of publishing "another small volume." He said he had "succumbed to vanity." In *The Good European* you encounter Blackmur in the middle of the journey, trying and mostly failing to find his way back.

For the record, he still put his poetry first. "There's no more engrossing work than writing a poem," he told the *Daily Princetonian* in 1951, "especially if you have a hold on it." His hold faltered and he worried minor points in work he had published. "The comma in line 14 of the third sonnet. . . . is the cross you will have to bear." He announced to a favorite student that he was planning another volume of poems. "I'm still working," he said, "I'm going to surprise you." He said the same thing to Sean O'Faolain, who had known him since early days in Cambridge and whom he brought to Princeton as a Gauss Seminarian. But when Ted Weiss wanted something for the *Quarterly Review of Literature*, he had to answer vaguely: "I may, or may not, have a group fit to print." He remarked of this group of poems, part of "a fairly long poetic project" on which he was working in the fifties: "I am not sure what I think of them now." Sean O'Faolain recollected the past and brought it to bear on the present. "One really had to have known the poor and struggling Keats boy of the 20's to feel the vastness of the change." He wondered did Blackmur's Fanny Brawne see this change "as a betrayal of their first dreams."

So Blackmur's career as a poet ended in sadness. He had prayed he might fall like a meteor "burnt in its own light." His fall was harder. He guttered and went out. By the time of his death, the memory of what he had made in poetry was already dying. The poems, said a recent reviewer, writing in the Sunday *Times*, "are no part of his power." Refusing their own ardors, they are only "pale ghosts, shadows of other men's ecstasies." I want to revise and say, the poems are shadows of Blackmur's own ecstasies. I mean the best in this kind are but shadows. What he saw and did really present in his poems is substantial: "the vestige brought out of turbulence" or the order that survives—here the metaphor shifts—"only by digesting disorder: the gravel in each mouthful that we eat."

There is plenty of this gravel in his poetry, too. He isn't coming on for his Nobel Prize acceptance speech. In 1936 he wrote to Robert Penn Warren: "The stable or uttermost place of imagination is the place where . . . disorder is given room." His tragicomic protagonist in "From Jordan's Delight," setting out his lobster pots along a breaking ledge where the undertow or backwash protects them—"finds by the very peril of his deed the piety of the stable place." So chaos lives at the heart of stability, and you can put it the other way round. The "fundamental disorder" declares its connection with "the eddying of order." What Blackmur called "the urban sensibility of the full response"—his response as a poet (being a state of Maine man was only his avocation, after all), a step up from the instinctual response of his hero—perceives this connection and makes ecstatic verses. Here is a verse, the last of Blackmur's "Scarabs for the Living":

> Quiet the self, and silence brims like spring:
> the soaking in of light, the gathering
> of shadow up, after each passing cloud,
> the green life eating into death aloud,
> the hum of seasons; all on beating wing.

The title of this poem glosses the best of Blackmur. "The scarab was a dung-beetle set by the Egyptians upon the heart of the dead. But poems under this title would be the furthest from the morbid." The comment, which points the "moral," isn't appended to the poem but reserved to a private journal. Blackmur made his juxtapositions, setting the dung-beetle on the heart of the living. The quickening, or was it the enervating, that followed was none of his business.

Most poets, except the very greatest, when they try the affirmative voice only persuade you of their hardness of heart. Grow cold along with me, the worst is yet to be. Blackmur's characteristic voice is not affirmative but acceptive. He knows all things are wholesome until you stiffen to meet them. So he keeps himself quick in the valley of the shadow. "Pone Metum," he begins:

> Be not afraid, if in the great fright,
> for all the ravage and the sack

> and the black frost,
> you find on a moonless night
> yourself intact.

He doesn't blink what he sees and doesn't venture to explain it. He bears witness. "See all we see." His phrase for his poetry is "the witnessing art." It brings him often on misery. The poems themselves, the ones you remember, are equable, though. The violence is in gear, so the whine of protest is absent.

"The quiet in his voice was drenched in strength." This line describes the man, not only the poet. For the poet, the stable place is midlight. Living in this place precludes the chance for certitude. Most truth-resembling poetry is located there, and is remote from the consolations of philosophy. Blackmur has this figure, in his poem "The Spear": "Salvation is a salmon speared . . . safe from the great safety of the sea." He doesn't want salvation. His agnostic prayer follows:

> O let my heart
> that spurns satieties
> be living hooked from the fresh flood
> but let my soul rehearse
> without benefit or curse
> of a saviour's blood
> its difficult and dangerous art.

He is an unbeliever, but "the seriousness of his unbelief rests on a desperate hope." I am quoting from his essay on Joyce's *Ulysses*. This hope is "to make an epiphany of the darkness shining in brightness."

Like Judas in his poem, Blackmur made a mirror of his deliberate purpose "where both the horror and the hope stood still." This is the source of his epiphanies:

> He whom this stillness breeds
> rejoices with a roving eye
> on thistles blown to seed,
> on hills against the sky,
> until in the sun's late haze
> the wild, neap-tidal air goes cold:
> hill and thistle equally old.

In this last of Blackmur's "Songs at Equinox," slack water meets the wild air. The order the conjunction makes is eddying or wayward. That is not what Blackmur wanted on his legislating side but it is what he achieved.

A haunting line of his reads: "we walk the earth of all we know." Blackmur glosses this line unconsciously in his *Essays in the European Novel*. He has been discussing in Flaubert the process of the objective imagination which "comes into existence and drags being after it." This process is involuntary, it is even subversive of the writer's intention, and suggests why we are satisfied by the great makers of nineteenth-century fiction. "Each fell on his own reality." Joseph Frank, enumerating Blackmur's touchstones—he cites Joyce, Yeats, Eliot, and Thomas Mann—describes them as "the artists who have felt and assimilated the greatest amount of the reigning disorder and have made the most strenuous efforts to dominate it." Blackmur in the poetry wants to dominate disorder but falls on his reality. What happens in the life is another graver story. It isn't domination for which you remember him. It is accommodation. "Your images will get ahead of your intentions," he wrote. This is all to the good and explains how "the objective mode tends to the dramatic." His successes in poetry are written in this mode.

Richard Eberhart:
Reading God's Fingerprints

Richard K. Cross

Yeats remarked, in the preface to *A Vision*, that his grand intent was "to hold in a single thought reality and justice." That project—reconciling man's tropism toward the light with his experience of a world that seems, as often as not, designed to thwart it—is, of course, a perennial concern of poets. Few have been more preoccupied with the task than Richard Eberhart, who is perhaps the most distinguished survivor of a tradition that remained potent well into this century but that has been partially eclipsed by the nihilist tendencies of the day, the tradition of religious romanticism whose greatest modern exemplars are Yeats, D. H. Lawrence, Dylan Thomas, and Roethke. If Eberhart sometimes strikes readers as an anomalous figure, it may be because his closest affinities have been not with his contemporaries, whatever their stripe, but with earlier Romantics—Wordsworth, Blake, and Hopkins in particular. I shall seek in this essay to indicate the direction of the poet's spiritual development and to probe critical stages of it as they become manifest in representative poems. The emphasis will fall on Eberhart's sense of the sacred as it discloses itself in nature and in human affairs and his efforts to harmonize that presence with the grim actualities of suffering and death.

"This Fevers Me," the lyric from *A Bravery of Earth* (1930) that opens the *Collected Poems* [New York: Oxford, 1976], is steeped in the early Wordsworth. The poem heralds a "Regenerate sudden incarnation," a spirit Eberhart apprehends first as energy, the dynamism of growth, and then as pattern, the correspondences that link all natural things:

> Primroses wear the pale dawn,
>
> . . . .
>
> The apple takes the seafoam's light.

From *Concerning Poetry* 12, no. 1 (Spring 1979). © 1979 by Western Washington University.

It has the power to quicken, to make lovely, and to destroy, although the last attribute is only touched upon lightly in this poem, which celebrates spring. The hallowing is a secret one, inferable because the poet participates, *tat tvam asi*, in its nature. And yet his God remains a purely numinous presence,

> Unununderstandable in grass,
> In flowers, and in the human heart.

"Unununderstandable" is a typical Eberhartism, awkward perhaps, but apt: the spirit is incomprehensible, since the poet in his finitude cannot view it from a nether—or a transcendent—standpoint. Such terms as "regenerate" and "incarnation" would seem to imply a Christian frame of reference; however, it is impossible to tell from a poem like "This Fevers Me" whether Eberhart believes in any sort of personal God. Other poems, early and late, indicate that he does. In the final section of "Suite in Prison," for example, he prays: "Lord, stabilise me. My legs / Fail in the white crevasses." The petition is moving, reminiscent in several lines of Hopkins's terrible sonnets, but it would still be difficult to characterize the God he addresses. The knowledge that Eberhart has been for many years an Episcopalian with, as he says, "some kind of a difference," offers the reader little help in interpreting his poems. There is no sign that his religious views have been much influenced by dogmatic theology as were, say, those of Eliot and Auden; Eberhart's brand of Anglicanism appears remote indeed from their orthodoxy. He has never been willing to be hobbled (or, for that matter, aided) by any system.

   Is Eberhart a mystic? In any but the broadest acceptance of the term, the answer must, I think, be no. Tempting as he might find the thought of an unmediated encounter with the *mysterium tremendum*, he ultimately rejects it as either impossible or unwholesome. He aspires not to the mystic's

> possession of the fire
> Annihilation of his own desire
> To the source a secret soaring
> And all his self outpouring

but rather to a "love discoverable here," a showing forth of the light within the human sphere ("The Goal of Intellectual Man"). The gods we conceive, he declares in "The Skier and the Mountain," mean to

> leave us in our true humanity,
> Elusive, shadowy gods of our detachment,
> Who lead us to the summits, and keep their secrets.

On few matters has Eberhart been more consistent than he has concerning the bounds of religious awareness.

   It was his mother's death from lung cancer in 1922, "her nine-month birth of death through utmost pain," that hurt Eberhart into making poetry his vocation. Among his attempts to close that wound, "Orchard" and "The Soul Longs to Return Whence It Came" are especially poignant. His most impressive early meditation on mortality is "The Groundhog." Indeed most of the verse initially collected in *Reading the Spirit* (1936) seems important now mainly as evidence of his struggle to find the voice and point of view perfected in that poem. The question he poses is whether the animal's demise represents, not just physically but also spiritually, a "senseless change." Eberhart treats death most effectively when he is able to gain a certain, though not too great, distance on it. The speaker in "The Groundhog" seeks to remain an observer: "watching the object," "strict of eye," "like a geometer." Such detachment is precarious, however, for distinctions between ego and other are merely provisional and the death of each living thing is implicit in that of every other. The superb finale

> I stood there in the whirling summer,
> My hand capped a withered heart,
> And thought of China and of Greece,
> Of Alexander in his tent;
> Of Montaigne in his tower,
> Of Saint Theresa in her wild lament

is Eberhart's variation on the theme of "Meru" and "Lapis Lazuli," without the transfiguring gaiety. The conqueror might well be stopping a bunghole; the philosopher's skepticism offers cold cheer; only the *unio mystico* of the saint, a blissful transcendence of self, could conceivably resolve the poet's quandary, except that he is, as I have indicated, unwilling to pursue that course to its end.

One finds a characteristic instance of Eberhart's recoil from transcendence in "I walk out to the graveyard to see the dead." With a wryness not much evident in the earlier poems but fairly common in the later work, he rejects the golden pheasant's invitation to contemplate the mysteries. Even if the bird should constitute a valid symbol of eternity, the poet has had enough of the "dark eye-smarting" such pursuits entail and will construct no artifice on his behalf:

> I cannot adore you, nor do I praise you,
> But assign you to the rafters of Montaigne.

One thinks of Frost's "Come In." Eberhart's poem concludes with a line at once declarative and imperative—"And action must be learned from love of man"—which should be read, perhaps, in the light of St. Augustine's *Ama et fac quod vis.*

"I walked out to the graveyard" strikes me as one of the three best poems in a generally strong volume, *Song and Idea* (1942). The others are "Now is the air made of chiming balls" and "If I could only live at the pitch that is near madness," which present a quite different side of Eberhart's sensibility. In "Now is in the air" a spring cloudburst has cleansed the doors of perception and allowed him to feel at one with the sublime setting of which he is, for the time being, a part. The seeds that "peep from the nested spray" respond to the same force that actuates the "naked necks of craning fledglings," and the speaker's "bunched anguish" yields to pleasure in the sun-dressed burdock's tightening. Nature is rounded and whole in this instant of cosmic consciousness: "the air made of chiming balls" echoes the music of the spheres. It is an access of grace virtually indistinguishable from one of Wordsworth's spots in time. Eberhart takes the transitoriness of such moments for his theme in "If I could only live at the pitch that is near madness." Against the delights of natal harmony, a timeless and unified realm in which one rests "immaculate in the Ego," stands a world of Otherness:

> time has big handles on the hands,
> Fields and trees a way of being themselves.
> I saw battalions of the race of mankind
> Standing stolid, demanding a moral answer.

The poet sacrifices his simplicity and enters the other side of childhood, an encounter with division, dependence, vulnerability—"the truth wailing there like a red babe." Whatever integrity he discovers in this new sphere will come as the result of arduous striving.

Next to his mother's agony the most severe test of Eberhart's faith in human prospects was his involvement in the Second World War. At the age of thirty-eight he enlisted in the Navy, serving as an aerial gunnery instructor, and out of that experience came the extraordinary war poems first collected in *Burr Oaks* (1947). "Dam Neck, Virginia" probes a discontinuity between aesthetic vision and belligerent fact: the luminous orbs that

> float out into space without a care,
> They the sailors of the gentlest parabolas,

are designed to kill. "Dam Neck" constitutes an effective prelude to a much more somber meditation, "The Fury of Aerial Bombardment":

> You would think the fury of aerial bombardment
> Would rouse God to relent; the infinite spaces
> Are still silent. He looks on shock-pried faces.

Eberhart has written no lines more powerful than these. One would be in error, I suspect, to read them as an indictment of God. What they register is a Pascalian sense of awe: His ways are not ours, but ours are no less baffling. The poem attains a rending intensity in its fourth stanza when the poet realizes that, implicated in the horror himself, he risks becoming as impassive as any deity:

> Of Van Wettering I speak, and Averill,
> Names on a list, whose faces I do not recall
> But they are gone to early death, who late in school
> Distinguished the belt feed lever from the belt holding pawl.

Among the American poets who wrote of World War II, Randall Jarrell alone seems to me to have produced work equal to "The Fury of Aerial Bombardment."

One other Eberhart war poem deserves comment. "Brotherhood of Men" a survivor's account of the Bataan death march and the subsequent years of incarceration in Japan, is cast in alliterative meter, and its jagged rhythms reinforce an almost Anglo-Saxon sense of doom. That feeling is relieved, however, by the unsuspected depths of compassion the speaker witnesses in his comrades, a revelation that leads finally to his resolve "To live for love, the lost country of man's longing." The poem is noteworthy chiefly because the speaker and intimate details of his story are fictitious; this sort of imaginative penetration into the life of another person does not occur in the earlier, inward-turning verse.

The 1940s, the time of Eberhart's marriage and the birth of his two children, of his relinquishment of teaching for a more active existence, first in the military and then in business, mark shifts in both his artistic sensibility and his orientation toward the scared. He retains the old themes, but his tone has altered and there are fresh concerns. This transformation is most evident in *Undercliff* (1953), particularly in such poems as "The Horse Chestnut Tree," "Seals, Terns, Time," and "Great Praises." The first of these is a captivating parable concerning schoolboy assaults on an ancient tree that belongs to the poet's father-in-law:

> Sometimes I run out in a kind of rage
> To chase the boys away; I catch an arm,
> Maybe, and laugh to think of being the lawgiver.
>
> I was once such a young sprout myself
> And fingered in my pocket the prize and trophy.
> But still I moralize upon the day
>
> And see that we, outlaws on God's property,
> Fling out imagination beyond the skies,
> Wishing a tangible good from the unknown.
>
> And likewise death will drive us from the scene
> With the great flowering world unbroken yet,
> Which we held in idea, a little handful.

That man's metaphysical reach exceeds his grasp is a familiar enough moral in Eberhart's poems. What distinguishes "The Horse Chestnut Tree" is the wit with which he draws it; a spirit of play qualifies his pensiveness, and the agonizing intimations of mortality that pervade the earlier lyrics give way to composed acceptance. The God of this poem is as remote, as little the loving father concerned with his children's lives, as he appears to be in "The Fury of Aerial Bombardment"; however, we have as compensation a kind of disinterested providence, his readiness to sustain "the great flowering world." Seldom has Eberhart managed so brilliantly to hold reality and justice in a single thought. It is an exercise in poetic theodicy worthy of a Hopkins. There are occasional relapses; nevertheless, the seven volumes that have succeeded *Undercliff* all testify to the durability of this new ripeness. Its humane virtues must, of course, be weighed against a price the poet has had to pay. As he has grown less self-absorbed, as his range of subject matter and sympathy has broadened, the anguish and the febrile joy that make poems like "The Groundhog" and "Now is the air made of chiming balls" so compelling have diminished.

Undercliff takes its title from Eberhart's vacation cottage in Maine, and much of his finest work over the past several decades is rooted in his attachment to that coast. Only Robert Lowell has written of it with comparable acuity. Consider in particular those of Eberhart's poems that reflect his imaginative rapprochements with marine life—"Sea-Hawk," "Ospreys in Cry," "Off Spectacle Island"—as well as those that record his sharp-eyed observation of both the natives and summer residents—"A Maine Roustabout," "Ruby Daggett." "A Wedding on Cape Rosier." Perhaps the most graceful of the Maine poems is "Seals, Terns, Time," in which the poet muses on the duplexity of human nature, the soul perhaps immortal fastened to a dying animal. Seals at play draw him "Back to a dim prehistory" while spiraling terns figure forth his urge to disencumber the spirit:

> Resting lightly on the oarlocks,
> Pondering, and balanced on the sea,
> A gauze and spindrift of the world,
>
> I am in compulsion hid and thwarted,
> Pulled back in the mammal water,
> Enticed to the release of the sky.

The Atlantic may be massively indifferent to the creatures who inhabit it or who return for visits, yet it also symbolizes the more bountiful world that has opened to a once-landlocked Minnesotan. Even its indifference seems at times a disguised form of benignity, for example, in "Sea Burial from the Cruiser *Reve*," which appeared in *The Quarry* (1964). In that poem, an exquisitely simple rumination on the strewing of a cousin's ashes over the waters, the speaker finds it possible to regard this "first hour of her new inheritance" as a "bright sinking." The soul's subjection to "unimaginable aftermaths" strikes a discordant note; however, nowhere in Eberhart's poetry does death have less sting.

One might be tempted to rest with this image of the youthful *héauton-*

timorouménos attaining a mature poise somewhere between stoic resignation and a romantic faith with Christian overtones more distinct than those in his early poems, a celebrant of the "light beyond compare" that constitutes "the wordless bond of all endings" ("The Incomparable Light"). It would be a poetically just life-trajectory for one who took Wordsworth as his first master, and it does seem a generally accurate representation. But it is not the entire truth. Lesions recrudesce. In "The Cancer Cells" the poet, examining a picture of these—his mother's—killers sees in them both the "murderous design of the universe" and a reflection of the artist's mind, his "own malignance in their racy, beautiful gestures." And at moments a dread of fatality nearly as potent as that in some of the early lyrics bursts upon him. "Trying to Hold It All Together," Eberhart's elegy for Auden, registers one such instance:

> Don't believe
> Will will help us, or religion, his civilized stance,
> A comic attitude, any saving grace,
>
> We cannot hold it all together, the depth,
> We cannot trick it out with word embroidery,
> Time is the master of man, and we know it.

The poem argues, ultimately, against its own being. Would Eberhart have written it had it no power to compose at least one corner of the flux, the agitation of his own grief? His stress on human finitude is unusually severe in "Trying to Hold It All Together"; nonetheless, the theme itself, at bottom a confession of creatureliness, comes close to being the leitmotiv of his *oeuvre*. Existing in time, the poet contends in "Vision through Timothy," we must reconcile ourselves to partially occluded views, Platonic shadows:

> Veils were drawn over our eyes
> When we were born or else
> We would have knowledge of eternity.

Perhaps, in the end, one will see God face to face, but for now a man has to settle for reading his fingerprints. One cannot, Eberhart insists, subdue the sky.

Louis Zukofsky: Eiron *Eyes*

William Harmon

If the Hindus are right and the destiny of every creature in the universe is governed by an inescapably just Karma that dictates the types and durations of an indefinite succession of reincarnations inflexibly delivering rewards and punishments that match what one has done in previous existences, then Harriet Monroe (1860–1936), founder of *Poetry* magazine, will by now have undergone any number of rebirths, via the wombs of a crawling insect (for her pedestrian imagination), flying insect (capriciousness and inability to sit still), jellyfish (occasional spinelessness and tendency to sting the innocent), tortoise (taking too much time with some important chores), jay (hysteria plus silly litigiousness), third-world churchmouse (to compensate for excessive wealth), and chairpersoness of the Greater Teaneck Arts Council and Begonia Guild (on general principles plus two counts of suffering Morton Dauwen Zabel gladly).

Any schoolchild today can look back at Ms. Monroe's errors in just the single year of 1915 and think, "Jesus! How could she have been such a ninny? She sat on 'Prufrock' for eight months before burying it in the back pages, all the while showcasing Arthur Davison Ficke and similar jive-turkeys. Deaf to the essential integrity of the original eight-stanza 'Sunday Morning,' she made Stevens omit three stanzas, so that he felt constrained to rearrange the remaining five. She was a poet of zero talent herself, and so overrated Masters, Sandburg, and Robinson that she had insufficient I.Q. left when the time came to give Hart Crane the appreciation and sympathy that he frantically needed."

We—you and I—can be sure, can't we, that *we* would never be guilty of such mistakes; we'd have "Prufrock" right up there in the front of the

From *Parnassus: Poetry in Review* 7, no. 2 (Spring/Summer 1979). © 1980 by Poetry in Review Foundation.

magazine with no eight month delay (if, that is, we had ever mustered the courage and resources to get a magazine going); we'd keep "Sunday Morning" intact all along without putting Stevens and his obviously brilliant poem through what must have been a humiliating and emasculating experience; if we had been calling the shots, Hart Crane would probably still be alive, surrounded by sycophants gaily helping to celebrate his eightieth birthday with a cake in the shape of a a big Life Saver; and . . . and, well and *everything*.

You bet.

My point is that, if the Hindus are right, Ms. Monroe ought to be about due for some release from her punishing passage through all those mortifying wombs, some recognition for the things she managed to do at least half-right. Death's first minister and chief of data processing, old Citragupta, will be on hand to recite evidence from his scrupulous printout that Ms. Monroe *did,* after all, found the magazine and run it vigorously for many years; she paid her contributors; she *did,* after all, print Eliot and Stevens and dozens of other first-rate poets; she *did* have the perspicacity to accept the advice of Ezra Pound when he was twenty-six (exactly half her age), even before he got so buddy-buddy with Yeats. And she *did,* early in 1924, publish a sonnet that had been written by a teenage prodigy in New York City:

> "Spare us of dying beauty," cries out Youth,
> "Of marble gods that moulder into dust—
> Wide-eyed and pensive with an ancient truth
> That even gods will go as old things must."
> Where fading splendor grays to powdered earth,
> And time's slow movement darkens quiet skies,
> Youth weeps the old, yet gives her beauty birth
> And molds again, though the old beauty dies.
> Time plays an ancient dirge amid old places
> Where ruins are a sign of passing strength,
> As in the weariness of aged faces
> A token of a beauty gone at length.
> Yet youth will always come self-willed and gay—
> A sun-god in a temple of decay.
>
> ("Of Dying Beauty")

You guessed it: Louis Zukofsky (1904–78). And your verdict is correct: not bad—for a kid (he turned twenty in January 1924 but the poem was written earlier) not bad at all. He may have absorbed too much Santayana, he may have affected the dark-fantastic too much, but he was no damned ego-freak (no "I" mars the poem) and he knew how to write a good dignified sonnet.

Scarcely seven years later, Ms. Monroe turned her magazine over to the same prodigy for a special number (February 1931) devoted to "Objectivist" poetry along with some modest polemics that provoked from her in the next issue a few condescending but indulgent remarks about the arrogance of youth (she was seventy, her guest-editor twenty-seven). But she *did* let Zukofsky edit a whole issue, even though nobody had any very prismatic idea of what an "Objectivist" poem may be (years later Kenneth Rexroth summarized the contributions as "anybody who would say yes and didn't write sonnets," but some of Zukofsky's own offerings were sonnets; and the point was in no way cleared up by the publication of Zukofsky's *An "Objectivists" Anthology* in 1932). Here is a poem from the special issue of *Poetry:*

> The moving masses of clouds, and the standing
> Freights on the siding in the sun, alike induce in us
> That despair which we, brother, know there is no
>   withstanding.

The note on the contributor of those lines says, by the way: "Whittaker Chambers, of Lynbrook, N.Y., was born in 1901. He has appeared in *The Nation, The New Masses,* and is a translator of note." Small world.

Zukofsky's own contribution to these "Objectivist" enterprises was a part of a long poem called *"A"* of which seven movements were finished by 1930. To approach a discussion of the whole poem, I want to start by looking at the original opening of the second movement:

> The clear music—
> Zoo-zoo-kaw-kaw-of-the-sky,
> Not mentioning names, says Kay,
> Poetry is not made of such things,
> Old music, itch according to its wonts,
> Snapped old cat-guts from Johann Sebastian,
> Society, traduction twice over.

The version, called *"A"*-2 in the eventual book form, shows some interesting adjustments:

> —Clear music—
> Not calling you names, says Kay,
> Poetry is not made of such things,
> Music, itch according to its wonts,
> Snapped old catguts of Johann Sebastian,
> Society, traduction twice over.

I want first to note that the poet had put his own name into the poem but in a mangled form, like the cries of beasts and birds: "Zoo-zoo-kaw-kaw-of-the-sky"; later he eliminated the name entirely, here and in other passages. Such a distortion of one's name followed by effacement of it impresses me as the gesture of a particular sort of personage, the *eiron* of antiquity who was both an ethical and a theatrical type.

Aristotle (*Nicomachean Ethics* 4) described the eiron and other such types so as to outfit a kind of Central Casting for life and literature. Zukofsky's generation, *Epigonoi* coming after a generation of giants like Stevens, Williams, and Pound, and Eliot, may seem particularly rich in pure types: Charles Olson a *philosophus gloriosus et maximus*, Beckett a tragic clown, Rexroth a lordly pedant of incredible erudition in sixty-seven languages, and Zukofsky himself, in person and in print, the classic eiron described in Northrop Frye's *Anatomy of Criticism:* self-deprecating, seldom vulnerable, artful, given to understatement, modest or mock-modest, indirect, objective, dispassionate, unassertive, sophisticated, and maybe foreign (all of these terms apply to the eiron both as author and as character). The derivation of eiron from a Greek word meaning "to say" (and kin to "word," "verb," "verve," "rhematic," and "rhetor") suggests that irony is chiefly a kind of speech and that the eiron is recognized chiefly by a manner or habit of speaking. He—whether Socrates, Swift, or Art Carney in the role of Ed Norton—says less than he means; now and then he says the reverse. He may be Prufrock, crying, "It is impossible to say just what I mean!" or Polonius, knowing how we "With windlasses and with assays of bias, / By indirections find directions out."

Now, from an objective or Objectivist point of view, epic contains history along with one or another measure of myth. The greater the measure of myth, the higher the status of the epic poet himself, so that Moses, Homer, and Vyāsa (who was said to have complied the *Mahābhārata*) are themselves legendary, as, in modern times, such poets as Milton, Whitman, and Pound have become. So grand is the epic enterprise, indeed, that the author thereof threatens to turn into a boastful *alazon*, ordering the Muses around and organizing gods and devils in overweening patterns. Besides, these poets make up among themselves a kind of hermetic society of trade secrets and inside dope, a tradition of precursors, guides, and counsellors, each one becoming *"mio Virgilio"* for the next one, who becomes *"il miglior fabbro"* for his associate, and so on. Since 1700, we have seen a succession of secularized or individualized epics or mock-epics, all of them more or less inconsistent and turbulent (if they are not outright flops), and they test the possibility of a sustained poem without a sustaining body of supernatural lore. The question seems to have been: What, other than a system of myth-dignified ideological conflicts and resolutions, can keep a long poem going?

The obvious answer from the eiron's viewpoint: *Nothing.* A somewhat less obvious addendum from the viewpoint of the modern eiron would be: *But it doesn't make any difference.* There persists an article of faith that supposes that we have somehow lost a paradise, that Homer or Dante or Milton could write tremendous poems because the poet and his audience *in illo tempore,* in that spell of magic and an organic oral tradition, shared a whole complex of beliefs capable of organizing and running an epic poem. That's a crock. If Homer, Dante, and Milton have anything in common, it is that they seem, fitfully, to have entertained beliefs that nobody could share. A cursory look at the debates among their audiences and successors will show very quickly that their appeal was not based on any shared system of beliefs, opinions, or even historical data. Their appeal was and still is based on their extremely powerful presentation of artworks so compelling that they overwhelm our disbelief with enchantment, and we—if we believe any-thing short of suicidal nihilism—assent.

Nothing is lost, but things can change and centers can shift around among comedy, tragedy, romance, and irony. It looks as though the general drift since 1700 has been toward irony, maybe because of the rise of science and the spread of middle-class commerce. In any event, we have been privileged witnesses to a prolonged flowering of ironies, some very amus-ing and some very touching. The general environment is a diachronic ma-trix, so to speak, in which mythic meanings have fled from literature to music, and a modernist-ironist like Zukofsky can best orient his own most ambitious literary work by going back two centuries—from 1928 to 1729—pick up a moment of metamorphosis ("traduction twice over," which means the two ironically contrasted meanings of "traduction"—from Old and New Testament to German to English—along with the transferral of energy from score to performance to repeated performance) and to chase that moment or movement as a fugue:

> A
> > Round of fiddles playing Bach.
> > > *Come, ye daughters, share my anguish—*
> > Bare arms, black dresses,
> > > *See Him! Whom?*
> > Bediamond the passion of our Lord,
> > > *See Him! How?*
>
> > . . . .
> > The Passion According to Matthew,
> > Composed seventeen twenty-nine,
> > Rendered at Carnegie Hall,
> > Nineteen twenty-eight,
> > Thursday evening, the fifth of April.
> > The autos parked, honking.

These lines of condensed polyphonic counterpoint enact the marriage of music and irony. For whatever reason (and reasons are legion), the eiron's art—irony—amounts to saying two or more things at one time, so that an auditor with 20/20 ears ought to hear an ironic utterance as a chord of sorts, one that displays its own meaning in its own sound as harmonies among *cord* and *chord*, *accord* and *a chord*, even *choral* and *coral*. (In the case of Zukofsky's introductory "Round," we are dealing with a fact. In 1928, Seder was Wednesday, April 4, and Passover began the next day, which was also Maundy Thursday for Christians and on that evening in Carnegie Hall there was a performance of Bach's *St. Matthew Passion* by the Detroit Symphony Orchestra and Choir, conducted by Ossip Gabrilowitsch. Olin

Downes's enthusiastic review the next day noted that the conductor "had requested plain dark dress and a silent reception of the masterpiece.")

At times, the drawing together of many meanings in one word amounts to an ecstatic joining of ostensible opposites, as when Hopkins, in "The Windhover," uses "buckle" to mean, simultaneously, both "fall apart" and "come together." Freud, in a note based on some pretty unruly speculations of the linguist Karl Abel, explored the possible psychic meaning of the "antithetical sense of primal words," such as the English "let," "fast," and "still" (or those contrasting twin daughters of a single mother, "queen" and "quean"). The presence of such Siamese chords permits the approach of monophonic language to polyphonic music. Oddly, "fugue" itself is fugal, because it means both "a polyphonic musical style or form" and "a pathological amnesiac condition" (both meanings derive from the concept of "chase" or "flight"). Whether perfidious or merely economical, the capacity in language for such halvings and doublings will give a high rhetorical valence to such figures as zeugma and syllepsis (which don't mean *quite* the same thing) and such devices as parallel plots and contrast-rhymes ("hire"-"fire," "town"-"gown," "womb"-"tomb," and so forth).

What the solo modern prose voice at the beginning of "*A*" accomplishes is, then, to suggest both irony and fugue complexly: by talking about a piece of vocal-instrumental polyphony and by doing so in ways that are themselves fugal or quasi-fugal:

A
Round of fiddles playing Bach.

"A" equals air (*aria*) with different values in ancient and modern English, or in English and other European languages, or in English itself variable according to stress. Prefixed in this way or that, it means "with" and it means "without." It means "one" and "he" and "they" and "of." Here, right off the baton, it plays "around" against "a round," which is iridescent with musical, poetic, geometric, and mundane meanings. The part-for-whole figure of "fiddles" (for "fiddlers") plays against the whole-for-part figure of "Bach" (for "a work by Bach"), and "playing," as I have been leaking none too subtly, means everything that both "work" and "play" can mean, including the ideas of performance and impersonation and contest. (At about the same time, Yeats was scrutinizing near-by ranges of meaning in "play" and "labor" in another poem that has to do with time, memory, age, youth, and music: "Among School Children," which moves from an ironic "I walk" to an ecstatic "dance?".

Then, hundreds of pages later, in an interpolation in "*A*"-21, Zukofsky resumes the theme of roundness by means of a related word, "rote":

there cannot be too much
music R—O—T—E
rote, fiddle

like noise of surf.

Let me confess that I went for most of my life with only one meaning for "rote," one phrase ("learn by rote"), and one circumscribed connotation (bad). I took that verbal poverty with me to a study of Eliot's "The Dry Salvages" and appraised the line "The distant rote in the granite teeth" as a very effective figure of speech that rendered the sound of water against a rock as a lesson mechanically repeated (*rota*: circle). In fact, English "rote" has three meanings, of which Eliot, writing in 1942, used two and Zukofsky, in 1967, used all three. It also means "medieval stringed instrument" and "the sound of surf breaking on the shore" (*American Heritage Dictionary*). (It could appear in the name of an enterprise called POTH, if that name be Greek.) The verbal chord may be tabulated:

	rote 1 routine	ME from Lat. *rota*, wheel	IE *ret*—to run, roll
rote	rote 2 surf	ON *rauta*, to roar	IE *reu*—to bellow
	rote 3 instrument	OF from Gmc.	IE *krut*—instrument

Such an etymological history of three words converging in a single sound—*rote*—may be seen as a model of Zukofsky's main themes and techniques in "*A*." No modern ironic poem of any length could possibly be self-standing, and Zukofsky's resembles those by Williams, Pound, and Eliot in including precursors and companions. A shrewd programmer should design a map that would show Pound appearing in Eliot's and Williams's poems (and, later, in Lowell's and Berryman's), Eliot and Williams in Pound's (and Lowell's and Berryman's), and so on, in a serial agon that is at the same time an old-boy network. As is noted in "*A*"-1, Zukofsky's poem gets going not long after the death of Thomas Hardy in January 1928. Some unconscious ironist says of the most conscious ironist of modern letters, "Poor Thomas Hardy he had to go so soon" (which is ironic because he had been born in 1840). But that note is enough to suggest that the long poem at hand will carry on the work of *The Dynasts*, Hardy's immense epic drama that could be called "The Convergence of the Twain," because it traces, in a somewhat fugal staggered form, the fate of two men born in 1769, Napoleon and Wellington, whose paths finally cross, or collide, at Waterloo. As Hardy is dying, the successors maintain the ironic dynasty, and Zukofsky launches his long poem by assimilating the techniques of Pound, Eliot, Williams, and Hardy. With Zukofsky, the focus is on technique and the fabric of the language itself, but the notion of telling ironic convergence remains as it had been in Hardy's poems.

Zukofsky begins his poem on a particular April evening in 1928, and for him—as for Whitman, Yeats, and Eliot before him—this paschal time of Passover and Passion, converging in the syncretism of Eos-East-Easter with its terrible beauty, furnishes an ideal prism for seeing the world clearly and for intelligently hearing its ironies and harmonies. (Of "When Lilacs Last in the Dooryard Bloom'd," "Easter 1916," *The Waste Land, Ulysses*, and *The Sound and the Fury* alike, one could say that the typical modern literary work begins and centers on a particular day in spring. Oddly, for both Faulkner and Zukofsky, the focus happens to be the same few days in

April 1928.) Given this matrix of ideal convergences, the eiron's eyes and ears can subject language to a detailed inquisition, though it hardly takes the full third degree to remove hide and hair from verbal surfaces. In a sixty-year career, Zukofsky experimented with every species of rhematic and thematic irony as ways of saying more than one thing at a time, and he devoted an inordinate amount of his genius to the transfiguration into English of various foreign texts. Since Zukofsky tried to preserve sound and sense alike—which is impossible—"translation" is not quite the correct word for this process. Pound's "creative translations" showed the path here, especially in versions of Old English and Latin (to which I shall come back in a few moments), but Pound is only one member of a large modern club that has trafficked in the Englishing and modernizing of many sorts of foreign and ancient texts. Some years ago, for instance, there was a black film version of "Carmen" called "Carmen Jones," in which Escamillo became "Husky Miller." Any number of modern characters, in their names if not otherwise, show this sort of metempsychosis: Shaw's John Tanner out of Don Juan Tenorio, O'Neill's Ezra Mannon out of Agamemnon, Eliot's Harcourt-Reilly out of Heracles, Faulkner's Joe Christmas out of Jesus Christ, Updike's Caldwell out of Chiron. Zukofsky's refinement, which may echo certain Talmudic or Cabalistic techniques of interpretation, has been to apply this principle of nomenclature to whole texts, typically ironic or comic-lyric, and to produce a complete *Catullus* by this method, as well as a version (appearing as "*A*"-21) of Plautus's *Rudens*, which is evidently a reworking of a lost Greek play by Diphilus.

One of those shipwreck-and-lost-daughter comedies, *Rudens* (i.e., *The Rope*) resembles Shakespeare's *Pericles* (although it is not, strictly speaking, the source of *Pericles*, as one critic has stated). At any rate, we may note here that volume 2 of Zukofsky's *Bottom: On Shakespeare* is a musical setting for *Pericles* by Zukofsky's wife, Celia. One may regard all of *Bottom* as a long poem that works as an appendix to "*A*." It is typically ironic of Zukofsky to see all of Shakespeare through the eyes of Nick Bottom, big-mouthed weaver and man of the theatre (not to mention part-time ass and boyfriend of the fairy queen).

Zukofsky's novel handling of Latin and other foreign languages has been duly admired by some, but I have to say that I think his Catullus and Plautus are dull distortions. Their purpose may be to breathe (literally) new breath through their consonants and vowels, but the result is a high-handed botch.

I am not qualified to discuss the fine points of this complicated problem of translation. It's just that sound and sense cannot be transferred from one language to another, and it may also be true that not even sense by itself can be moved. Now and then, as in the acoustic and semantic nearness of Hebrew *pāsah*, Latin *passiō*, and English *pass*, there seems to be a linguistic kinship that resembles the connection among *Pesach*, *Passion*, and *Passover*; but such harmonies are rare. More commonly, even "cognates" from closely related languages may not be good translations for one another, especially in the realm of abstractions. *Stupor Mundi* just isn't "stupor of the world."

Consider these two lines from *Rudens*, in which Charmides (a *senex*) is needling his friend, the pimp Labrax, about a shipwreck:

> *Pol minime miror, navis si fractast tibi,*
> *scelus te et sceleste parta quae vexit bona.*

"Pol" is a faint oath that abridges something like "by Pollux." "Minime" is an adverb meaning "least" (or "not at all"). "Miror" (as some may recall from their high-school Latin version of "Twinkle, Twinkle, Little Star") is the present first-person singular declarative of a deponent verb (hence the passive form) meaning "I wonder." "Well, by God, I'm not a bit surprised," as you might say. The Loeb translation by Paul Nixon captures all of these meanings: "Gad! I don't wonder at all that your ship was wrecked, with a rascal like you and your rascally gains aboard." Zukofsky:

> Pole! minimal mirror! the ship
> fractured from your ill-begot goods.

Well: Pole! minimal mirror!" does preserve the general sound pattern of "Pol minime miror," and it may preserve some of the sense (if calling one "Pole" and "minimal mirror" suggests that he doesn't do much reflecting). But at what price? This: the subordination of sense to sound, which is exactly what Imagists and Objectivist complain about in the verse of sonneteers and what Olson complained about in Pound's later Chinese translations. And this: the sacrifice of the character's personal style. Kept up doggedly for seventy pages, Zukofsky's Plautus's Diphilus's *Rudens* is the most tiresome part of "*A*."

The next most tiresome part is "*A*"-24, which is another fugal experiment. "*A*"-21 amounts to a superposed transmogrification of the folk theme of the recovered daughter with Greco-Roman voices joined by synthetic English (a tricky sort of technique that Pound was intelligent enough, in Canto I, to limit to seventy-six lines and to carbonate, ad lib, with matter, rhythms, and "cross-lights" from sources other than his Greek-Latin-English triad). "*A*"-24, which was composed by Celia Zukofsky (with help from the Zukofsky's brilliant son, Paul) before Louis Zukofsky wrote "*A*"-22 and "*A*"-23, is not so much the real conclusion of "*A*" as a kind of addendum called *L. Z. Masque*, "a five-part score—music, thought, drama, story, poem." The score is presented contrapuntally with music in two staves (treble and bass) above four verbal lines in type of varying sizes. The music is Handel's, the words from Zukofsky's *Prepositions* (thought), *Arise, Arise* (drama), *It was* (story), and "*A*" itself (poem). The two acts are divided into nine scenes named for characters and musical forms (Cousin: Lesson, Nurse: Prelude & Allegro, Father: Suite, Girl: Fantasia, Attendants: Chaconne, Mother: Sonata, Doctor: Capriccio, Aunt: Passacaille, and Son: Fugues). The text is about 240 pages, with an indicated duration of about

70 minutes. Presumably, a harpsichord plays while four voices speak the words ("The words are NEVER SUNG to the music. . . . Each voice should come through clearly"). I have taken some pains to describe "*A*"-24, because I don't want to be judged indifferent or careless when I say that the thing is unreadable. I have done my best, line-by-line and also measure-by measure, and in my cranial studio I get only the effect of five non-profit educational stations going at one time. I'll keep at it, but for the present I can't find anything to admire. In both "*A*"-21 and "*A*"-24 the fugue fails.

That failure is more than disappointing. It is heartbreaking. As the ironic poem progresses through its early and middle phases, its moments of greatest tenderness and beauty coincide with the moments of most concentrated attention on Zukofsky's marriage to Celia Thaew in 1939 and the birth, on 22 October 1943, of their son, the *Wunderkind* violinist Paul Zukofsky, whose childhood experiences contributed to Louis Zukofsky's novel called *Little*. *Baker's Biographical Dictionary of Musicians*, edited by Nicolas Slonimsky, praises Paul Zukofsky's sympathy for contemporary music and the "maximal celerity, dexterity, and alacrity" of his playing. Even so, the Plautus translation, which was probably done as the Catullus was—by Louis and Celia Zukofsky together—and the five-part happening of "*A*"-24, in which all three Zukofskys had a part, subtract from all the overall integrity and intensity of "*A*."

The remaining twenty-two sections add up to about five hundred pages of poetry that takes the initial fugal subjects and styles through a forty-five-year development, conditioned by external historical and personal events but never, I think, completely irrelevant to the promises potently implicit in

> A
> Round of fiddles playing Bach.

Earlier I suggested a number of the possible meanings, but I did not mention the chance that the fiddles are playing B A C H, which, in a peculiar German style of notation used at one time before the seven-note nomenclature was adopted, would sound as B-flat, A, C, B-natural. J. S. and C. P. E. Bach used this sequence as a musical subject, as did Schumann, Liszt, Rimsky-Korsakov, and a score (ha) of other composers. Zukofsky's use of this musical acrostic to organize the very long (135 pages) "*A*"-12—

> Blest
> Ardent
> Celia
>   unhurt and
> Happy—

brings us back to the alphabet and its gifts and challenges to the ironic poet.

Bach's adding his "signature" to a piece of music is an uncommon but not a unique phenomenon. It is recorded that Bach, who may have written a four-note "cruciform" motif for the Crucifixion in the *St. Matthew Passion*, once sketched out a canon formula for a friend named Schmidt. Translating *Schmidt* into the Latin *father*, Bach then canonized his friend in the form of F A B E Repetatur, then signed the formula with the tribute, *Bonae Artis Cultorem Habeas*. It is said that the *paytanim*, composers of Hebrew liturgical poetry, "signed" their works by placing their names or anagrams thereof as an acrostic at the beginning of each line. It is also said that certain Jewish names may have been formed as acronyms drawn from devotional formulae, as "Atlas" from *akh tov leyisrael selah* ("Truly God is good to Israel") and not from the Greek name of the world-bearing Titan or the German word for "satin." That may belong in the same uncertain category as the oddity of the King James version of Psalm 46, written when Shakespeare was 46 years old: the forty-sixth word from the beginning is "shake," the forty-sixth from the end "spear." It is certain, however, that writers now and then have used their own names or initials to "sign" their works internally, as it were, as well as on the title page. Shakespeare and Donne used "will" and "done" in poems as puns on their own first or last names. Robert Browning used his initials for *The Ring and the Book*, and T. S. Eliot may have had a variation of the same policy in mind when he titled a play *The Elder Statesman*. J. D. Salinger once named a character Jean de Daumier-Smith, and Martin Gardner's fascinating column in *Scientific American* is called "Mathematical Games." In modern prose's grandest ironic epic, Mann's *Doktor Faustus*, the composer Leverkühn repeatedly uses certain notes, Bach-fashion, to trace nonmusical meanings over musical themes; and at the end of the book, in the *Nachschrift*, the author's own names rises touchingly through the prose of his rather foolish narrator, "Dr. phil. Serenus Zeitblom": *Es ist getan*," he says. He now writes as *"ein alter Mann, gebeugt. . . . "* Pound reversed the process once, in Canto IV, when he alluded to Whitman's "Beat! beat! . . . whirr and pound" but changed the wording to "Beat, beat, whirr, thud." Later, though, he made up for this avoidance of his own name by putting three archaic Chinese characters on the title page of *Thrones: pao en tê*, pronounced, more or less, "Pound."

So what? So the work of art inherently resists being used for autobiography or any other kind of direct representation. Only by certain tricks can an artist register his own presence in a self-willed medium, especially if he is an eiron approaching that medium and its social environment from below or outside. The eiron's infra-structural position resembles the alien's extra-structural condition, so that if one has to be both—a talented son, say, of Yiddish-speaking immigrants—then one's ears will, with luck, be attuned to speech as a foreign entity and, particularly, to American English as the native property of others. "Abcedminded," then, as it says in *Finnegans Wake*, verbal comedy leads ironic outsiders of various sorts to write *The Comedian as the Letter C* and an uproarious novel called *V.* and a long poem called *"A"* (just as Stephen Dedalus contemplated calling his novels by letters of the alphabet). This is elevated comedy, a plane of discourse where linguistic perspicuity and literally broken English are joined in rapturous wedlock. Here Gandhi, mindful of the gentry's "plus fours," will describe his loincloth as "minus fours," and Vladimir Nabokov will notice how, on more than one level, "therapist" may equal "the rapist." The fine ear of Zukofsky's Wisconsin friend Lorine Niedecker will pick up and decoct the miraculous fission of language when it is forced through the double warp of music and translation:

> O Tannenbaum
> the children sing
> round and round
> one child sings out:
> atomic bomb.

(This is, incidentally, part of a garland, *For Paul*, written for Zukofsky's son.) Poetry tests the language as language tests the world.

An ironic epic, accordingly, is going to be partly an ordeal for words themselves, starting, conventionally enough, with the virtually pure air of the first letter and first vowel, *a*. The purpose of the ordeal, from the viewpoint of ironic skepticism, will be to follow the contours of language without undue distortion, so that most of Zukofsky's prosody is a natural-seeming measure of syllables-per-line or words-per-line with no twisting, chipping, or padding to fit an imposed meter that may depend on an arbitrary Morse of qualitative or quantitative dots and dashes given further shape by a rhyme scheme. Once the measure by syllable-unit or word-unit is established along with a modest devotion to short lines, however, the purest music of consonant and vowel, stress and pitch, fancy and plain can come through with an effect, usually, of delicacy, eloquence, accuracy, and fidelity.

Such an idiom works best with its inherent data of ambiguity, inquisition, and multiple irony. These data are most lucidly presented in fairly short poems (like Zukofsky's, and like those of Cid Corman and Robert Creeley, both of whom owe much to Zukofsky's example) in which the courtesy and modesty can balance the potentially injurious clarity of perception and memory. The idiom does not work so well in longer flights, in which it tends to become otiose or academic. ("*A*" comes equipped with an index, but it quirkily omits some important items. Lorine Niedecker seems to be in the poem . . . but is not in the index; neither is "A friend, a Z the 3rd letter of his (the first of my) last name". . . who I think must be Charles Reznikoff.) Yet another difficulty with this idiom is the way it refreshingly insists on seeing everything anew, with unprejudiced eyes; but that means the propagandist for the idiom, whether in lyric or in critical writing, had better be sure he is original. Often, however, Zukofsky seems merely derivative. His *A Test of Poetry*, for instance, promises to chuck out academic biases but winds up as little more than a replay of Pound's "How to Read" and *ABC of Reading*, even to the extent of repeating Pound's dogmatic concentration on book 11 of the *Odyssey*. A teacher can get a funny feeling when a bold student merely repeats the once-original gestures of Creeley, say, and justifies them on principles that really are "academic" in the worst sense: "I do this because Creeley does, because Olson and Zukofsky told him, because they got it from Pound, because Pound thought Fenollosa was right," etc. I am not sure that originality is very important. I am not even sure it is quite possible. But if you make a fuss about it, then you ought to be able to do some other thing than imitate, echo, and repeat.

At his best, Zukofsky dissolves illusion and punches sham to pieces. He breaks things up into particles and articles; under his testing, for example, the ambiguity-loaded *anathema* is analyzed into *"an, a, the.* Once the alphabet has been taken apart, though, the problem is how to put it back together with honest energies and designs. Zukofsky's life must have confirmed some of his early ironic suspicions; after twenty years at a technical school, he retired as an associate professor, and for a long time he "was not well." The one time I met him, in June 1975, he was frowning through the sickliest-looking yellow-green complexion I think I have ever seen; but his voice was very youthful, his wit intact. On the whole, though I think he found himself on the receiving end of an enjoyable destiny. He was brilliant, he loved his noble father, he found the perfect wife, his son appeared with the New Haven Symphony at the age of eight, and his work tended after all in the direction suggested by the title of a late poem: "Finally a valentine."

As *"A"*-24 is arranged, the whole book ends on a nicely cadenced C-minor chord in the harpsichord, the drama voice saying, "New gloves, mother?" and the poem voice repeating the end of *"A"*-20, "What is it, I wonder, that makes thee so loved." Finally, with "love" sounding simultaneously in "gloves" and "loved," a valentine, indeed.

Well, I must be churlish. I prefer consigning *"A"*-24 to the status of appendix or addendum, because I think the poem itself (if not the life of the poet) finds a more authentic and convincing conclusion in the end of *"A"*-23, which was the last part written by Zukofsky. It does not end, *Heldenleben*-style, with a survey and synthesis of the artist's life-in-work, but with a return to the alphabetical keynote that started *"A"*-1. What we have is a scrupulously measured twenty-six-line alphabet-stretto:

> A living calendar, names inwreath'd
> Bach's innocence longing Handel's untouched.
> Cue in new-old quantities—'Don't
> bother me'—Bach quieted bothered;
> since Eden gardens labor, For
> series distributes harmonies, attraction Governs
> destinies. Histories dye the streets:
> intimate whispers magnanimity flourishes: doubts'
> passionate Judgment, passion the task.
> *Kalenderes enlumined 21-2-3, nigher . . . fire—*

Land or—sea, air—gathered.
Most art, object-the-mentor, donn'd one—
smiles ray *immaterial Nimbus . . . Oes*
sun-pinned to red threads—thrice-urged
posato (poised) 'support from the
source'—horn-note out of a
string (Quest returns answer—'to
rethink the Caprices') *sawhorses silver*
all these fruit-tree tops: consonances
and dissonances only of degree, never-
Unfinished hairlike water of notes
vital free as Itself—impossible's
sort-of think-cramp work x: moonwort:
music, thought, drama, story, poem
parks' sunburst—animals, grace notes—
z-sited path are but us.

This garland names names (Bach, Handel) and suggests others without quite pronouncing them outright (Landor, Mozart, maybe Anaximander, John Donne inwreathed, as is fitting, with Don Juan). It covers instruments, voices, plants, animals (including a goat inside "Caprices" and an A-shaped sawhorse that is a Wooden Horse too: a running theme through the poem, so to speak). I don't know what all is included in "z-sited," aside from the author's and alphabet's final monogram, but I suspect it may include a reminder that the early Semitic and Greek character for *zayinzeta* looked like this: I, which may be pronounced "eye" or "I," which is roughly what the Hebrew *zayin* still looks like—hence "eyesight." "Are but us" looks and sounds like a re-vision of "arbutus" with an adumbration of widespread (if not universal) identity, community, and harmony.

That hermetic hint is, I think, a more satisfying conclusion than an adventitious pun on "love." We have come too far through too many agonies and mazes at too much intellectual and emotional expense to accept at the end the weakly established assertion that love matters or some similar Hallmark sentiment. It's like the Calvin Coolidge whom one can imagine in Purgatory taking a look at Pound's sweet little Canto 120 "What's it about, Cal?" "Forgiveness." "What's he say?" "He's for it."

One of these days a scholarly critic with time on his hands is going to discover or invert a tabular schema. In *"A"*-12 there is evidence that Zukofsky had the twenty-four-book plan in mind by 1950 and possibly somewhat earlier. There too there is a recognition that both of Homer's epics have been divided into twenty-four books by scholars, and it would not surprise me to learn that Zukofsky knew that Bach's *St. Matthew Passion* can be divided into twenty-four scenes: Schweitzer calculated it as "twelve smaller ones, indicated by chorales, and twelve larger ones, marked by arias." But Zukofsky's general design does not gracefully fall into twenty-four shapely parts. With or without the marginal "*A*"-21 (*Rudens*) and "*A*"-24 (*L. Z. Masque*), the shape of the whole is asymmetrical. The contour may match that of a diary or revery, but there is no essential literary progression. Such development as may emerge is more along the lines of an experimental fugue and variations, with room along the way for one poem 135 pages long ("*A*"-12) and another four words long ("*A*"-16). "*A*"-16 asks:

> *Can*
> The design
> Of the fugue
> Be transferred
> To poetry?

When the "plot" has to include a piece of history—such as the death of Williams or the assassination of President Kennedy—then the writing slackens, and the grief seems perfunctory. In other stretches, the author's vigor and sincerity seem to thin out and his wordplay ("Pith or gore has" for "Pythagoras") nosedives towards the asymptote of crossword puzzles and tricks like Henny Youngman's superseding "diamond pin" with "dime and pin."

The scholiasts have their work cut out for them. For all I know, the audience for poems like Zukofsky's may be nothing but scholiasts. I hate to think that world poetry today amounts to nothing more than a hundred people writing something for an audience of a hundred (probably the same hundred). The dismal situation would be no less dismal if that figure were a thousand or even a million, because the proportion is so small up against the whole human race. Maybe the University of California Press ought to keep a few copies of the full "*A*" available for specialists, and they may be wise to market it in an ugly Clearasil-pink dust jacket, to keep amateurs at arm's length. But maybe the publisher should also issue a 250-page volume of selections. I would suggest that 1–7, 9–11, 15–18, and 20 could be kept as wholes, 21 and 24 done without, and the rest given in generous selections. That sort of book would reach more people with a more concentrated representation of a fine poet's best work.

Stanley Kunitz:
The Stubborn Middle Way

Robert Weisberg

"The easiest poet to neglect is one who resists classification." Had he spoken of himself, Stanley Kunitz might rather have said that we neglect the poet who becomes classified too early and too narrowly. Since a brief, if sympathetic, article by Jean Hagstrum in 1958 [in *Poets in Progress*], Kunitz's impressive canon has aroused no critical interest. Instead, he has been dubiously honored, by almost universal agreement, as a strange phenomenon called the "poet's poet," and the only recent study of him, by Marjorie Perloff in the *Iowa Review*, explicitly sustains this official view. In what sense is Kunitz "the poet's poet"? The title first assumes that his verse is of minor interest in itself, but that his literary relationships as peer and mentor have merited him a grateful, if condescending, nod from the historians of contemporary poetry. More specifically, the title has generally implied fixed critical views of the nature of his verse. In his early work as represented in *Selected Poems* he is a skillful but derivative practitioner of the modernist-metaphysical mode, limited in subject, a bit abstruse in imagery, and interesting chiefly as a technician. In the late poems in *The Testing Tree* he is again the skillful derivative, this time as a late convert to the confessional mode. . . .

Selected Poems 1928–1958 is organized, the poet tells us, not by chronology, but by similarities of "argument," of theme. Two outstanding themes appear in it, and perhaps a third emerges to unite the two. The first theme unifies a great number of poems that make the agonies of love a metaphor of mortality in general. The poet pictures these agonies through complex metaphysical imagery as a wound, or, more often, a festering disease from which we may seek escape into pure vision, but to which we return as the *felix culpa* of poetry: love and life are a venereal disease. The

From *Modern Poetry Studies* 6 (1975). © 1975 by Robert Weisberg.

second major theme is that of generation, of the poet's three-phase struggle with his past. First, the poet tries to escape the responsibility that the ghosts of the past place on him; then he ecstatically embraces them in a transcendent illumination; and finally, as in the first theme, rejecting a rarefied vision for the salvation he finds in the fecund ditch of life, he learns to "endure" (a central word in Kunitz) the agonies of the generative process. This does not mean to make peace with the past by transcending time, but to make peace with time itself. Ultimately, the wound and the generative process are one, and it is the poet's job to celebrate them.

It is the poems of the first theme that undoubtedly caused critics to type Kunitz as an extreme formalist, but it is important to see a substantial change within them even in *Selected Poems*. We might say that Kunitz does begin with poems that *do* all too self-consciously offer themselves as reincarnations of John Donne:

> And even should I track you to your birth
> Through all the cities of your mortal trial,
> As in my jealous thought I try to do,
> You would escape me—from the brink of earth
> Take off to where the lawless auroras run,
> You with your wild and metaphysic heart.
> My touch is on you, who are light-years gone.
> We are not souls but systems, and we move
> In clouds of our unknowing.
>   ("The Science of the Night")

Kunitz here displays the typical dilemma of his generation—an excess of sheer stylistic talent all too vulnerable to strong influence—as if he were too enthusiastically filling Eliot's request for a re-association of sensibility. The burden of talent and influence produces an immensely interesting and rich lyric which yet seems to stifle the poet's true voice, as if an almost unconscious insincerity may have been the curse attached to the Eliot-Auden inheritance. At other times we may feel the poet fully to blame for conceiving himself as the restorer of the Elizabethan world picture:

> So intricately is this world resolved
> Of substance arched on thrust of circumstance,
> The earth's organic meaning so involved
> That none may break the pattern of his dance.
>   ("So Intricately Is This World Resolved")

The problem is that at the base of a good metaphysical yoking-conceit must be some sort of conflict between an order and a violence, and if the violence is insufficiently realized in the poem, if it seems just a tame, cultivated violence and not the genuine violence of a convincing emotional experience, the order in the conceit will seem more clever than dynamic.

But as *Selected Poems* progresses, a more sincere voice does emerge in the poems of this first theme; a more forceful, less genteel, violence of language reveals a genuine emotional core, and Kunitz seems to achieve the difficult synthesis he may well have thought Eliot was asking for. He manages to bring his immediate experience a Renaissance sense of wit and decorum, including metrical formality, and use it to express and contain his personality, not suppress it through derivative stylization. We might even imagine him in these poems conducting a secret argument with Eliot. The poet has acknowledged himself a respectful adversary of Eliot: "His definition of poetry as an objective act, a depersonalized performance, was contrary to my own conviction that art and life were bound together. I sought a more passionate voice. And I scorned his politics." Kunitz undoubtedly is wrong in seeing a crude art-life split in Eliot, but he takes Eliot at his word in making a poetry of intelligence and emotion possible again, very close to the original Renaissance model. This is opposite to what Eliot did in his own verse, which was to transform the metaphysical mode so thoroughly into modernist-free verse as to make the metaphysical influence more a critical catalyst than a true poetic model.

The new voice emerges gradually. We see in "No Word" still the almost excessively thick imagery, yet the wit in this poem conceals a contemporary, common subject—the "no word" is the telephone call that does not come— and so the metaphysical style begins to connect with a true experience:

> No message. May the mothering dark,
> Whose benediction calms the sea,
> Abater of the atrocious spark
> Of love and love's anxiety,
> Be kind; and may my self condone,
> As surely as my judge reprieves,
> This heart strung on the telephone,
> Folded in death, whom no voice revives.

At the end here, the poet moves toward Eliot in weaving an object of common experience into the conceit, and the effect is startling and emotionally convincing. Recalling Eliot's distinction between the "rhetorics" of Henry James and John Milton, we might see the twists and turns of the verse approaching the vacillations of an active emotional mind, and not just self-consciously elaborating the conceit. The woman of the poem remains as remote as in "The Science of the Night"—but remote as a real woman might be to a man and not, as in the previous poem, remote merely because abstract. Here she is simply distant and cold, and takes on some implied substance through the poet's own tension.

We see another advance in "The Words of the Preacher." The diction is no more contemporary, and in some ways the emotional experience no more precise. But the poem has an *energy* that other of Kunitz's metaphysical lyrics lack. And so it succeeds as one of Ezra Pound's early experiments in traditional forms succeeds, by investing the form with new vigor and whole, yet being, in a sense, a purely imitative poem. Equally important though, the poem begins to develop the disease conceit that will dominate the rest of the volume:

> Taking infection from the vulgar air
> And sick with the extravagant disease
> Of life, my soul rejected the sweet snare
> Of happiness; declined
> That democratic bait, set in the world
> By fortune's old and mediocre mind.
>
> To love a changing shape with perfect faith
> Is waste of faith; to follow dying things
> With deathless hope is vain; to go from breath
> To breath, so to be fed
> And put to sleep, is cheat and shame—because
> By piecemeal living a man is doomed, I said.

This verbal energy, or, more specifically, this invigorating sense of a speaking voice, is precisely what most imitative verse lacks. Many poems of the thirties compound the weakness by seeming uncertain of *who* is speaking at all. The potential energy in a good "homage" may be dissipated by the poet's anxiety to force sincerity, and the result is the insincerity we have seen already. Here, the poet displays a rare Pound-like sense of play with the metaphysical style. The poem deals with his serious theme, yet borrows from the early Pound the redeeming power of play in rejuvenating the old form. This sense of play is a significant movement for Kunitz, for the poems get richer as they turn from a forced Elizabethan elegance to the sharper emotional thrust that is more natural to him.

For Kunitz, the *felix culpa* is man's attachment to this "extravagant disease" (the metaphor has the metaphysical *vigor* of such Yeats metaphors as "dying animal" and "fecund ditch") and like W. B. Yeats, he gradually lays claim to this middle ground, this scrimmage of mortality between nihilism and rarefied vision as the distinct arena of his poetry. Kunitz's best poems refuse to decorate the physical life with Elizabethan elegance, or transcend it for a permanence he finds all the more threatening. Again, the poems are strongest where the commitment to this mortal arena is most honest, where the metaphysical images heighten rather than tame the tension. . . .

Much as the first theme is of a journey through pain, the second is a journey through guilt; pain and guilt are the loci of the poetry. In this theme of guilt we may see a parallel development from an agonizing awareness, to a magniloquent vision of transcendence, and finally to a middle ground that does not undermine the vision but balances it with a subtler possibility of enduring a bitter, but liberating, tension between the guilt and the vision. Thus may the development be seen in bare outline, but as with the first theme, a very close reading of the poems reveals a complicated journey in and out of these three phases, with an emerging emphasis on the last phase toward the end of the volume and in the finest poems in *The Testing Tree*.

As the pain came from love, so the guilt comes from time, and in "The Signal from the House," the poet boldly announces the theme, and immediately casts it into its central metaphor. His "father's house" is the repository of ghosts who fail him, as we shall see, in not offering him a clear spiritual heritage, in not giving him a word to take into the future, and whom he fails in his refusal or inability to make peace with them. The poems of what we might thus call the generation theme oscillate between these two failures, but it is the latter failure that provides the drama for this first announcement:

> I said to the watcher at the gate,
> "They also kill who wait."
>
> I cried to the mourner on the stair,
> "Mother, I hate you for those tears."
>
> To mistress of the ruined hall,
> The keeper of the sacred heart,
>
> I bought the mind's indifference
> And the heavy marble of my face.
>
> For those who were too much with me
> Were secretly against me:
>
> Hostages to the old life,
> Expecting to be ransomed daily
>
> And for the same fond reason
> From the deep prison of their person.
>
> Their lantern shining in the window
> had signaled me, like a cry of conscience.
>
> Insisting that I must be broken
> Upon the wheel of the unforsaken.

Aside from being another example of a work intensely personal while in no clear way being confessional, the poem succeeds as a conscious metaphysical conceit where earlier ones failed, in that again, it energizes an old form: here what we might call the dramatic reversal structure of such a George Herbert poem as "The Collar." The reversal arises from the speaker's defiant but uncertain attitude toward the dead, exemplified by his attitude to the mourners, whom he chides for mediating between him and the father he wants to forget but cannot. He resists identifying with the mourners—who are imagined as respectful worshippers as well as the bereaved—and adopts the pose of "marble indifference."

The action significantly connects with the well-known poem "The Thief," in which Kunitz ultimately rejects the marble past of Rome for the squalid and fertile modern city that stands on its ruins. In "The Signal from the House," the same pose is offered only to be shown in its futility. The undertone of guilt and paranoia at the center of the poem turns suddenly at the end to direct acknowledgement of the wheel, the medieval torture of time to which he is committed. The father-haunted-house metaphor is woven into the metaphors of the sacred chapel and of the psychological kidnapping, and all merge in the final torture which the poet presents in impressive understatement. Here, as in the next poem of the theme, we begin with an ironic Miltonic echo, which reminds us at the end, that the poet must join those "waiting," enduring the responsibilities the unburied dead foist on us.

Now it is just this stance of serving and waiting that "Open the Gates" contradicts, and it is important to see this as a very deliberate contradiction, as Kunitz establishes the opposite pole of the theme. "Open the Gates" is a poem of visionary impatience with time, a storming of the door out of the haunted house and into heaven, and through its goal is rejected by later poems it still stands as a brilliant, terse revelation of a *possibility*. Even if modified later, this possibility by its power, still remains a constant valence in Kunitz's mind. Without this poem as opposite pole, even "King of the River" might be weakened in its dramatic placement in his canon:

> Within the city of the burning cloud,
> Dragging my life behind me in a sack,
> Naked I prowl, scourged by the black
> Temptation of the blood gone proud.
>
> Here at the monumental door,
> Carved with the curious legend of my youth,
> I brandish the great bone of my death,
> Beat once therewith and beat no more.
>
> The hinges groan: a rush of forms
> Shivers my name, wrenched out of me.
> I stand on the terrible threshold, and I see
> The end and the beginning in each other's arms.

The past, personal as well as cultural, is even more clearly a guilty burden in this poem. Kunitz creates an impersonal sense of visionary possibility of unity rising out of the personal theme of "The Signal from the House," which is reiterated in the sense of skulking guilt and shame at the end of the first stanza here. An earlier poem, "Among the Gods," had platonically celebrated "the sound / Of matter pouring through eternal forms," as if the music of that cascade will be his true poetry. In "Open the Gates," in the final metamorphosis of the concluding scene of St. Augustine's *Confessions* into a brilliant, Yeatsian sexual metaphor, the process reverses, and the forms ecstatically rush *out* of the speaker, and he stands, purged, before "the terrible threshold" through which he sees time embraced into a unity. The commitment to physicality in such poems as "Among the Gods" seems coldly abstract compared to the sexual excitement of the return to Platonic purity in "Open the Gates," his "Byzantium." . . .

Selected Poems, Kunitz tells us, is classified into themes and arguments, and the absence of chronological structure teases us into abstracting a line of development that the arrangement of poems may obscure. As such, having discerned the two basic themes of disease and generation, we may have to add a third, not just to tie our two themes into a conclusion, but to account for a number of impressive poems which fall in between or outside these themes. Let us call it the theme of monstrosity.

Kunitz has explicitly defined for us a concept of the contemporary artist as a potential monster:

> What is it in our culture that drives so many artists and writers to suicide—or, failing that, mutilates them spiritually? At the root of the problem is the cruel discrepancy between the values of art and the values of society, which makes strangers and adversaries out of those who are most gifted and vulnerable. The artist who turns in on himself, feeds off his own psyche, aggrandizes his bruised ego, is on the way to monsterdom. Ambition is the fire in his gut. No sacrifice is judged too great for his art. At a certain point he becomes a nexus of abstract sensations and powers, beyond the realm of the personal.

He then refers to two poems in particular, "Approach to Thebes," and "The Artist," from *The Testing Tree*, which elaborate this notion. The Oedipus figure of the latter poem lives to tell his story, and so, though "spiritually mutilated" by his incest with his "flagrant source" (the pun suggests, in terms of the generation theme, the dangers of the beginning and the end embracing), survives as a poet to bequeath his monstrous legend to his posterity. And such would be a tolerable notion of the role of the poet, as bequeather except we see a more terrifying picture of the poet as monster in Mark Rothko's suicide in "The Artist," and most especially in an amazing poem that Kunitz does not mention, "Prophecy on Lethe."

> Echo, the beating of the tide,
> Infringes on the blond curved shore;
> Archaic weeds from sleep's green side
> Bind skull and pelvis till the four
> Seasons of the blood are unified.

Anonymous sweet carrion,
Blind mammal floating on the stream
Of depthless sound, completely one
In the cinnamon-dark of no dream—
A pod of silence, bursting when the sun

Clings to the forehead, will surprise
The gasping turtle and the leech
With your strange brain blooming as it lies
Abandoned to the bipeds on the beach;
Your jelly-mouth and, crushed, your polyp eyes.

A poem like this may explain why the poet resists what he calls elsewhere "the Faustian dog that chews my penitential bones," why he resists a poetry of visionary prophecy, to which he is clearly attracted, why he sets against the great monsters of poetry such figures as William Carlos Williams and Boris Pasternak "who were whole, who excelled in their humanity, who fulfilled themselves in the life as well as in the work." It explains, in fact, the whole middle way of Kunitz's poetry, a refusal to embrace "the Truth" so violently that he will ruin himself into abstracted monsterhood—the danger being, of course, that it *is* the truth that he fears. But the poet is honest enough to acknowledge what he is willing and not willing to do, and "Prophecy on Lethe" suggests that he has come close enough to the terror of the truth to know what he would choose to keep clear of.

"Prophecy" makes monstrosity much more precise and suicidal than "Approach to Thebes." It alludes to the myth of Echo and Narcissus and makes the poet a bit of each, doomed to inwardness, reduced to two separate parts: a carrion and a voice. Like Oedipus, the implicit poet figure bequeaths a poetic legend to posterity. The bequest turns out to be his own frightening monster-self, tossed on the shore of normal reality from the sea of Truth—inward truth—that the self has descended to. It is swollen, decayed, contorted; it has seen some Medusa, and it cannot tell the story but only offer itself as a warning. Yet the warning cannot even be heard or understood, since the animal imagery of the poem pictures the poet as having passed into a wholly new species, inexplicable to "the bipeds on the beach." He has passed, in fact, all the way through poetry to silence, the visionary embrace having separated itself from the voice it left underwater. Instead of the beginning and the end in each other's arms, we get the "skull and pelvis" bound and blurred beyond human recognition and denied voice and vision. The heroic poet has been harmonized into grotesquerie. Kunitz acknowledges that not every poet can be a monster, that it "takes a special kind of greatness," such as Sylvia Plath had, and here we have the poet's refusing to join what has become the post-confessional suicidal school. We can only say that if it seems he lacks that "greatness," his poetry is ennobled nevertheless by the way he refuses to desire it.

So perhaps the truest final note of *Selected Poems* comes in the wry realism of "Revolving Meditation," which tries to put poetry into a perspective of the larger question of the whole, healthy life, arguing that there may be something "beyond all this fiddle."

> Imagination makes
> Out of what stuff it can,
> An action fit
> For a more heroic stage
> Than body ever walked on.
> I have learned,
> Trying to live
> With this perjured quid of mine,
> That the truth is not in the stones,
> But in the architecture.

Kunitz is willing to risk that his poetry may suffer the consequences of his believing that mere [truth] is something worth more than poetry, though it is that risk which ironically produces many of his best poems. To those who cry for a leap into the Truth, he responds:

> But I fly towards Possibility, . . .
>
> Careless that I am bound
> To the flaming wheel of my bones,
> Preferring to hear, as I
> Am forced to hear,
> The voice of the solitary
> Who makes others less alone,
> The dialogue of lovers,
> And the conversation of two worms
> In the beam of a house,
> Their mouths filled with sawdust.

We can relate the worm-riddled house to the Broken Tower here, and see the poet making what he can of the decaying process, which is also the march of pure stain upon stain toward the sun. He wants poetry to bring him fulfillment *in* life, not beyond or beneath it.

The Testing Tree shows us some of the fulfillment in the possibilities of poetry once the struggle with "the brave god" has been relaxed, the battles for the truth over. "The Artist," the poem on Rothko, provides us with a bridge to Kunitz's latest volume, since it reassures us that the poet is now beyond any interest in self-consumption:

> At last he took a knife in his hand
> and slashed an exit for himself
> between the frames of his tall scenery.

> Through the holes of his tattered universe
> the first innocence and the light
> came pouring in.

It takes a full appreciation of the early Kunitz to receive the full ironic bite of those lines. The artist here is denied even the grotesque legacy of "Prophecy on Lethe"; he achieves not even destruction, but pure dissolution. *The Testing Tree* is the offering of a poet who has learned—and hopefully taught—his lesson, and the appealing personal—*not* confessional—warmth of the volume is model of what a deliberately, maturely limited aesthetic can produce.

"Illumination," which in some ways recapitulates "Open the Gates," uses a light tone to make a serious new point about the possibilities of vision—in fact, to deliberately deepen the ambivalence of the value and feasibility of the visionary embrace he once tried so resolutely to assert. The poet here, with obvious irony, catalogs the ills of his life:

> the parent I denied,
> the friends I failed,
> the hearts I spoiled,
> including at least
> my own left ventricle.

Then, with even subtler irony, the illumination is promised, but not delivered. And yet the poem leaves him—and us—with the strangest feeling that perhaps the illumination was accomplished—but not as intended:

> "Dante!" I cried
> to the apparition
> entering from the hall,
> laureled and gaunt,
> in a cone of light.
> "Out of mercy you came
> To be my Master
> and my guide!"
> To which he replied:
> "I know neither the time
> nor the way
> nor the number on the door . . .
> but this must be my room,
> I was here before."
> And he held up in his hand
> the key,
> which blinded me.

This poem subsumes all the conflicts about vision shaping the earlier poetry in a healthy irony exactly opposed to the deadly irony of his Auden-influenced work. Having moved among extremes of feeling and thought, the poet has created as the great sanity and health-inducing element of his poetry the manipulation of tone as the great limiter and negotiator among extremes. There is a lessened risk here; after all, "The Artist" did see a light the poet cannot allow into this poetry. But Kunitz finds ample poetic freedom in dramatizing the vicissitudes of the mind and heart tracing out their boundaries, and his subtlest and most mature manipulation of tone is also his most lucid map of the geography of the mind and heart, and finally the richest poem of his career.

"King of the River" fuses the emotional intensity of the early poems with the terse and yet conversational style of the other poems of this volume. It is his most distilled statement and most finely crafted lyric. Ironically, both Kunitz and Lowell (in "Waking Early Sunday Morning") have been moved by Yeats to write about *salmon*. Yeats, a great influence on the early poems, may be seen as an antagonist here. "Sailing to Byzantium" itself is, of course, ambivalent in its nostalgia and desire for the fish-filled sensual river of generation—or we might say simply its nostalgia *for* desire. But the thrust of Yeats's poem is to assert the primacy of monuments of unaging intellect as the right goal of the imagination. Kunitz, in effect, is reconstituting Yeats's "Dialogue of Self and Soul" and throwing it in the face of Byzantium, by actively committing himself to corruption. The bruised, battered human muscle of Kunitz's poem, "glazed with madness," is only slightly less grotesque in physical form than the polyp-eyed corpse of "Prophecy on Lethe," yet it becomes a figure not of terror, but of heroic endurance and imagination. The poet embraces, not the dissolving of the beginning into the end, but his constant oscillation on the "two-way ladder / between heaven and hell." And the waving orchestration of the poem, parallel to the coiling and uncoiling of this generative human muscle, celebrates the same ambiguities of his attitude toward time and eternity. Kunitz renews Yeats's "fecund ditch" in his "orgiastic pool," and the rapid and almost grotesque birth, copulation, and aging toward death of the salmon becomes the happiest metaphor of the poet's career. As in "The Illumination," where he subsumed the dilemma over vision, here he perfectly dramatizes the tensions of nostalgia and desire in the contours of the verse—in the "if-but-then" sequence which builds irony into the very structure of the poem:

> If the power were granted you
> to break out of your cells,
> but the imagination fails
> and the doors of the senses close
> on the child within,
> you would dare to be changed,
> as you are changing now,
> into the shape you dread
> beyond the merely human.

The finest irony of all is that the visionary poet fails to see that the shape he aspires to assume, he may be assuming all his life. To be visionary for Kunitz is to want orgiastic death, which is what we are having all along if we will slow down our senses to notice. Normal experience is all the orgy toward death a poet needs, and all the monstrosity he can afford. We are going nowhere as rapidly and as grandiloquently as we need to, so to endure is to be as apocalyptic as we need be.

"Songs of a Happy Man": The Poetry of Theodore Roethke

Charles Molesworth

Though it is plainly heterodox in beliefs and forms, American poetry gathers much of its strength and interest from a recurrent concern: the individuation of the poet. This individuation mediates between the burdens and the possibilities of selfhood, since the American poet is clearly postromantic and sees himself (we might even say *sings* himself) free of the circumstances of continuity. As an individual, the poet insists on shaping himself; on the other hand, the song he gathers begins its pulse in a given world, and nothing short of the *compass* of this world can measure the song's totality. Emily Dickinson says her business is circumference. Emerson, in "Circles," claims, "Permanence is a word of degrees. Everything is medial. Moons are no more bounds to spiritual power than bat-balls." The very sufficiencies of a centering self, its limitations in time, thrust against its insistent growth; its memory-haunted thrownness is obliterated by its indefatigable autonomy: these are the songs our poets bring forth, partly as curses, partly as interdictions, and partly as celebrations. Theodore Roethke's poetry participates in this "medial" tradition, and broadens its range as well, for Roethke was above all a poet of selfhood, or more exactly, a poet of the self-as-problematic. Therefore, he was a poet of growth, a singer who needed to gather up his origins as he moved further and further toward the completion of his entelechy. He needed, in other words, to encircle himself while he was desperately bursting all containment.

The concern with origins in Roethke's poetry is transformed into a fascination with metamorphoses and gestures. The original template might never be recoverable, but at each stage of growth both the seed and the wet sheath it has sprouted forth can claim new origins. The procedure,

95

however, is crucial, for Roethke was to realize that the poem can easily become "loosely oracular" and that real recovery can be obfuscated by the too-ready dazzle of feigned madness. The poet must be somewhere between Ophelia and Lear, partly lyrical and partly accursed in his meanderings. This is why the innovative language of "The Lost Son," for example, is by turns catechetical and tentative and passes through several other shades of firmness in between. The sequence's mélange of rhetorical modes confesses Roethke's uncertainty at the same time that it claims his authority; the poet becomes both self-effacing initiate and self-taught master. Like Pound in *Pisan Cantos,* Roethke must confess his crimes and reveal his strengths; but unlike the mastery of Pound's allusiveness and historical placements, Roethke's *periploi* describe a voyage more inward and less specifically located. The surface of Pound's text is almost archeologically horizontal, whereas Roethke's text forms like a crystal, its overall shape often distorted by accretions of insolvent matter. Pound's criticism renders sensory data accurate to the point of photographic clarity; Roethke's images of natural phenomena are more ecstatically presented. Pound wants to illustrate, Roethke to celebrate.

The title sequence from *The Lost Son* exemplifies a surrealist texture and structure that has since become commonplace in American poetry. In some senses, to the reader of the seventies this sequence might seem contemporary; though it would surely stand out among its later epigones, its true inventiveness might be obscured. But a few reminders will partially reset the context of Roethke's innovation. When "The Lost Son" appeared, "Notes toward a Supreme Fiction" was only a few years old; *The Pisan Cantos* had just come out; and Eliot had not yet completed all of *The Four Quartets.* In other words, the "masters" of modernism were producing the capstones of their careers, and the next generation had just begun to find its voice; Lowell's *Land of Unlikeness* was contemporary with Roethke's *Lost Son,* for example, though the distinctive mode Lowell was to develop was not securely in hand until *Lord Weary's Castle,* two years later. So when we read in Roethke's essay "How to Write Like Somebody Else" that "one dares to stand up to a great style," we know he is not just reiterating apothegms or offering a concealed defense of his own imitativeness. "The Lost Son," whatever it produced in his later style, however it shaped the course of his self-definition, was surely a daring exploration. Rather than simply continue in the mode he had already brought to such high polish in his first book, *Open House,* Roethke took a much-heralded plunge into his own psyche. The heralding came later, to be sure, though Roethke himself, as he shows in the "Open Letter" discussing the "sources" of his procedure, thought of the plunge as a recovery rather than a discovery, as a reclamation by the ego of those marshy, imbedded roots of feeling and association. It is as if Roethke discovered the seeds of several modes that were later to dominates contemporary poetry: confessionalism, neosurrealism, deep images. In speaking of looking for "some clue to existence from the sub-human," Roethke describes the poet as one who looks from an angle of vision ordinarily closed to public or discursive language. "He sees," Roethke says, trying to formulate an approach rather than a definition, "and yet does not see: they are almost tail-flicks, from another world, seen out of the corner of the eye." These "clues" are just that, traces of a previous or incipient existence or presence, something not yet, or just under or beyond. "The experience . . . is at once literal and symbolical," and its medial frames of reference, the epistemological status of its observations, keep shifting, now certain, now whimsical, part revelation, part willed invention. In this sense Roethke may also be recognized as one precursor of "composition by field," or "projective verse" as Charles Olson called it, whereby the poet situates himself in an attitude toward his or her consciousness and, mixing attentiveness and abandonment, strives to create the *feel* of thought in all its multifariousness and interconnectedness.

> By snails, by leaps of frog, I came here, spirit.
> Tell me, body without skin, does a fish sweat?
> I can't crawl back through these veins,
> I ache for another choice.
> The cliffs! The cliffs! They fling me back.
> Eternity howls in the last crags,
> The field is no longer simple:
> It's a soul's crossing time.
> The dead speak noise.

The journeying here starts from impulses evolutionary and mystical, and the senses are both the means to and the impediments of new knowledge. The progress of the sequence is often humorous and is not above a certain self-deprecatory undercutting of its own vatic yearning, as the second line here shows. In any more or less typical stretch of "The Lost Son," the mode of discourse may shift often and abruptly. We can move from a rhetorical question, to what seems a scrap from a nursery rhyme, to a quick axiomatic stab. In each case the language will be dominated by simple, often one syllable nouns, there will be a relative absence of adjectives, at least of a sophisticated or precise sort, and the verbs will frequently be of simple physical scope: crawling, whispering, or sleeping. One line of bare description will spark another that is apparently symbolic, the spark jumping across a "mythical" association, or a pun; as soon as a discursive context is generated by some clause of subordination or apposition, it is suddenly abandoned for a string of three or four sentences randomly connected. Clearly the total effect of this must be cumulative, for while the sense and feel of the poem's central thrust (or of that of one of its sections) may be forceful, the precise shape and texture of the poem's argument become most distinct after several readings, and Roethke's insistence on the necessity of reading the poem aloud makes sense when we realize the nature of the poem's affective structure. It is made of language that is at once obsessive and anonymous; its shifting gestures become the poet's inchoate attempt to make up, and make up *for*, his unacknowledged fears. The poem's theme, if it can be formulated succinctly, might be called the struggle of the self to circumscribe itself, fighting off the equally tempting but equally fallacious notions of solipsism and determinism. By turns the "I" in the poem fears and flaunts its own self-generation and its own hereditary "tunnel"; "I've seen my father's face before / Deep in the belly of a thing to be," says Roethke, making the father something realizable instead of given, a future to be grown toward rather than a past to be fled. Later he says, "A son has many fathers," as if a mediating refuge might be found in emotional polytheism.

Roethke included in *The Lost Son* volume, besides the long title sequence, three other sections. The middle sections of the book contain several lyrics written in the mode of his first book, *Open House:* imagistically straightforward, fairly tightly argued, and conventionally rhymed and metered. Some few of these, such as "Dolor" with its "duplicate grey standard faces" from the world of bureaucratic clerical employees, introduce a more mundane and less pastoral subject matter into Roethke's work, but the overall effect here is of an unsuccessful attempt to revitalize a past mode. However, the opening section of *The Lost Son and Other Poems* exhibits Roethke's sensibility in one of its most distinctive modes, as beautiful and as challenging in many ways as the surreality of "The Lost Son" sequence. The subject in these poems is the greenhouse environment of his childhood, the root cellar, the steam pipes, the rich loam and dank air of horticultural activity. This is Roethke's world of "underness," as Frederick Hoffman calls it, a world of slow movement below the surfaces of vision, a world highly tactile and olfactory in its moist complexity. Everything becomes instinct, pushing upward toward light; all the processes of change are as determinedly gradual as they are invisible. Virtually every poem here ends with a gesture on or toward the borders of transformation. Roethke uses the carefully modulated personification and allegorization we can see in an early poem like "Night Journey"; the "merely" human order of consciousness is never triumphant over the vegetable existence it nurtures but whose subhuman mysteries it only fitfully comprehends.

> I can hear, underground, that sucking and sobbing,
> In my veins, in my bones I feel it,
> The small waters seeping upward,
> The tight grains parting at last.
> When sprouts break out,
> Slippery as fish,
> I quail, lean to beginnings, sheath-wet.

The present participles here shade into a present tense that seems almost optative rather than declarative, as the wish for participation *becomes* the main source of awareness and intention. In "Moss-Gathering," his version of Wordsworth's "Nutting," he says, "But something always went out of me when I dug loose those carpets / Of green." Taken all together, the poems are a loose system of conduits; they are poems not of origins, but of mediations and thresholds. The sequence might recall Wordsworth's Lucy poems, not in its subject or manner to be sure, but in the special revelations it provides about its author. We see and hear in these lyrics part of a peculiar psychological configuration that resists explication yet must be taken into account in any overall "portrait" of the author. "Even the dirt kept breathing a small breath," Roethke says, and we realize that our sense of scale must be adjusted. In the poetry of natural history, the reader must often reconstruct the sequence of biologic events with a metaphoric bridge, since the poet, in his efforts not to betray the otherness of the observed world into blurring sentimentality, has had to guard himself against a reductive taxonomy. (Emerson complains of the young men who go into the fields with their Latin nomenclature and remain blind.) And if the natural world is appropriated simply to illustrate some initially subjective crisis, the system of naming will be equally benighted. The pressure of mind Roethke uses in these poems prepares us in a way for "The Lost Son," with its anonymous yet intimate revelations, for these poems are also spoken from a self-concealing premise—they are constantly pointing out *there*—yet their hushed, almost reverent testimony stands out as clearly personal. They form a key part of Roethke's work; by blending almost seamlessly with other parts of his sensibility, the sources of his awareness in these poems were to nourish the final success of the "North American Sequence."

Roethke's poetry rests on a body of sentiment rather than an articulated network of ideas; but in two of his major sequences, "The Dying Man" and "Meditations of an Old Woman," we can glimpse through his poetic formulations some of the philosophical elements of existentialism. Both of these sequences concentrate on process, and they view the self as problematic, as a construct that constantly gives itself over to other forces; and, in its attempts to mediate between the inner and outer reality it faces, this self is sustained more by a trust in its faculties than by any lasting pride in its accomplishments. "I am that final thing / A man learning to sing," as the dying man says, so finality appears as a formative process, and reality is a form of instruction rather than a lesson to be mastered. And the old woman, near the end of her meditations, says:

> To try to become like God
> Is far from becoming God.
> O! but I seek and care!
> I rock in my own dark,
> Thinking, God has need of me.
> The dead love the unborn.

If these sequences test the assumptions of existentialism about the primacy of existence over essence, of process over product, they also explore the sense existentialism fostered that only through and in death are our values truly revealed. Ordinary waking consciousness structures itself through the aid of several convenient deceptions: truth will make itself clear; the universe is consistent and explorable by rational methods; we know our own minds. But death, especially in the form of the mortality of the individual, threatens these deceptions with an unsettling redefinition. Instead of the testing growth of metamorphosis, death's transformation redefines the whole series of changes; the truth of process, once a comfort and a potentially heroizing struggle, threatens to become a final, inert product. "The dead love the unborn," perhaps because the ongoingness of the species makes death less terminal, more explicable. The lines also suggest that the dead God of existentialism mockingly loves the shapeless humanity it has deserted. But the sequence "The Dying Man" ends with these lines, probably the bleakest Roethke ever wrote:

> The edges of the summit still appal
> When we brood on the dead or the beloved;
> Nor can imagination do it all
> In this last place of light: he dares to live
> Who stops being a bird, yet beats his wings
> Against the immense immeasurable emptiness of things.

Poetry will not avail; the bird of romantic transcendence, whether Shelley's skylark or Yeats's bird made of "gold and gold enameling," deceives us. Death and love, those enchanting, twin nightmares, still present a summit, however; we must stop being a bird, but we must not cease the birdlike action of "beating against," for only in critical struggle is the sleight of hand we call reality checked and illuminated.

In these sequences, the dying man and the old woman both seek a place for themselves, a place that will itself be the culmination and the vindication of their experience. But this place becomes only as revealing as the light that floods it. In these sequences, Roethke comes closest to a tragic vision of life, and he does so in the images of light. Vision—the natural light and mystical illumination beyond the borders of the physically seen— centers all of Roethke's major poetry; it is for him what memory is for Wordsworth, the occasion and the result of his deepest love, his strongest affective energies. "Who would know the dawn / When there's a dazzling dark behind the sun?" The "would" here can mean either that no one would choose to know the dawn, or else that no one would be able to see the order of diurnal world once they had glimpsed a transsolar perspective. The dying man, whether he chooses to pass beyond his boundaries or has them shattered, can imagine only a "dazzling" dark, for even nonexistence must have a visually energized aspect. The visual field becomes for Roethke almost equivalent to the self; or rather, as the visual faculty takes shape, has appetites, and is challenged by both outer and inner disequilibriums, so also does the self.

> Though it reject dry borders of the seen,
> What sensual eye can keep an image pure,
> Leaning across a sill to greet the dawn?
> A slow growth is a hard thing to endure.
> When figures out of obscure shadow rave,
> All sensual love's but dancing on the grave.

Again, "the visible obscures," as the eye wants to see *into* things, not just their surfaces; likewise, the self wants possession of the world, not just contact with it. Both eye and self want the "not yet," the transference into a new order; at the same time, they both know that the unseen, the unformed confront them with a threat to order that can only be relieved by defiantly excessive sensual indulgence, "dancing on the grave." "I want more than than the world, / Or after-image of the inner thing," cries the dying man, who, though he realizes "all exultation is a dangerous thing," nevertheless knows,

> What's seen recedes; Forever's what we know!—
> Eternity defined, and strewn with straw,
> The fury of the slug beneath the stone.
> The vision moves, and yet remains the same.
> In heaven's praise, I dread the thing I am.

Dissatisfaction with the self, if not indeed self-loathing, becomes the origin of the transcendent; the crawling, sluglike self is furious in the presence of stonelike necessity, and that fury *is* eternity. As Camus's Sisyphus comes to love his rock, so the underness of Roethke's world flowers at the borders of the visible.

The structure of "Meditations of an Old Woman" makes use of the associative movement Roethke discovered in "The Lost Son." While "The Dying Man" uses the traditional verse forms and tightly ironic sentences that were such a dominant part of the prevailing idiom in American poetry in the 1950s, Roethke's "other" confrontation with death looks forward to a freer, less rational language. The first two poems in the "Meditations" sequence are fairly traditional, and they use the motif of the journey to picture the reminiscences and reverie of the old woman. But with the third of the five meditations, the structure changes and becomes more associative—or perhaps, more dissociated, since Roethke is clearly trying to suggest a weakening of the old woman's faculties as she approaches death. But here the ambiguity of structure parallels the ambiguity of "meaning," since the closer the woman comes to death the clearer her "vision" becomes.

> In the long fields, I leave my father's eye;
> And shake the secrets from my deepest bones;
> My spirit rises with the rising wind;
> I'm thick with leaves and tender as a dove,
> I take the liberties a short life permits—
> I seek my own meekness;
> I recover my tenderness by long looking.
> By midnight I love everything alive.
> Who took the darkness from the air?
> I'm wet with another life.
> Yea, I have gone and stayed.

This resembles the language of "testifying," that public proclamation of newfound evangelical fervor. (The speaker, like the woman in Stevens's "Sunday Morning," is clearly haunted by the "encroachment of that old catastrophe.") Earlier in the sequence Roethke had begun to rely on rhetorical questions and self-questionings to propel the poem forward. This reversion to the mode of surreal catechesis, used so frequently in "The Lost Son," doesn't untrack the poem, however. In fact, the last two meditations have a gentle, formulative quality about their statements; they seem less driven, less haunted, as if the woman knows ahead of time the false dawns that will break to confuse and mislead her. The poem's magnificence comes in large measure from this sense of full struggle with a never-ending, and never-changing, problem:

> Beginner,
> Perpetual beginner,
> The soul knows not what to believe,
> In its small folds, stirring sluggishly,
> In the least place of its life,
> A pulse beyond nothingness,
> A fearful ignorance

and a few lines later:

> O my bones,
> Beware those perpetual beginnings,
> Thinning the soul's substance.

The old woman's acceptance of the need for "beginning" results in no easy comfort, yet the temptation toward surcease never triumphs: "I live in light's extreme; I stretch in all directions; / Sometimes I think I'm several."

The self imagined as several offers a riveting image for the language that Roethke was to develop in his poetry and that was to become so severely important to later poets. Roethke's work is permeated by a consciousness of being body-centered. Yet the poet's body, gestural, supple, organic, and instinctual as it is, never rests in oneness. For Roethke, it is always searching for the other in order to achieve its own completion. This "other" can be a place, or a time, or a stage of growth, as well as an-other body. Indeed, the body, because of its very resiliency, needs a multiplicity of "others" in order to complete itself. Roethke's body-centered mysticism is echoed in the poetry of Robert Bly and Galway Kinnell. His confessionalism, his offering of his body as the irreducible evidence of his scarred world, has its analogues in the work of Berryman, Lowell, and even Diane Wakoski. As Roethke's body bears metaphorically the traces of its own seeds, as it is linked through the species to that "other" time of myth, his poetry suggests later developments in poets as diverse as W. S. Merwin and Gary Snyder. In each of his long sequences, from "The Lost Son" to "North American Sequence," Roethke achieves a fullness of voice that derives in part from a fondling irony, a playing with appearances and stances that avoids dogma and ideology, but also in part from an "openness to experience," a testing of consciousness in both its circular and threshold configurations, which allows him to celebrate his gatherings and test his limitations with equal force. The structuring of these sequences relies on several obvious devices—such as the persona, or imagistic clustering, or mythical reverberations—but on no single aesthetic program. Because of their pluralism, the sequences, seen as a group, are the perfect embodiment of the poet's bodily growth and psychical sinuosities, since the thematic coherence we experience behind them never becomes dry or forced; they sacrifice neither their wisdom for experimentation nor their daring for mere consolation.

The language of the "North American Sequence" gathers up the exfoliating parts of Roethke's sensibility; and, while this integral speech is something new and distinctive in Roethke's work (as well as in contemporary American poetry), its roots are many and traditional. Biblical rhythms, the long line and catalogue of Whitman, the ecstatic litany of Smart, the meditative energy of Stevens, and the commonplace grandeur of Eliot's *Four Quartets:* all these elements grace the sequence, though none dominates it. Roethke is here both litanist and botanist, to use terms Karl Shapiro once employed to distinguish the symbolist aesthetic of Poe from the native strain of Whitman. Roethke's work doesn't fit into any neat categorization of contemporary poetry, in part because he wasn't interested in theory and hence took little concern with groups or schools of poets, but also because he drew widely and unabashedly on both traditional and innovative currents of poetic energy. Nowhere is this more apparent than in the language of "North American Sequence," yet most appreciative readers of Roethke consider it his "authentic" voice, the fruition of his lifelong attempt to come to terms with his burdens and possibilities.

Not only the language but also the formal structure of this sequence rests on a complexity at once densely affective and semantically straightforward. The central image is that of a journey, both as a movement to a new place and as a change to a new form; the natural cycles and stages of physical growth are gracefully, almost tangentially aligned with emotional growth. Much of the pleasure of reading the sequence comes from the lyric and equitable distribution of its parts into circular meditations and unfolding exultations. Either the circle or the threshold subtends most of the poem's images and thematic developments. Both of these "figures" can be reassuring or threatening in their immediate thrust or their larger implications; for example, the cyclical return of plant life is counterposed by the circular spins of the wheels of an automobile stuck in a snowdrift, return balanced by frustration. Mixing the traditional tropes and arguments of landscape poetry and mystical literature, the sequence draws on a resonant symbolic background, but it never courts obscurantism for its own sake; though it has clear "autobiographical" contexts, it never becomes plangently confessional. But perhaps a brief look at each of its six sections, and their relationships, will show how measured and yet how powerful are Roethke's journeyings.

In the first section, "The Longing," movement is clearly stymied: "On things asleep, no balm." The quiescence doesn't so much threaten as stultify, and this is the only section to use the rhetorical self-questionings that appear in much of Roethke's earlier work. From the questions—"What dream's enough to breathe in? A dark dream."—Roethke moves to the optative mood. "I would with the fish . . . , I would believe my pain . . . , I long for the imperishable quiet at the heart of form": these faint stirrings of desire occur in the last part of the poem, where the "disorder of this mortal life" is called an "ambush" and a "silence." The poem ends with a mocking reference to Eliot's *Four Quartets* and what we can read as a gentle, self-deprecating use of the rhetorical question:

> Old men should be explorers?
> I'll be an Indian.
> Ogalala?
> Iroquois.

The humor here reveals that Roethke's search will, if possible, avoid violence in favor of some medial, settled means of transference. Also, the tone of the affirmation here quivers with reticence, as the poet takes up his "duties" with a diffidence and a shred of "free choice" to conceal his desperation. The next section, "Meditation at Oyster River," turns from the interrogative mood to one of quiet observation. The images are all of faint movements: the turn of the tide, the thawing of a river. The speaker rocks "with the motion of morning," while lamenting, "The self persists like a dying star, / In sleep, afraid," as most forms of life are extinguished before the surfaces record the cessation. But, likewise, the sources of renewal are in motion beneath the frozen face of things:

> The sudden sucking roar as the culvert loosens its debris of
> branches and sticks,

Welter of tin cans, pails, old bird nests, a child's shoe riding
    a log,
As the piled ice breaks away from the battered spiles,
And the whole river begins to move forward, its bridges
    shaking.

"Water's my will, and my way," he sings in the last few lines of the poem, and this will be one of the most recurrent of the sequence's natural images, taking on the force and scope of a mythical symbol, though first introduced at the level of the "naturally commonplace." The tone of this second section retains, however, some of the diffidence of the first: "The flesh takes on the pure poise of the spirit, / Acquires, *for a time*, the sandpiper's insouciance" (italics added). At this point the journey and the transformation are beyond will, beyond control.

In "Journey to the Interior," the third section of the sequence, Roethke shifts to an automobile journey for his metaphoric base, and the theme of the sequence is expressed in terms of the difficulties of the journey or, to use the terms of the metaphor, in terms of the detours and hazards of the road surface. In the second part of this section, the poet adroitly shifts to natural images as they are seen from the car—"I am not moving but they are." Then in the last part of this poem the voice of testimony enters: "I see the flower of all water, above and below me." This is symbolic of the "soul at a stand-still," for the visionary moment is "the moment of time when the small drop forms, but does not fall." This moment resembles a rehearsal for death, it is terminal but not necessarily transformative. "On one side of silence there is no smile," the poet says, and the images of sound and silence begin to gain dominance as they become a further mediating agency, yet another measure of growth and cessation. "And the dead begin from their dark to sing in my sleep," this section concludes, and the possibilities of integrating the moment of silence into the noise of everyday life remain problematic. The fourth section of the sequence, "The Long Waters," demonstrates a journey to new forms of life, but does so in a specially qualified context, having as its symbolic location a landlocked bay, in which growth and decay seem comfortably self-encircling, yet which is "a vulnerable place." Here the poet "acknowledges his foolishness" and says, "I still delight in my last fall." The phrase *last fall* can portend the end of his mortal life, it can refer simply to the preceding season, or it can suggest that mythical event that produces his alienated but singing consciousness, content at least to know there is no more fall once he accepts his mortality, his humanness. The language in the fourth section is among the most melodic, the most Whitmanesque of the whole sequence. The return from the still moment of silence in the third section is gradually recognized here as a triumph, and the fourth section ends with the strongest affirmation so far:

> I, who came back from the depths laughing too loudly,
> Become another thing;
> My eyes extend beyond the farthest bloom of the waves;
> I lose and find myself in the long water;
> I am gathered together once more;
> I embrace the world.

Both self and world are here encompassed, as circular embrace and linear expansion become congruent. Transformation of the self, occasioned by new sensory powers, a self-surrender that is identical with self-definition, all culminate in an acceptance of reality: the complex of awarenesses and changes we have seen before, but here the almost understated surety of it gives a fresh force to the healing.

Almost as if to avoid the sense that the healing was too easily achieved, Roethke returns in the fifth section, "The Far Field," to images of a stalled journey and to imagery from the preceding four sections in order to test and measure the validity of his "embrace" of the world. "I have come to a still, but not a deep center," he says in this protoclimactic poem, and he dwells on recollections and meditations of how "All finite things reveal infinitude." This section brings to fruition Roethke's interest in edges, in the consciousness of an object or event that is most truly revealed only at the border of its outline or form. "I feel a weightless change" he notes at one point, and the poem has an especially lovely tentativeness, relying in part on present participles and gerunds (there are six in one seven-line stretch) and in part on a tone that hovers between calm acceptance and rapt indifference:

> A man faced with his own immensity
> Wakes all the waves, all their loose wandering fire.
> The murmur of the absolute, the why
> Of being born fails on his naked ears.
> His spirit moves like monumental wind
> That gentles on a sunny blue plateau.
> He is the end of things, the final man.

The last phrase here recalls Stevens's "single man" from "Notes toward a Supreme Fiction," but the quietly resolved tension between the implicit agnosticism of "fails on his naked ears" and the firm faith of "monumental wind" remains distinctly Roethke's. "What I love is near at hand / Always, in earth and air," he tells us, giving to airy nothingness not only a local habitation and a name, but also a place in relation to his own corporal awareness. The old man in this section is pictured in "robes of green, in garments of adieu," and the sense of acceptance becomes more pervasive.

The final, sixth section of the poem, "The Rose," revolves around images of place more than of journeying; but again, as in the "vulnerable place" of the fourth section, the location is one where change and process can be fully revealed. The rose, "flowering out of the dark," is Dante's rose, and Blake's, and Eliot's, but also Roethke's father's:

> And I think of roses, roses,
> White and red, in the wide six-hundred-foot greenhouses,
> And my father standing astride the cement benches,
> Lifting me high over the four-foot stems, the Mrs. Russells,
>   and his own elaborate hybrids,
> And how those flowerheads seemed to flow toward me, to
>   beckon me, only a child, out of myself.

Ecstasy and transcendence have very local origins: "What need for heaven, then, / With that man, and those roses?" he asks, in the highest spirits of the sequence. He calls up an image of a "single sound" when "the mind remembers all," and this sound leads him to recognize his self-sufficiency: "Beautiful my desire, and the place of my desire." The place here, for the son who has at last found himself, is at once geographic, temporal, and cognitive. He sees now where he belongs, where he fits in, and realizes his love has brought his world close at hand.

This last section builds its complexity by resolving the journey motif into images of place, but also by raising the images of sound and silence to a new level of importance. "I think of the rock singing, and light making its own silence," he tells us, as the ordinary sensory order is transposed and the solid, the placed, become harmonious while the seen, the visible, becomes hushed. The poem's conclusion reiterates the central theme of self-transformation and self-acceptance:

> Near this rose, in this grove of sun-parched, wind-warped
>   madronas,
> Among the half-dead trees, I came upon the true ease of
>   myself,
> As if another man appeared out of the depths of my being,
> And I stood outside myself,
> Beyond becoming and perishing,
> A something wholly other,
> As if I swayed out of the wildest wave alive,
> And yet was still.
> And I rejoiced in being what I was.

The vision of the poem is created in terms of a locatable place where the movements of the wind are harmonized into a music that alternates with, and thus defines, a totally dazzling stillness:

> And in this rose, this rose in the sea-wind,
> Rooted in stone, keeping the whole of light,
> Gathering to itself sound and silence,
> Mine and the sea-wind's.

At the end the poet's voice achieves a status commensurate with a natural force. It is almost as if Roethke were reversing the story of Orpheus and, instead of leading the rocks and trees, joining *them* and being gathered at last into the first of rhythms, into himself.

And so the rage that warped his clearest cry to witless agony in the opening poem of his total book is here mediated into a different form, a "true ease" of himself, and the search concludes. Roethke's career, by which we mean the intersection of his life and his genius as he is able to record it in his poetry, is as perfect as that of any other modern poet. Its intensity is posited on a search for individuation; though the career is limited by its lack of a sustaining audience and by the concomitant absence of any socially oriented vision, Roethke did all he could to make his vision clear, to publicize, in the good sense of the word, his agony and his ease. It's possible to see him as he saw Stevens, as the father of the next generation of poets. For one can trace and sense in various parts of Roethke's work many of the modes of poetry that were to dominate the 1960s and early 1970s, such modes as deep imagery, confessionalism, neosurrealism, and the return to a kind of pastoral ecstasy, as well as the use of mythical parable. Merwin, Bly, Strand, Kinnell, Levertov, Wakoski, Ashbery, Ammons: the list of his debtors is extensive, and ironic, considering that his reputation was once limited by those who argued he was too derivative. It is difficult to be either traditional *or* as modern as possible, to write either spiritual autobiography in a heroic vein *or* naturalistic lyrics with anonymous ease, without borrowing something from Roethke's poetry. No doubt his place in contemporary poetry will become clearer with time, and we can surmise that this one last transformation would have pleased him, for we have his word for it that "The right thing happens to the happy man."

Theodore Roethke: Death and Rebirth in a Modern Landscape

James Applewhite

In approaching Romantic landscape poetry in terms of a typical tension between conscious structure or figure and wild or unconscious moorland or sea, we are participating in a psychological interpretation that has already been made, in effect, by intellectual and artistic developments in our own century. Our time, after all, is that of the discovery of the unconscious. Henri Ellenberger, in the book from whose title this phrase comes, has traced the psychoanalytic movement from its origins in Romanticism. Awareness of the doctrines of Freud, Jung, and their followers has permeated modern life and marked modern art and criticism. Maud Bodkin's *Archetypal Patterns in Poetry* represents a pioneering attempt to apply the concepts of C. G. Jung to the interpretation of poetry—an attempt that appears to have influenced the thinking of the modern American poet Theodore Roethke. Our artistic inheritance is Dada, surrealism, and abstract expressionism, movements wherein artists have sought deliberately to introduce change, illogic, and emotional association into their work, to free it from the dominance of the conscious will so that more primal powers may be manifest. The presence of African masks and various totemic deities in our galleries and as influences in the work of painters, sculptors, and other artists attests to our time's fascination with the primitive, the irrational, the unconscious.

The theme of psychological death and rebirth in the context of a landscape imagery symbolizing access to the unconscious comes to an especially clear formulation in the work of Roethke. As a poet who imbibed the central modernist influence (his work is clearly marked by both Yeats and Eliot) and who also returned sympathetically to Romantic predecessors, Roethke is representative of the Romantic and post-Romantic themes we have traced

From *Seas and Inland Journeys*. © 1985 by the University of Georgia Press.

as they arise in a new but recognizable form in the period following World War II—a time that saw a reaction to, and reformulation of, the modernist version of the poetic act. We will find in Roethke an explicit interest in the unconscious, as well as a pattern resembling the Romantic resuscitation ritual, and the house and ship imagery symbolizing consciousness in its interaction with the unconscious.

In an "Open Letter," published in 1950 with a selection of poems from *The Lost Son and Other Poems*, Roethke acknowledges the poet as "conscious instrument," as opposed to "some kind of over-size aeolian harp upon which strange winds play uncouth tunes," yet sees the poet's task as to "fish, patiently, in that dark pond, the unconscious, or dive in, with or without pants on." The rather playful tone of this beginning does not disguise the essential seriousness of what Roethke is saying, for as he speaks of "The Lost Son" sequence, something of the agony behind these poems of psychic breakdown and regeneration becomes apparent: "Each in a sense is a stage in a kind of struggle out of the slime; part of a slow spiritual progress; an effort to be born, and later, to become something more." The psychic birth to which Roethke refers is a form of that separation of individual consciousness from the unconsciousness of nature that we have identified as central Romantic motif.

Roethke sees the movement of these poems as cyclic, as hard-won progressions founded upon a reimmersion of the adult psyche in the primal, chaotic, unconscious world symbolized by memories of his Michigan childhood and its landscape with marshes, rivers, and ponds. "I believe that to go forward as a spiritual man it is necessary first to go back." Thus, as the poems dramatize, there is a regression amounting to breakdown, to a dissolution of the old restrictive consciousness, then an almost deathly absorption in unconsciousness (symbolized by landscape) followed by a painful, difficult journey back into the conscious personality, as if the stages of evolution were being retraced in the life of a single man: "Some of these pieces . . . begin in the mire, as if man is no more than a shape writhing from the old rock." The antiquity he feels in this psychic landscape suggests C. G. Jung's concept of a collective unconscious: "Sometimes one gets the feeling that not even the animals have been there before; but the marsh, the mire, the void, is always there, immediate and terrifying."

This muddy marsh before human history corresponds both to Wordsworth's oceanic reservoir and begetter of individual souls in the "Intimations" ode and to W. B. Yeats's "frog-spawn of a blind man's ditch" in "A Dialogue of Self and Soul." Roethke's source, like Yeats's, is presented so as to acknowledge the terror and misery associated with this primordial symbolic water, as well as its fertility. Thus, Roethke's image of the origin of consciousness resembles that of his much-admired W. B. Yeats more than that of Wordsworth. Roethke did, however, name the book of this following *The Lost Son* with a phrase from Wordsworth. "Praise to the end!"

occurs in *The Prelude*, book 1, in a passage dealing with exactly this process of cyclical separation/return of a developing consciousness in respect to nature/unconsciousness, which Roethke treats in more explicitly psychological terms.

Karl Malkoff points out that Maud Bodkin's *Archetypal Patterns in Poetry* (with its long exegesis of "The Ancient Mariner" in terms of the "rebirth archetype") was the "application of Jung's ideas to poetry with which Roethke was unquestionably familiar." In his analysis of two other short poems from *The Lost Son*, "Night Crow" and "River Incident," Malkoff establishes the connection between those "unconscious forces" within the mind, the psychic residue of ancestral experience (which Bodkin deals with as "archetypes") and the poetic method of Roethke. Like "Night Crow," he argues, the "atavistic imagery of 'River Incident' probes still further into the nature of the collective unconscious. The protagonist, with sea water in his veins, is taken back to his origins, to man's origins":

> I knew I had been there before,
> In that cold, granitic slime,
> In the dark, in the rolling water.

The return to this "slime" and "water" is seen as the necessary regressive journey for the man who has encountered an obstacle "with which he cannot cope."

Both his own experiences and intuitive inclinations and Maud Bodkin's Jungian analysis of "The Ancient Mariner" appear to have prepared Roethke to deal in poetry with "a state of introversion and regression, preceding a kind of rebirth." And Bodkin had made explicit for Roethke a connection between Jung's "unconscious contents . . . disfigured by the slime of the deep" and Coleridge's "slimy things" that lived within the shadow of the Ancient Mariner's becalmed vessel. Having adduced some of the many references to slimy yet glowing seas that J. L. Lowes found as sources for the poem in Coleridge's reading, Bodkin suggests the paradox that meaning and beauty were to be found in things initially repulsive and alien. "We begin to see what kind of symbolic value the imagination of Coleridge, ever seeking a language for something within, would feel in those shapes, slimy and miscreate in the stagnant water, that yet glowed with gemlike colour and strange fire." In psychological terms, the value of the slime of the unconscious is made clear when the more conscious self, forced by crisis, comes back to this primal origin and is fertilized, reborn through its contact. But such a return, such a "night journey," associated by Bodkin with Jonah's trip into the whale's belly, is dangerous and repugnant to the conscious personality. Returns to the unconscious and its primal sea, therefore, are seen as episodes of death and rebirth.

In the beginning of "The Lost Son," Roethke makes explicit what has to be fished for with some ingenuity in "The Ancient Mariner": that the journey away from the world of the expected, into a different order, is psychic. There is an initial indication of death, a death that pulls the poet downward, into contact with underground spaces of the landscape.

> At Woodlawn I heard the dead cry:
> I was lulled by the slamming of iron,
> A slow drip over stones,
> Toads brooding wells.

The death was perhaps that of the poet's father, although we cannot know it at this point. Here we feel primarily the sense of absorption into another level of being: somnolent, identified with subterranean "drip," close to the perspective of toads. "All the leaves stuck out their tongues" makes us sense that nature is vital yet taunting. Feeling himself incorporated into decay, the poet invites creatures of this minimal, unconscious level to aid him.

> I shook the softening chalk of my bones,
> Saying,
> Snail, snail, glister me forward,
> Bird, soft-sigh me home,
> Worm, be with me.
> This is my hard time.

The conscious self feels soiled, humiliated, useless, and has to call on elements of nature's unselfconscious process for models of how to adapt to the world of dissolution, of loss of the former identity.

The poet is becalmed, like the Ancient Mariner—in a fertile place but in a sterile condition.

> Fished in an old wound,
> The soft pond of repose;
> Nothing nibbled my line,
> Not even the minnows come.

The self-absorption is isolation.

> Sat in an empty house
> Watching shadows crawl,
> Scratching.
> There was one fly.

The house of consciousness is emptied of the old contents. Yet nothing else has taken the place of adult interaction. The protagonist must continue to question, to ask for direction. Finally "Dark hollows" and "The moon" reply, cryptically. Then "The salt said, look by the sea." He must abandon the world of conversation, of external events, for the regressive quest: "You will find no comfort here, / In the kingdom of bang and blab."

At this point the sequence of images seems to shift suddenly into

childhood memory—a specific time and place as in the recollections of
Wordsworth.

> Running lightly over spongy ground,
> Past the pasture of flat stones,
> The three elms,
> The sheep strewn on a field,
> Over a rickety bridge
> Toward the quick-water, wrinkling and rippling.

Here is motion rather than brooding stasis, and lightness rather than the
downward, bone-softening heaviness of the beginning. Childhood offers
an opening to the way back, then, a "bridge" from this sterile present to
the "quick-water"—where *quick* suggests "alive" as well as "fast-moving."
The search into the unconscious wears a healthier aspect as the poet becomes again his childhood self,

> Hunting along the river,
> Down among the rubbish, the bug-riddled foliage,
> By the muddy pond-edge, by the bog-holes,
> By the shrunken lake, hunting, in the heat of summer.

His instinctive boyhood activities provide a model for this return to primal
origins now forced upon him by a crisis in adult life. Like Wordsworth in
The Prelude, book 1, he finds in the native self, before the sophistications
of conscious intellect, a pattern for a unified being that incorporates conscious and unconscious dimensions of personality without a disastrous
conflict.

Though the model of a more unified psyche is available, however,
certain earlier traumas have now to be relived before healing can occur.
The phallic, underwater principle of sexuality and its connection with the
unconscious is evoked through a kind of altered nursery rhyme.

> The shape of a rat?
>   It's bigger than that.
>   It's less than a leg
>   And more than a nose,
>   Just under the water
>   It usually goes.

Freudians may have their field day with the rat, leg, nose (and later eel
and otter) images. But clearly this poet is aware of the symbolism and is
dramatizing, through a half-playful, almost child-like voice, the uncomfortable attraction-repulsion surrounding that part of the boy's physical
being whose roots are most obviously in the unconscious.

Sexual conflict continues into the present in part three of "The Lost
Son," as "Dogs of the groin / Barked and howled." The poet feels an
alienation so strong that weeds, snakes, cows, even briars "Said to me:

Die." The central wound, his father's early death and his own unresolved feelings about that matter, have now to be faced."Rub me in father and mother," he asks, cold and alone, needing comfort like a child. But he feared his father. "Fear was my father, Father Fear." The following appears to be a dream version of his father's death from cancer during the poet's adolescence:

> What gliding shape
> Beckoning through halls,
> Stood poised on the stair,
> Fell dreamily down?

This primordial fall seems to unglue the very structure of matter.

> From the mouths of jugs
> Perched on many shelves,
> I saw substance flowing
> That cold morning.

This scene is set, no doubt, in the house of childhood, but it is also the house of consciousness, and that structure is dissolving as the dream ends—"As my own tongue kissed / My lips awake."

"The Lost Son" sequence was continued in *Praise to the End!* (Roethke's next volume), and a section from the poem entitled "Where Knock Is Open Wide" helps clarify the scene of fall and dissolution looked at above. Section four presents a memory of the father, beginning with a fishing trip.

> We went by the river.
> Water birds went ching. Went ching.
> Stepped in wet. Over stones.
> One, his nose had a frog,
> But he slipped out.

The language here is more obviously representative of a child's point of view. A crane, perhaps, has speared a frog with its beak ("One, his nose had a frog"). Memories of the father are no longer fearful. He throws back a fish when the child is "sad" for it.

Then there is the lovely image of the florist-father as virtually God-like sustainer of the garden-greenhouse.

> He watered the roses.
> His thumb had a rainbow.
> The stems said, Thank you.
> Dark came early.

His premature death, suggested in the last line above, leads to the following mournful cry:

> That was before. I fell! I fell!
> The worm has moved away.
> My tears are tired.

The fall of the father, then, leads to the fall of the son, and to a mythic sense of fall so apocalyptic that the very structure of consciousness was partially dissolved.

According to our paradigm, individuation itself, the separation of consciousness from its source, as of the child from the womb, is perceived as a fall. But in the case of Roethke (as well as of Sylvia Plath), this archetypal sense of exile, on the child's part, from the "watery cradle" of childhood was reinforced by the untimely death of a father. "The Lost Son" and those related poems represent Roethke's attempt to modify the finality of that fall by a modern, psychological version of Wordsworth's return to the "immortal sea" of origin. For Roethke, a commitment to psychic turmoil, to the breaking down of the old self, was required.

In "The Lost Son," following the dream-vision of the falling figure, ordinary psychic coherence (as well as the normal structure of the landscape) appears to break down.

> Is this the storm's heart? The ground is unstilling itself.
> My veins are running nowhere. Do the bones cast out
>   their fire?
>
> . . . .
> All the windows are burning! What's left of my life?

The narration of psychic process moves through an associative, often obscure progression from image to image, phrase to phrase, as fragments of nursery rhyme and nonsense are conjoined with suggestions of boggy landscape and phallic animal life to suggest with maximum directness the less structured perceptual flow of a personality in turmoil, regressing toward childhood. But as "the time-order is going," under "the last of primordial milk," the protagonist begins to find a way back, through childhood and again toward the present. He revisits the greenhouse of his florist-father, remembering the coming of light and heat after the night. The structure of consciousness is reaffirmed in this house of cypress and glass, with the dirt and slime underfoot. Creation is reaffirmed, reiterated, as the father and order come after the night.

> Once I stayed all night.
> The light in the morning came slowly over the white
> Snow.
> There were many kinds of cool
> Air.
> Then came steam.
>
> Pipe-knock.

Scurry of warm over small plants.
Ordnung! ordnung!
Papa is coming!

A fine haze moved off the leaves;
Frost melted on far panes;
The rose, the chrysanthemum turned toward the light.
Even the hushed forms, the bent yellowy weeds
Moved in a slow up-sway.

The poet is inviting us to view this scene through the child's eyes but also in mythic terms. As Roethke said of this passage, "With the coming of steam and 'papa'—the papa on earth and heaven are blended—there is the sense of motion in the greenhouse, my symbol for the whole of life, a womb, a heaven-on-earth." But it is a heaven approached through a kind of hell, a structure of consciousness made fertile again by reunion with the primal ooze of "that dark pond, the unconscious."

Through images suggestive of the original act of creation and thus, by extension, of the conscious psyche's birth from the unconsciousness of nature, the artist revisits or relives the process of his own individuation at a quite early stage. Courage is needed to face the world before creation has finished, for chaos represents an unconscious and threatening condition. Yet here the rank vegetation and slime of the earlier sections are successfully incorporated within a more stable house of glass. Even the lowest "hushed forms" respond to the benign illumination, with an "up-sway" as if moving in water.

The symbolic separation of the conscious from the unconscious, seen by Jung in the creation story in Genesis, is to be found in the landscape structures of both Wordsworth and Roethke. For Roethke it is the celebration of sunrise illuminating the greenhouse, assimilating the dark materials of ooze and slime into a single, unitary round, "A Womb, a heaven-on-earth." For Wordsworth, most centrally, it is the moon-illuminated sky above Mount Snowdon in *The Prelude*, book 14, into which lighted space, from

A fixed, abysmal, gloomy, breathing-place—
Mounted the roar of waters, torrents, streams
Innumerable, roaring with one voice
Heard over earth and sea, and in that hour,
For so it seems, felt by the starry heavens.
(ll. 58–62)

These are triumphant reconciliations of the dualities of consciousness and unconsciousness, of human psyche and the objective landscape. These are assertions of a vital correspondence between an inner structure and an outer world of experience into which we are able to project the ordering and unifying ability of imagination. Such moments transcend alienation and say, in effect, that the poet is immersed in a collective origin where nature and the deep psyche are continuous and now claims the right to interact with the landscape on a level of reidentification yet creative freedom. The resuscitation ritual, in bringing the poet's psyche back to life, makes nature live again for the senses, as fertile source of those symbols that allow artistic expression.

Thus, the regressive journey back into the minimal, the inarticulate, has ended in a return to the greenhouse-consciousness by a poet now possessed of a new body of imagery, a new language. Those minimal, unconscious things—stems rooting, shoots "Lolling obscenely from mildewed crates" ("Root Cellar"), even "bacterial creepers" in wounds ("The Minimal"), have been incorporated into a more unified consciousness and given names and meanings in the total drama of the psyche, which now claims nature as a part of itself, as its source. A very similar claim for nature as origin of the psyche's vitality, and of symbolic language, is urged by Wordsworth in the Snowdon scene we have looked at above. Those "higher minds" who are properly attuned to nature "build up greatest things / From least suggestions." They inhabit "a world of life," and, while not "enthralled" (or enslaved) by "sensible impressions," are nevertheless "by their quickening impulse made more prompt / To hold fit converse with the spiritual world" (*Prelude* 14:101–8).

Robert Pinsky argues that the Romantic impulse toward loss of self in the landscape, as seen in Keats's "Ode to a Nightingale," continued into the twentieth century, has made the poem pursue "the condition of a thing." Roethke is singled out as the contemporary poet who has carried furthest this "attempt to get back to the plainest roots of the situation." Certainly Roethke's vocabulary of lowly particulars seems to assemble things into poems, yet the poems would not affect us as they do had these particulars no symbolic power. Pinsky wishes to reemphasize the necessarily abstract quality of language, to point out the illusion involved in words as objects. Yet words do evoke objects, and the discovery or dramatization of an intelligible correspondence between objects and psychic states creates a fresh artistic excitement. Eliot has said that the "only way of expressing emotion in the form of art is by finding an 'objective correlative'; in other words, a set of objects, a situation, a chain of events which shall be the formula of that *particular* emotion." His own life-measuring "coffee spoons" in "Prufrock," the butterfly upon the pin, as well as the "white hair of the waves," are all objective correlatives.

The question, of course, is how the object comes to be correlated with the emotion. A name such as Lazarus, traditionally associated with resurrection, is one sort of symbol—a symbol, we might say, out of civilization's collective consciousness. Eliot, and to a lesser (but still important) extent, Sylvia Plath, depend upon these symbols. Another category of symbols was first brought into importance by the Romantics: images drawn from direct observation of nature, from personal experience and the immediate environment. Such symbols depend upon interrelationships in the developing context of the poem—that is to say, upon the total structure of landscape imagery and upon the reactions of the observer. As we have seen, a typical division or tension separates images of the observing self from that which the self observes, and which it more and more closely approaches as the poetic action progresses. As Coleridge said, "In looking at objects of Nature . . . I seem rather to be seeking, as it were *asking* for, a symbolical language for something within me that already and for ever exists, than observing anything new." The drama of the Romantic self's approach to the not-self of nature depends upon just this obscure intuition that the self and the not-self, at some deep enough level, are coextensive and correspond.

The drama in one sense is that of the creation of language—thus the fascination of Adam's naming of the animals in Genesis, and, more generally, of the creation story as a whole. The drama is also that of escape from isolation, transcendence of the psyche/world, mind/matter separation made threatening by the development of science and philosophy. Roethke, like the Romantics, attempts to get back to "the plainest roots of the situation" precisely because he feels those roots in danger. Sterile consciousness threatens to enclose him, along with the many other "duplicate grey standard faces" ("Dolor"). But the experience of return to the minimal, the memory of response from mere things remains, perhaps as memory from childhood. So the drama unfolds again, the civilized man shucking off his inhibiting garments of convention and learned mind/world separation.

> Must pull off clothes
> To jerk like a frog
> On belly and nose
> From the sucking bog.
> ("The Shape of
> the Fire")

When light comes to the greenhouse in "The Lost Son," we feel the freshness of creation having begun over again, of consciousness having risen into the light directly from its sources, and still in contact with them.

The question of archetypes is central, of course, and not finally answerable. Yet we can assert that certain situations, divisions, tensions, and contrasting types of structures are traceable from Romanticism. This scenario of individuation, this coming into light from the dark, this identification of the separateness of the self beside the all-embracing sea, or in relation to the "muddy pond-edge," is inevitable in landscape poetry deriving from Wordsworth and Coleridge. The self realizes its separateness and expressive autonomy in relation to the environment with which it formerly identified, and which it still carries within itself in the unconscious, just as we carry a residuum of ancient sea water in the salt of our blood. The language with which the new self is born is partly that of the biological facts of its condition of life and history, and partly that of the innate patterns of its development. Thus, for Roethke, objects such as stems, roots, and bacteria are caught up into a "situation, a chain of events"—which is con- sciousness' dissolution or loss of identity, followed by reindividuation— and thus correlated with emotion. There is nostalgia/disgust for the slime of this biological origin, and exhilaration/elegiac regret at the reseparation into freedom, autonomy, and limitation. Part of eternal, mindless nature falls into the freedom to realize itself, to act and to die. The garden of Genesis is the scene of the oldest drama.

Pinsky's evaluation of the Romantic impulse toward unconsciousness, as seen also in Roethke, is not quite fair because it fails to comprehend just how closely the mind of the poet is related to this landscape that calls him to itself. Keats feels not merely aesthetic charm and the hope of escape from personal cares in the bird's timeless song, he also feels the nostalgia of having formerly belonged to this "warm South," this Provençal land- scape of collective song and underground wine. But he is committed, as we all are, to the "alien corn" of our individual adult lives. In *A Study in the Process of Individuation*, Jung describes a "fantasy-image" of one of his patients, who imagined herself "with the lower half of her body in the earth, stuck fast in a block of rock." Just as for Wordsworth, the scene of this psychic birth is beside the ocean: "The region round about was a beach strewn with boulders. In the background was the sea." With the help of the good doctor himself, in his guise as sorcerer, the stone is burst open and she is able to step free. Keats has had to be both sorcerer and figure released, and his return at the end of "Ode to a Nightingale" leaves him partly undecided between vision and dream, waking and sleep. From the perspective of the collective sea, ordinary reality may be the illusion from which we awake in vision and in death.

What disturbs Pinsky in Roethke's poetry is probably the relative ab- sence of that more rational, abstracting consciousness that he feels should be acknowledged as a legitimate and inevitable part of the poetic act. Roethke's triumph as poet of the primal does tend to leave him perhaps too continuously in the realm of sense perception and visceral intuition, with too little of the specifically human wisdom we find in the Eliot of *Four Quartets* or in Auden or in Yeats. But we must also remember that intel- lectual self-consciousness has become, in our time, a potential imprison- ment, a bell jar or bottle enclosing the ship of the psyche. Roethke exercised his particular genius in escaping this trap by presiding over the destruction of something in himself. Having fled from abstraction to childhood and the particular, he must assert his ultimate values through symbols rather than concepts. It is therefore particularly interesting to see how, in Words- worth's terms, he uses the "least suggestions," the "sensible impressions" of lowly organic life, "to hold fit converse with the spiritual world."

The cyclic struggle "out of the slime," the "effort to be born, and later, to become something more," of "The Lost Son," is repeated over and over in the poems that continued that sequence into Roethke's next book, *Praise to the End!* We need not follow this movement in its repetitive detail and variation. Yet the poem that ends *The Lost Son* and so served as the original conclusion to development presents images that deserve our attention. The boat, a vehicle for psychic voyaging upon the "enchafed flood" of the Romantics that became Roethke's own greenhouse-ship of "Big Wind," appears in the second stanza of "The Shape of the Fire."

> Water recedes to the crying of spiders.
> An old scow bumps over black rocks.
> A cracked pod calls.

The recession of water suggests psychic sterility, the "crying of spiders" psychological torment and perhaps personal neurosis. The psychic ship is aground, an "old scow." The sounds convey effort, heaviness, drought. The association of a "cracked pod" with this vessel more becalmed than the Ancient Mariner's implies that out of its wreck may come the kernel of a rebirth, just as a pod must crack open to release its seed.

But the immediate context of rebirth is the suffering of dissolution. "What more will the bones allow?" the poet cries out. "These flowers are all fangs"—his central image of the spirituality in physical things has become venomously threatening. The agony is partly that of chaos. A few stanzas on we meet "Him with the platitudes and rubber doughnuts, / Melting at the knees, a varicose horror." This figure may be recalled from the mental institution where Roethke underwent treatment during his psychic collapse, but it is also, we suspect, a potential image of the self for this poet who stands appalled by the "melting" he must undergo. And the agony is also the threat that the human dimension, the sense of spirituality and sacredness, may be wholly lost in this descent into the primordial slime of the unconscious. "Where's the eye?" he asks, questioning a more conscious sensory function. "The eye's in the sty," he replies. The human identity may be lost entirely.

> Who, careless, slips
> In coiling ooze
> Is trapped to the lips,
> Leaves more than shoes;
>
> Must pull off clothes
> To jerk like a frog
> On belly and nose
> From the sucking bog.

Yet in the triumphant sections four and five, Roethke transmutes the base metal of sensuality and unconsciousness into a kind of spiritual gold. Water is the central image, as it unobtrusively pervades memory from childhood—in particular, the shoreline world of herons and "little crabs" in "silvery craters." The climactic image in section five is of a Wordsworthian moment of transcendence (like the boat-rowing episode in *The Prelude*, 1:357–400) wherein the physical, unconscious water shines with a numinous presence.

> To stare into the after-light, the glitter left on the lake's
>   surface,
> When the sun has fallen behind a wooden island;
> To follow the drips sliding from a lifted oar,
> Held up, while the rower breathes, and the small boat drifts
>   quietly shoreward;
> To know that light falls and fills, often without our knowing,
> As an opaque vase fills to the brim from a quick pouring,
> Fills and trembles at the edge yet does not flow over,
> Still holding and feeding the stem of the contained flower.

Here the water is purified, and spiritualized by light. The psyche as "old scow" in the beginning has been transformed into a "small boat" that moves now without conscious effort, supported by the light-filled lake, just as a rose is sustained in its vase by water filled even above the brim. A beautiful balance is suggested by the boat's drifting quietly with lifted oars, and by the water above the edge of the vase that "does not flow over." The boat and the rose are images of the ego, now in contact with the source of fertility.

Harmony between opposed dimensions of personality, like that created by God with the separation of light and land (the "wooded island") from darkness and water (the lake) produces a Yeatsian Unity of Being, and the ooze or slime of earlier sections of "The Lost Son" sequence has been transformed, as by the moon's effects upon "the rotting sea" in "The Ancient Mariner." Spiritual value is thus symbolically represented as the harmonizing reconciliation between the limitlessness of "the whole air" and water (part five), versus the small boat that drifts in this surround; between the unconscious childhood when "Death was not," when the poet "lived in a simple drowse" (part four), and the mature perspective of this memory; between water and the light of this present intelligence. The boat of ego, like a rose in a vase, drifts on the surface between above and below, waking and sleep, where the unconsciousness of nature touches articulating consciousness and language.

Charles Olson:
Violets and Bridge-Work

Sherman Paul

There are many measures of *The Maximus Poems*. Perhaps the most obvious is that it makes good the very thing Olson, in his earliest criticism, objected to in reviewing Babson and Saville's *Cape Ann: A Tourist Guide* (1936)—the want of serious attention to Gloucester and chiefly to the "significant centre . . .—the fishing industry, its myth, even its economics." Olson, like Frances Rose-Troup, gave Gloucester "place in the genetic world." He made it stick; and, as Warren Tallman says, "in and through [him] it begins . . . to shine on its hill again." It is as much a place possessed—an inalienable possession—as Walden Pond.

One reason for this is that in completing the symbolic action begun in *Call Me Ishmael*, Olson spelled out his obsessive words (*space, myth, fact, object*) and notably achieved the project he had spoken of to Ferrini in [*Letters of*] *Origin* no. 1:

> the only object is
> a man, carved
> out of himself, so wrought he
> fills his given space, makes
> traceries sufficient to
> other's needs.

By filling his given space and thereby making it place, he made traceries that we find useful.

Of the seven essential human offices, Olson performed especially those of teaching, giving pleasure, and consoling. For him, as has been remarked of Jane Austen, the true relation between people was pedagogic—and it

From *Olson's Push: Origin, Black Mountain, and Recent American Poetry*. © 1978 by Louisiana State University Press.

was chiefly in the generous way of his teaching that he gave pleasure and consolation. Such pedagogy—an antonym for demagogy?—is one of his conspicuous New England traits. Kenneth Burke, whom I cite on the essential offices, replaces "console," his initial choice for the last office, with a word that better explains its function: "pontificate; that is, to 'make a bridge.' " This reminds us that Maximus, in the first instance and always a teacher, is also a Pontifex Maximus. When asked why he went to another culture to get his myth, Olson replied, "I just thought I bridged the cultures." Bridge-work, as for Crane, was his work. There is much to connect. He makes (restores) connections, and this gives us hope.

But Olson's pontificating is not of the transcending kind Burke chiefly has in mind in treating Emerson. The symbolic action of Olson's work follows the path of descendence rather than transcendence. It does not provide a bridge from here to elsewhere—to a realm beyond, higher, heavenly: transcendent. Nor does it rely, as such bridging does, on generalization. Whether imaginatively or physically, in visionary flight or westward expansion, it resists such restlessness and willfulness. Instead it bridges down and back, from here to beneath ("to a hard bottom and rocks in place," Thoreau said; to Olson's "Ragged Arse Rock Earth"), to the ever-present archaic fundament, to particulars, *things* that have meaning not by way of subsumption but because they exist through themselves—because, at bottom, in his cosmology, as in Whitehead's, things stand forth, "there is nothing in the real world which is merely an inert fact." Olson is one of the pioneers of *back/down*, a direction of increasing significance in the American imagination. He provides a measure of his own achievement, when writing in 1956 of Williams's *In the American Grain*, he said that "the Pelasgian [synonymous for him with "archaic"], & exactly geographically as of Arkadia, is an American's 'home,' his original departing point" and that Williams "was on the truest path an American can follow if he wishes to go back by the feel of his own texture to his starting place." Williams, he thought, simply didn't go back far enough, take the steps from Eric the Red to Arcadia. He did.

This pontificating may be put in another way. At the end of his lecture on *Causal Mythology*, Olson said that he wanted to use the "papal blessing" that, as a Catholic, still impressed him. He wanted to bless the city and the world, the *urb* and *orb* that figure so prominently in his discussion. Now earth for him is an *orb*, a *"One,"* a thing "knowable" and "seizable," as "familiar to me," he says, "as the smallest thing I know," and, like every thing, alive with its own meaning. Earth is not the world, that is, the whole of creation, the universe. It is only a part of the universe, as perhaps we have begun to realize in an age so much concerned with both space and ecology. To see it in this way, or to see it, as Olson does, as Mother Earth, is to acknowledge dependence on something living, finite, and destructible. Conversely it is to acknowledge and so respect a marvelous bounty. *An actual earth of value*—to have given us this is indeed a pontifical blessing,

an immeasurable gift. In Olson's poem, as in Whitman's, we may find that
a poem is more than its meaning:

> Have you practis'd so long to learn to read?
> Have you felt so proud to get at the meaning of poems?
> Stop this day and night with me, and you shall possess the
>   origin of all poems;
> You shall possess the good of the earth and sun—(there are
>   millions of suns left;)
> You shall no longer take things at second or third hand, nor
>   look through the eyes of the dead, nor feed on the
>   spectres in books;
> You shall not look through my eyes either, nor take things
>   from me:
> You shall listen to all sides, and filter them from yourself.

Olson gives us the good of the earth (and the sun)—he restores the priceless
things—and, like Whitman, he gives us a way to know earth intimately.
In teaching us to live in the world, he teaches us, as Whitman had, to live
in the body, to know the world, as Thoreau said, by direct intercourse and
sympathy, with the senses, proprioceptively.

And what of *urb? Urb* is polis, and polis is not society. Olson told
Elaine Feinstein, "I find the contemporary substitution of society for the
cosmos captive and deathly." The substitution is captive and deathly because society, as all of us know, is not organized, as both cosmos and polis
are, in a living coherent ecological fashion. Present society, itself a product
of the old discourse, does not liberate a beneficent transference of energy.
Because its syntax isn't vital—because its sentences, in Olson's summary
of Fenollosa, are not "governed by mother earth"—it consumes energy and
fosters entropy. Polis is community where society is not. Polis uses people,
as Paul Goodman says, as resources; uses them without using them up,
in the very exchange of their energies adding to them. Olson's conception
of polis is of this generous, generating kind: it is the human order of the
cosmos founded, like the cosmos, on the notion of process and necessary
vital exchange. As he said in speaking of the organization of Black Mountain
College, "function, process, change . . . interaction and communication"
is the premise of modern thought; "the universe—including man and his
interests—is . . . in microcosm and in macrocosm . . . the continuously
changing result of the influence that each of its parts exerts upon all the
rest of its parts." Olson's poetics expresses this view and proposes an
ecological model for poem, polis, and cosmos. What happens between
things, relations (as Emerson knew), transfer of energy (enactment: drama)
are its prominent features—all making possible a turning, to play on the
trope in entropy, that is not entropic. In bringing cosmos and polis together,
in connecting them in *cosmopolis*, he defines a new kind of cosmopolitanism.

This is what Olson had in mind when he said, "I compell Gloucester

/ . . . / to change." He would make it the community that Emerson before him had hoped Concord might become, a generative place. To be made so, I might add, by conversation—a fundamental notion of American social psychology, succinctly expressed by John Dewey: Democracy [polis] begins in conversation. For an interval Olson found such community at Black Mountain College. Thereafter, community was what this teacher and talker—consider what it means to talk to live, the hunger to give and take involved—hoped to find by establishing lay monasteries and universities (universe-city: another cosmopolis). In the space of *The Maximus Poems*, he created a cosmopolis by making Gloucester place, a navel of the world as perhaps all true cities must be. His first will, his will to change, was the will to such coherence, to find and found such a city, an *urb* that had not yet succumbed to urbanization.

But Gloucester had succumbed. Urban renewal was destroying it even as Olson was writing about it. "Rubbish of creation," his brilliant phrase, recognizes this, and it reminds us, as his poetics already has, that Olson's vision is not only ecological in its assumptions (drawn from the earlier ecological visions of the great nineteenth-century New England writers, from Feñollosa, from Lawrence, from Whitehead's philosophy of organism) but in its application. With him ecological consciousness is inevitably ecological conscience, and stirs the will to change. That is the use to which he turned "American tales . . . of man against earth."

We must not fail to consider him a nature poet, one of our best, to be placed in the tradition that includes Thoreau and Snyder, and we must acknowledge among his poems those, like "For a man gone to Stuttgart" or "When do poppies bloom," that explicitly treat nature and merit Frank O'Hara's appreciation of the delicacy of Olson's sensibility. We should also remember his immediate push in response to the "city of mediocrity and cheap ambition destroying // . . . renewing without reviewing [re-*viewing*]"—his "screams" in the Gloucester *Daily Times*, his reminders that "demolition / and service organization" is "not the same as / participatory experience. It / blinds out people into / mice." He told his vision in our time of "Tell-A-Vision" when "the true troubadours / are CBS," and that it didn't do any immediate good didn't deter him. His vision had been formed in response to greater disasters, to that of World War II, which both precipitated present conditions and forced him to review the entire history of humankind, and in that reviewing to find ways (the Way) of renewing.

In the last year of his life, in talking with Herbert Kenny, Olson recalled that he had once been asked why he was writing about a city that was going to disappear. His reply, not to his interrogator but to Kenny, was that he considered Gloucester "a redeemable flower that will be a monstrance forever, of not a city but of City, and stay because she wasn't urbanized." He knew she had been, but he insisted, as *The Maximus Poems* do, that "it's a fishtown, that's all." That *that's all* is everything: cosmopolis.

Which is why, in answer to "what do you think the future of Gloucester on Cape Ann will be?" he replied, "An image of creation and of human life for the rest of the life of the species."

This summarizes admirably the Gloucester of his own work, and in elaborating it Olson explained its migratory theme and ecological ultimatum. Gloucester, he said, was "the final movement of the earth's people"; migration ended there; "Gloucester was the last shore." He had used it "as a bridge to Venice and back from Venice to Tyre, because of the departure from the old static land mass of man which was ice, cave, Pleistocene man and early agricultural man, until he got moving, until he got towns." So, he believed, "the last polis or city *is* Gloucester"—and "man now is either going to rediscover the earth or is going to leave it."

These, we realize with diminishing sense of melodrama, are the alternatives of human history, alternatives of the kind Olson confronted in response to the atom bomb and his own "fatal male small span." For us the inevitable choice is easier because Olson himself has made it and enables us to do so: to rediscover the earth. As early as 1947—early, that is, in his career—he wrote: "It is of nature that we are bereft, the old mother." His project was to "arch again / the necessary goddess," to create a poetics and poetry equal to this, one that restored the function of poetry, which, according to Francis Ponge, another poet of things, is "to nourish the spirit of man by giving him the cosmos to suckle." The enabling means is an open poetics, which, in Ponge's words, requires that we "lower our standard of dominating nature and . . . raise our standard of participating in it" and become "not just the site where ideas and feelings are produced, but also the crossroad where they divide and mingle." This means enables because the path (crossroads) the poet indicates between reality and the soul (self)—to cite Whitman's formulation of the task—is a pathway to the Way, the source of energy, and because it restores what may be called matriarchal ways of thought. An open poetics is ecological by virtue of serving the Great Mother, by standing against the patriarchal consciousness that estranges us from the familiar world, the actual earth. ("Creation is crucial," Olson said; "If you don't stay close to it you lose everything.") And it has another virtue of ecological importance: It reminds us that "acts are value" and that, having to act, we must, as Olson said at Berkeley, believe in our action.

Olson himself heartens us by his own demonstration. His incredible effort to recover a usable past, to make available the resources of scholarship, to offer a vision (an image of the world) accords with the idea of the poet he may have acquired in reading Bruno Snell's *The Discovery of Mind.* If the Greek poets discovered the mind, he (a learned poet, after all) might do something equally worthy, equally momentous in human history. In this sense of the large work to be done, we may find less outrageous his remark, "the poet is the only pedagogue left, to be trusted."

We expect too much from poets, even that they singlehandedly do the work of our time. It is enough if they generate images and transfer energy, if they set us the necessary tasks, set us in motion, and give us hope. Olson does this in many ways and sometimes, as in the following, in ways that appeal to us as Americans.

1. He said that we were the last *first* people, meaning that in the course of human migration westward we were the last people to have the fresh opportunity to use space that the first people had. Or had had, since we failed this opportunity. Nevertheless, he persisted in thinking of us as a first people and tried, imaginatively, to recover for us the space of that possibility. He learned from Jung that we fill space with our own projections and that we explore it in order to achieve wholeness. And so he read the history of the discovery and settlement of America in this light. We were the *last* first people in the sense that we had the opportunity to recover the wholeness that had been lost in the progress of civilization—and for Olson as for Jung that meant contact with the Great Mother. In reading *Psychology and Alchemy*, Olson simply inscribed beneath figure 97, a picture of the "Grand Peregrination" by ship, the word "John Smith." With Jung's explanatory comments, this named his (our) work: "an odyssey in search of wholeness." Such an odyssey, needless to say, differs from those told in Homer, Dante, and Melville, the last, Ahab's, putting an end, as Olson said, to the individual responsible only to himself."

2. Olson's birth and childhood coincide with America's coming-of-age. His earliest teachers, academic or otherwise, had engaged—were still engaged—in the most important critical battle since transcendentalism. In this battle between the modernist Americans and the New Humanists, the factions that Emerson had called the Party of Hope and the Party of the Past were renamed by the New Humanists, the defenders of tradition. The Party of Hope became the Party of Nature, and the Party of the Past the Party of Culture, Culture having its Arnoldian meaning. As a result we see more clearly what all along had been the American critical issue: Nature vs. Culture. And we see where Olson, with his push against European Culture, stands.

But what distinguishes Olson from those who precede him in this debate—and also suggests a difference between the postmodernists and their modernist predecessors—is his extension of the terms, so that the issue is no longer within the western tradition but now involves the western tradition as one of its terms. Western tradition—now American as much as European—acquires the meaning of Culture, and Nature, long since lost as the unique advantage of America—we are no longer "Nature's Nation," in Perry Miller's phrase—Nature is "backward and outside," the sources or origins wherever they can be found in all time and all place. Now the issue is worldwide, of that magnitude of importance.

Nature vs. Culture. We recall from Levi-Strauss's study of Amerindian myth and G. S. Kirk's study of Sumerian and Greek myth that this opposition provides the primary structure of many myths and may be the fundamental contradiction that myth accommodates. Olson recognizes the ever-presence of myth in experience. This enables him to recover those times and places when myth itself arose, and to ask us, in returning to these origins, to begin again with the primary issue of human experience.

> The whole question & continuing struggle to remain civilized Sumer documented in & out: I imagine you know the subtle tale of how Gilgamesh . . . was sent the rude fellow Enkidu to correct him because he, even Gilgamesh, had become a burden, in his lust, to his city's people. As I read it, it is an incredibly accurate myth of what happens to the best of men when they lose touch with the primordial & phallic energies & methodologies which, said this predecessor people of ours [the Sumerians are the first first people] make it possible for man, that participant thing, to take up, straight, nature's, live nature's force.

3. Gloucester was once "frontier," a paradigm of the Westward Movement; and it was left behind in its course. Olson never wrote the long poem on the West that he had proposed early in his career. He didn't have to because he rehearsed much of it in the history of Gloucester and found there the task presented by it: how to stay put, dig in and down. He awoke in the morning, as he said, "after the dispersion," in a New England whose urban erosion was of the pattern of previous agricultural erosion. And in the old, misused, and cast-aside—"the waste and ashes of pioneering," as Van Wyck Brooks said earlier of the old American towns—he showed us how to find place; how, in fact, it is more likely to be a place because it has a history, because human life there has, in whatever ways, altered space. We repossess place in repossessing the experience of it. *Polis is eyes:* caring and attending are the best means of urban renewal. It is possible to refound even with the sacred and profane worn out. By digging in (a) place we recover not only America but all origin, and in doing this we remake our places.

Olson traveled much in Gloucester, discovering, as Thoreau had, that "the nature which inspired mythology still flourishes," and that such discoveries may help us clear away the junk of history and open the springs of being.

> I told the woman
> about the spring
> on the other side of Freshwater
> Cove which lies
> right on the edge of the
> marsh and is flooded
> each high tide by
> the Ocean which it then
> expells it runs so fast itself
> from its sources and to drink it
> the moment the tide has pulled off even one little bit
> is a water untasteable elsewhere.

Pushing Olson

Calvin Bedient

The poems of Charles Olson are distinguished by a hard, dry medium, a seashell medium cool and crusty to the touch. Olson sought this disembowelment as if raging against romantic heat, mire, change. "Juicy" was his most dismissive word. That he preached a philosophy of organism (after Whitehead) was ironic; his practicing sensibility was standoffish, distrustful, fussy, irritable, attitudinizing, pompous, terse. On querulous terms with the body, his vulgarity a blurting schoolboy's, pinioned in a 6'7" frame with a freakish pituitary, shy and arrogant, as loquacious as he was inarticulate, he used words as a means of crossing, high and dry, the white water of instant reality. A few lyrics in *The Maximus Poems, Volume Three* call from the living element itself—but for the rest the remoteness of history and hifalutin allusion are the rule. Never a buzz or alarm of surplus connotation, a thaw or flow, or even a risky little skip of rhythm. Life does not tempt this man from inside. His verse is bent up and raised narrowly on life like the slat of a venetian blind. His poetry, like "polis," is "eyes"— those angels among the senses, those spook holes. And eyes for archives as much as for streets and a harbor. He snapped phrases across line breaks, dis*organ*ized syntax, dispelled momentum by maniacal parentheses, and alluded laconically, all to back the mind up before the problematic novelty of his medium. But why make so much of the medium itself when it is clearly not fashioned for pleasure? It must be largely to check empathy and replace the organic with a mental contrivance—to fence out the wildness both of the world and the mind. (For the rest, it was to quash facility, conceived as an overripeness.) Olson's verse is an ascetic's retreat.

There is appeal to this asceticism. Rereading some of *The Maximus*

From *Parnassus: Poetry in Review 7*, no. 2 (Spring/Summer 1979). © 1980 by Poetry in Review Foundation.

Poems, one may find the verse lighteningly removed from the present struggle of life, satisfyingly ugly, like autumn grass. Times when the breath of
the moment blows thrillingly in, as here—

> It is undone business
> I speak of, this morning,
> with the sea
> stretching out
> from my feet

> And now the shadow
> of the radiator on the floor
> is wolf-tits, the even row of it
> fit to raise
> feral children

are rare. Otherwise he might be tapping his fingernails against a lacquered
box, the sense of being safely on top, outside, is so marked. The inden-
tations and spacings bespeak control, calculated variation and emphasis.
At the same time, the line breaks, the wooden rhythms, are all finicky
haltingness. "How I got to / what I say" is a monosyllabic graph of slow
progress, and "there are only / eyes in all heads, / to be looked out of" is
all downright insistence, and outward moving, in its poking ugliness. "I'd
not urge anyone back. Back is no value as better" tugs back even as it
makes its disclaimer; it has Olson's characteristic woodpecker rap. Frequently common but seldom humble, his words bite matters off. Their
value is "containment." Even the shrill

> o kill kill kill kill kill
> those
> who advertise you
> out

is metallic rhetoric.

The question, then, is how much containment, as against presentment,
one wants. My own sense of Olson is that he punishes sensibility. His
average is a trying fracturedness:

> Eyes
> & polis,
> fishermen,
> & poets
>> or in every human heave I've known is
>> busy
> both:
> the attention, and
> the care
>> however much each of us

> chooses our own
> kin and
> concentration.

In saying it new, this says it awkwardly and bleakly. There is no absence of skill, only of a joy of perception and style. The writing is not free, not a freshet. It is foxed and foxing. And the twists and gaps, even the diction, are a little precious. Egotism of manner.

And what is to be had besides the manner? Wisdom? I should say, of no noticeable degree—that a few pages of Thoreau, not to mention La Rochefoucauld, are more telling than all the *Maximus* poems put together. History? Only the local history of Cape Ann, chopped and shuffled around. And Olson's sources—generously quoted in George F. Butterick's *Guide to the Maximus Poems*—make more flavorful and coherent reading than his uses of them. Spirit of place? Gloucester remains something of a rumor. The stars, the sea—mere rumors. Olson seems to seize on Gloucester with a fierce and shaking intent. The place bleaches in the glare of his demands on it. The latitudes of long and genuine love are barely evident. Nothing remotely like the glowing concresence of Agee's rural Alabama, Thoreau's Walden, Dinesen's Africa.

Instead, attitudes and propositions, as well as historical and geological transcriptions, make up the substance of the volumes. And the attitudes are a bit tough or, on occasion, sentimental ("They should raise a monument / to a fisherman crouched down / behind a hogshead, protecting / his dried fish), the propositions less than "lures for feeling." In Whitehead's somewhat indiscriminatory argument in *Process and Reality*, propositions are "not primarily for belief, but for feeling at the physical level of unconsciousness." Literature, he says, should teach us this. Thus of Hamlet's speech "To be, or not to be" he observes, "The speech, for the theatre audience, is purely theoretical, a mere lure for feeling." It is, rather, a speech *from* a character and *in* a play, more situational than theoretical. A real, if fine, distinction lies between literary and nonliterary propositions. But the thing to note about the propositions in *The Maximus Poems* is that they function like nonliterary propositions. Our judgment of them is not, in Whitehead's words, "eclipsed by aesthetic delight." And no persona, hotly engaged in life, gives them "inevitability." They are accidental and (not to make much of the term) anti-poetic. Here is a sampling:

> Polis now
> is a few, is a coherence not even yet new . . .

> In the face of sweetness,
> piss
> In the time of goodness,
> go side, go
> smashing, beat them, go as

as near as you can

tear

What weeds
as an explanation
leaves out, is
that chaos
is not our condition.

Not that relaxation.

All,
has no honor as quantity.

The first and third of these are pretentious and make little effort to guide feeling; they are assertions, at the opposite pole from the negative capability, the laboratory slide, of Hamlet's soliloquy. The second is all macho push. None is in the mode of discovery. Ours but to entertain them, like contentious guests.

This self-declared "Objectivist" was, I think, too egotistically cerebral to give us poems full of objects to be experienced. His self-regard rides herd on his words. His language is not raised to the tenth power by incorporating any romance with what is other than himself. I quote from Max Picard:

> When the word is the object, the word seems like a blessed overflow: the object exists but through the word it exists all over again. In this overflow, language . . . is free and therefore beautiful. Whenever a word succeeds in expressing the object completely, man is both happy and sad. The yearning for the Wholeness that man has lost is present in language.

Shakespeare's "the uncertain glory of an April day" is an object in this sense, free and beautiful. But Olson's art is, in a phrase Robert von Hallberg takes from Wallace Stevens [and uses in *Charles Olson: The Scholar's Art*], a "scholar's art," and deliberately object-less. Poetry *is* the scholar's art, said Stevens, who, however, turned even abstractions into objects. Olson is more concerned to teach by making of language a hard school-bench. "Poet-pedagogue," von Hallberg calls him. But I must hasten to explain that he does not mean it as a criticism and even seems to mean it as praise.

His premise: "Olson deserves close attention precisely because his poems do not conform to what modern critics have argued is essentially poetic." "Some of the intentions of Olson's poetics that now seem unpoetic," he adds, "might be more familiar to us if we still consented to the poetic conventions that flourished in the eighteenth century and perished in the nineteenth." Are the modern critics wrong, then, in finding Olson unpoetic? Let us consider. "Olson never conceived of poetry's effect as pleasurable," writes von Hallberg. This is clearly a heresy whether from the point of view of Pope or Pound. Again: "his verse is willfully prosaic, both metrically and thematically, because he hoped to destroy the category of Poetry itself." Now, what remains after destroying this swollen capitalized entity: the "essentially poetic" or the unpoetic? "It is not always apparent that Olson's poems . . . need to be poems." The unpoetic, then.

"Questions of poetic theory," von Hallberg states, "rather than the poems themselves, are my subject." He goes on to enumerate three concerns: "What are the attractions of an expository poetics? What ends are served by expository poems? Why should a didactic poet use so exclusive a rhetoric?" But not only does he avoid theorizing about poetry as such; a single obvious answer, "the communication of thought and meaning," makes do for all three questions. The "attractions of an expository poetics" are not elaborated, nor does this critic's neutral tone betray any enthusiasm for particular charms or achievements. His book is more rhetorical than diagnostic. Without the trial of argument, it contends that "the communication of thought and meaning" is acceptable in poetry. This cannot be granted. The real question is: when is this communication poetic or not poetic? And this question, again, he avoids.

Of the poems, von Hallberg writes: "Many critics would persuade us that they are poems of a minor order, especially those critics who believe meaning is not the business of poetry." But of course few critics stand behind a meaningless poetry. The issue lies, rather, in what is meant by meaning. Von Hallberg himself seems to link it with "information" and "abstraction." "This is a poetry," he notes, "in which attitudes and personalities matter less than information." "At its best," he adds, "Olson's poetry records a mind committed to abstraction and general understanding feeling its way through language." "Information," however, isn't meaning; it's what passes for fact. As for Olson's "general understanding," I have suggested that it lacks the *bloom* of meaning. How could it be otherwise when he "resolutely avoided" "striking and apt figures, sonorous or well-turned phrases, unity of texture and structure"? These are the rivers and engines of experienced meaning. Torque and timbre and overtone and convergent images, after all, are meaning, too. A page of Keats is more meaningful than a page of Whitehead because poetry is more instinct than prose with "the Wholeness" that man desires. In any case, von Hallberg is not much exercised either to paraphrase or to propose Olson's meanings. "Meaning" functions in his book largely as a neoclassical shibboleth. It has also an unspecified humanistic value, as if simply to communicate a thought, any thought, were humanizing. But what matters is the quality of the thought communicated.

Is Olson really effective in communicating thought? Consider that his propositions are not only thin but twisted. "Olson," as von Hallberg notes, "is a mannerist"; and mannerism interferes with pedagogy. For Olson, his critic observes, "poetry is first of all language, a means to an end: communication, the establishment of common knowledge." But what von Hall-berg details as "phrases ending with the preposition 'of,' dozens of commas blocking passage through a single poem, stresses clotted by assemblages of monosyllabic words, unnecessarily abstract diction, barrages of appo-sition and clausal parallelism" obviously briar-patch communication. As he himself acknowledges, "Olson's mannerisms show that he has moved through the poem forcefully, and sometimes that is very nearly the whole point." His manner was in fact an effort to create a limited experience, an experience of language as artifice. "The thinking and weighing in of the quantity," to borrow his own words on Shakespeare, "stop twist and in-tensify the speech, thus increasing the instancy"—the instancy of the lan-guage itself. But this practice tore at his intention to instruct.

Still and all, von Hallberg judges Olson almost as severely as one would like. Recall him on Olson's all too forceful manner. Here are other strictures:

> What makes Olson different from Pound in his handling of [his-torical] material is his willingness to make—actually, his frequent insistence on making—his point directly and explicitly, only too often at the expense of flat and uninteresting language.

> What began as an effort to change American culture by establishing common knowledge and values ended, as most such attempts end, with the achievement of a personal order, but one presented, as in "A Note for Anyone Able to," as something larger.

And connected with this last:

> It is too easy and uninstructive to say that Olson's elitism made him a cult-figure with a heuristic poetics. The more fruitful ques-tion, to which easy answers are unconvincing, is how America (unlike England, say) breeds such ambitious poets and yet at the same time persuades them to settle for so little.

As to this, a gamier critic might have had a shot at answering the "fruitful question"—and a more cautious one might not have used "persuades." But all three excerpts point to a certain authority, a certain toughness of mind. Certainly von Hallberg is (nor need one add, for so young a critic) a knowledgeable, urbane, and practiced writer, whose comparisons of Ol-son with Pound, Williams, and Zukofsky are excellent and whose analyses of Olson's manner are precise. He will be, I think, a critic worth keeping up with.

This "boom" year in Olson studies [1980], as George F. Butterick calls it, bears two other critical books, as well as Butterick's own *Guide to the Maximus Poems*. Having made much of history, Olson, who died in 1970, is himself now history, rating, for one thing, a page or two in the story of the transformation of poetic form into a mode of quest, or at least into a quarrel with silence. A page or two only, because "field composition" was ill-suited to so dogmatic a poet. Nothing much lives or surprises in his field; he just scatters his material across it. Not the recalcitrance of the subject but his pick-a-daisy method explains his fragmentary work. The sequence of Yeats's "Vacillation" or Geoffrey Hill's "Mercian Hymns" is, Olson might say, an extension of their content; by contrast, *The Maximus Poems* is sequential because Olson wanted a form coterminous with his interests. A few late poems aside, it betrays, not a nostalgia for Wholeness, but a scholar's combination of concentration and desultoriness.

Has Olson not misled his critics? When (in "Projective Verse") he spoke of "no track other than the one the poem under hand declares," he invoked a philosophy of organism, and not his own collector's atomism. Paul Christensen, in *Charles Olson: Call Him Ishmael*, describes *Maximus* as "an allegory of a person seeking understanding"; but this misconstrues the poem, or, conversely, allegory and seeking. For what is Olson seeking? If we say, a way out of the "pejorocracy" of commercial America, he is out of it from the beginning. If we say, the Great Mother (as analyzed by Jung and Erich Neumann), then he has already found her. And in fact the references to her in *The Maximus Poems* are not only littered about but literary, and lack the impact of revelation. Then Christensen goes one up on "allegory" by speaking of *Maximus* as "a modern mystery play." But Olson's methodology—the transcription of records, the reminiscences, the rebukes to the present, the random order, above all the quirky, distancing style—is even less a medium of drama than of quest. Certainly it keeps at bay all that he thought he stood for: the moment, energy, the senses riding "this joy in the mortal particulars" to find a "spiritual dimension" satisfying to the soul.

Christensen also shows a perhaps unwarranted faith in the coherence of *The Maximus Poems*. Here is his description of the second volume:

> The way is long and the cues of connection are not pronounced. The foreground is so crowded with detail that the reader never glimpses the whole subject of the work. Narrative does not sweep us forward, as it does in other poems of this length. We must infer a narrative, even struggle for one, as though we were made to cross a mosaic floor on all fours and guess what figure the tiles make up.

But what meaning does narrative keep when applied to so disjunctive a work? An inferred narrative is a self-contradiction, a story that does not get told. Christensen's willingness to "struggle" for connections says more for his zeal and earnestness than for the singleness of the work. But to him the connections, such as they are, are all important; they save the poems:

> Even when we acknowledge the frequent dullness of passages, the unreasonable difficulty of allusions, the purely personal details to which we have no access, the long catalogs of facts and minutiae,

all of which clutter up and destroy a smooth flow of language and "plot," the discovery of the poet's control over his material at any juncture is a pleasure that beckons us onward.

This "discovery" seems a rather bleak return for enduring the dullness and difficulty so devastatingly detailed. "The poet's control over his material" becomes wonderful by default of what is more accessible, and more certain, in the poems. Still, how real and extensive *is* Olson's "control"? I should say that the following law applies: the more ingenious the organization detected by the critic, the more it is likely to be his own and not Olson's. File together fragments of material related by subject matter and point of view, and of course connections can be formed. But the poem *is* still a drawer of files.

Christensen's book is otherwise a balanced scholarly introduction to the *oeuvre*. It takes one patiently through the prose and the short poems and *Maximus* and then, rather gratuitously, right on to "the Black Mountain Poets." Apart from the fanciful notion that the poems have significant vertical and horizontal axes, the technical analysis rings true. Even the faults of the book are the defects of a virtue—the critic's generosity. Perhaps he is too easily overwhelmed. "The poignance of this long, awesome poem," he writes, "comes from the sense that he cannot enjoy the splendor of earth alone; his words are the song that would lure humanity out of doors." But this hardly fits so arrogant and unlyrical a poet, whose rejection of "description" curtained off the "out of doors." Christensen is so soft on Olson as to attribute his own romantic nature ("splendor . . . song . . . lure") to the poems.

Of course, Olson might be indexed in our histories under R for Romanticist or O for Originalist, as well as under O for Open Form or P for Projectivist (though this last is, I think, a puffed-up notion). At least he was Romantic in his "projected" outlook, if anti-Romantic in his poetic practice. Sherman Paul, in *Olson's Push*, celebrates Olson's stance toward reality:

> Olson, of course, is not outrightly Emersonian; his work is a reaction to elements of transcendentalism and romanticism, and yet more than he realized, or admitted at this time, it is continuous with them. . . . Like Emerson, Olson would renew our experience, quicken our sense of life here and now, in the present world, and by repossessing us of our dynamic—"Man is, He acts"—enable us to cope with the occasions the world presents us.

He adds:

> Unlike Emerson, he does this not so much in terms of "nature" as in terms of "history"—and by breaking the egg of history, the mythic metaphor evoking the shock of primal creation.

But Paul, I think, is still another critic who takes Olson's word for his words. His eye is on the theorist, not the poet. Olson the poet regrets history more than he breaks the egg of it. (By contrast, Whitman and Lawrence are true egg-breakers.) Again: "An open poetics is ecological by virtue of serving the Great Mother, by standing against the patriarchal consciousness that estranges us from the familiar world, the actual earth." But there is more refamiliarization with the earth, I suggest, in the slenderest volume of Marianne Moore or Elizabeth Bishop than in the whole of *Maximus*. Then, in "what all along had been the American critical issue: Nature vs. Culture," Paul rejoices to find Olson in "the Party of Nature." Yet to my mind *Maximus* is overwhelmingly, even self-defeatingly, a work of culture, more egotistical than sublime. And that Paul is concerned with what Olson says at the expense of how he says it may lead him to praise passages for the wrong reason. He describes the following as "brilliant":

> When I think of what Fitz Lane didn't do
> painting all this light which almost
> each day is enough, at least at twilight,
> to rouse one as a change of air does
> to the direct connection our lives bear
> to the mathematic of Creation surrounding us,
> I love him more for his attempts pre-
> Hawthorne to draw in silk the pinks and
> umbrous hills and rocks surround
> on their reflexive & reflexing
> Harbor—light sits under one's eye
> & being as the saucer to the in
> the instance of this evening high al-
> most exactly perfect half moon al-
> ready going westward too.

Paul finds this "remarkable enough (and so patently intended) to stand beside Emerson's famous passage in *Nature* on the transparent eyeball." But as romantic epistemology it seems to be moth derivative and murky. What by contrast *is* brilliant, or "almost," is the strategy of letting the reader draw from the syntactic chaos something intelligible and picturable—as if snatching the honey and escaping the bees. What is "remarkable" is the writing. So much confidingness mixed with so much reserve ("what Fitz Lane didn't do") and so much stateliness with so forfending a novelty. Never mind why the light is only "almost . . . enough." Why is "pinks" paralleled with "umbrous" instead of "hills," and why jam the syntax with "surround"? And, passing over the Latinate play and diffusion of "reflexive nd reflexing," what justifies the grotesquerie of "light sits under one's eye / & being as the saucer to the in"? But the clear moon suddenly stands high and westward, an "almost exactly perfect half," and the problems are all cast into shadow. The method both costs and pays. Faced with such exciting and strenuous writing (few passages in *Maximus* are its equal), how distracted one must be not to be struck, first and last, by the poetry as such.

The first wave of Olson criticism is predictably introductory, sweeping, scholarly, and divided between reserving judgment as to the "final success" of *The Maximus Poems* and assuming that Olson's importance is large. What is needed, at least now, is a shrewd look at the poems—one that neither resorts to the dodge that a work should be judged in its own terms (the bootstrap theory) nor takes for granted that the poems coincide with the poetics, or the poetics with the philosophy. Fanned by his self-importance, the smokescreen of Olson's rhetoric still rolls across his lines.

In his *Guide to the Maximus Poems*, George F. Butterick (the Curator of Literary Manuscripts at the University of Connecticut, which houses the Charles Olson Archives) is on comparatively pedestrian, if very useful, ground. All he needed was to be patient, thorough, tireless, and judicious as he annotated "all three volumes of Olson's epic work, page by page, line by line, identifying names of persons and places, foreign words and phrases, and supplying the precise sources of the many literary and historical allusions and borrowings"—and so he has been. His handbook "does not seek to analyze or interpret, but to allow the reader to participate actively in the poems" (in other words, gain information). It is exemplary, and the introduction, while not drawing one up to the poems as to a fire, duly tells the story of their making.

Preposterous, however, that our academic machine has fired this 816-page work down the chute before making the third volume of *Maximus*, and even the second, readily available to library users, let alone to bookstores. (I went to two major university libraries before finding *Volume Three*, which was sequestered in Special Collections.) A vast closet poem, even if now lit up by 4,000 or so annotations. But where a *Guide* appears, can the primary work be far behind? Butterick's squat book may do a tugboat's service.

Meanwhile, within the Special Collections of large libraries, sleep most of Olson's most moving poems, for instance this:

> When do poppies bloom   I ask myself, stopping again
> to look in Mrs. Frontiero's yard, beside her house on
> this side from Birdeyes (or what was once Cunningham
> & Thompson's and is now O'Donnell-Usen's) to see if
> I have missed them, flaked out and dry-like like
> Dennison's Crepe. And what I found was dark buds
> like cigars, and standing up   and my question is
> when, then, will those blossoms more lotuses to the
> West than lotuses wave like paper and petal by petal
> seem more powerful than any thing except the Universe
> itself, they are so animate-inanimate and dry-beauty not
> any shove, or sit there poppies, blow as crepe

paper. And in Mrs. Frontiero's yard annually I
expect them as the King of the Earth must have
Penelope, awaiting her return, love lies
so delicately on the pillow as this one flower,
petal and petal, carries nothing
into or out of the World   so threatening
were those cigar-stub cups just now, & I *know*
how quickly, and paper-like, absorbent
and krinkled paper, the poppy itself will, when here,
go again and the stalks stay like onion plants oh
come, poppy, when will you bloom?

A curiously pell-mell, happily clumsy, lumberingly loving poem. Refreshing to find Olson writing on this small, personal, needful scale, as if no
more (and no less) ambitious, if no less eccentric, than Charles Sisson or
W. S. Graham. The naked eye replaces the telescope of history and those
cigar-stub poppies, that krinkled paper, have really been seen. The ego,
the "I," is half-mythicized and mellow. Olson's lines, "nakedness / is what
one means / that all start up / to the eye and soul / as though it had never
happened before," are at last illustrated by the poet himself.
  Or take "Celestial Evening, October 1967":

                              the

full volume of all which ever was which we
as such have that which is our part of it,
all history existence places splits of moon
& slightest oncoming smallest stars at
sunset, fears & horrors, grandparents'
lives as much as we have also features
and their forms, whatever grace or ugliness our legs
etc possess, it all

comes in as also outward leads
us after itself as though then
the horn of the nearest moon was
truth. I bend my ear, as,
if I were Amoghasiddi and,
here on this plain where
like my mole I have
been knocked flat, attend,
to turn & turn within
the steady stream & collect which
within me ends as in her hall and I
hear all, the new moon new in all
the ancient sky.

Paul's observation, "By digging in (a) place we recover not only America but all origin, and in doing this we remake our Places," partially glosses this lovely mutant of a poem. Here Olson's anti-lyric upheavals break and lift our speech into something new—then let it subside into lyricism. (It is the same strategy as in the lines on Fitz Lane, only heated up.) Inarticulateness transcends itself as a startled eloquence. An old-style smoothness ("of all which ever was," "slightest," "smallest" "whatever grace or ugliness," etc.) contends against abrupt phrasing, missing punctuation, pull-away syntax, confused imagery, and refractory line breaks. Inventing a mode of wonder, the writing is literally distracted. The lines contract at being knocked flat and attending—then expand not least through rhymes, here aural windows in the Great Mother's hall, openings upon openings. In these rhymes, the poet, the man of harmonious words, lovingly hears all—had he not implied in "The Ring Of" that words and love are born of like "elements"? Here Eros is released not as myth so much as the desire for the Wholeness implicit in language. The god-like concentration and tranquility of the Tibetan Amoghasiddi is the flowering of this human need, the benediction of a celestial evening.

I shall hasten on to another neglected beauty from *Volume Three*, "Hotel Steinplatz, Berlin, December 25 (1966)":

> And light increases, in my room falls thickly erasing
> gloom. But brings terror the sky itself is falling the End
>
> of the World Tree has come! Oh, white hart of the Tree's
>   boughs
> oh rotten side of the tree's side   oh Serpent, of the Earth
> do not make this the Epoch simply that man has—oh now
>   the snow
> has swung back, no longer falls as though the top has gone,
>   tries
> itself once more lessly—It is not good, I want
> the snow, I want need, hail and ice, need-nail fingernail of
>   Abwehr
>
> the staves
> the three staves of my giants, I need two sweet
>   environments, of procreation,
> creation
> and
>
> TiuBirka's bebt, Tiubirka
>   s shaking, of the top and
> dew dew aurr sprinkling until she cries
>   who is this man who drives me   all the way
>   who drives me on down this weary path?
>
>   Snowed on by snow, beaten by rain
>   drenched with the dew, long I lay dead

> And pressed me, as he went
> not caring, so soon as he had heard
> What he had forced out of me
> the Tree itself alone—ah now no snow at all.

This poem flattens a little on rereading. That many of the details come from H. R. Ellis Davidson's *Gods and Myths of Northern Europe* (as Butterick notes) somewhat tames it as an act of imagination: tree, hart, snake, rotten side, need and nail, the three staves, the sacred birch tree Tiubirka, the four lines beginning "who is this man," are Nordic or Norman borrowings. But the point I would make is that the poem overshadows almost all Olson's other work in imaginative attack, river-run inevitability, adventure of mind and language. A modern man has touched myth and made it tingle all through; it becomes, for the moment, his racing pulse.

All three poems belie "Objectivism"—what in "Projective Verse" Olson spoke of as "the getting rid of the lyrical interference of the individual as ego, of the 'subject' and his soul, that peculiar presumption by which western man has interposed himself between what he is as a creature of nature . . . and those other creations of nature which we may, with no derogation, call objects." But perhaps Olson got it wrong: perhaps objects are dead, unbefriended, unredeemed, unless apprehended lyrically. Even a dispassionate appreciation of them trembles on the threshold of passion. To attend is to create and begin to love. So it is in these three pieces, and so it is not in much of the rest of *Maximus*. Olson's preoccupation with methodology, the egotism and masculine self-importance of it, hurt his gift. It arrogated far more to itself than does lyricism, which by contrast is an unusual openness. As his "great master" Whitehead said: "All is there for feeling. All *does* flow."

Vision and Mastery
in Elizabeth Bishop

Bonnie Costello

Some poets provoke their readers into commentary. I find myself wanting to fight with Williams, to explain Stevens, to sort out Moore, to pin down Ashbery. But Elizabeth Bishop first inspires in me, and I suspect in many readers, a contemplative silence. We gaze rather than reply. Critics have remarked on Bishop's reticence, but while the voice is restrained, most seem to agree, the vision compensates. The bulk of critical writing on Bishop deals with her sense of the visual particular in one way or another—her sense of place, her preoccupation with mapping and geography, her descriptive discipline. No one claims, any more, that she is "merely" descriptive, but all agree that Bishop gathers and communicates knowledge through the eye. Such an emphasis on the visual particular in Bishop can be misleading, however, when taken as confidence. Randall Jarrell, in *Poetry and the Age* (New York: Knopf, 1953), insists "all her poems have written underneath, *I have seen it*." But this sounds like a kind of boast, a Romantic absolute invested in the physical world. Bishop's vision is not ample; it is not meant to fill in the void left by voice. She is more likely to write "I have seen it leaving," for mutability is her theme, Darwin her guide. No Grand Design reveals a Master Hand. Depth is an illusion carved by time into the face of things. It is that sad face that she studies, with what she called Darwin's "self-forgetful, perfectly useless concentration." Of course such concentration is not useless, but it separates vision (or "looks" as she preferred to call it) from mastery, resists the desire of contemplation to become commerce. But the imagination cannot entirely resist that logic of desire. The eye seeks amplitude and composure, but finding it, seeks again deprivation, flux, and freedom. It is this rhythm of vision—receding and yielding—that interests me in Bishop's work.

From *Twentieth Century Literature* 28, no. 4 (Winter 1982). © 1983 by Hofstra University Press.

But what is the point of describing landscapes, if not to render a vision of God's Work, or find a transcendental meaning? Descriptive poetry provides the mind (of reader and writer) with a scene of action. Its meanings are in one sense highly specified and focused (sights, sounds, smells) but partly because these meanings are specified in a context relatively empty of human content, they offer a broad range of suggestion and more room for association. With less formal and less thematic closure than other genres, the description of the landscape becomes a means for the release of motions and tensions which might otherwise be precluded or overlooked.

What we experience, then, is not so much the particular streak of the tulip, or the particular mountain or cave or field, but a series of tensions and movements, a range from close focus to wide prospect, and so on, which invites us to enter the poem each with his own range of more individual feelings and thoughts. We cannot say what the meaning of open space is, and yet a wide skyscape or valley often seems powerfully significant. For one who has little trust in a closed system of meaning or symbolism, the landscape offers an important locus of self-discovery. The shapes Bishop traces there are unfinished to the human eye, merging into one another, deviating from every pattern assigned to them. And yet she can bring to the landscape and dramatize there her basic imaginative needs and tendencies.

A distinct cycle of feeling forms repeatedly in the shapes and rhythms of Bishop's landscape description, and it is that cycle I wish to explore here. In the most general terms: Bishop begins by dismantling or pushing back some resolved or comprehensive vision, some former mastery, releasing or dispersing it into images of flux or retreat. As the eye moves over these dynamic forms, they first seem iridescent, but become increasingly hazardous, until the eye seeking rest settles on a place of impenetrable, or vacant darkness. Out of this darkness emerges (either directly, by juxtaposition, or as fantasy) a mundane figure or image—usually an animal— which offers the eye a momentary composure (not as articulate order but as ineffable coalescence) before it too retreats or recedes. I want to stress that this is a pattern of feeling (sometimes only implicit), not a determinate meaning or conclusive process in Bishop, though by the end I hope to suggest at least tentatively some conceptual coordinates to it.

By way of introduction I'd like to explore two early poems, "Brazil, January 1, 1502" and "Over 2,000 Illustrations and a Complete Concordance," which display some of this movement and tension and establish the visual context of Bishop's skepticism. In ordering her experience Bishop encounters many of the same problems and employs many of the same solutions as landscape painters. I want to show how she works with the materials of landscape, with wide and narrow prospects, static and dynamic form, background and foreground, horizon and vanishing point, light and color, in displaying her theme of mutability, her shifts of loss and consolation. In conclusion I will read closely two late poems, "The End of March" and "The Moose," which employ these techniques and display the full cycle of feeling I have outlined.

The artist/explorer, undertaking treacherous expeditions in quest of primal vision, provided a rich mythology for nineteenth-century American painting, as Barbara Novak has pointed out in *Nature and Culture* (New York: Oxford, 1980). Bierstadt, Church, Moran, and other Luminists pursued the virgin territory of the American West and even Labrador and South America in search of a natural antiquity, a new vision of Genesis, by which they might, as artists, partake of the power and completeness of the Creation by representing it in original form. They indeed wished to write "I have seen it" beneath every canvas. Their ambition suffered from a double irony, for not only did their gaze anticipate a trail of gazers who would defeat Nature's primacy, but since their vision was not innocent, they saw only belatedly. Their images of these exotic places fit the baroque and sublime conventions of Claude Lorrain, Salvador Rosa, and others.

While Bishop's "Brazil, January 1, 1502" is about Portuguese conquistadors, it describes a similar ironic will to impose compositional order on wild nature.

BRAZIL, JANUARY 1, 1502

> . . . embroidered nature . . . tapestried landscape.
> —*Landscape Into Art*, by Sir Kenneth Clark

Januaries, Nature greets our eyes
exactly as she must have greeted theirs:
every square inch filling in with foliage—
big leaves, little leaves, and giant leaves,
blue, blue-green, and olive,
with occasional lighter veins and edges,
or a satin underleaf turned over;
monster ferns
in silver-gray relief,
and flowers, too, like giant water lilies
up in the air—up, rather, in the leaves—
purple, yellow, two yellows, pink,
rust red and greenish white;
solid but airy; fresh as if just finished
and taken off the frame.

A blue-white sky, a simple web,
backing for feathery detail:
brief arcs, a pale-green broken wheel,
a few palms, swarthy, squat, but delicate;
and perching there in profile, beaks agape,
the big symbolic birds keep quiet,

each showing only half his puffed and padded,
pure-colored or spotted breast.
Still in the foreground there is Sin:
five sooty dragons near some massy rocks.
The rocks are worked with lichens, gray moonbursts
splattered and overlapping,
threatened from underneath by moss
in lovely hell-green flames,
attacked above
by scaling-ladder vines, oblique and neat,
"one leaf yes and one leaf no" (in Portuguese).
The lizards scarcely breathe; all eyes
are on the smaller, female one, back-to,
her wicked tail straight up and over,
red as a red-hot wire.

Just so the Christians, hard as nails,
tiny as nails, and glinting,
in creaking armor, came and found it all,
not unfamiliar:
no lovers' walks, no bowers,
no cherries to be picked, no lute music,
but corresponding, nevertheless,
to an old dream of wealth and luxury
already out of style when they left home—
wealth, plus a brand-new pleasure.
Directly after Mass, humming perhaps
L'Homme armé or some such tune,
they ripped away into the hanging fabric,
each out to catch an Indian for himself—
those maddening little women who kept calling,
calling to each other (or had the birds waked up?)
and retreating, always retreating, behind it.

The epigraph, from Kenneth Clark's *Landscape into Art*, "embroidered nature . . . tapestried landscape" is reinforced by the first description, in
which nature seems to "greet" the viewer as a virginal hostess (it is January,
the new year), nevertheless well trained to deck herself out in baroque
opulence. All, initially, seems foreground: "every square inch filling in with
foliage— / . . . solid but airy; fresh as if just finished / and taken off the
frame." But such a moment of completion, filled in and balanced, is always
precarious in Bishop. She immediately looks for a recalcitrant element,
creates a distance, before the plenitude becomes cloying. Here the epigraph
quickly becomes ironic as the eye, possessed by an illusion of depth, pur-
sues its object and tries to "rip away into the hanging fabric." The visual
organization of the scene gradually leads away from rather than confirms

the viewer's initial conquest. Nature which seemed to greet our eyes frontally has now turned its profile and has become secretive:

> And perching there is profile, beaks agape,
> the big symbolic birds keep quiet,
> each showing only half his puffed and padded,
> pure-colored or spotted breast.

To call these birds symbolic is still to possess them. But if this scene is emblematic rather than decorative as it seemed at first, it represents the viewer's own defeat, for as her eye gloats over the surface it settles on an old memento mori: "Still in the foreground there is Sin." Within this primal vision is the reminder of its original loss, to which the eye is soon fastened. This lower part of Bishop's tapestry, described in the second stanza, parodies the upper part as the "hell-green flames" of moss and "five sooty dragons" repeat in darker contrasts, the curls and windings of the lilies and ferns. But a demonic hand seems to have "worked" the tapestry here as the moss "threatens" and the oblique, serpentine vines "attack" the rocks. The introduction into the foreground of "Sin" in the form of "five sooty dragons" thematically and visually establishes the sense of background, of a receding Eden. For the focal point of the tapestry, to which "all eyes" represented in it are turned, is the hot little female lizard "back-to," her seductive tail "straight up and over." With this image the entire orientation of the canvas reverses and Nature turns her back on us.

This reversal throws us back on our position as beholders, and reminds us, now in an ironic spirit, that Nature "greets our eyes / exactly as it must have greeted theirs:"—the eyes of the Conquistadors—that we, in a sense, have fallen into the same trap as they. This third stanza is richly ambiguous, for the "Just so" which opens it can stand for the entire description of the first two stanzas, uniting our experience with that of the Christians; or more specifically it can stand for the lustful lizards, who then become comic surrogates of human pursuit and undermine our moral superiority.

The Portuguese pursuing the Indian maidens "found it all, / not unfamiliar" because they saw what they imposed on it, and "old dream of wealth and luxury / already out of date when they left home—." They never get their "brand-new pleasure" because it is newness itself they seek, which recedes as they approach, irreconcilable with the mercantile wish for wealth and luxury. It is "not unfamiliar" in a second sense as well, for they repeat an ancient story of desire. By enfolding the beholder in the scene Bishop makes the innocent eye a symbol of an infinite regress, receding as the landscape does. Indeed the Portuguese have become part of the composition they thought to possess, and function, with their incongruous glinting weaponry, as emblems of Sin in the foreground. "Hard as nails" in their aggressive wish for wealth and luxury, they are also "tiny as nails" in the vast fabric of Nature, crucifying their dream of redeemed vision "directly after Mass." The sky is indeed "a web" and they are caught in it, for the Indian maidens retreating behind it may be an illusion created by the birds waking up, part of the changing fabric of the moment, not the immortal genii of the place.

The literature of travel is, as Bishop implies in "Questions of Travel," always a skeptical literature, seeking out proof for its beliefs, pursuing the particular rather than the general. It is the literature of "epistemic gloom," in contrast to the literature of laws and symmetries, the dictionary, the thesaurus, the concordance, full of epistemic happiness. Bishop explores such a contrast in "Over 2,000 Illustrations and a Complete Concordance." For this speaker, in the aftermath of travel, the pictorial harmonies have already been refuted. "Thus should have been our travels: / serious, engravable" she sighs in response to the epistemic happiness of the boasting title, thinking back over the irreverent, ephemeral world she witnessed. The poem begins by looking over the religious scenes which

> granted a page alone or a page made up
> of several scenes arranged in cattycornered rectangles
> or circles set on stippled gray,
> granted a grim lunette,
> caught in the toils of an initial letter,
> . . . all resolve themselves.

But even as she yearns for these orders they become uncomfortable, confining, (grim toils), and the imagination begins to return to a memory of flux, at first enticing. Just as the travelers in the last poem would tear away at the hanging fabric, this speaker casts her memory beneath the two-dimensional surface, into the sea of life, painfully relinquishing pictorial order.

> The eye drops, weighted, through the lines
> the burin made, the lines that move apart
> like ripples above sand,
> dispersing storms, God's spreading fingerprint,
> and painfully, finally, that ignite
> it watery prismatic white-and-blue.

Unlike the symmetries of the concordance, these memories are connected only by "and" and "and," never yielding a sum. But this is precisely the biblical connective, and the ephemeral footprints of meaning, if not permanent inscriptions, play across the varied historical surface of memory. Each scene is a parodic reflection of some biblical illustration, the old schematic meanings comically released into a life heartily indifferent to them. There are no holy revelations at St. John's, only glimpses of goats leaping up cliffs. The poppies irreverently split the mosaics, the dead volcanoes "glistened like Easter lilies," and the golden length of evening proffers for epiphany a "dripping plush." The Annunciation is an English woman pouring tea and observing that the Duchess is going to have a baby; Magdalenes appear as "little pockmarked prostitutes" who "flung themselves / naked and giggling against our knees." These comic images do not simply refute the serious, engravable biblical stories, however; they return them to the world. Mutability is an undeniable fact of that world, and as this fact looms larger Bishop's imagination is drawn away from the prismatic play of life toward an ashen center.

> It was somewhere near there
> I saw what frightened me most of all:
> A holy grave, not looking particularly holy,
> one of a group under a keyhole-arched stone baldaquin
> open to every wind from the pink desert.
> An open, gritty, marble trough, carved solid
> with exhortation, yellowed
> as scattered cattle-teeth;
> half-filled with dust, not even the dust
> of the poor prophet paynim who once lay there.

This grave is indeed serious, engravable, but not in the way of the pictured scenes. Into this keyhole we go like the Christians pursuing the pagan maidens, but we find no immortal presence, no shelter from loss. The speaker's imagination retreats from this terrifying memory and returns to the shelter of the "heavy book." But the book, too, has become part of the dispersal: "(The gilt rubs off the edges / of the pages and pollinates the fingertips.)"

It is also, perhaps, the guilt of which the Bible speaks, so that we know the answer when Bishop asks "Why couldn't we have seen / this Old Nativity while we were at it?"

> —the dark ajar, the rocks breaking with light,
> an undisturbed, unbreathing flame,
> colorless, sparkless, freely fed on straw,
> and, lulled within, a family with pets,
> —and looked and looked our infant sight away.

Explicitly we are denied this vision, but rhetorically it does provide a moment of composure and shelter against the frightening scene that precedes it. We don't simply return to the strained pictorial order the poem begins with, for the figures are elemental and familiar ("a family with pets"), not at all grim or tortuous in the unity they represent, and not at all cryptic. Of course we cannot remain in that lair. Sight itself is not innocent, so that to look is indeed to look "our infant sight away."

In both of these poems we see a movement away from visual mastery or revelation and a nostalgia for innocent sight. But the eye is not innocent and it sees mutability in everything. Depriving itself of momentary plenitude, unable to compose and portion out the world, or to behold it in its primal condition, vision remains for Bishop in a state between memory and expectation, where everything is deteriorating or becoming. The Christian framework in which she sets her desire in these two poems provides a context rather than an explanation. Her losses are weighed in no teleological balance; they mark the fundamental quality of living form.

I'd like now to outline some of the recurrent compositional elements in Bishop's descriptions, which define this pattern of dismantled vision, dispersal, darkness, and compensatory glimpse. We should notice first that the view of experience, as opposed to the view of expectation, dream, or art, is minimal and messy. Expecting the balanced, frontal, filled-in tapestry, the eye finds an ungenerous and slovenly world. "Arrival at Santos," for instance, another quest poem, begins in complaint rather than exaltation. This is certainly not Cathay, but it *is* a composition of sorts.

> Here is a coast; here is a harbor;
> here, after a meager diet of horizon, is some scenery:
> impractically shaped and—who knows?
>   —self-pitying mountains,
> sad and harsh beneath their frivolous greenery,
>
> with a little church on top of one. And warehouses,
> some of them painted a feeble pink, or blue,
> and some tall, uncertain palms. Oh, tourist,
> is this how this country is going to answer you
>
> and your immodest demands for a different world,
> and a better life, and complete comprehension
> of both at last, and immediately.

Hardly a new heaven, new earth, to state the hungry eye. "Florida" begins similarly. The "state with the prettiest name" turns out to be "held together by mangrove roots," its swamps strewn with skeletons of oyster clusters. Fading shells "arranged as on a gray rag of rotted calico," delicately ornament its "monotonous, endless, sagging coastline." At night "the careless, corrupt state is all black specks / too far apart, and ugly whites; the poorest / post-card of itself" rather than the sublime tapestry of the imagined place. And yet I think she likes it better for its shabby minimal appearance. Opulence and symmetry can suffocate.

Bishop's landscapes are almost always "withdrawn, indrawn." You have to squint to see. The old man's net in "At the Fishhouses" is almost invisible in the gloaming. No sublime ocean waves smack the eye; it is usually low tide. The eye cannot rest in such deprivations; the skimpiness of the landscape tends to pull us into the space, making arrival scenes into departures as the foreground dissolves. "Ports are like soap or postage stamps"—wasting and slipping away, drawing us into the interior. In "A Cold Spring" Bishop uses a technique of time-lapse photography, making the gradual change of season (the temporal filling in of Nature's tapestry) correspond to a movement from foreground to background.

A cold spring:
the violet was flawed on the lawn.
For two weeks or more the trees hesitated;
the little leaves waited,
carefully indicating their characteristics.
Finally a grave green dust
settled over your big aimless hills.

Bishop begins to see on the horizon what had seemed impossible right at her feet. This visual movement of hope occurs in almost every landscape, the eye, searching out in the receding or dismantled surface some line of pursuit, finds a road disappearing into mountains, a figure edging toward mist, birds dissolving into pinpoints of sky. Such images tease the sight; Bishop knows with the landscape artist that nothing excites so much as that which is hidden.

The word "contemplation" bears the root suggestion of a temple. The landscape for nineteenth-century artists was a place of worship, and they often emphasized massive frontal effects of steep cliffs and high suns or moons in order to make a timeless altar of nature. But landscape is always primarily horizontal; we gaze across rather than up, travel rather than transcend. Bishop emphasizes this quality by making dynamic forms dominate over static ones. Roads, rivers, waterfalls, tides (weaving and rolling in repeated gerunds) carry us through the scene, enhanced by buses, trains, boats. But such constant motion troubles the eye, which begins to seek out places to pause or settle. In Bishop's poems the only stable objects appear as casualties of movement rather than respites from it. "Questions of Travel" begins:

There are too many waterfalls here; the crowded streams
hurry too rapidly down to the sea,
and the pressure of so many clouds on the mountaintops
makes them spill over the sides in soft slow-motion
turning to waterfalls under our eyes . . .
But if the streams and clouds keep travelling, travelling,
the mountains look like the hulls of capsized ships,
slime-hung and barnacled.

Living form, in Bishop's canvas, always implies flow; stasis implies ruin. Simile reinforces the sense of muted catastrophe. In "Little Exercise," the vertical palm trees "all stuck in rows," in neat, civilized avenues, are "suddenly revealed / as fistfuls of limp fish-skeletons." The little churches in Cape Breton "have been dropped into the matted hills / like lost quartz arrow heads," and the little (all human things are little in Bishop) white boats in "The Bight" look like "torn open, unanswered letters." The mossy oyster shells in "Florida" form "green hummocks / like ancient cannon-balls sprouting grass."

Weather, light, and season atmospherically enhance the drift and dispersal in the dismantled shapes of the landscape. There are few burning midday suns or luminous sunsets in Bishop. She more often records a foggy twilight or "unsympathetic yellow" dawn. Cold springs and rainy seasons dominate over other climates. There are no cumulus clouds or angelic gestures of cirrus but only a quiet sublimity in pervasive gray. One suspects Bishop was a student of Dutch painters—Ruisdael in particular— more than of Americans. The ubiquitous mist in Bishop's scenes makes everything ghostly, indeed, looks rather ghostly itself "like rotting snow-ice sucked away / almost to spirit; the ghosts of glaciers." Sometimes this mist gathers into storm, and the static shelters shrink under its weight, the specklike clapboard houses offering little reassurance to the eye as it perceives a hazard.

Just as there are no prominent architectural forms giving verticals to the landscape (as in Poussin, for instance) and a sense of permanence and security to culture, so other signs of humanity are reduced to relics and fragments. The human world is as indrawn as everything else, represented only by relics of activity. The abandoned bulldozers in "Cape Breton," the fishtubs in "At the Fishhouses," suggest a time when the human figures who give these objects meaning will be permanently absent. Bishop's landscapes, when they show signs of civilization at all, look like archeological sites. The "frowsy" sponge boats in "The Bight" seem almost without sailors, and their destiny is mirrored in other boats piled up as wreckage from the last storm. What figures we do see are usually dwarfed, and engaged in futile efforts to secure some order—the "specklike boy and girl" in "The Squatter's Children," for instance, digging holes in the silting earth, the old man in "At the Fishhouses" mending nets in the twilight, his knife blade almost worn away.

In a Bishop landscape, then, often in contrast to a frontal, vertical, tapestried perfection, we find a predominance of horizontal and dynamic form, strewn with the detritus of previous life. This drift in which all things are tentative, while picturesquely loosening the eye, works to produce a feeling of anxiety in the viewer so that she eventually seeks a new place of composure. The eye settles, though, not on a place of shelter, but on a dark area, usually introduced about two-thirds of the way through the poem, in a muted climax of fear. Visually and rhetorically, this place defines a destination. In "Seascape," though, this place forebodes rather than follows the dismantling of an old pictorial harmony. The poem about a "cartoon by Raphael for a tapestry for a Pope" describes in detail a sprightly vertical scene in which "the whole region, from the highest heron / down to the weightless mangrove island" "does look like heaven." But "a skeletal lighthouse" in clerical black and white thinks heaven "has something to do with blackness and a strong glare."

"At the Fishhouses" perhaps best illustrates this movement to a dark focus. The poem begins by drawing the eye vertically away from obscurity and flux to the "steeply peaked roofs" of the fishhouses, but we are not allowed to remain at that constructed height, for "gangplanks" pull us down onto the docks where the view takes us across a silver surface. At first the viewer delights in the "beautiful herring scales" which cover everything in "creamy iridescent coats of mail," the prismatic sheen of living form. But soon these images mingle with images of death and mutability— the rust on the ironwork of the old wooden capstan looks like dried blood; the sequin scales on the vest and thumb of the old fisherman lead to the old black knife which has scraped them from unnumbered fish. And the "thin silver / tree trunks . . . laid horizontally / across the gray stones" lead the eye to the water, the "cold dark deep and absolutely clear, / element bearable to no mortal." These waters offer no reflection, figurative or literal, for they represent the essence of motion and change. No glassy lakes mirror a permanent heaven in Bishop (in "Florida" the "pools seem to have slipped away"). Meaning has abandoned the landscape and though the eye may look for it in these dark centers, it finds none.

In "Cape Breton" this area is defined by the "folds and folds of fir . . . / dull, dead, deep peacock-colors," not at all ambiguous like the rest of the mist-covered scene, it is in its impenetrability, "certain as a stereoscopic view," an image of necessity. The speaker imagines, behind these dark folds, a geological timetable, a kind of natural scripture etched by loss, this is:

> in the interior,
> where we cannot see,
> where deep Lakes are reputed to be,
> and disused trails and mountains of rock
> and miles of burnt forests standing in gray scratches
> like the admirable scriptures made on stones by stones.

But "these regions now have little to say for themselves." These places in Bishop's landscape seem like black holes ready to swallow us up. Indeed, in "At the Fishhouses" she imagines the icy water rising "above the stones and then the world." Something must yield to the eye or release it from this paralyzing gaze. And something almost always does in Bishop. No lightning carves commandments, no archangel appears to bugle judgment day, but something very common and delightful seems to emerge from this darkness and releases us from it. "Just when I thought I couldn't stand it / another minute longer, Friday came," says Crusoe in "Crusoe in England." In "At the Fishhouses" a seal "stood up in the water and regarded me / steadily, moving his head a little." Like all primitive and animal life in landscape art, these figures belong to nature and yet, closer on the scale of life to man, help him overcome some of the distance between his intelligent life and the "rocky breasts" of the earth. These figures offer no possessible knowledge. They are quotidian, and vanish back into the dark. Friday cannot be brought back to England, the fish die out of the water.

They are only glimpsed, and their orders are ephemeral and meaningless, but they provide a cheerful release from the darkness.

In "Cape Breton" for instance, though the natural scriptures are unread the region yields "thousands of light song-sparrow songs floating upward / freely, dispassionately, through the mist, and meshing / in brown-wet, fine, torn fish-nets." (Fish nets, in Bishop, as in many poets, are a sign of ordered life: torn ones let life escape.) In "Florida" "fireflies map the heavens in the marsh." In "The Bight" the dredge "brings up a dripping jawful of marl," "awful but cheerful." In "Over 2,000 Illustrations" Bishop imagines (and wishes to see) a "family with pets." These primitive images stand against the dismantled compositional orders as compensatory glimpses of wholeness. But the compositional orders must be relinquished for these moments to arise at all. They are, in a sense, the goal, not just compensations, though they seem diminutive next to the old dream of wealth and luxury. Some critics have called them epiphanies, but I don't think Bishop would approve of so grandiose a term. They are never accompanied by transcendent knowledge. They are not images of permanence (as is Keats's bird) but of complete being in a passing moment, from which the human mind, denying itself that direct completeness, can nonetheless draw cheer and vicarious satisfaction.

I have been describing what Bishop encounters in her visual quest: disorder, darkness, momentary being. But where the viewer stands is crucial to the proportions and limits of what she sees. Traditional representational landscape identifies reality with a single point of view, and provides the viewer with a feeling of mastery. Bishop manipulates perspective to disrupt this confidence in a variety of ways. Sometimes she simply parodies it, as when she imagines the world as seen by the sandpiper or crab. Other times she will erase the illusion of being in the scene by taking a detached, aerial, often cinematic prospect from which hazard is enlarged and shelter shrunken. Such omniscience yields little security in the absence of an overarching order or compositional balance to which the eye can appeal. The relentless rhythm of tension and release in "Little Exercise" climaxes, finally, when we find a surrogate of ourselves "sleeping in the bottom of a row-boat," "uninjured, barely disturbed" after the storm we have been following around.

The subtlest and most compelling manipulations of perspective occur when the poet places herself in the landscape and finds her old masteries turned upside down. In "The Bight," for instance, the water is "absorbing, rather than being absorbed" and looks "the color of the gas flame." She finds no comforting new unity of resemblance in this, for the place is "littered with old correspondences," old ways of ordering experience. Next to the "pilings dry as matches" the whole maritime scene seems ready to go up in flames. In "At the Fishhouses," too, the dark cold water seems a "transmutation of fire," And there, too, the "heavy surface of the sea" looks opaque and solid, while human constructions, the benches, buildings, masts, appear translucent. In "Florida" the buzzards drifting "down, down, down" in the air look "like stirred-up flakes of sediment / sinking through water." Such disruptions of faith in our view usually accelerate the losses in Bishop's landscapes.

The representational painter depends upon our ability to recognize his shapes and dots as objects in life, but in Bishop "things fly away from their names" and easily metamorphose or slip from recognition. Thus in "Sleeping on the Ceiling" a chandelier becomes a fountain in a park and in "From the Country to the City" a road becomes a giant jester. All identities are dubious. Relinquishing one-point perspective means shaking up the relation of size to distance. If a cow is smaller than a man we think it is farther away. But in Bishop close up and far away are not secure orientations. In "12 O'Clock News," for instance, she looks down at her typewriter as if from an aerial height and discovers an alien civilization. These techniques of disorientation derive from Bishop's early interest in surrealism, especially the work of Giorgio de Chirico and Max Ernst, who worked with multiple vanishing points and perspectives within a single surface. In "The Monument," after a wood rubbing by Max Ernst, Bishop disorients the viewer by conflating several points of view into one surface as Ernst himself did with images. "The view is geared / (that is, the view's perspective) / so low there is no 'far away,' / and we are far away within the view." "The Monument" works because of the immediacy of dialogue and richness of thematic material. But Bishop sometimes uses these techniques crudely or naïvely (as in "12 O'Clock News"), in which case the effect seems superficial and contrived.

"Crusoe in England" represents Bishop's most mature use of this technique, centered in a disturbed consciousness that cannot make the "constant readjustments" life requires. The poem owes as much to Swift as to Defoe in describing the relativity of the human view. The poem begins with "a speck on the horizon" which may be a fly on the telescope, and our sense of proportion is immediately thrown off. Such uncertainty of size and identity is precisely the condition of life on the island. Crusoe's efforts to relate the landscape to himself and thus master it are futile:

> Well, I had fifty-two
> miserable, small volcanoes I could climb
> with a few slithery strides— . . .
> I'd think that if they were the size
> I thought volcanoes should be, then I had
> become a giant;
> and if I had become a giant,
> I couldn't bear to think what size
> the goats and turtles were.

Metaphor itself is, as Kenneth Burke, said, perspective. And Bishop always gains perspective by incongruity.

The problem of the beholder, the unsteady status of perspective, leads us back to a question raised at the beginning. What is the purpose of describing a landscape? Contemplation, of course, but of what? to what end? The word implies expectation and intention. If landscape does not provide Bishop with an idyllic retreat or a vision of God's Work, what can it provide? For Darwin, the scientific observer, the question of purpose was taken care of. But for the artist? Is expressiveness, the release of feeling and desire into the mutable world, enough? Bishop works hard in her poems to remove commerce from contemplation, but the urge to harvest something from the labor of the eye is strong.

The kind of static composition in her great-uncle's "Large Bad Picture" will not satisfy, certainly. Like the Spaniards, this uncle traveled to a corner of the earth, here "the Strait of Belle Isle or / some northerly harbor of Labrador," in search of a "comprehensive, consoling" vision, a "perpetual sunset." But the waves look too perfect, the birds too artificial, and the masts of the ships suggest burnt match sticks. He has confused commerce with contemplation, though the poet can still trace some of the life. More appealing is his small sketch of a local Nova Scotian scene which only frames mutability. Her own "Poem" takes after the painting it describes. "About the size of an old-style dollar bill, / . . . [it] has never earned any money in its life" and offers no collateral against loss as it is "handed along collaterally to owners / who looked at it sometimes, or didn't bother to." The work is not comprehensive or consoling; it depicts another cold, misty March. Nor does it offer an immediate knowledge of nature, for the original scene has receded into the mutations of memory and like Crusoe's island is "unrenameable, unrediscoverable." Indeed, it seems to have loss written into it "the yet-to-be dismantled elms" barely there. But as the eye moves back and forth from illusion to painted surface, the loss of the landscape unites Bishop asynchronously with the other who had seen it and with his act of composition. "Up closer, a wild iris, white and yellow, / fresh-squiggled from the tube. . . . / the hint of steeple, / filaments of brush-hairs, barely there." In this way "the earthly trust" is extended just a little. By the simple addition to "two looks" (not visions—there is nothing permanent to see) the crisp iris lasts a little longer. "Not much." In place of metaphysical or aesthetic transcendence Bishop discovers the transitory moment, given extension and duration through memory and desire.

But that very mode of duration also presents Bishop with a problem of incomplete being. In seeking relief from this feeling Bishop makes reference to two kinds of completeness—one a consciously fictive totality in which things are cleared up finally, the other a vicarious experience of nature's complete being in the moment, making no reference to an anterior source. In neither form of completeness can her mind abide for long, but together these reference points offset the vision of necessity which troubles her sight.

In her last book, *Geography III*, in which "Poem" is included, Bishop displayed astonishing control over the expressiveness of landscape description. And the rhythms of feeling become distinctly organized around the configurations I have been describing. Two poems in which we find the poet in the landscape ("The End of March" and "The Moose") will summarize my argument.

"The End of March" is, like the Brazil poems, a quest for something "comprehensive and consoling," in this case a "proto-dream-house," a shelter from the "the rackety, icy, offshore wind." But the immediate scene, as usual, is "withdrawn as far as possible, / indrawn: the tide far out, the ocean shrunken, / seabirds in ones or twos." The eye meets deprivation. Though it is the beginning of spring, it is another unpromising start, the wind threatens to push spring back, disrupting "the formation / of a lone flight of Canada geese." The familiar order of things is, again, inverted: "The sky was darker than the water / —*it* was the color of mutton-fat jade." Following out the traces of departed life, the viewer notices "a track of big dog-prints (so big / they were more like lion-prints)," and the hint of fear in this image is confirmed in the disheartening image that follows.

> Then we came on
> lengths and lengths, endless, of wet white string,
> looping up to the tide-line, down to the water,
> over and over. Finally, they did end:
> a thick white snarl, man-size, awash,
> rising on every wave, a sodden ghost,
> falling back, sodden, giving up the ghost. . . .
> A kite string?—But no kite.

This is emotionally the darkest moment in the poem, the meandering line of the kite seeming to mimic the viewer's own path, leading to a desolate end. And indeed the walkers never reach the dream house (it remains a "crypto" dream house), though this image of a sodden ghost heightens the wish for it. The speaker's mind retreats from this ghostly omen to the dream house as it retreated to the picture of the Old Nativity, and the two have something in common—they are places of comfort and stasis, lit from within, "perfect! But—impossible." The house resembles a kite itself, "limply leashe[d] . . . / to something off behind the dunes." But there is "no kite" and this house is "boarded up." She is not permitted to retreat from life. The journey soon becomes a departure and, still in the elements, the faces of the walkers freeze on the other side. But we know by now that Bishop rarely denies vision without some kind of consolatory glimpse. What releases her from the fear of darkness is always, as we have seen, something ordinary and mutable, no divine intervention but an experience of nature's living form. Both eye and fancy find something for their cravings.

> The sun came out for just a minute.
> For just a minute, set in their bezels of sand,
> the drab, damp, scattered stones
> were multi-colored,
> and all those high enough threw out long shadows,
> individual shadows, then pulled them in again.

Here is the pleasure in life's prismatic sheen, like the scales of the fish, its "principal beauty," something she might have missed in her proto-dream house, where no shadows are cast. But while the eye enjoys this glimpse, the imagination fills in more.

This is a poem of questions as well as quest. Indeed, questions are a part of most ritual journeys. The wishful speculations Bishop makes about the house are never confirmed. But the questions raised out of experience and fear are cleared up, at least as myth, compensating for the deprivation of the eye. What dangerous creature has walked this beach before us? How did this ghostly kite string come to be here? Why are these shadows darting out?

> They could have been teasing the lion sun,
> except that now he was behind them
> —a sun who'd walked the beach the last low tide,
> making those big, majestic paw-prints,
> who perhaps had batted a kite out of the sky to play with.

Such personification gives us no shelter from or power over the whims of nature, but makes them seem less predatory, precluding other more terrifying myths. Bishop cannot escape into this comprehensive myth, but she can make reference to it in a moment of fear. The lion-sun, like the seal of "At the Fishhouses," the song-sparrows of "Cape Breton," the fireflies of "Florida," does not change experience, but releases us from terror. The moose functions in the same way.

The word whispered throughout the opening landscape of "The Moose" is "flow." This poem focuses on departure rather than destination, as in "The End of March," and it moves from light to dark rather than dark to light. This home of "fish and bread and tea" is eroded not only by the tide and the river, but again in the sky (usually a place of permanence), itself a river, "where, silted red, / sometimes the sun sets / facing a red sea, / and others, veins the flats' / lavender, rich mud / in burning rivulets." The volcano metaphor only hints at fear, as the giant paw prints and ghostly kite string did, but fear will build as the poem proceeds. The neat domestic verticals of "rows of sugar maples" and "twin birches" are overcome by the horizontals of road and river. What doesn't flow withdraws inward, the bees creep into the foxgloves. But the churches "ridged as clamshells" are as tightly shut. The bus which travels along the road is going West, of course, and gradually the signs of domesticity wane. (The usual Bishop progression.) A woman shaking out a table cloth is a "pale flicker" in the distance as darkness encroaches. Signs of danger arise: "a loose plank rattles," "an iron bridge trembles," "a red light / swims through the dark," until we enter the dark place, again about two-thirds into the poem. The New Brunswick woods are wolflike, predatory, "hairy, scratchy, splintery," the mist "caught in them like lamb's wool."

But "the moose" that comes "out of / the impenetrable wood" softens this image. She (the moose is female) is "perfectly harmless," "towering, antlerless, / high as a church, / homely as a house / (or, safe as houses)." Of course we can't enter this house, but are relieved to see it in the landscape. By their juxtaposition in the poem we associate the moose with the dreamed "conversation in Eternity" in which things are as with the lion-sun "cleared up finally," a fictive knowledge leading not to power but to acceptance. Imagination (the lion-sun, the conversation in Eternity) fills in a background to the transitory joy (the iridescent stones, the moose). Bishop does not disparage our mythmaking faculty, but since our "knowledge is historical" these images must recede, and the smell of travel overtakes the smell of Eternity once again.

> For a moment longer,
>
> by craning backward,
> the moose can be seen
> on the moonlit macadam;
> then there's a dim
> smell of moose, an acrid
> smell of gasoline.

My words have confirmed the idea that Bishop is a poet of the eye. Her thinking is visual, her expressive techniques easily parallel to those of the visual arts. Images tell us more than statements can about the deep structure of this poet's mind. In an age of psychological submersion, Bishop celebrates surface. But that surface is not sublime, and the eye itself is a limited instrument. What can be seen stimulates the imagination's hunger.

While I have concentrated on Bishop's relationship to landscape painters, she belongs primarily to a family of writers. In a letter to Robert Lowell she described herself as the last in a Wordsworthian line of nature poets. Bishop quotes Wordsworth in her work, shares his preoccupation with memory, his interest in figures absorbed into landscape, his explorations of poetic identity. But Wordsworth's nature is his exclusive guide, the world is all before him, the spots of time await his arrival. Bishop would like to see the world as Wordsworth does, but like Crusoe's her memory is imperfect, and Wordsworth's lines forgotten. Her stronger kinship, I think, is with Keats (and his wary descendant Wallace Stevens), the line of reticent chameleon poets. Hers is indeed a negative capability, not an irritable seeking after truths of reason. She shares Keats's aesthetic of melancholy, his joy in ephemeral things. Her young imagination surely must have quickened to the departing landscape of Autumn, to the Nightingale disappearing over the next hill. But these closing moments in Keats are where Bishop's meditations often begin. She does not entertain his moments of plenitude. Nor does she display as much confidence in the consolation of art, the sublimity of the human achievement, that can harvest something lasting. Just as she picks the small sketch over the large picture, she would feel more at ease with Stevens's anecdotal jar than with Keats's Grecian Urn. But Bishop is not so autumnal or elegiac as Stevens. She does not descend into darkness but returns to "all the untidy activity," "awful but cheerful."

Reference to the visual does not offset, but rather reinforces Bishop's feeling of transience. Diversification is associated with loss for her—"and" a connective which finds no staying sum. Though the eye searches out a source or creative center, it finds none, nor any law but necessity, written like a curse into the generic code. But deterioration is not so bad when she can witness a being in the moment. If living form is not serious or engravable, it is free, fluid, iridescent. It would be a mistake to privilege this cheer, for accepting loss means as well accepting the loss of certain moods and kinds of knowledge. Still, among the human seasons, Bishop's favorite is early Spring.

Elizabeth Bishop's Dream-Houses

David Bromwich

In a very striking passage of "Rooster," Elizabeth Bishop turns to address the shiny, gloating, and definitively male creatures whose cries disturb her sleep:

> each one an active
> displacement in perspective;
> each screaming, "This is where I live!"
>
> Each screaming
> "Get up! stop dreaming!"
> Roosters, what are you projecting?

The sleeper, as she tells us in another poem, eventually recovers from these assaults and continues to inhabit "my proto-dream-house, / my crypto-dream-house, that crooked box / set up on pilings." She has taken in enough of the roosters' admonitions to concede, "Many things about this place are dubious." But the force of her rhetorical question—"What are *you* projecting?"—suggests a reserve of personal strength. Bishop's own poems are active displacements of perspective. They too project a warning about where she lives, and they have the authority of dreams rather than awakenings.

That she was praised throughout her career for a humbler kind of success is doubtless just as well: charitable misunderstandings help an artist to go on working quietly. Yet it is worth recalling the standard terms of this praise, for they reveal how little had changed in the years that separate Bishop's first appearance from that of Emily Dickinson. Admirers of "Suc-

From *Raritan: A Quarterly Review* 4, no. 1 (1984). © 1984 by *Raritan: A Quarterly Review*, New Brunswick, New Jersey.

cess is counted sweetest" (who thought it probably the work of Emerson) were replaced by encouragers of the best woman poet in English. And a sure ground of appreciation for so special a performer was taken to be her "accuracy." What did that mean? Not, evidently, that she adapted the same style to different situations, and not that she changed all the time, with a relentless originality. It was an esthetic compliment, difficult to translate into English. Similarly, Bishop was prized for her "charm." In the sense of a warm sociability, she certainly was not charming, least of all when she meant to be, as in her poems about the poor. In any other sense, charm is a tedious virtue for a poet, just as accuracy is an impracticable vice. And yet, in spite of their evasiveness, both words converge on a trait which all of Bishop's readers have felt in her poems: the presence of an irresistible self-trust. To her, art is a kind of home. She makes her accommodations with an assurance that is full of risk, and, for her as for Dickinson, the domestic tenor of some poems implies a good-natured defiance of the readers she does not want. The readers she cares for, on the other hand, are not so much confided in as asked to witness her self-recoveries, which have the quality of a shared premise. Her work is conversation which never quite takes place but whose possibility always beckons.

My point of departure in testing what this feels like in practice is an early poem, "The Monument." Bishop appears to have conceived it as an oblique eulogy for herself, and she frames it deferentially enough to suit a posthumous occasion. The poem's authority and weight have less in common with modern inventions like Joseph Cornell's boxes than they do with an older tradition of immortality—"Not marble, nor the gilded monuments / Of princes, shall outlast this pow'rful rhyme." We are well-advised at the start not to measure a sure distance between those lines and these.

> Now can you see the monument? It is of wood
> built somewhat like a box. No. Built
> like several boxes in descending sizes
> one above the other.
> Each is turned half-way round so that
> its corners point toward the sides
> of the one below and the angles alternate.
> Then on the topmost cube is set
> a sort of fleur-de-lys of weathered wood,
> long petals of board, pierced with odd holes,
> four-sided, stiff, ecclesiastical.

Irony, in one of its meanings, is a pretense of concern in a speaker, for the sake of revising a listener's whole structure of concerns; the pretense here is that Bishop's listener, in order to cherish the monument need only hear it described just so. She patiently adjusts the description ("It is X. No. Like several X's") to anticipate any complaint, as later in the poem she will give the listener a more official embodiment by composing speeches for him.

All this self-qualification is a gravely enacted farce. When it is over we will find ourselves still staring at the monument and rehearsing what she has said about it, until we see that the object of the poem was to compel our attention without giving reasons.

In the course of the one-woman narration, with its imagined interruptions, we listeners are permitted exactly four objections to the monument. These may be summarized abstractly: I don't understand what this thing is trying to be; I've never seen anything hang together like this; It's just too makeshift to succeed; and, What are you trying to prove, anyway? In short, museum-boredom ("Big deal; take me somewhere else"), which the poet meets at first with a curatorial delicacy. But her final speech, which takes up almost a third of the poem, overcomes all defensiveness and simply expands the categorical authority of her earlier statement, "It is the monument."

> It is an artifact
> of wood. Wood holds together better
> than sea of cloud or sand could by itself,
> much better than real sea or sand or cloud.
> It chose that way to grow and not to move.
> The monument's an object, yet those decorations,
> carelessly nailed, looking like nothing at all,
> give it away as having life, and wishing;
> wanting to be a monument, to cherish something.
> The crudest scroll-work says "commemorate,"
> while once each day the light goes around it
> like a prowling animal,
> or the rain falls on it, or the wind blows into it.
> It may be solid, may be hollow.
> The bones of the artist prince may be inside
> or far away on even drier soil.
> But roughly but adequately it can shelter
> what is within (which after all
> cannot have been intended to be seen).
> It is the beginning of a painting,
> a piece of sculpture, or poem, or monument,
> and all of wood. Watch it closely.

This ending allies "The Monument" with other American appeals to the power of metaphor to shape a life, particularly Frost's "A Star in a Stone-Boat" and Stevens's "Someone Puts a Pineapple Together." Even in their company, Bishop's poem keeps on growing as one thinks of it. It has perhaps less invention than they have; but then, it presumes a questioner suspicious of all that is new; and its persistent skepticism is a grace equal to any exuberance.

Earlier in the poem, still explaining the look of the monument itself,

Bishop had composed a diagram of the viewer's relation to what he sees, which may also be read as a geometric proof of her own power over her readers.

> The monument is one-third set against
> a sea; two-thirds against a sky.
> The view is geared
> (that is, the view's perspective)
> so low there is not "far away,"
> and we are far away within the view.

I take the first five lines to mean that our eye is placed just above horizon-level, so that the whole sky and sea appear as a flat vertical backdrop, without depth and therefore without any far or near. But in what sense can we be said to be "far away within the view"? It must be that the view looks out at us too, as through the wrong end of a telescope, from a perspective capable of absorbing everything; it takes us in as it pleases. Indeed, the monument can contain the world, by implication. That is the sense of the listener's disturbed question, "Are we in Asia Minor, / or in Mongolia?"—site of "Kubla Khan," where a kindred monument was decreed by imaginative fiat. So the poem says here, with the metaphor of perspective, what it says at the end by the rhetoric of conjecture: an active mind alone makes the world cohere, as "Wood holds together better / than sea or cloud or sand could by itself, / much better than real sea or sand or cloud." The flat declaration, "It chose that way to grow and not to move," only seems to announce a faith in the autonomy of art objects; Bishop returns us to the human bias of the thing, by her emphasis on those features of the monument which "give it away as having life, and wishing; / wanting to be a monument, to cherish something." Before it can be, it must want to be something. And we read it for whatever spirit it communicates; we cannot do more than watch. But we are accompanied by the prowling sun which also keeps watch—a casual sublimity, the reward of the poet's discovery of a shelter uniquely right for herself. It is an image to which Bishop will return in "The End of March," where "the lion sun . . . who perhaps had batted a kite out of the sky to play with," is mysteriously connected with the wire leading out from her dream-house "to something off behind the dunes."

The monument will do for a figure of a poem, which turns out to be an allegory of what it is to *make* anything in the optative mood. A figure of a poet appears in the more straightforward allegory called "The Man-Moth." In a brief note, Bishop traces the title to a newspaper misprint for "mammoth," but the reason for its appeal to her is plain when one remembers the man-moth of Shelley's "Epipsychidion":

> Then, from the caverns of my dreamy youth
> I sprang, as one sandalled with plumes of fire,

> And towards the lodestar of my one desire,
> I flitted, like a dizzy moth, whose flight
> Is as a dead leaf's in the owlet light,
> When it would seek in Hesper's setting sphere
> A radiant death, a fiery sepulchre.

Part of Bishop's aim is to translate this image of the poet to a less radiant climate—that of the modern city—where his quest can take on the shape of an almost biological compulsion.

> Up the façades,
> his shadow dragging like a photographer's cloth behind him,
> he climbs fearfully, thinking that this time he will manage
> to push his small head through that round clean opening
> and be forced through, as from a tube, in black scrolls on the
>   light.
> (Man, standing below him, has no such illusions.)
> But, what the Man-Moth fears most he must do, although
> he fails, of course, and falls back scared but quite unhurt.

Where the monument chose a certain way to be, the Man-Moth acts without a will: his quest is merely a condition of existence. It is as if he were born knowing, *there is a creature (and you are he) who does all of this*—climbs sky-scrapers because he "thinks the moon is a small hole at the top of the sky"; travels backward in underground trains, where he dreams recurrent dreams; and through all his risks, looks on mortality as "a disease he has inherited the susceptibility to." He is defined not by his activity but by the contrast he makes with man, who

> does not see the moon; he observes only her vast
>   properties,
> feeling the queer light on his hands, neither warm nor cold,
> of a temperature impossible to record in thermometers.

Man's shadow is no bigger than his hat; the Man-Moth's is almost palpable, trailing "like a photographer's cloth behind him"; and one is reminded that "shadow" is still our best English word for *figura* and *typus*. In a way that can be shown but not said, the Man-Moth, by being what he is, interprets man to himself. But the poem makes a lighter fable of this. Like any other second-story artist, the Man-Moth abstracts a few choice possessions from his victim and flees the scene.

How his theft may be retrieved is the subject of Bishop's final stanza, which is addressed to man, still "observing" and coldly pragmatic.

> If you catch him,
> hold up a flashlight to his eye. It's all dark pupil,
> an entire night itself, whose haired horizon tightens
> as he stares back, and closes up the eye. Then from the lids

one tear, his only possession, like the bee's sting, slips.
Slyly he palms it, and if you're not paying attention
he'll swallow it. However, if you watch, he'll hand it over.
cool as from underground springs and pure enough to
        drink.

The Man-Moth's eye is "an entire night itself," a complete image of that world of the earth's surface in which he seeks what is most different from himself. The object of his quest he calls a tiny hole of light; man, less interestingly calls it the moon. To reach it would mean suffusion by the light and hence, to an eye all pupils, destruction. The Man-Moth, however, is sustained by the fantasy of an ascent through "that round clean opening," and of being forced "in black scrolls on the light." In this dream of consummation he would become his writing.

One may interpret the dream as at once expressing and concealing a hope that some principle of self will survive the dissolution of the body. Of course, the fallacy is easy to expose: immortality is not a form of health to which one can inherit a susceptibility. Yet this analysis gives no comfort to man, about whom we have heard it said that "Man, standing below, has no such illusions"; for the compliment holds in reserve a fierce irony: "Man, standing below, has no such ambitions." Nor does Bishop herself want to unbuild our illusions. She is interested in the use we make of everything the illusion-bound creature brings from his journeyings. This is figured in the poem as a hardly calculable refreshment, with the character almost of bodily secretion. The Man-Moth's "one tear, his only possession, like the bee's sting," may be his gift to us. The image comes close to a hackneyed sentiment about perfection and pain, and hovers near an allusion to Keats's "Melancholy," but slips free of both. It is hard not to read it poignantly—the reader, like the map-printer in another of Bishop's poems, "here experiencing the same excitement / as when emotion too far exceeds its cause." But the tear is not really a possession, the light that produced it after all was man's, and both parties seem amenable to the exchange. Our acceptance of every curiosity in the poem owes something to its conscious urbanity: the opening line even gives us the "battered moonlight" of a cityscape—battered by too much jingling in the pockets of too many songwriters, but still salvageable by one poet. Elsewhere, the same word appears to evoke a larger freedom with imagery that looks worn or already found: the fish that is "battered and venerable / and homely"; the big tin basin, "battered and shiny like the moon." "The Man-Moth" and "The Monument" go beyond the dignity of statement—the somewhat ponderous naturalism—that such diction has usually aimed to license and keep honest. They stand apart from the poems of Bishop's generation in the stubbornness with which they try ingenuity by the test of prosaic heft.

To an exceptional degree in modern poetry, Bishop's work offers resistance to any surmise about the personality of the author. One reason is that the poems themselves have been so carefully furnished with eccentric details or gestures. These may seem tokens of companionability, yet a certain way into a poem the atmosphere grows a little chill; farther in, as the conversation strolls on, one senses the force field of a protective ease. Some day, a brief chapter in a history of poetry will describe Lowell's misreading of Bishop as a voice of resonant sincerity, and his appropriation for journalistic ends of her more marked traits of syntax, punctuation, and anomalous cadence. But to the reader who returns to these poems for their own sake, the question likeliest to recur is: what are they concealing? It helps, I think, to frame this as a question about a different passage—for example, about the pathos of some lines near the end of "Crusoe in England," in which Crusoe describes the objects that recall his years of solitude.

> The knife there on the shelf—
> it reeked of meaning, like a crucifix.
> It lived. How many years did I
> beg it, implore it, not to break?
> I knew each nick and scratch by heart,
> the bluish blade, the broken tip,
> the lines of wood-grain on the handle . . .
> Now it won't look at me at all.

Like many comparable passages of her work, the description is weirdly circumstantial. What does it mean for a poet who is a woman to write, as a man, of an object so nearly linked with masculine assertion, with this mingling of tenderness, pity, and regret?

The poetic answer, which has to do with the cost of art to life, does not exclude the sexual one, which has to do with an ambivalent femininity. The poet's own weapons in art as in life have been more dear to her than she can easily confess. The punishment for deserting them is that they refuse to return her gaze; they lose their aura, and she ceases to be a poet. A similar recognition is implied in other poems, where a wish to conquer or dominate—resisted at first, then acted on—darkens the celebration of having come through every challenge. Thus, "The Armadillo" moves from horror of a creature, quite distinct from the poet, to wonder at the same creature, which in the meantime has been implicitly identified with her. She devotes a poem to the armadillo because it is a survivor, forearmed against any catastrophe. Like her, it watches in safety a dangerous and beautiful spectacle, the drifting of the "frail, illegal fire balloons" which at any moment may splatter "like an egg of fire / against the cliff." As for the poet herself, the poem is proof of her armor. In the same way, in "Roosters" she is a second and unmentioned crier of the morning; the poem, with its "horrible insistence" three notes at a time, announces exactly where she lives.

These identifications go deep. Such poems are not, in fact, animal-morality pieces, in the vein of Marianne Moore. They more nearly resemble Lawrence's "Fish," "The Ass," "Tortoise Shell," and "Tortoise Family Connections"—protestant inquests concerning the powers of the self, which have the incidental form of free-verse chants about animals. Bishop writes without Lawrence's spontaneous humor, and without his weakness for quick vindications. Indeed, there is something like self-reproach in a line that begins the final movement of "Roosters": "how could the night have come to grief?" By a trick of context, this phrase opens up an ambiguity in the cliché. It warns us that there has been matter for grieving during the night, before the first rooster crowed, at a scene of passion which was also a betrayal. "The Armadillo" too reveals the complicity of love with strife, in its italicized last stanza; here the last line and a half is a chiasmus, in which strength is surrounded by a yielding vulnerability.

> *Too pretty, dreamlike mimicry!*
> *O falling fire and piercing cry*
> *and panic, and a weak mailed fist*
> *clenched ignorant against the sky!*

"Weak" and "ignorant" are meant to temper the surprise of the "mailed fist clenched," and they cast doubt on those three central words: the fist, emblem of contest, is defended by weakness and ignorance, its only outward fortifications. The gesture of defiance, however, becomes all the more persuasive with this glimpse of a possible defeat. The way "The Armadillo" comes to rest has felt tentative to some readers, and yet the only question it asks is rhetorical: "See how adequately I shelter my victory?" In other poems just as surely, an elaborate craft gives away the poet as always present, at a scene she has painted as uninhabitable. The repeated line in a very late poem, "One Art," will declare her control by rhyming "disaster" with "The art of losing isn't hard to master"; as if we could expect her endurance to be taxing of course, but no more doubtful than her ability to pair the words for a villanelle.

Sexuality is the most elusive feature of Bishop's temperament—before writing any of the poems in *North & South*, she had learned to allegorize it subtly—and the reticence of her critics alone makes its existence worth noting. Like other habitual concerns, it interests her as it joins a care for what she sometimes calls the soul. This is an argument carried on from poem to poem, but its first appearance, in "The Imaginary Iceberg," is startling.

> Icebergs behoove the soul
> (both being self-made from elements least visible)
> to see them so: fleshed, fair, erected, indivisible.

Until these concluding lines the poem has been a light entertainment, a "Convergence of the Twain" told from the iceberg's point of view. The lines shift our perspective on everything that came before—in effect, they translate a poem which did not seem to need translation. "Fleshed, fair, erected, indivisible": the words, we see at once, belong to the human body rather than the soul. They are monstrously beautiful because they are a lie. For in the metaphor about the soul which has been perfectly built up, the comparison rightly demands instead: cold, white, immense, indestructible. This yields a pleasant description of an iceberg which, when we ponder it, is replaced by a sublime representation of the soul.

It is characteristic of Bishop's wit that she should have begun the same poem fancifully: "We'd rather have the iceberg than the ship, / although it meant the end of travel." Translating, as the poem suggests we do, this becomes: "We'd rather have the soul than the body, / although it meant the end of life." Yet for Bishop travel is not a chance metaphor. It stands for all that can divert the soul from its prospects. To hold fast to what it knows may mean for the soul to remain always "stock-still like cloudy rock"; or like a mariner, curled asleep at the top of a mast or seated with his eyes closed tight, untouchable by the charms of the voyage. This is the condition of "the unbeliever" in the poem of that title: believing only in himself, he knows "The sea is hard as diamonds; it wants to destroy us all." With his intensity perhaps, the soul may be equal to the imaginary iceberg which "cuts its facets from within. / Like jewelry from a grave / it saves itself and adorns / only itself." The phrase "from a grave," as it finally seems, is not fanciful at all but descriptive. It says that a guarding of the soul's integrity may also be a defense against death. And the sense in which this is especially true for a poet is the sense that matters to Bishop.

The titles of three of Bishop's volumes (*North & South*, *Questions of Travel*, *Geography III*) show how far she accepted—at times rather flatly—the common opinion that travel was her distinctive subject. Yet few readers are likely to know even a single region as intimately as she knew two hemispheres; and to make her geography poems interesting we have to read them as poems about something else. With this need of ours, a whole tract of her writing refuses to cooperate: poems about squatters and other half-cherished neighbors—efforts of self-conscious whimsy (like "Manuelzinho") or of awkward condescension (like "Filling Station"). I think these are the only poems Bishop ever wrote that dwindle as one comes to see them more clearly. One has to move away from these in order to learn what must have been clear to her from the first: that geography carries interest as a figure of the soul's encounter with fate (or as she puts it, with "what we imagine knowledge to be"). Occasionally, in the terms she proposes for this encounter, Bishop echoes the hero of Stevens's "The Comedian as the Letter C," who sought

> an elemental fate,
> And elemental potencies and pangs,
> And beautiful barenesses as yet unseen,
> Making the most of savagery.

But the poems I have in mind all end in a distrust of these things. In them, the dream of freedom, under the aspect of a perpetual self-renewal, is interpreted as a helpless revolt against the conditions of experience. The poet, however, offers no hope that we shall ever escape the enchantment of the dream.

"Brazil, January 1, 1502" marks the conquistadors' first step into a trap, a vast mesh of circumstance disguised as a jungle, and cozily misnamed "the new world." The poem starts off, innocuously, with an epigraph from Sir Kenneth Clark, "embroidered nature . . . tapestried landscape."

> Januaries, Nature greets our eyes
> exactly as she must have greeted theirs:
> every square inch filling in with foliage—
> big leaves, little leaves, and giant leaves,
> blue, blue-green, and olive,
> with occasional lighter veins and edges,
> or a satin underleaf turned over.

It is all, she goes on to say (confirming her epigraph) "solid but airy; fresh as if just finished / and taken off the frame." Courteously artful, we are like the conquistadors in supposing that we can make Nature over in a language we know—for them, the language of tapestry, for us that of naturalistic description. In either case we reproduce the nature prized by a Western connoisseur of art; and the poem is about how we cannot ever effect the conversion without loss. Nature will always take its revenge by drawing us still farther in, and suspending our knowledge of the thing that claims our pursuit.

So, in the nest stanza, the tapestry is described as "a simple web"— a moral text, its foreground occupied by "Sin: / five sooty dragons near some massy rocks." Even after these have been naturalized as lizards, Bishop tells us "all eyes / are on the smaller, female one, back-to, / her wicked tail straight up and over, / red as a red-hot wire." Between then and now, the allegorical and the natural, the poem admits no disparity— none, anyway, to compete with the similarity implied by such imperial habits of seeing. Hence the appropriateness of the poem's grammatical structure, its "*As* then, *so* now." This structure is completed only in the third and last stanza, which reverses the order of the comparison. As we find it now, not unfamiliar,

> Just so the Christians, hard as nails,
> tiny as nails, and glinting,
> in creaking armor, came and found it all,
> not unfamiliar:
> no lovers' walks, no bowers,
> no cherries to be picked, no lute music,
> but corresponding, nevertheless,

to an old dream of wealth and luxury
already out of style when they left home—
wealth plus a brand-new pleasure.
Directly after Mass, humming perhaps
L'Homme armé or some such tune,
they ripped away into the hanging fabric,
each out to catch an Indian for himself—
those maddening little women who kept calling,
calling to each other (or had the birds waked up?)
and retreating, always retreating, behind it.

In the light of this ending, the poem may be read as a colonial dream of all that seems infinitely disposable in the colonized.

But it is also about something that evades our grasp in every object that appeals to the human love of conquest. The Indian women, "those maddening little women who kept calling, calling to each other"—but not to their pursuers—only repeat the attraction of the female lizard, "her wicked tail straight up and over, / red as a red-hot wire." Both alike appear to beckon from behind the tapestry of the jungle fabric. They entice, and bind their spell. Another retreat will always be possible to them, since the jungle has gone opaque to the men hunting them, who believe at every point that it is transparent. This is another way of saying that the invaders have become victims of their own conquering perspective. They recreate here "an old dream of wealth and luxury"; yet the dream was "already out of style when they left home"; and the new place, as disclosed to other eyes, has seemed far from home-like. In the end their crossing of this threshold, "hard as nails, / tiny as nails," says most about their sense of home, which was equally marked by a failure of knowledge. What they take to be an act of possession is not, therefore, even a successful repossession, but the enactment of a familiar ritual of self-seduction.

This poem shows Bishop moving well outside the limits of the travel sketch. By itself, it is almost enough to persuade us that she exploits the genre elsewhere chiefly to break with it, from an impulse comparable to Dickinson's in revising the poem of "home thoughts." At any rate, the sketch that goes furthest to appease the worldly taste of her readers carries a suspicious title, "Over 2,000 Illustrations and a Complete Concordance," and the steady mystification of its narrative seems bent on protracting our suspicion. The poem, with an unsettling confidence, treats worldliness as a form of literal reading that is death—but the title is worth pausing over. What is a concordance? A system of reference to all the uses of every important word in the bible, or for that matter in any sacred book, including the work of a great poet. The illustrations accompanying it may be pictures—the picture-postcard atmosphere of much of the poem will toy with this—yet they are as likely to be passages longer than a phrase, which give a fuller context for the entries. When reading a concordance, we do not look at individual words to be sure of their reference, but to satisfy ourselves of a fateful pattern of choice. From the sum of an author's repetitions, we may learn a tact for whatever is irreducible in his character. "Over 2000 Illustrations" owes its force to the propriety with which one can substitute both "reader" and "traveller" for "author," and view a place in the world as denoting a locus in a text.

The thought that troubles Bishop at the start is that the book of nature and history may not be either a clean text or an already canonical one, whether bible or secular fiction, but something more like just such a concordance, with occasional glimpses into its depths coming from the illustrations alone.

Thus should have been our travels:
serious, engravable.
The Seven Wonders of the World are tired
and a touch familiar, but the other scenes,
innumerable, though equally sad and still,
are foreign. Often the squatting Arab,
or group of Arabs, plotting, probably,
against our Christian Empire,
while one apart, with outstretched arm and hand
points to the Tomb, the Pit, the Sepulcher.
The branches of the date-palms look like files.
The cobbled courtyard, where the Well is dry,
is like a diagram, the brickwork conduits
are vast and obvious, the human figure
far gone in history or theology,
gone with its camel or its faithful horse.
Always the silence, the gesture, the specks of birds
suspended on invisible threads above the Site,
or the smoke rising solemnly, pulled by threads.

The broken, randomly spliced rhythm of this opening, the discreteness of its sentences, as well as the words "often" and "always," suggest the episodic quality of the moments chronicled in the illustrations. They tell a story, apparently senseless, and in no particular order, which the poem later names the story of "God's spreading fingerprint." Only the Christians in the illustrations make a connection from place to place; and in the margin, everywhere, are faintly sinister Arabs, plotting or "looking on amused": together, these figures give it the unity it has. But as the account moves on, it grows still more oddly inconsequential: "In Mexico the dead man lay / in the blue arcade; the dead volcanoes / glistened like Easter lilies. / The jukebox went on playing 'Ay, Jalisco!' " The blare of the jukebox comes in when the story's meaning appears to have been surely lost, and it signals a transition. Now, the tone of the illustrations (which somehow have become cheap guidebook images) drifts toward the hallucinatory:

And in the brothels of Marrakesh
the little pockmarked prostitutes
balanced their tea-trays on their heads
and did their belly dances; flung themselves
naked and giggling against our knees,
asking for cigarettes. It was somewhere near there
I saw what frightened me most of all:
A holy grave, not looking particularly holy,
one of a group under a keyhole-arched stone baldaquin
open to every wind from the pink desert.

By the first five lines of this passage, every worldly fact has been rendered exchangeable with every other, and the loss is of nothing less than the history and the pathos of the things one may come to know.

Bishop is frightened "most of all" by the suddenly exposed grave in the desert because it reminds her of a life emptied of causes and consequences, with "Everything only connected by 'and' and 'and.' " The conclusion of the poem brings together author, reader, and traveller a last time, and envisions a sort of text that would return attention to something beyond it.

Everything only connected by "and" and "and."
Open the book. (The gilt rubs off the edges
of the pages and pollinates the fingertips.)
Open the heavy book. Why couldn't we have seen
this old Nativity while we were at it?
—the dark ajar, the rocks breathing with light,
an undisturbed, unbreathing flame,
colorless, sparkless, freely fed on straw,
and, lulled within, a family with pets,
—and looked and looked our infant sight away.

Much less than everything is restored by this ending. Though the holy book, once opened, confronts us with an ideal representation of our origins, we have to read it uninnocently. We know how thoroughly we have revised it already by our later imaginings, by every arrangement which makes the end of a life or work distort its beginning. To deny our remoteness from the scene would be to cancel the very experience which permits us to pass through "the dark ajar." Thus, we stand with the poet, both in the scene and outside it, uncertain whether pleasure is the name for what we feel. Her wishfully innocent question—"Why couldn't we have seen / this old Nativity while we were at it?"—has the tone of a child's pleading, "Why couldn't we *stay* there?"—said of a home, or a place that has grown sufficiently like home. Some time or other we say that about childhood itself. The book, then, is hard to open because it is hard to admit the strength of such a plea; harder still, to hear it for what it says about our relationship to ourselves. Any place we live in, savage or homely, dream-house or rough shelter, we ourselves have been the making of. And yet, once made, it is to be inherited forever. Everything may be connected by "because" and "therefore," and every connection will be provisional. The last line accordingly yields an ambiguous truth about nostalgia: to look our sight away is to gaze our fill, but also to look until we see differently—until, in our original terms, we do not see at all. The line, however, warrants a more general remark about Bishop's interest in the eye. In common with Wordsworth, she takes the metaphor of sight to imply the activity of all the senses, and these in turn to represent every possibility of conscious being. Sight is reliable because it can give no account of itself. We make it mean only when we look again, with "that inward eye / Which is the bliss of solitude" (words, incidentally, which the hero of "Crusoe in England" tries reciting to himself on the island, but can remember only after his rescue). It is in the same poem that Wordsworth says of the daffodils, "I gazed—and gazed"; and the action of "The Fish" turns on this single concentrated act: "I stared and stared," and the colors of the boat changed to "rainbow, rainbow, rainbow," and she let the fish go.

In passing from sight to vision, or to "what is within (which after all / cannot have been intended to be seen)," Bishop always respects the claims of unbelievers different from herself. Her mood is almost always optative, in its readiness to inquire into not-yet-habitable truths; and I want to conclude with an especially full expression of that mood, from "Love Lies Sleeping." She writes there of a dawn in a city, with eleven lines of a soft introductory cadence, good enough for the opening bars of a Gershwin tune; with a memory of the waning night and its "neon shapes / that float and swell and glare"; with a panoramic view and a long tracking view that ends in the window of one dwelling, where the poet asks the "queer cupids of all persons getting up" to be mild with their captives:

> for always to one, or several, morning comes
> whose head has fallen over the edge of his bed,
>   whose face is turned
>   so that the image of
>
> the city grows down into his open eyes
> inverted and distorted. No. I mean
>   distorted and revealed,
>   if he sees it at all.

The words are as serious and engravable as an epitaph. At the same time, with a doubt exactly the size of a comma, they point to a revelation that may have occurred, and, for the sake of its distortion as well as its truth, keep it living in surmise.

J. V. Cunningham's Roman Voices

Jack Hill

The Roman voice, uttering its close-woven language, tends towards the lapidary, the epigrammatic. It distrusts the paradisal, for had not Rome acquired great power and wealth while still leaving the Roman subject to violence, fear, lust and hangovers? Its love-poetry is sharp, knowing, passionate, but realistic; its lovers are clearly defined both in their beauty and in their imperfections, for the Romans believed neither in the perfectibility of the individual nor in the ecstatic contemplation of the individual's guilt. Each person was original, but not an original sinner. All were fools, some wicked; and to ask a beautiful body to provide a simulacrum of infinity or a solution to the problems of history and personality was a silly way of preventing the body from providing what it could provide, namely a thoroughly pleasant evening, often rendered more sharply enjoyable by the inevitable preliminary difficulties. To express this the Roman began not in paradox, that Christian mode, but in epigram, the short poem in short lines, and Cunningham, almost alone among American writers of this century, is an epigrammatist, having written more than a hundred of them. (Even his sequence on driving westward *To What Strangers, What Welcomes* is a set of short poems in short lines, and such a topos does not usually stir the American writer to brevity either of whole or unit.)

Among his epigrams there are first the good simple jokes, as in No. 68:

> *Arms and the man I sing*, and sing for joy,
> Who was last year all elbows and a boy.

The neat, brisk metre takes Cunningham here closer to Ogden Nash than

From *Modern American Poetry*, edited by R. W. (Herbie) Butterfield. © 1984 by Vision Press Ltd.

to Martial, but the double mockery of the Roman hero and the adolescent is effective enough. In No. 42, however, we are on different ground:

> Soft found a way to damn me undefended:
> I was forgiven who had not offended.

A sharp formulation of a peculiarly obnoxious form of moral hypocrisy acquires an added complexity from the world-weary cadence of the feminine rhyme. The characteristically Latin separation of the relative clause from the nominative pronoun gives a legal formality and inevitability, the sense that the poet is summing up once what has often happened before, and will as often recur. And the scansion of the second line moves us forcibly out of a potential pastiche of English Augustanism into Roman muscle, consisting as it does of dactyl and trochee (the end of a hexameter), followed by pyrrhic, spondee and trochee again:

$$/\ \smallsmile\ \smallsmile\ /\ \smallsmile\ \big|\ \smallsmile\ \smallsmile\ /\ /\ /\ \smallsmile$$

> I was forgiven | who had not offended.

In No. 49 we are back to iambs, but to Cunningham's favourite octosyllabic iambs, favoured also by seventeenth-century epigrammatists:

> Lip was a man who used his head.
> He used it when he went to bed
> With his friend's wife, and with his friend,
> With either sex at either end.

Stripped of the connotations which are liberatedly hyped into the vocabulary normally chosen to glamourize such coitions, these plain words combine with the comic relentlessness of the metre to expose the activity (the fashion, one might add) as absurd, mechanistic and vulgar. The tone is not repelled and fascinated, but aloof, amused, and contemptuous: in a word, aristocratic.

The best of Cunningham's epigrams succeed because of this neat bluntness, this inscriptional quality involved in the meaning of the Greek word *epigramma*, a short verse written on tombstones or votive offerings. The form combines with astute social and self-knowledge to present a final judgement, a usually humorous summing-up of those inescapable limitations of human life which always underlie the human being's sexual or moral posturings:

> Jove courted Danäe with golden love,
> But you're not Danäe, and I'm not Jove
> (No. 4)

or

> This humanist whom no beliefs constrained
> Grew so broad-minded he was scatter-brained.
> (No. 43)

or

> You ask me how Contempt who claims to sleep
> With every woman that has ever been
> Can still maintain that women are skin deep?
> They never let him any deeper in.
>
> (No. 62)

Since this style is destructive of hyperbole, of the glorious mendacity which is the very essence of other more opulent modes, it does not easily allow the broad evocative sweep, the bravura gesture. The lyric can encompass it, for song, however far removed from incantation, still moves us away from general social knowledge towards individual inspiration. The epigram does not, and when Cunningham injudiciously tries to mix the two forms, the result is unhappy:

> This garish and red cover made me start.
> I who amused myself with quietness
> Am here discovered. In this flowery dress
> I read the wild wallpaper of my heart.
>
> (No. 14)

Our discovery is more, and less, than the poet intended. Even worse, since more is at stake, is:

> I had gone broke, and got set to come back,
> And lost, on a hot day and a fast track,
> On a long shot at long odds, a black mare
> By Hatred out of Envy by Despair.
>
> (No. 55)

The conceit is laboured, the rhythm, all-too-obviously setting up the last line, banal, and the sentiment both hyperbolic and commonplace. The personifications give a general wash of indulgent gloom rather than information, and in the facile chiaroscuro of pseudo-Romantic agony the epigrammatist's knowledgeable hauteur and humour are quite lost. Not only does the form demolish its content, as in the preceding poem, but one pose destroys another—Gibbon cannot be Poe, especially in four lines. (The only man who successfully fuses the two is Byron, and then only in very long poems.)

This is not to say that the epigram cannot be tender, or sad; its first function was elegiac, and when Cunningham writes his own epitaph, he correctly blends an almost seventeenth-century octosyllabic wit with a half-pound resignation:

> When I shall be without regret
> And shall morality forget,
> When I shall die who lived for this,

> I shall not miss the things I miss.
> And you who notice where I lie
> Ask not my name. It is not I.

The "this" in line 3 may refer either to poetry or to the general condition of being alive or to the skill which has gone into the writing of this very poem, but the non-specificity is a source of strength, not weakness. Cunningham is writing an American *exegi monumentum*, where he asserts that what Ovid called the "better part" of him is not limited by the body, the grave, or the epitaph, but survives in what may be known of his life, and what he has written. Horace asserted that he would not wholly die ("*non omnis moriar*"), Ovid that the better part of him would live, and Ronsard demanded that his name survive almost as a natural phenomenon:

> *Et voyant mon pays, a peine pourra croire*
> *Que d'un si petit champ Ronsard se vante ne.*

But Cunningham's crisp finale asserts the value of a life and a metier, a value which has nothing to do with name or with survival, though it obviously hopes for the latter. And the conventions of the Greek epitaph (the passing stranger, the chosen anonymity), scrupulously observed, root the poem in a deep historical awareness of the poetic tradition (the metier) to which the individual is indeed important, but strictly speaking incidental, just as a link is a constituent but not a definition of a chain. It is a fully classical poem.

In many of his (slightly) longer poems, Cunningham begins from epigram. For example, in "For My Contemporaries" he opens with a brilliant one,

> How time reverses
> The proud in heart!
> I now make verses
> Who aimed at art

successfully binding self-mockery and general satire. But the wry and sharp-edged stance cannot, if it is to succeed, be mistaken for that very unaristocratic posture, disappointed pique. And in the next stanzas the poet, although expressing an understandable distaste for the vulgar rhodomontade of some of his contemporaries, falls into vulgarity himself:

> But I sleep well.
> Ambitious boys
> Whose big lines swell
> With spiritual noise,

> Despise me not,
> And be not queasy
> To praise somewhat:
> Verse is not easy.

The lines about the ambitious boys are meant to sound *as* empty as the boys' own poems, but they just sound bad-tempered, and the queasy/easy rhyme is itself queasy, especially as Cunningham here is asking for praise, which is not a gentlemanly thing to do. And the slickness of the last stanza expresses not a precisely-poised balance of knowledge and wit, but ungentlemanly self-satisfaction:

> But the rage who will.
> Time that procured me
> Good sense and skill
> Of madness cured me.

In another poem, "The Predestined Space," however, Cunningham brings off a technical tour-de-force, using an only slightly longer stanza to express the identical operations of human behaviour, theology and the craft of the poet.

> Simplicity assuages
> With grace the damaged heart,
> So would I in these pages
> If will were art.
>
> But the best engineer
> Of metre, rhyme, and thought
> Can only tool each gear
> To what he sought
>
> If chance with craft combines
> In the predestined space
> To lend his damaged lines
> Redeeming grace.

The basic premise of the poem is that fallen man may occasionally express a perfection which he cannot perform—or, in other more secular words, that language may realize potentials outside the scope of action, the works of imagination thereby surpassing those of reality. Such occasional perfected expression may not be achieved by "will" but by craft and chance which combine to add aesthetic grace to the bare form, just as the grace of God redeems the damaged heart from sterile predestination. The repetition of the adjective "damaged," applied to both "heart" and "lines," associates them inextricably together, just as repetition of the adjective "green" in Marvell's "The Garden" inter-identifies "thought" and "shade," though Cunningham risks a much bigger gap between the doubled epithet than Marvell. This repetition beautifully sets up and reinforces the final splendid double entendre of "grace" (aesthetic and theological) and the silky perfection of rhythm and rhyme in the last stanza gives an optimistic certainty which refutes the tentative opening with the conditional "If." The argument (fundamentally syllogistic) harks back both to mediaeval Christianity and to the English poets of the seventeenth century, but Cunningham goes further than either for he is not reworking a simple syllogism ("Had we but world. . . . But. . . . Therefore. . . . Thus") or refuting a proposition (as Aquinas refutes, for example, in the *Summa contra Gentiles* the proposition that happiness consists in the practice of art): his poem is asserting that identical logical (and hence inescapable) processes inhere in the creation of a poem and in the operancy of grace. And the clear, formal stanza is the only form which can enact this. Just as Shakespearean hyperbole may express an over-reaching vision which neither the actor's human physique nor the details of plot can embody, or as a Petrarchan oxymoron may express the simultaneous co-existence of emotional antitheses which resists reasonable formulation, so may the neat verse, with the "exclusions" of its rhymes, express the inevitable certainty of rational process—granted A, therefore B, if C. It is a Latin way, more Christian and Catholic than Augustan and Horatian, but Latin nonetheless.

Again using a blend of theological and literary vocabulary, though less successfully, Cunningham admits to scepticism of

> the new
> Regenerate elect
> Who take the social view
> And zealously reject
> The classic indignation
> The sullen clarity
> Of passions in their station
> Moved by propriety.
> ("The Symposium")

But his classic-Christian disbelief in the natural virtue of humankind saves him from facile whatever-is-is-rightery; the clarity is sullen, and the indignation may be classic but is still indignant, Faced with eternal verities, and Cunningham believes in them, innovation is rash:

> The hot flesh and passionless mind
> In fancy's house must still abide
> Each share the work, its share defined
> By caution under custom's guide.
> ("Fancy")

And literary education provides, he points out gently but firmly, neither a *modus vivendi* nor a scrutiny of self, but a trade:

> For you have learned not what to say
> But how the saving must be said.
> ("To a Friend on Her Examination
> for the Doctorate in English")

Cunningham in many quotations and references, more deeply in his selection of forms (and, one should add, in his translations from Latin), acknowledges his roots. (One of his most unfashionable lines—"Radical change, the root of human woe"—must be that rarity in a modern poet, an opinion which would attract nods of approbation from Horace, Saint Jerome and Burke.)

He rarely quotes from non-Latin writers, and it is odd that in one of his early poems he should mention Beardsley and Dowson, characterizing them in these lines

> Their verse, sepulchral, breathes
> A careless scent of flowers in late July,
> Too brief for pleasure, though its pleasure lie
> In skilled inconscience of its brevity.
> ("Obesquies for a Poetess")

The words offer a kindly critical appraisal of the feel of '90s' poetry, but they also refer both in matter and manner to a whole long tradition of lyric verse, itself defined less by form than by one of its dominant topoi—carpe diem. Awareness of the evanescence of pleasure may destroy pleasure, but may also sharpen it, as the sharpness of form of the best carpe diem writers deepens the reader's pleasure both emotionally (this delight is the more to be loved since it is short) and aesthetically (so much said in so little). The apparent contradiction of the phrase, "skilled inconscience," contains, beneath the criticism of Dowson, both the effortless ease of the skilled technician and the poise, the *sprezzatura*, of the knowledgeable and fashionable man of the world. And since this poem is being addressed by one poet to another about their predecessors, we may legitimately infer that these qualities are important to him. (It might also be pointed out that as the poem was written in the early '30s, its apparently anachronistic references and opinions are in fact polemic.)

But the phrase itself, "skilled inconscience," takes us further into another aspect of Cunningham's classicism. The late J. B. Leishman pointed out that one of the important strands of a certain type of classical verse, and one which unites writers as chronologically distant as Horace and Marvell, is a kind of witty play. But this witty "play" is not merely frivolous, but a manifestation (one might also say a re-enactment) of that condition of mind when the creative intellect, emancipated from the doings of the mundane world (what Shakespeare called "all these"), is able to form those imaginative insights which are given by such meditative freedom into a delightful artifice. It is the result of *otium* rather than of *negotium*, and may only be expressed by wit in the Renaissance sense (the surprising but irresistible formulation of a novel imaginative insight in a melodious but sequential form). It is, through humour, removed from the narrowly personal, and a precondition of its success is a quick awareness of the true, as opposed to the apparent (daily or conventional), importance of things. (Among other scholars Huizinga, Rahner and Levin have written on this theme at length.) The witty delight is achieved not *despite* but *through* the acceptance of rule, just as delight (and the only possible efficiency) in a game of rugby or bridge is expressed through a sequence of accepted limitations. Such "play" does not mean that the poet is bound to be a comedian, though he must have many of the comedian's qualities, and it does not mean that he cannot write of unhappiness and failure; it does mean that jokes shall be economically phrased and timed, and it also means that the unhappinesses shall not ramble, but be checked by the same proprieties of expression as the jokes. In other words, both the form and the style transmit grief as a facet of sanity, not as a periphrasis of *in*sanity. The psychiatric ward may be the setting for an egocentric memoir, which we may agree for the purposes of convention to call a poem, but the quatrain, octosyllable and sonnet are better settings for a definition of life. Only the brake makes the efficient car, just as only the rules of play enable personal feeling to be expressive of general truth. And only a sane man may simultaneously receive into his consciousness both immediate personal feeling and an objective awareness of its relative importance in history and scale. Cunningham always adopts that most classical and difficult of postures, and the one without which very little truly great verse can be written: that of the sane adult writing for an audience of equals. The general truths, the *sententiae*, are newly present, and must emerge neither from obediently followed commonplace nor from an illogical novelty, for the sane and educated reader can spot both; and the reader's good eyesight, just as much as the difficulty of the Stanza, is one of the constituent difficulties of the classical poet, which he has to accept, with (one hopes) both pleasure and success.

As Petronius points out, the poet must

> take care that his sententiae do not seem to detach themselves from the body of his discourse, but that they shine like colours which have been woven into garments.

Cunningham's entire poetic output seems to obey, or at its worst unsuccessfully to try to obey, Petronius's rule. Stanzas and whole poems are organized so that the final statement or sententia, whether it be literary heir to the Romans or to the English metaphysical wits, emerges as naturally as the colours shine from a garment. His last lines often seem like quotations, though they seldom are, partly because of the precision of phrasing, and partly because, as one reads the poem as a whole, they seem to be arrived at by a process of indisintricable logic. Here are a few examples:

> Your mute voice on the crystal embers flinging.
> ("The Phoenix")

> Nor live curiously
> Cheating providence.
> ("A Moral Poem")

> Naked you lie in an unknown grave.
> > ("The Helmsman, an Ode")

> Love's wilful potion
> Veils the ensuing,
> And brief commotion.
> > ("Ars Amoris")

> And David equally with Venus
> Has no penis.
> > ("I too have been to the
> > Huntingdon")

> Was it unforgivable,
> My darling, that you loved me?
> > (*To What Strangers,*
> > *What Welcomes*)

Through the arguments, the rhymes, and the play, exercised for neither therapy nor reward

> Insight flows into my pen
> I know nor fear nor haste.
> Time is my own again.
> I waste it for the waste
> > ("Coffee")

a cannily ancient voice is heard. It needs and accepts drink, sex, travel and art, but never mistakes them for absolutes, or avers that the pleasures and pains they bring are themselves absolute. It does not believe that in the acts of enjoying and speaking about these pleasures any grand gestures should be struck, or, using a less virile participle than struck, pirouetted. It distrusts statistics as much as ecstasies:

> Error is boundless
> Nor hope nor doubt,
> Though both be groundless
> Will average out.
> > ("Meditation on Statistical
> > Method")

It mocks itself. It depends not on sensuousness for its effect, but on a knowledge of sensuousness's bounds. It is logical, partly Christian. It is sometimes stoic, more often epicurean. It is humorously resigned to the limitations of man's small pleasures, but also knows that the limitations of pleasure do not stop it from being pleasurable:

> Reader goodbye. While my associates
> Redeem the world in moral vanity

> Or live in the casuistry of an affair
> I shall go home: bourbon and beer at five,
> Some money, some prestige, some love, some sex,
> My input and my output satisfactory.
>
> (No. 100)

Despite the references to bourbon, cars and Montana, this voice comes from Rome—or if not from Rome as it was, from Rome as it was understood by Horace and Ovid, by Saint Thomas Aquinas, and by the wits of the seventeenth century.

I do not consider Cunningham a great poet, though I am sure he has written poems such as the world will not willingly let die. It might seem strange to set him in a tradition which includes Horace, Ronsard, Shakespeare and Marvell. But we should make our judgements in comparison with what Matthew Arnold called "the glorious company of the best," and I believe that Cunningham himself would require, indeed demand, such comparisons. And it is only by a continual reference to the classics, whether of antiquity or of our own vernacular tradition, that poets and critics may avoid becoming provincial in their judgements. If wit, poise, sadness, clarity and shape are the virtues of Roman verses and voices at their best, and I believe they are, then at *his* best Cunningham is a classic.

William Everson (Brother Antoninus): The Inner War

Paul A. Lacey

Two stages are readily discernible in William Everson's life as a poet. For fifteen years he published poetry as William Everson—farmer, printer, conscientious objector of no particular religious persuasion in World War II; for nearly twenty years he was Brother Antoninus—convert to Catholicism, Dominican lay brother. That second stage represented by the name in religion is now over, since he has given up his annual vows as an oblate, left the Order, and married.

The pre-Catholic poetry reflects the same preoccupations which mark all his later work. It is rooted in awful awareness of nature and history, the two matrices in which man either finds himself or knows himself trapped. Both nature and history are violent; both represent outwardly and universally the inner war which Everson experiences. Kenneth Rexroth says in his introduction to *The Residual Years* that all of Everson's poetry, including the later, Catholic poetry, "is concerned with the drama of his own self, rising and falling along the sine curve of life." Coming to terms with the self also means coming to terms with the savagery of men and the savagery of the natural world. And poetry is both a means of coming to terms and the product of the conflicts out of which the self is being shaped. Poetry has pattern, created by the tug and pull of emotions and events, refined and perfected in the frustration of human fallibility and incapacity. "The Answer," a poem from"The Impossible Choices" (1940–46), explores these themes. The poet labors over his lines, drawing on the pain which has afflicted him from birth—failure, guilt, the tyranny of sex—but no poem comes, "nothing converges." Only later, when some sense experience or casual word evokes a response from the inner depths, do "the inner locks

From *Benchmark and Blaze: The Emergence of William Everson*, edited by Lee Bartlett. © 1979 by Lee Bartlett. Scarecrow Press, 1979.

open." Conscious labor is replaced by unconscious growth: "The thought stirs in its seed; / The images flower"; and the poem emerges,

> Freighted with judgment,
> Swung out of the possible into the actual,
> As one man's insight matches mankind's at the midpoint of
>   language;
> And the meeting minds reduplicate in the running vowel
> Their common concern.

The inner war is a necessary prelude to the act of creation, but creation itself comes from those depths in the self where individual and race meet, where convergence occurs. The poem does not belong to the poet alone; it confirms and is confirmed by the language of the race.

> Then here rides his triumph:
> Caught in his doom he had only his anguish,
> But the human pattern imposes across his stammering mind
> Its correctional hand.

"Delicate structure," "midpoint of language," "the human pattern": all speak of the individual's link with others, but for Everson these links are most frequently created by guilt and violence, the outer wars which reflect the inner. In "Attila" and "Fish-Eaters" Everson speaks of the violent past from which individuals and social forms alike spring. Attila's outer wars failed—though only because there have been so many others—but he has made his mark on the deeps of life, in the genes of the race and in the unconscious. The poet cannot trace his blood to its single source; it has mingled in thousands as a result of conquest, war, and lust. But, thinking of the fish-eaters, he knows that what he wants, his longing for peace, somehow has its roots in that past he must explore and affirm: "I, the living heir of the bloodiest men of all Europe."

What has made structure—the human pattern, language, social institutions—is violence. In "The Roots" the poet meditates on the English, gaunt raiders, broken in turn by waves of conquest, who shape the words of our language from their history: "The single rhythm of the ancient blood / Remembers the anguish, the hate and desire." Trying to write, the poet feels behind him this trial and error, the shaping for experience, the awareness of generations coming to form in his mind.

A poem has both structure and freedom; it is both personal and universal; it is made from the stuff of violence but transformed into peace and beauty; it is a midpoint of language where minds meet. A poem grows out of the tangle and struggle of opposites. Light comes out of darkness:"I feel the power rising out of the dark sources, / Those unknown springs in the sea-floor of the self." *War* is a constant motif in the poetry, whether Everson is writing about the act of making poetry, his consciousness of history, or his response to the natural world. The poem "Sun" begins "Season on

Season the sun raiding the valley / Drowns it in light." The storms speak "furious words" and "syllables of thunder"; the music of nature, like the music of poetry, grows out of the dark impulses, danger, destruction.

Everything is at war, but the poet's end is to find peace without sloth. The early acts of Everson's drama of the self are played out against the backdrop of the rise of fascism in Europe and the approaching world war. Two poems in particular memorialize the drama: "The Sides of a Mind" and "Invocation." In the first, the spiritual struggle expressed in the conflict of *sides* of a mind parallels the physical struggles being played out in war, the march of squadrons, and "the smell of misery and rot and the filth of the poor." Behind the battle to build shining cities and obliterate poverty there still lies the doubt that any human action matters. "But there is no God, nor was ever a God, / And that is the root of our trouble." Working over his futile poem, the poet feels the power to write surging in him but lacks a theme: "Belief made foolish, the pitiless hunger unfulfilled, / The mind crying for anchor." He surveys his heritage and knows only guilt and inadequacy; he turns to nature and sees only the destruction on which his life is predicated. Working in the fields, breathing, eating, his body is inescapably engaged in warfare against other creatures.

> Every sucking breath that I drew
> The long border of warfare ran down my lungs,
> Furious soldiers of my blood warring and killing.

The poet turns inward so radically that he becomes conscious of the oozing of his pores, the sloughing of dead skin from his feet, and the growing of his nails, and asks whether this ugly decay can justify his poetry. The poem reaches two conclusions, the first that "life feeds on life," so that what we make of our existence means everything and nothing. This thematic rounding off leaves unresolved the conflict represented by the "sides of the mind." The second conclusion loses the conflict in a lyrical celebration of the close of a decade and the opening of something new. Nature for itself, not as a symbol of any inner meaning, soothes the poet; the night flows and the river rolls, "the decade wears itself out," and the unsubstantiated hope for the future closes the poem.

"Invocation" also sums up a decade, in this case the completion of the poet's third decade. Now, however, he has made his affirmations, recorded for example in "The Vow," never to take life wantonly, to atone in his soul for the past he had no control over, to show pity and mercy to all life precisely because he knows its ultimate dissolution. He now sees the spring fructification, the summer fulfillment of nature, and asks for himself a part in that fertility and harvest. He is still at war, "in which neither the foe nor myself is known," a war within the self which finds its double in the war between men. To answer his questions "And I? What am I?" the poet must strip away the ease and pleasure, the lack of imagination, the habitual frameworks which conceal the warfare.

> There runs the war,
> In the half-perceived but unattended,
> There at the marginal edge of perception,
> There must it be met.

He promises his pity for all living things, so that the spirit will be cleansed, the ego chastened, the senses hushed. He pictures the terrible struggle of evolution, where the self is locked in its inner struggle and "the extensional conflict," but where the perception of its need and its partial attainment can partially redeem the waste of the past. And out of that vision of the war of evolution he prays that his thirtieth year might yield him fulfillment.

Of Everson's early poetry it might be said that his theme is finding a form, while his forms express a persistent struggle to find a theme. The war in the self has as its purpose finding a truth to speak and to live by. But war is always destructive; Everson's poetry is marked by disgust for the physical—especially human sexuality—shame, guilt, imperfectly controlled violence. That this should be so in the writing of one so sensitive to the times in which he lives is not to be wondered at. What he longs for is meaningful pattern, a framework within which life makes sense. History provides one framework, nature another, and many of Everson's poems grow out of the attempt to measure and value the self against the patterns of family history, racial history, or natural history.

The verse patterns and language he uses in these poems illustrate the theme-form problem. He favors long poem-sequences where the separate stanzas and parts often relate to each other like separate poems within a book. End-rhyme or regular metrical patterns rarely occur; instead Everson uses alternations of long and short lines to represent the rise and fall of emotion or activity. Lines are frequently built up in the loose parallelism of the Hebrew Psalms. Phrases and words modify each other simply by being placed side by side. The poetry frequently tends toward slackness—in the line, the stanza, and poem—which duplicates the emotional sprawl. The language he uses serves to counteract this effect, but not without exacting its own price. Anglo-Saxon monosyllables predominate, often harsh, blunt words which convey images and feelings through tactile impressions. Nearly every noun has its adjective, but often they are past participles which lend a sense of physical action to the phrase.

> The whispering wind,
> The erect and tensile filaments of weeds,
> The fallen leaf,
> Half-consumed near the igneous rock,
> All keep accordance,
> Strung on the rays that leave no trace,
> But sift out the hours
> Purling across the deaf stones,

> While the exactitude of each entering star
> Chronicles the dark.
>   ("A Privacy of Speech" 9)

Intense but unfocused emotion, language in which physical reality and intellectual abstractions jostle with one another, form and theme in search of one another, an aura of violence surrounding even the most pastoral poems: these are the characteristics of Everson's earliest verse. Perhaps no recent poet better exemplifies the longing for and resistance to form.

In 1949 William Everson became a Roman Catholic, in 1950 he began working with the poor as part of the Catholic Worker movement, and in 1951 he entered a Dominican monastery. An intense conversion led to a series of callings, first away from secular success, and finally away from the secular life itself. With his new name, symbolizing a new life and changed nature, Brother Antoninus also received a new, tight, and finely articulated framework into which he needed to fit his whole life. His next book of poems, *The Crooked Lines of God: Poems 1949–1954*, testifies to the importance of that framework, as do the "Pages from an Unpublished Autobiography" which appeared in *Ramparts* in September, 1962, and the interviews he has given.

> The first thing about a vocation is that there is a need for per-
> fection. . . . If you come to the religious life, you come to do
> sacrifice. This is imperative. If this is not understood, woe to the
> man who comes; if his inner search, his grasp of reality, does not
> exceed his other concerns, even his art becomes a trifling thing.

The terms in which Brother Antoninus describes the religious life set the conditions for a more intense inner war than he has experienced before, except that the adversaries cannot claim an equal right to win. To practice the vocation of artist in opposition to the religious vocation is to commit the sin of disobedience. The dedication of the artist becomes willful pride. God writes straight; man—the poet—writes crooked. "My crooked lines, tortured between grace and the depraved human heart (my heart) gouge out the screed of my defection. Everywhere about me the straight writing hems me in, compresses me, flattens my will."

The Crooked Lines of God shows a number of organizing principles at work. There is, of course, Roman Catholic theology, stressed and heightened by the convert's zeal. Following that organizing principle, Brother Antoninus has arranged the poems in three parts, "each corresponding to a particular phase of spiritual development, and each dominated, more or less, by the psychology of a particular saint." The first section he sees dominated by the psychology of Saint Augustine, focusing on guilt, repentance, and the contemplation of the Passion; the second section, corresponding to his time with the Catholic Worker, he sees as Franciscan in psychology; the third is Dominican, moving through "the full development of the erotic religious psychology of the Spanish Baroque." This three-part division also roots in Brother Antoninus's development chronologically, taking us from the conversion through its first fruits, to the monastery and to the point where the clash of crooked and straight choke out poetry. Finally, Brother Antoninus set the type for the book, giving as we shall consider later, yet another important shaping influence on the poetry, "concretizing" the spiritual states it testifies to.

The book opens with "Triptych for the Living," the first poems of his conversion, and they reflect the intense compression of that subjective experience in the form of the Christmas story, the mature, skeptical mind reflecting on and appropriating the most naive elements of the Christian mythos.

"The Uncouth" is a meditation on the shepherds to whom the angel announced the birth of Christ. The subject is almost mandatory for the Christian poet, but for that reason a successful handling is difficult. The story always raises the same questions, approached and answered in hundreds of poems and thousands of sermons each Christmastide: Why were these simple people first given the Good News? What does this story say to our own time? Unfortunately, the range of responses to these questions has narrowed down over the years. W. H. Auden makes the shepherds represent the Lumpenproletariat, a void to be filled, a force to be given direction. That is one kind of updating. Brother Antoninus gives us another kind—straightforward, unironic—making the shepherds a symbol for the perennial outcast, the uncouth who is unknown and unknowing. Once this connection is made, however, there is nothing more to do with it—no shock of recognition, no admiration of a witty comparison, nothing but the working out of details.

Recognizing this, Antoninus paints a picture reminiscent of an altar-panel, where our interest is engaged more by craftsmanship than by the story. The scene becomes California, the shepherds become the sheepherders, "in the folklore of the West . . . of all types the most low."

> As for them, the herdsmen,
> They'd rather hug out the year on a juniper ridge
> Than enter now, where the hard-bitten settlers
> Fenced their acres; where the merchants
> Wheedled the meager gain of summer;
> Where the brindled mastiffs
> Mauled the wethers.

They become types of the "prime, animal amplitude for life," the representation of unchanneled energy, the body and "naked intelligence" awaiting a soul. Grace comes first to them, in Antoninus's poem, *because* they have retained the purity of ignorance and have no knowledge of either the world or the angel.

Since Antoninus leaves the story untouched, except to place it in an

American setting, we must look to the details of form to determine whether he has made something new. The poem has six stanzas of varying lengths, from one line to thirteen, loose verse paragraphs built on irregular iambic lines. Only the diction gives any sense of energy to the poem, and it is rooted in physical description, monosyllables, and strong verbs. Some coined words effectively surprise the reader: "pastures / Greened again with good verdure," "Wind northed for cold," "wilderness-hearted earth." Alliteration and assonance operate to give the poem a quiet music.

When we compare this poem, a quiet, pious rendering of a traditional Christian story, with the prose account of its genesis, we see some of the difficulties Antoninus faces in working with the framework he has chosen. In "Pages from an Unpublished Autobiography" he speaks of attending midnight mass, Christmas of 1948, sitting in the church and feeling his customary estrangement from it. He smells "the resinous scent of fir trees" coming from the crib which the nuns had set up in the cathedral. He seizes on the scent with "true realization," and without the rebellion it would ordinarily call up. "Now out of the greatness of my need I sensed in it something of a verification, a kind of indeterminate warrant that I need not fear, were I to come to Christ, that He would exact the dreaded renunciation of my natural world." The verification, only a scent mixed with the incense, draws him into meditation on the scene in the crib. He reflects on the shepherds until "I saw the correlation." This, the key to his conversion, is also the key to the poem; the California sheepherder becomes a confirmation of the meaning of the Incarnation, for the Good News comes first to the man of the wilderness, the ignorant sheepherder subdued to what he works in. All this Antoninus renders for us through constant reference to the odors of the fir and the recalled odors of the sheepherders. The *evidence* which wins his assent to Christianity comes through "the odor of fir, the memory of sheepdung and mutton grease, cutting across the closed interior air of the Cathedral." After the logical structure of a faith has been affirmed, he says, there remains a blankness of those areas of association "which make in the mind the living thing a religion must be," and this blank filled for him when the odor of fir persuaded him that Christ would not deprive him of "the natural kingdom and the great sustaining Cosmos."

Turning from the crib to the woman beside him, whom he loves, the poet reflects on the feminine receptivity to the Mystery. The woman becomes a symbol for intuition, openness, "vibrant expectancy." Alternating between her innocent waiting and the crude primitive subjectivity of the sheepherder, Antoninus weaves his mediation, searching for the correlations. In turn he stands in the Mystery of Christ and the Mystery of the Church: "The once sinister Church, seen only as evil, becomes in a trice the resplendent Mother of Men, the Christ as pure beneficence, and he skips in singing."

Paraphrasing his description of the moment of conversion cannot do

Antoninus justice. In a few pages he shows us the convergence of forces and experiences and the discovery of "correlations" so vividly that we stand within the conversion situation with him. Intellectual insights and affirmations of faith receive some final confirmation for him through his senses; the smell of fir and the remembered smell of sheepherders become signatures for a spiritual truth. And we participate in this with him. Unfortunately, the poem which grows out of this experience is thin and abstract by comparison. Perhaps the simplest explanation for the difference is that the autobiographical passages must be in the first person, the discoveries must be personal, while the third-person telling in the poem distances events. But, more importantly, there is a world of difference between discovering a correlation or link in one's past which brings a truth home to oneself, and elevating that correlation into a general truth. Antoninus tries to translate the emotional and spiritual profundity of his experience into a rational profundity in the poem, and it does not work.

In this we see the chief difficulty facing Brother Antoninus as a poet and us as his readers. The conversion has been accomplished and is in the past:

> Nothing remains to show now but the poetry, and what is that?
> Something of the energy is contained there, but also something
> of the shapelessness, something persisting in the mystery of form,
> the mystery which blankets and obscures the outline of its tem-
> porality, but somehow releases the abiding energy, the force, and
> the inherent motive that made the act what it was.

Form is ambiguous for Antoninus. Energy and shapelessness come together; the mystery of form stands over against them, acting to release energy but also to obscure and blanket the "outline of its temporality," which apparently means all the slight details of sensory experience, the stuff out of which poetry, and conversions, is made. Form comes, *ab extra*, imposed by a theory or a theology. The poems must be introduced with a foreword to blanket and obscure the torment of unworthy thoughts and human temptations by announcing that the crooked lines will eventually be made straight. The foreword reports that the inner war, out of which the poems come, is over, or has ended in armistice.

"The Coming" and "The Wise," the other poems of the Triptych, are like "The Uncouth" in employing vigorous, kinesthetic language to explore relatively simple correlations between past and present. The "freshness, raciness and energy of immediate observation," which Samuel Johnson demanded of poetry, are there in abundance, but we must conclude, also with Johnson, that so far as theme is concerned "there is no nature, for there is nothing new." What is said is familiar, orthodox.

A number of problems arise in any treatment of biblical stories. The most obvious is that one has little latitude with a sacred fable; the details must be faithfully reproduced or any deviation thoroughly justified by its clever contemporaneity. Of course, in the richest literature, details occur for themselves and for the deeper significance they offer the rest of the work, but when the details of a story are so sacred that the only acceptable use of the artist's imagination is to make every one of them plausible in a new telling, no matter what the demands of the new work are, we see the heaviest weight of tradition.

Perhaps a more difficult problem to deal with for the artist who wishes to explore Christian themes is one we find in the New Testament itself, namely, that every action and speech must be explained through the benefit of hindsight, by reference to types and prophesies. So every surprising act or word of Jesus is explained by reference to the crucifixion and resurrection which are in the future, from the narrative's point of view, but already accomplished for the narrator. Or the hard sayings are explained as fulfilling a prophesy from the Old Testament. Saint Paul's reading of the Old Testament as providing types and shadows of Christ illustrates the difficulty of reading a text free of this sacralizing tendency.

A third problem in dealing with a sacred fable is that it must be made to bear theological or spiritual freight. It must mean more than the events themselves. Frequently the artist meets this demand by a resort to dramatic irony of the "had-we-but-known!" kind, underplaying the events while hinting at their cosmic significance. T. S. Eliot's "The Magi" is an example of the type, as are "Triptych for the Living" and other poems in *The Crooked Lines of God*. The generalizing of "The Flight in the Desert" illustrates the point:

> This was the first of his goings forth into the wilderness of
>   the world.
> There was much to follow: much of portent, much of dread.
> But what was so meek then and so mere, so slight and
>   strengthless,
> (Too tender, almost, to be touched)—what they nervously
>   guarded
> Guarded them. As we, each day, from the lifted chalice,
> That fragile Bread the mildest tongue subsumes,
> To be taken out in the blatant kingdom,
> Where Herod sweats, and his deft henchmen
> Riffle the tabloids—that keeps us.

The look forward here requires turning the infant Jesus and Herod into symbols at the cost of their humanity. So much is made of the deeper significance of the flight into the desert that we lose sight of the personal drama, and even the final stanza, picturing the Holy Family around a campfire while Jesus feeds at his mother's breast, fails to persuade us that these are real people. Anyone reflecting on his sacred stories will discern in them both a universal and individual significance; seeing the world's history and the history of his own life converging in each story. It is harder to recognize that what gives them their vigor is that they are first of all the history of the people they speak about. In "Gethsemani" Brother Antoninus describes Christ fainting with fear as he contemplates the approaching crucifixion. The language is vivid and excites our compassion, but then the theological tidying-up begins. "Power has proved his Godhead," the poet says

> But that the God was man,
> That the man could faint,
> This the world must know.

The human suffering becomes an object lesson and loses its credibility in the process. "Whatever the world will suffer / Is here foresuffered now." The second and third parts of this long poem become steadily more discursive and correspondingly less interesting poetically. Rhetorical questions and exclamations become the chief devices for importing excitement into the poem. Finally the object lesson swallows everything else.

His subject has deep importance to Brother Antoninus, and he clearly has brought to it a wealth of reading and reflection. He is personally engaged throughout the work, but the poem is not personal and fails to engage the reader personally, for where there should be discovery and revelation, there is only explication.

When Coleridge published his "Reflections on Having Left a Place of Retirement," he attached to it the epigraph *sermoni propriora*, "in his own voice," which Charles Lamb preferred to translate as "properer for a sermon." For though Coleridge was deeply engaged with his reflections— tentative religious opinions and ideas and resolutions for future action— poetic form was more a convenience than a necessity for them. For the poet to speak "in his own voice" will not make the result poetry, if the voice he uses is a schoolteacher's or the village explainer's. A constant difficulty with Brother Antoninus's poetry is precisely that what matters most to him, what brought him to his faith and his vocation as a Dominican Friar, cannot be directly translated into poetry. When he speaks sermoni propriora as a Dominican, what he says may be "properer for a sermon." At least, in the practice of his art, a tension actually exists between the demands of form and those of content.

The short, choppy line and a largely Anglo-Saxon vocabulary characterized Brother Antoninus's pre-Catholic poetry, as it does much of his later work. In *The Crooked Lines of God* he also tries a number of canticles, songlike poems composed in long, flowing lines. Here the influence of Catholic liturgy is most clearly seen, but it is enriched by other streams which have fed the poet, including Robinson Jeffers, Whitman, and the Song of Songs which has such a direct influence on the liturgy. The long accentual line and loose parallelism of the canticle form offer an ideal medium for one of Antoninus's favorite themes, celebrating the plenitude of nature. His "Canticle to the Waterbirds" in the second section of the book, glories in the creation, symbolized by the strange waterbirds of California. The early stanzas of the poem illustrate what Gerard Manley Hopkins meant when he spoke of "stress" and "idiom," whatever strongly accentuated individuality and set one thing off from another, and "inscape," how the details of external nature reflect an inner, spiritual shape.

> Clack your beaks you cormorants and kittiwakes,
> North on those rock-croppings finger-jutted into the rough
>   Pacific surge;
> You migratory terns and pipers who leave but the temporal
>   clawtrack written on sandbars there of your presence;
>
> . . . .
>
> Break wide your harsh and salt-encrusted beaks unmade for
>   song
> And say a praise up to the Lord.

Detail, difference, individuality, and their beauty take the center of the poem, but once again Antoninus turns from describing things as he sees and loves them to explaining what they are *there* for. And a long, loose line is the worst possible medium for discursive writing: "But mostly it is your way you bear existence wholly within the context of His utter will and are untroubled."

In the final section of his book, Brother Antoninus explores most freely the sensual language and compressed intensity which were common to his earliest poetry. Here he takes his warrant from the Spanish Baroque and particularly from Saint John of the Cross and Saint Teresa of Avila. Saint John can be a particularly lucky influence on a poet still newly converted enough to suffer from scruples about literary creation, for he was able to separate the system-building aspects of his theology from the intense personal experience from which it drew its evidence. *The Ascent to Mount-Carmel* and *The Dark Night of the Soul* are prose treatises on the spiritual life; the poems render the sensual and emotional experience of religious ecstasy. And, as Saint John says in the preface to *The Ascent to Mount-Carmel*, all the stages of the spiritual journey to be explicated in the prose work are revealed in one poem in which the soul perceives itself as the Bride of Christ.

His influences allow Brother Antoninus to write about violence and sex, subjects which have always held a threatening fascination for him. Now he can bring them together, as in his canticle for Mary Magdalene, and speak of "A Savagery of Love." Mary Magdalene's saintly purity, her sacrificial love of Christ, are the redirecting of her sexuality, not its abnegation. The crucifixion becomes truly the Passion of Christ as we view it through her eyes, taking on some of the sexual significance of suffering for love of others. As Mary Magdalene poured out her body for the delight of others, she poured out the oil to anoint Christ's feet and finally pours out her grief at the foot of the cross. As her sexual nature is completed when her body has been penetrated, so Antoninus makes the lance's penetration of Christ's body a symbol for the completion of his passion, love of mankind.

> What plenitude of power in passion loosed,
> When the Christ-love and the Christ-death
> Find the Love-death of the Cross!

If sex and violence threaten Brother Antoninus, following the example of Saint John of the Cross gives him a way to exploit the themes and still keep distance between this poetry and his earlier, pre-Catholic work, for in these poems he imagines himself feminine, receiving the mark of God as the barren doe receives the blaze of the buck. In "A Canticle to the Christ in the Holy Eucharist" he speaks of Christ as the mark, the kill, the wound, and describes himself sucking the wound as a fawn sucks milk from its mother. "Thy word in my heart was the start of the buck that is sourced in the doe." Sexual conquest unites violence and sensuality; when God is the conqueror, the man who must otherwise assert his aggressiveness through sexual conquest may justify his passivity and even pray "Annul in me my manhood, Lord, and make / Me woman-sexed and weak." At the risk of appearing to psychoanalyze or explain away Brother Antoninus's poetry, we may say that these poems of the final section of the book attempt to sublimate material and personal drives which have been the source of both anxiety and intense power in his earlier work. These personal issues are by no means resolved through the poetry, though the intensity of the struggle confirms his wish to change his nature. They are among the most striking of his poems, but they testify eloquently to the constructions which finally shut off the poetic flow with which his conversion began.

Brother Antoninus wanted to create a double work of poetry which would balance out his earlier work. In this plan either his inspiration or God failed him. What stands out clearly is how the claims of the religious life and those of the artistic impulse interact to provide what he calls "creative tension," the "tension which is union."

Whether speaking about the religious life, artistic creation, or the structure of the human psyche, Brother Antoninus always begins with paired opposites: active and contemplative, conscious and unconscious, rational and nonrational, intellect and imagination, male and female. In discussing the tensions which beset the artist in a religious community, he develops an extended and evocative contrast between the institutional and the charismatic. This becomes the key distinction for talking about all the creative tensions he experiences; the tug between these two characterizes the church as well as the individual within it. "Any religion can only develop by refining the tension between its charismatic and institutional elements. . . . When the charismatic finally breaks through an institutional matrix and makes its pronouncement, it brings down upon itself the whole wrath of an almost unconscious terror from the opposite side."

It would be unfair to treat this distinction as an attempt to speak with philosophical precision, for Brother Antoninus is using it to discover how the conflicts and interactions of opposites have fructified his own life and where they have caused paralysis. "Charismatic" as he uses it always roots back to the literal meaning of the word, a divinely inspired gift of supernatural power or a capacity to lead others. The charismatic side he identifies, therefore, with the Dionysian, the irrational, the artistic, the creative, and the mystical. Inwardness, contemplation, and the imagination are all associated with it. "The artist is an imaginative man, and the whole mode of an artist is freedom. The imagination, strictly speaking, knows no laws." The charismatic must always be ambiguous and dangerous; it always threatens to dissipate its gifts in the pursuit of freedom.

For Brother Antoninus the struggle between religion and art seems far less the result of a tension between the charismatic and the institutional, though that plays its part, than between contrary aspects of the charismatic itself. The charisma presses toward fulfillment of its own nature, toward some kind of perfection. Here is the source of a deep conflict within the charismatic as Brother Antoninus understands it, for if the artist fulfills his gift through freedom, the religious man fulfills his through restraint. The Dionysian man, opening himself up to the mystical even at the risk of madness, stands opposed to the contemplative, whose goals are calm vision. "The problem for the spiritual man, the man seeking perfection, is to curb the sensibility; for the artist, to liberate the sensibility." But the artist too seeks perfection of his gifts.

In his interview with David Kherdian [*Six Poets of the San Francisco Renaissance*], however, he describes a complex attitude toward perfection in art. As his poetic craft matured until it became something unconscious, he turned to printing so that he might have another craft to develop in. He speaks of approaching facility in a craft, having it become unconscious, but perfection seems more threatening than encouraging as a goal, perhaps because it suggests a *willed* achievement which consciousness controls. He speaks of perfecting the work as an act of *concretizing* or *memorializing* the craft. "You write a perfect poem, a perfect book of poems, and concretize it in a perfect format established on absolutely authentic materials."

He renounces the search for perfection in either printing or poetry, however, arguing that the norms of perfection finally work against themselves and become a demand for *perfectionism*. "To go beyond it is worse, believe me, than to fail to reach it . . . . What is over-done is more than finished, it is finished off, 'finalized'—the thing that has happened to so much modern poetry." Perfectionism is the violation of the tomb, he says, whereas imperfection, "as for instance in the gash, actually liberates the charisma."

The terms "memorialize," "concretize" have to do primarily with finding the right form for what he wants to do or say in art. But form means something more than patterns created by technique here, for facility in the craft only signals an intermediate stage in the artist's development. "The craft has to be memorialized in the flesh, and the flesh has to be memorialized in the spirit, the life principle. Then you are free. . . . She, perfection, delivers you." *Perfection, Sophia*, Divine Wisdom, and the Muse become the same figure, the feminine principle, the receptor of the charisma. When he speaks of learning to print, Brother Antoninus speaks of it as having to do with what Jung calls Sensation, the concrete side of experience. He needs first to learn techniques, which means to be straitly confined by them, but only so that at a later point he will have internalized them sufficiently to be free even to violate them. *Form*, whether it derives from a religious commitment, a theological framework, the liturgical year, a schema tracing his conversion through the psychological stages represented by Saint Augustine, Saint Francis, and Saint John of the Cross, or the psychology of Jung, stands over against *technique*. It becomes the synthesis of craft and content for him.

Such an explanation must not be taken to minimize the importance of Antoninus's religious commitment. Whether or not the reader understands why he needs to contain his poems within the frameworks established by the forewords to his books, there can be no doubt that the poet's need for form, in this larger sense, is so genuine that we could not have the poetry without it. And if a number of poems seem deeply flawed because of the framework, others owe their great success to it.

Quite aside from the influence of a religious vocation on the development of his charismatic side, his need for framework would help explain Brother Antoninus's attraction-repulsion for the institutional life. The institution links a solitary person to others; it provides a conventionalized lifestyle which balances the undisciplined life of the charismatic; it develops the intellectual and rational faculties to keep pace with the intuition, emotion, and sensation; finally, it is, in his terms, the *active* life, as over against the contemplative life of the artist.

Especially as the institutional life requires that the individual submit his inspirations to the judgment of the collective, represented both by the tradition and the superior, it also provides such a counterweight to the charismatic that when Brother Antoninus speaks of the "creative tension between the point of view of the superior and the point of view of the subject," he says "That tension is the crucifixion." The point of union for the creative artist in the religious life is a cross, he says elsewhere.

In *The Hazards of Holiness* (1962), the stream of poetry which had been choked out in the early years of his religious vocation flows again, for he had taken as theme the spiritual aridity which shut off poetry. Once again the reader is introduced to the poetry through a foreword which explains it in theological and personal terms. This time the poems are also framed by Jungian psychology.

The foreword is in two senses an apology for the poetry. Antoninus justifies it as "objectification of inner experience" which he calls "the most efficacious of all acts of relief, except prayer," and he appeals to W. B. Yeats for support: "We gaze not at a work of art, but the re-creation of the man through that art." From T. S. Eliot he takes the image of the poet as one who writes to exorcise his demons, not to communicate with others. Brother Antoninus offers poems which seek to *objectify, concretize, or memorialize* his inner experience. His poems represent a victory over himself, and he argues for judging them on that basis.

The second apology seeks to explain away the material from which the poetry comes, for fear that it will seem offensive or blasphemous, especially coming from a Dominican brother. Here he resorts to two explanations, the first an invocation of "that famous Dark Night of the Soul," the second the dream world of depth psychology.

> Against the grain, compounded of the hallucinatory and the obscene, no less than of the transcendental and the sublime, the imagery seeks back against the primordial anguishes, encounters the mute demon and the vocal ghost.

Once again he fights his inner war as a battle to discover a form for his poetry, but once again the form is theological rather than literary. The paired opposites occur again, this time with much greater debt to Jung's psychology, so the tension also exists, but over everything there is the reassurance, *cum permissu Superiorum.*

The Hazards of Holiness has three sections, titled "Friendship and Enmity," "The Dark Face of God," and "Love and Violence." Seven of the poems are introduced by dreams which generated them. A number of others have epigraphs or explanations which link them to the same kind of nonrational source. The dreams are about traveling—on caravan, on pilgrimage, returning for the poet's mother's funeral—and about death. Journeys, darkness, graves and coffins, erotic images and impulses, being swallowed up, dominate the imagery of the dreams.

The relation of freedom and guilt is the theme of both his dream-life and his poetry. "Jacob and the Angel" sets the tone for the entire book. In his dream, the poet is on caravan to the Holy Land but also returning home from exile. He and his guides make camp beside a river, intending to cross over in the morning. He has a dream-within-a-dream that he has come home to his father's house but finds it "deathly vacant"; he wakes to find the caravan gone and the way across the river barred by a tall defender with a rifle. Because he has been used by his guides, who are thieves, the poet is indistinguishable from them and the servant shoots him. As the bullet flies across the distance, "like a meteor from outer space," the poet feels within himself "the whole destiny of the human race in its struggle toward realization, . . . incredibly concretized within my one tormented life-span, and actualized in my very flesh." As he sinks into the water, the poet tries to communicate to the faithful servant "a gesture of desperate truth" to establish "the authentic character of what is real." He does not know whether he has succeeded, but his final affirmation is that the energies within him have been purged and transformed so that the water can have no final power over this "core of absolute existence."

The poem describes the interconnectedness of liberation and guilt in the Jacob story. Jacob the supplanter is driven into exile because of his mother's fondness, but there he sees "the laddered angels in their intercourse with earth,"the liberating sign which frees him "from the mother's death-hug." But then his mother's brother, who tricks him into marrying Leah instead of Rachel, becomes a symbol of guilt. "Deep down the offended father / Lived on symbolic in the maid's evasive sire." Through service to the father-substitute he gains strength to gain the next liberation, receiving another sign of angels that he has become "father-freed." Now he can turn toward home to offer restitution to his brother. Now he meets the angel, whom he mistakes for Esau, and struggles with his twin. This must be both his ultimate restitution and his ultimate liberation; he must both win and lose the battle, for this twin identity is both an angel and Esau's champion.

The poem is very different from the dream. What they have in common is the imagery associated with struggling to cross the stream to confront the defender. The obscure guilt-feelings of the dream, hinted at in images of exile and the vacant family home, ramify in the Jacob myth to include both the poet's parent-child conflict and the theme of fraternal conflict which dominates Genesis. The relationship between dream and poem is such, however, that the latter becomes a Jungian homily on the bible story rather than a re-creation of its meaning.

> One queasy crime—and the score-long exiled years!
> How many mockeries of the inscrutable archetypes
> Must we endure to meet our integration?
> Is it fate or merely malice that has made
> Us overreach our brother in the burdened womb?

The struggle with the angel becomes a symbol of political development and the integration of the personality as aspects of one another. As "the night-wombed nations murmur into birth" while the wrestling match goes on, Jacob's wives, "twin aspects of his dark divided life" huddle in the dark and pray for the outcome. He wins his final liberation, a blessing from the angel, "who seized / In the heart's black hole the angel of intellection," and receives his new name, "Israel, striver with God." Now he can go to his reconciliation with his brother, who recognizes his new nature.

As always, Brother Antoninus is at his best when handling violent language and physical sensation and at his weakest when he makes his fable serve a doctrine. That the doctrine in this case is about the integration of personality makes no difference; it is intrusive on the fable and awkward when poeticized. Nothing in the events in the poem prepares us for the explanation of the struggle with the angels as the calling up of intellection from the unconscious, represented by the "heart's black hole." The language of the poem becomes abstract and sermonic when the theme needs to be explored through physical imagery. The questions are rhetorical in the worst sense—they are neither taken seriously as requests for information nor open enough to make the answers interesting to us.

A number of the poems show the same difficulty of reconciling the discursive and nondiscursive. "Saints," for example is built up of short, choppy lines which convey the emotion through explosives and harsh monosyllables. But the discourse is all orthodoxy.

> Not even God
> Has power to force an evil act
> But man does!

And the reader cannot respond to the emotional tension, no matter how genuine he believes it, in such a line as "God? Saints? Faith? Rapture? Vision? Dream?— / Where?" "The Word" is an example of the most abstract discourse broken up into short lines and made into a kind of shorthand to give the impression of poetry. No physical imagery, no metaphor or simile borrowed from the senses appears in the poem; the reader has nothing to draw him into the poem except the argument, which is as obscure as it is abstract. The poem begins:

> One deepness,
> That mammoth inchoation,
> Nothingness freighted on its terms of void,
> Oblivion abandoned to its selflessness,
> Aching for a clue.

Once more we recognize the energy in the verbals, but they do not take us anywhere. The Word was made flesh and dwelt among us precisely so it need not be so abstract and unavailable to human understanding and perception. Here the senses are utterly starved. What the poem says of the Word would baffle the most severe Platonist. Where he has a metaphor by which he can develop the inner struggle with God, Brother Antoninus can make his craft work for him. "In the Breach," for example, speaks of God as both the killer and the midwife. The reluctance of the child to leave the womb and its compulsion to do so, for the sake of life, work together in his elaboration of the images of birth.

In "A Frost Lay While on California," a dream of finding a raped dead woman and realizing that he had committed the crime stimulates a poem in which the poet engages in a colloquy with God throughout the frozen night. The figures of the woman and the dog, which appear in the dream, become images by which God describes his relationship to the poet. Stanzas alternate in which God speaks and the poet reflects on his inner state and links it to the cold darkness around him, but the power of the poem comes through the poet's reflections, for the begging of God seems diffuse and elaborate—too much what we might imagine ourselves giving him to say in a dialogue we wrote. "I am your image."

> Close your eyes now and be what I am.
> Which is—yourself!
> The *you* who am I!

Operating underneath this inner dialogue, however, is something akin to Coleridge's "silent ministry" of frost. The rain which has been threatening all through the hours of the poet's vigil, comes with the dawn, "a slow spilth of deliverance," breaking up the frost; "it was falling, I knew, out of the terrifying helplessness of God." The poem works because it relies ultimately on natural imagery and the feel of human experience to convey what is happening spiritually, rather than giving us arguments for, or opinions about, the mercy of God.

Brother Antoninus wishes to use his poetry to gain victories over himself, but the best poems, and perhaps the surest victories, are those like "In All These Acts" and "God Germed in Raw Granite," where he focuses his attention on describing the goings-on of nature with all the precise detail he can achieve. Here he might be said to follow the example of Gerard Manley Hopkins, whose finest nature poems grow out of the discovery, *in the scene*, that the Holy Ghost works through it, and whose finest poems about people grow from his discovery that Christ is in each of them. "In All These Acts" chronicles with horrified fascination a wind storm in the forest which tosses logs in "staggering gyrations of splintered kindling." An elk, caught between two crashing logs, is torn open and dies in spasms of agony:

> Arched belly-up and died, the snapped spine
> Half torn out of his peeled back, his hind legs
> Jerking that grasped convulsion, the kick of spasmed life,
> Paunch plowed open, purple entrails
> Disgorged from the basketwork ribs
> Erupting out, splashed sideways, wrapping him
> Gouted in blood, flecked with the brittle sliver of bone.

Vigorous verbs and verbal adjectives, explosive monosyllables, tight linking of words through alliteration and inner rhyme, bring the scene before us in overpowering fashion. But the scene does not stand alone: it parallels the river's violent "frenzy of capitulation" as it destroys itself in "the mother sea." And in a counter movement, the poet describes the salmon leaving the sea about to make their way to the place they were born, to "beat that barbarous beauty out" in their urge to spawn. The elk's death-throes, the river's self-destruction to feed the sea, the salmon's immolation-propagation become symbols of

> the wakeful, vengeful beauty,
> Devolving itself of its whole constraint,
> Erupting as it goes.

The poet sees the ambiguities suggested by *wakeful, vengeful beauty*, implied by the constellation of violence and sex, and he affirms them, seeing Christ in them, "the modes of His forth-showing, / His serene agonization." This is as theologically orthodox as any poem Brother Antoninus has written, but here we believe the insight to have come from the poem itself. Christ does not stand over against this violence; he is not escape from the world of nature or compensation for it. "In all these acts / Christ crouches and seethes." He is the way things are; and fascination with the barbarous beauty expended for the continuation of the race finally turns to affirmation of him.

What makes the poem effective is suggested by the phrase "These are the modes of His forth-showing." The poet argues his poem in the images, and their larger significance arises from this unsentimental look at what they are. To use one of the simplest critical distinctions, the poem has *shown* us, rather than telling us.

Similarly, "God Germed in Raw Granite" shows us through images the emergence of outward shape from inner nature. Word choice and length of line distinctively shape a poem whose theme is shape. Freedom and constraint, expressive form, the tug of paired opposites—all these preoccupations of the poet's life as artist and religious enter the poem through his description of rock, that most fixed and static aspect of the creation. He sees into its source, its germ, "the tortured / Free-flow of lava, the igneous / Instant of conception." The germ is feminine, "Woman within!" and the love of man for woman partakes of the desire for inner coherence and the desire for God.

> In the blind heart's core, when we,
> Well-wedded merge, by Him
> Twained into one and solved there,
> Are these still three? Are three
> So oned, in the full-forthing . . . ?

Theological commitments influence it—e.g., the doctrine of the trinity and the conception of marriage as a type of Christ's love for the Church—but nothing occurs in the poem *because* a doctrine exists to cover such a situation. The wonder of sexual love generates the meditation on the mystery that two can become simultaneously one and three; it requires no explicit reference to liturgy or scripture, no allegorizing of the Song of Songs. We go back to the experience which was the source of the allegory and realize afresh why human love symbolizes the divine.

The Hazards of Holiness is a flawed but powerful book. The flaws seem greatest where the poet cannot let experiences—dreams, temptations, sins, insights—stand by themselves and make their own meanings. The allegorizing spirit lets things stand for other things too easily, especially when a Dominican brother is publishing *cum permissu*.

Brother Antoninus acknowledges that the religious artist also struggles with the inner censor, which may tell him that words and attitudes are unacceptable coming from him. Those elements in his poetry which make for the reader's dissatisfaction even in the most vigorous, deeply felt and sincere poems, carry the cum permissu stamp on them. The retelling of biblical stories—even the bloody tales of John the Baptist and Judith and Holofernes, where his warrant for speaking of sexual enticement is clear— the meditations on saints, the canticles, have been hedged round by explanations from the inner censor. Perhaps the clearest example is "The Song the Body Dreamed in the Spirit's Mad Behest," where the title, an epigraph from the Canticle of Canticles, and a gloss on the imagination introduce the poem in such a way as to neutralize any shock caused by the explicitly sexual imagery.

Speaking of prayer, Martin Buber describes the tension between spontaneity and the subjectivized reflection which assails it. "The assailant is consciousness, the overconsciousness of this man here that he is praying, that he is *praying*, that *he* is praying." A similar overconsciousness seems to operate in Brother Antoninus's poetry: he writes to objectify inner experience and to gain release from inner torment, but he also writes to instruct, to give *exempla* acceptable to his readers, his superiors, but primarily to that inner assailant which tells him he is writing a poem.

Not uncommonly, the worst poems written by an able poet fail not because of a change in subject matter or a change in technique but because they miss the fragile balance between extremes which he accomplishes in his best work. The characteristic techniques and attitudes, the diction and imagery, remain, but reduced to stock response. All the tensions which have shaped Brother Antoninus's poetry stand most starkly opposed in his latest book, *The Rose of Solitude* (1967), but now, under the pressure of his subject or of his obligation to make something affirmatively Christian of it, his poems express the worst emotional excesses and technical gaucheries of which he is capable. He calls the book a love-poem sequence and tells us it is an interior monologue continuing from "In Savage Wastes," which concluded *The Hazards of Holiness*. That poem tells of a monk who returns to the world when a dream shows him that he has not escaped its temptations by fleeing to the desert. His "travail of self-enlightenment" continued in *The Rose of Solitude*.

Behind the poems is a love affair between a monk and a divorced woman, a dancer. When a situation which must not be, is, the suffering is intense. Two kinds of fidelity clash, for each is good and bears the stamp of the divine, yet they are inimical to one another. Breaking the vows is sin, but renouncing the human love is not virtuous; something lies deeper in this conflict which must be worked through for the sake of a more profound understanding of faithfulness.

The man of God and the woman of the world are, from the point of view of the normative consciousness, polar opposites. But like all polar opposites they are drawn together by an ineluctable attraction and mutual fascination, verifying their distinctness each on the other's being. . . . When these inner realities emerge and move together, what happens is an expansion of awareness beyond the code of manners that society has established for either, and a profound crisis in the moral life of two people.

As this passage indicates, two kinds of doctrines will need to find expression and resolution in the poetry, orthodox Catholic theology and Jungian psychology. The handling of dreams in *The Hazards of Holiness* and the interview with David Kherdian would have prepared us for the Jungian emphasis. We can expect, therefore, as the foreword emphasizes, that the masculine-feminine dichotomy will operate on many levels and that a great deal of attention will be given to archetypal figures, images, and relationships.

These ways of ordering experience to comprehend it result in two kinds of poetry in *The Rose of Solitude:* long poem-sequences made up of terse stanzas which are closer to entries in a spiritual diary than they are to lyrics; and long canticles exploiting a long line and loose verse-paragraph in a fashion "half rationale and half celebration." The characteristic weaknesses of each are evident in the book.

Part 1 of the book, "I Nail My Life," made up of three poem-sequences, gives us the data of the relationship. This is the spiritual diary, a documentary account of a developing relationship and the poet's attempt to put it in context. The separate poems are made up of the simplest subject-verb sentences put together in the simplest parallels. While the first poems, in "The Way of Life and the Way of Death," give us the sensual accompaniments of the relationships, the woman's signatures—poinsettias, the flesh of mangoes and guaves, rum—the later ones become increasingly sparse and vacant of sensory imagery.

The canticle form calls for a rich sensual fabric, the piling up of colors, sounds and tastes and luxuriating in them for their association with the loved one. Liturgies derived from the Song of Songs celebrate Mary in the language of a lover. The form tends toward shapelessness and emotional sprawl, however, since it develops out of the loose parallelism of Hebraic poetry and has no necessary conclusion or rounding off. "The Canticle of the Rose" joins emotional sprawl to theological abstraction, asserting as doctrine about the woman he loves what we could, at best, grant only as an extravagant expression of one's personal feelings. As a consequence, we withhold our assent from both the theological and the personal assertions.

> And if I call you great, and if I call you holy, and if I say
>   that even your sins enforce the sheer reality of what
>   you are,
> Know that I speak because in you I gaze on Him, by you I see
> Him breathe, and in your flesh
>   I clasp Him to my breast.

From the first poems, the speaker claims to recognize something redemptive in this relationship; he call it both *necessitum peccatum* and *felix culpa*. The woman becomes a type of Christ, a symbol of divine love, a bearer of grace to be identified through the image of the Rose with the Mother of God. If we are to take all this as unambiguously true, we must then ask what the issue of the book is. Surely the torment of breaking vows must disappear in the light of such a revelation. If that is too simpleminded an approach to take, are we to read the book as we would read other interior monologues—as an account of spiritual development from confusion to clarity, from self-deception to honesty? Such a stance would demand of us a certain ironic detachment and awareness of moral and intellectual ambiguities when the speaker makes extravagant claims for the woman he loves. Nothing in either the poetry or the foreword, however, indicates that the poet wishes us to take the book at anything other than face value.

"My art can err only in insufficiency, my fierce excesses crack on the ineluctable reality of what you are," he insists. To take him seriously on his own terms, therefore, means to indict him for inflating his subject beyond credibility. The poignancy of his forbidden love for a beautiful woman gets lost in the extravagance of his claims for it; she becomes a symbol of divine love the same way the bullfrog became a bull. We might say of the poetry that is has the meaning but missed the experience; events are so rapidly turned into their significance that we lose the feel and texture of experience itself, despite Brother Antoninus's lifelong preoccupation as a poet with the blunt, harsh word, the vigorous verb. Here every noun has its Latinate-sounding adjective; lines and phrases are strung out to prolong a mood of hectic excitement. Striving for the vatic, the poem achieves only the bathetic.

> I have said before:
> All the destinies of the divine
> In her converge.

What creates difficulties in the canticle form operates in the simple poem-sequences as well. Clearly the poet wants to make her a symbol of many things having to do with the opening up of his spiritual life, but once again he runs into difficulties because the psychological-theological form he accepts demands that she be pure archetype. Symbols are built up by slow accretion—the history of the rose in Western literature illustrates the point—not by appropriation. The woman the poet loves does not *participate* in the reality she points to; the middle ground between tenor and vehicle of a metaphor does not exist.

There are poems and passages from poems in *The Rose of Solitude* which move us by their spiritual perception and poetic tact: when the balance is struck, the poetry is effective in Brother Antoninus's characteristic ways. And even when the reader feels obliged to find greatest fault with the poetry, there is never any doubt of the poet's intense sincerity or that he has suffered through everything he writes about. If his poetry achieves the victory over himself that he wishes, we must be grateful for that, and wish him well. But if we bring to our reading the expectation that form and content support each other in such a way that poetic problems are solved poetically and not doctrinally, we must remain dissatisfied with much of Brother Antoninus's work. The inner censor, whether operating from the standpoint of Catholic doctrine or Jungian psychology, closes too many ways to Brother Antoninus; the overconsciousness that tells him he is *writing* imposes too heavy a burden on his work—and perhaps on the man as well. Externally imposed form, which accompanies the cum permissu stamp, wrestles with the material of his life as the angel wrestles Jacob in his poem, with equally unclear results. Among the chief hazards of holiness for him seems to be the incapacity to be free as a poet. His tragedy may be that there can be no final victories in his inner war except at the cost of his poetry.

Covenant of Timelessness and Time: Symbolism and History in Robert Hayden's *Angle of Ascent*

Wilburn Williams, Jr.

The appearance of Robert Hayden's *Angle of Ascent* is something of a problematic event for students of the Afro-American tradition in poetry, for while it gives us occasion to review and pay homage to the best work of one of our finest poets, it insistently calls to mind the appalling tardiness of our recognition of his achievement. A meticulous craftsman whose exacting standards severely limit the amount of his published verse, Robert Hayden has steadily accumulated over the course of three decades a body of poetry so distinctive in character and harmonious in development that its very existence seems more fated than willed, the organic issue of a natural principle rather than the deliberate artifice of a human imagination. But in spite of official honors—Hayden is now the poetry consultant at the Library of Congress and a Fellow of the Academy of American Poets—and a formidable reputation among critics, Hayden has received surprisingly little notice in print. Unless we suffer another of those sad fits of inattention that have so far limited Hayden's readership, *Angle of Ascent* should win for him the regard he has long deserved. With the exception of *Heart-Shape in the Dust*, the apprenticeship collection of 1940, poetry from every previous work of Hayden's is represented here, and we can see clearly the remarkable fertility of the symbolist's union with the historian, the bipolar extremes of Hayden's singular poetic genius.

Robert Hayden is a poet whose symbolistic imagination is intent on divining the shape of a transcendent order of spirit and grace that might redeem a world bent on its own destruction. His memory, assailed by the discontinuities created by its own fallibility, is equally determined to catch

From *Chant of Saints: A Gathering of Afro-American Literature, Art, and Scholarship*, edited by Michael S. Harper and Robert B. Stepto. © 1979 by Wilburn Williams, Jr. University of Illinois Press, 1979.

and preserve every shadow and echo of the actual human experience in which our terribleness stands revealed. In poem after poem Hayden deftly balances the conflicting claims of the ideal and the actual. Spiritual enlightenment in his poetry is never the reward of evasion of material fact. The realities of imagination and the actualities of history are bound together in an alliance that makes neither thinkable without the other. Robert Hayden's poetry proposes that if it is in the higher order of spirit that the gross actualities of life find their true meaning, it is also true that that transcendent realm is meaningful to man only as it is visibly incarnate on the plane of his experience.

Viewed as a theory of poetics, Hayden's characteristic method of composition will hardly strike anyone as unique. His preoccupation with the relationship between natural and spiritual facts puts him squarely in the American tradition emanating from Emerson; we are not at all amazed, therefore, when we find correspondences between his work and that of figures like Dickinson and Melville. The brief lyric "Snow," for instance:

> Smooths and burdens,
> endangers, hardens.
>
> Erases, revises.
> Extemporizes
>
> Vistas of lunar solitude.
> Builds, embellishes a mood

recalls the Dickinson of "It sifts from Leaden Sieves—." But the brooding presence of death lurking behind the brave outward show of a playful wit that is common in Dickinson is uncharacteristic of Hayden, and a comparison with Melville casts more light on his habitual concerns. In "El-Hajj Malik El-Shabazz" Malcolm X is likened to Ahab—"Rejecting Ahab, he was of Ahab's tribe. / 'Strike through the mask!' "—and "The Diver" closely parallels chapter 92 of Melville's *White-Jacket*. To be sure, Hayden's speaker and Melville's narrator are impelled by distinctly different motives. The former's descent is a conscious act, a matter of deliberate choice, whereas White-Jacket's one-hundred-foot fall into a nighttime sea cannot be ascribed to his sensible will, however strong his subconscious longing for death might be. Yet the underlying pattern of each man's ordeal is the same. The approach to death is paradoxically felt as a profound intensification of life. Death takes, or at least seems to promise to take, both men to the very core of life. Thus White-Jacket in his precipitous drop "toward the infallible center of the terraqueous globe" finds all he has seen, read, heard, thought, and felt seemingly "intensified in one fixed idea in [his] soul." Yielding to the soft embrace of the sea, he is shocked into revulsion of death almost purely by chance—"of a sudden some fashionless form" brushes his side, tingling his nerves with the thrill of being alive. In like manner, Hayden's diver's longing to be united with "those hidden ones" in a kind of well-being that lies so deep as to be beyond the reach of articulate speech, his passion to "have / done with self and / every dinning / vain complexity," can be satisfied only if he tears away the mask that sustains his life. The intricate contrapuntal development of the poem brings an overwhelming extremity of feeling to the critical moment that finds the diver poised between life and death. His going down is both easeful and swift, a plunge into water and a flight through air. The flower creatures of the deep flash and shimmer yet are at the same time mere "lost images / fadingly remembered." The dead ship, a lifeless hulk deceptively encrusted with the animate "moss of bryozoans," swarms with forms of life that are themselves voracious instruments of death. And what liberates the diver from this labyrinthine and potentially annihilating swirl of contradictory instincts and perceptions is never clear. As is the case with White-Jacket, he "somehow" begins the "measured rise," no nearer to winning the object of his quest but presumably possessed of a deeper, more disciplined capacity for experience. ("Measured" is decidedly meant to make us think of the poet's subordination to the rules of his craft.)

The most fruitful area of comparison between Hayden and Melville is to be found in their tellingly different attitudes toward the symbolistic enterprise itself. Committed to reconciling within the ambiguous flux of poetic language the warring oppositions created by the divisiveness of discursive logic, the symbolist finds himself necessarily presupposing the very terms of order—subject and object, mind and matter, spirit and nature—his method seeks to erase. Because the symbolist's stance is such a difficult posture to keep, the idea of the artist as acrobat and the conception of his craft as a dance of language are conventional figures in modern literature and criticism. In Hayden, however, the drama of the symbolist's tightrope walk is objectified infrequently. The symbolist's striving for balance is not seen in what Hayden's speakers do but is heard in how they talk: tone assumes the burden that topic might bear. Hayden's characteristically soft-spoken and fluid voice derives much of its power from the evident contrast between the maelstrom of anguish out of which it originates and the quiet reflecting pool of talk into which it is inevitably channeled. Interestingly enough, when Hayden does write poetry in which the action is clearly analogous to the symbolist's task of wizarding a track through a jungle of contraries, the prevailing tone is not his customary seriousness. In "The Performers," the modesty of two high-rise window cleaners subtly mocks the speaker's misuse of their daring as a pretext for a kind of absurd metaphysical strutting that his own desk-bound timidity will not allow. In "The Lions" an animal trainer whose mentality is a peculiar blend of Schopenhauerian wilfulness and transcendentalist vision breaks out into an ebullient speech that is at once divinely rapturous and somehow wildly funny:

And in the kingdom-cage
as I make my lions leap,
   through nimbus-fire leap,
oh, as I see them leap—
   unsparing beauty that
creates and serves my will,
   the savage real that clues
my vision of the real—
   my soul exults and Holy cries
and Holy Holy cries, he said.

Yet whenever Robert Hayden loses his artistic balance, his fall is not likely to be in Melville's direction. The enormous gulf between the unified paradise of the symbolistic imagination and the outright hellishness of a world rife with division, the gulf which drew Ahab and Pierre to their deaths and drowned Melville the writer in silence, poses no threat to Hayden. Hayden's peril comes from a different quarter, and it comes disguised as his salvation. It is precisely Hayden's faith in the ultimate redemptiveness of the universal and timeless order of spirit that threatens to kill the life of his art. Insofar as his poetry is concerned, Hayden's God and Devil are one. The blinding light of faith can shrivel up the sensuous specificity of poetry just as surely as it can enkindle the life of the world of inert fact. Hayden's divergence from Melville here is nowhere more apparent than in "Theme and Variation." Readers of Hayden will recognize the voice of the Heraclitus-like stranger who delivers the poem's wisdom as the poet's own:

I sense, he said, the lurking rush, the sly
transience flickering at the edge of things.
I've spied from the corner of my eye
upon the striptease of reality.

There is, there is, he said, an imminence
that turns to curiosa all I know;
that changes light to rainbow darkness
wherein God waylays and empowers.

Set the above lines against this sentence from the famous last paragraph of "The Whiteness of the Whale" in *Moby-Dick:*

And when we consider that other theory of the natural philoso-
phers, that all other earthly hues—every stately or lovely embla-
zoning—the sweet tinges of sunset skies and woods; yea, and the
gilded velvets of butterflies, and the butterfly cheeks of young
girls; all these are but subtle deceits, not actually inherent in substances, but only laid on from without; so that all deified Nature
absolutely paints like the harlot, whose allurements cover nothing

but the charnel-house within; and when we proceed further, and consider that the mystical cosmetic which produces every one of her hues, the great principle of light, forever remains white or colourless in itself, and if operating without medium upon matter, would touch all objects, evaj tulips and roses, with its own blank tinge—pondering all this, the palsied universe lies before us a leper; and like wilful travellers in Lapland, who refuse to wear coloured and colouring glasses upon their eyes, so the wretched infidel gazes himself blind at the monumental white shroud that wraps all the prospect around him.

Hayden's stranger reverses Ishmael on every point. His perceptions nourish belief: Ishmael's skepticism and doubt. He is pious and Ishmael is blasphemous. Melville's Nature dresses while Hayden's disrobes. The former's adornment is emblematic of a diabolical deceitfulness; the latter's nudity points to a sanctuary of grace. Where Melville's eye strips away delusory hues to gaze in horror upon the "blank tinge" of a "palsied" and leprous universe, Hayden's eye spies out an indwelling spirit that transforms an undifferentiated light into a sacredly tinged darkness wherein man discovers his hope and his blessing. But here Hayden can no more be accused of a naive optimism than Melville can be charged with blind cynicism. The ironic intimation of violent assault reverberating in "waylays" checks the stranger's rush into the plenitude of divine imminence, maintaining the poem's complexity and integrity.

Nevertheless, the point remains that the beneficent banditry of Hayden's divinity has far more in common with the onslaughts of Donne's Three-Personed God than with anything ever done by the maddeningly elusive Jehovah of Melville. Hayden's supreme highwayman is more apt to strip the poet of his facts than to rob him of his faith, which might be heaven for religion but certainly hell for poetry. As much is evident in the increasingly sparing detail and more cryptic utterance that marks the poet's recent work. At his best Hayden composes poetry that is paradoxically both rich in statement and ascetic in temperament. In "Stars" and the Akhenaten section of "Two Egyptian Portrait Masks," however, an abstract and unconvincing expression of acute religious belief shows only a marginal relation to the concrete particularities of human experience. The latter verse segment plainly suffers in contrast to the paean to Nefert-iti that precedes it. Meditating on the carving of a woman

> whose burntout
> loveliness alive in stone
> is like the fire of precious stones
>
> dynastic
> death (gold mask and vulture wings)
> charmed her with so she would never die

the poet tersely harmonizes a succession of discordant sensations. But in the Akhenaten companion piece, the poet's contemplativeness has no equivalent object on which it can focus—admittedly, it would take an extraordinary imagination to bridge the gap between the majesty of Akenaten's dream of human oneness and the fat hips and bloated abdomens of the Pharaoh's Karnak colossi—and consequently the poetry lacks force:

> Aten
> multi-single like the sun
> reflecting Him by Him
>
> reflected.
> Anubis howled. The royal prophet reeled
> under the dazzling weight
>
> of vision,
> exalted—maddened?—the spirit moving
> in his heart: Aten Jahveh Allah God.

Certainly there is nothing in this like the faultless description of death as "dynastic," a brilliant conceit whereby Hayden associates the idea of the unbroken hereditary transfer of power from generation to generation with the eternal dominion of death, thus finding death's very indomitability dependent upon the principle of generation, or life. What Emerson, the one indispensable figure in any discussion of American symbolism, once said about the poet's duty is patently applicable to Robert Hayden, and it can serve both as an accurate representation of what Hayden does in his best work and as a necessary corrective to the etherealizing proclivities of Hayden's symbolist genius:

> The poet, like the electric rod, must reach from a point nearer the sky than all surrounding objects, down to the earth, and into the dark wet soil, or neither is of use. The poet must not only converse with pure thought, but he must demonstrate it almost to the senses. His words must be pictures, his verses must be spheres and cubes, to be seen and smelled and handled.

II

However much we might like to dwell on the manifold possibilities of Hayden's symbolism, particularly in relation to the practices of Yeats and Eliot (to whom he sometimes alludes) and to Auden (whom he has said was a key factor in his growth as a poet), no discussion of his poetry can avoid the question of the place a sense of history occupies in his work. Every reader is quick to detect a pervasive sense of the past and a powerful elegiac strain in his work. In the most thorough examination of Hayden's poetry we have, Charles T. Davis has recounted the crucial contribution of Hayden's extensive research in the slave trade to "Middle Passage," and he has called attention to the importance of Hayden's grasp of the Afro-American folk tradition to "O Daedalus, Fly Away Home," "The Ballad of Nat Turner," and "Runagate Runagate." Aware of the paradox, Hayden has referred to himself as a "romantic realist," a symbolist compelled to be realistic and Michael Harper has called him a "symbolist poet struggling with the facts of history." Now, nothing is perhaps more tempting or more mistaken than to infer from all this that the historian in Hayden is at odds with the symbolist. A close reading of the poetry will not support such a conclusion. Because of the popularity of "Middle Passage" and "Runagate Runagate"—poems unmistakably black in subject matter and sometimes identifiably black in use of language—the historical impulse in Hayden is understandably allied in the minds of many readers with the poet's pride in his own blackness. Since Hayden's recognition of his blackness is widely (and, we think, most aberrantly) perceived as a grudging one, the symbolist in Hayden is often viewed as the enemy of his essentially historical, and black, muse. If that Bob Hayden only knew better, the argument (it is hardly reasoning) goes, he would leave that symbolism stuff alone (the poetry of *The Night-Blooming Cereus,* for example) and get back to his roots. Certainly Hayden's insistence that he be judged as a poet and not as a Negro poet only exacerbates this misapprehension, and no appeal to the extensive exploitation of symbolism in the spirituals and the blues is likely to quiet the suspicion that Hayden's symbolist clings parasitically to the creativity of his black historian.

But while it is easy to see that the symbolistic method is operative in poems as disparate as "Middle Passage" and "The Night-Blooming Cereus," it is not so evident that Hayden's historical sensibility is also at work in poems that have no obvious connection with historical incidents. To apprehend the unity of Hayden's entire body of work, it is necessary to understand that his fascination with history is but one part of a more comprehensive entrancement in the mystery of time. Robert Hayden is clearly more intrigued by the process of change, the paradoxes of permanence and evanescence, than the particular substances that undergo change. Here we are interested in the psychological and artistic implications of his dramatic re-creations of historical events, and not just in the nature of the events themselves. Throughout the poetry of Hayden we encounter a memory and an imagination pitted against the losses time's passage inevitably entails. We meet a consciousness struggling to retain the finest nuances of its own experience and seeking to enter into the experience of others from whom it is alienated by time and space. The fundamental source of Hayden's productivity, the wellspring of his poetic activity, lies in the ability of the human memory to negotiate the distance between time past and time present and the capacity of a profoundly sympathetic imagination to transcend the space between self and other. The complex interactions generated by the life of memory and imagination define the basic unity of Hayden's work.

But while we think that Hayden's obsession with time is, in a sense, larger than his deep involvement in the Afro-American past, it would be foolish to deny the special place black American history occupies in his development as a poet. The 1940s, the years in which Hayden patiently studied the annals of his black past, are also the years in which he matured as artist. To simply live in a culture with a sense of the past as notoriously shallow as this one's is burden enough. A black like Hayden, the fierceness of whose need to know his history is matched only by the ponderousness of the mass of distortion and fabrication under which his past lies buried, finds that even the truthful accounts of the black American experience, which cannot really take him farther back than the eighteenth century anyway, give him the composite picture of a collectivity, rather than detailed portraits of individuals. It can hardly seem an accident to him that historians have until recently slighted the value of the slave narratives, documents that shake him with a revelation more awesome than any truth contained in the most complete compilation of data seen even in the wildest dreams of the maddest cliometrician. When he looks at his mental picture of Representative Afro-American Man, he sees that it is a mosaic formed of bits of the lives of many men, and there are moments when he wonders whether the portrait typifies the truth of art or the deceit of artifice. The face is formed of fragments themselves faceless; the sacred text of his people's experience an accretion of footnotes culled from the profane texts of another's. His past is pregnant with a significance that it is incapable of giving birth to. It is a speechless past peopled with renowned personalities who are ironically impersonal:

> Name in a footnote. Faceless name.
> Moot hero shrouded in Betsy Ross
> and Garvey flags—propped up
> by bayonets, forever falling.
>   ("Crispus Attucks")

Viewed in this somber light, the primary significance of Hayden's famous poems of Cinquez, Turner, Tubman, and Douglass resides in the poet's imaginative attempt to reforge his present's broken links with the past. The past, Hayden says, need not be past at all. His speakers confront their history as active participants in its making, and not as distant onlookers bemoaning their isolation; the past is carried into the present. Although the poet's mind ventures backward in time, the poems themselves invariably close with a statement or action that points forward to the reader's present. The progress of "Middle Passage" is through death "to life upon these shores," and the reader leaves the poem with his attention riveted to *this* life on *these* shores just as much as it is fixed on the historical reality of the slave trade. The man we leave at the conclusion of "The Ballad of Nat Turner" has his revolution still before him. "Runagate Runagate" ends with an invitation, "Come ride-a my train," whose rhythm subtly anticipates the action to be undertaken, and the powerful assertion of yet another intention to act—"Mean mean mean to be free." The accentual sonnet to Frederick Douglass is poetry that moves like the beating of a living heart. The poet emphasizes that the dead hero is still a vital force. The first long periodic sentence seems to resist coming to an end. The poem celebrates not a man who has been, but a man still coming into being. Although commemorative in nature, it does not so much elegize a past as prophesy a future. Frederick Douglass, the poet, and all enslaved humanity are united in one generative process:

> When it is finally ours, this freedom, this liberty, this
> > beautiful
> and terrible thing, needful to man as air,
> usable as earth; when it belongs at last to all,
> when it is truly instinct, brain matter, diastole, systole,
> reflex action; when it is finally won; when it is more
> than the gaudy mumbo jumbo of politicians:
> this man, this Douglass, this former slave, this Negro
> beaten to his knees, exiled, visioning a world
> where none is lonely, none hunted, alien,
> this man, superb in love and logic, this man
> shall be remembered. Oh, not with statues' rhetoric,
> not with legends and poems and wreaths of bronze alone,
> but with the lives grown out of his life, the lives
> fleshing his dream of the beautiful, needful thing.

A great deal of Hayden's success in undoing the dislocations of time and space can be attributed to his poet-speakers' uncanny ability to give themselves over to the actuality they contemplate. They become what they behold; known object and knowing subject unite. Like psychic mediums, his speakers obliterate distinctions between self and other; the dead and distant take possession of their voices. Take for example these lines from "The Dream (1863)":

> That evening Sinda thought she heard the drums
> and hobbled from her cabin to the yard.
> > The quarters now were lonely-still in willow dusk
> after the morning's ragged jubilo,
> > when laughing crying singing the folks went off
> with Marse Lincum's soldier boys.
> > But Sinda hiding would not follow them: those
> Buckras with their ornery
> > funning, cussed commands, oh they were not were
> > not
> the hosts the dream had promised her.

The poem is obviously a third-person narrative, but the space separating narrator and actor is frequently violated. The speaker's voice modulates effortlessly into the cadences of the slaves. "Marse Lincum," "Buckra," and "ornery" are words heard in the accents of the slaves. The pathos of the cry "oh they were not were not" is so extraordinary because, syntax notwithstanding, it is Sinda's own voice we hear, and not the poet's. In six lines in "The Rabbi" Hayden gives a virtuoso demonstration of the resources of his voice:

> And I learned schwartze too
>
> And schnapps, which schwartzes bought
> on credit from "Jew Baby."
> Tippling ironists laughed and said
> he'd soon be rich as Rothschild
>
> From their swinish Saturdays.

In the first two lines the poet's retrospective view of the blacks of his youth is clearly refracted through the cultural lens of the Jews he knew. By the end of the third line, however, his perspective has shifted, and it is now the Jews who are being looked upon from a black point of view. "Credit" is the pivotal term in this transition, for it not only allows the speaker to describe objectively the economic relationship of black to Jew but also lets him draw on the powerful connotations this word has in the Afro-American speech community. The last three lines of indirect quotation, framed by two jocularly incongruous phrases that are clearly of the poet's own making, indicate that the speaker finally assumes an amused posture independent of the viewpoint of either black or Jew, but remarkably sensitive to both. And there is a social morality implicit in this display of Hayden's multivocal talents. What might at first seem to be merely a technical device has enormous ethical implications. When the poet says in the last stanza,

> But the synagogue became
> New Calvary.
> The rabbi bore my friends off
> in his prayer shawl

he means for us to see that the loss of his childhood friends Hirschel and Molly is part of a wholesale separation of black and Jew, a separation that will brook no opposition from considerations as flimsy as one human being's love for another. "New Calvary," tellingly isolated in a single line, is not only the name of the black church that succeeds the synagogue. It represents too a place and an action. It is the hill where Christianity and Jewry part ways, the site where Hayden's ideal of human oneness is sacrificed, a modern reenactment of that old attempt at redemption that ironically, bitterly, only sped man in his fall out of unity into division.

But there is a sinister dimension to this intercourse between self and other, present and past. Robert Hayden knows, and this is a sign of his strength, that openness is also vulnerability, that the past in which one finds possibilities of inspiration and renewal can exert a malignant influence on the present. In "A Ballad of Remembrance" the poet is besieged by specters pressing upon him the value of their individual adaptations to American racism. The Zulu King urges accommodation, the gunmetal priestess preaches hate, and a motley contingent of saints, angels, and mermaids, blind to the realities of evil, chime out a song of naive love. These competing voices drive the poet to the brink of madness. In "Tour 5" an autumn ride into the country becomes a frightening excursion into a surreal world alive with ancient conflicts between black, white, and red men. In "Locus" the Southland lies wasted under the blight of its own history. The present abdicates to the superior force of the past. The redbuds are "like momentary trees / of an illusionist"; there is a "violent metamorphosis, / with every blossom turning / deadly and memorial soldiers." Life here is stunted, reality the bondsman of a dream of disaster. The past forecloses its mortgage on the future:

> Here spareness, rankness, harsh
> brilliances; beauty of what's hardbitten,
> knotted, stinted, flourishing
>   in despite, on thorny meagerness
> thriving, twisting into grace.
> Here symbol houses
> where the brutal dream lives out its lengthy
> dying. Here the past, adored and
>   unforgiven. Here the past—
> soulscape, Old Testament battleground
> of warring shades whose weapons kill.

Closely related to Hayden's interest in the cunning ironies of history is his anxiety for the fate of myth and religion in the modern world. This concern provides the motivation of some of his best poetry. Take "Full Moon," for example, which we quote in full:

> No longer throne of a goddess to whom we pray,
> no longer the bubble house of childhood's
> tumbling Mother Goose man,
>
> The emphatic moon ascends—
> the brilliant challenger of rocket experts,
> the white hope of communications men.
>
> Some I love who are dead
> were watchers of the moon and knew its lore;
> planted seeds, trimmed their hair,
>
> Pierced their ears for gold hoop earrings
> as it waxed or waned.
> It shines tonight upon their graves.

And burned in the garden of Gethsemane,
its light made holy by the dazzling tears
with which it mingled.

And spread its radiance on the exile's path
of Him who was the Glorious One,
its light made holy by His holiness.

Already a mooted goal and tomorrow perhaps
an arms base, a livid sector,
the full moon dominates the dark.

The world we encounter here is radically impoverished. The slow process by which the rise of positivistic science has emptied Nature of all religious significance is recapitulated in the fall of childhood's illusions before the advance of adult skepticism. For contemporary man, the moon exists only as a means of flaunting the triumphs of his technological vanity. But the poet seems in this diminished moon an analogue to the deprivations death has exacted from him, and with this crucial recognition of a mutuality of fates begins the movement toward recovery. Like the breathtaking expansion of meaning we witness in Eliot's "Sweeney among the Nightingales" when we leap from the nightingales "singing near / The Convent of the Sacred Heart" to those that "sang within the bloody wood / When Agamemnon cried aloud," there is a startling intensification of feeling in the transition from a light that "shines tonight upon their graves" to the light that "burned in the garden of Gethsemane." But Hayden knows that this age looks upon Jesus Christ and the prophet Baha'u'llah (The Glorious One of the penultimate stanza and the founder of Hayden's Baha'i faith) with a cynical regard, and that any appeal to them to restore the significance of a degraded Nature would sound highly artificial and entirely unconvincing. Like Flannery O'Connor, who frequently discerns in overt denials of faith ironic avowals of the existence of God, Hayden subverts the materialism of technology to make a claim for the reality of spirit. The moon that is now meaningless will once again become all-meaningful, he says, not as the throne of a benign deity or as an object of harmless childish fancies, but as an arms base that can end all life. The meaning that has been lost to the achievement of science reasserts itself with a vengeance by means of that very same achievement. This ironic turn of events is itself fully in keeping with the traditional view of the moon as the symbol of eternal recurrence. The full weight of this paradox is felt in the critical word "livid," on which a whole world of ambiguities turns. As meaning ashen or pallid, livid is both a forthright description of a full moon and suggestive of the moon's fearful retreat before the press of technology. As meaning black and blue, livid, in conjunction with the reference to the moon as "the white hope of communications men," suggests a moon bruised and discolored by the assaults of the Jack Johnsons of science. As a synonym for enraged or angry, livid further elaborates upon the implied meanings of this prize-fighting metaphor, and, by connecting it to the ominous possibilities of the moon's use as an arms base, subtly transforms the earlier reference to the moon as victim into an image of the moon as aggressor. And when we finally consider livid as meaning red, that satellite's consequence as an object of martial reverence is fully revealed, for the red moon is the moon foreseen by John of Patmos, and its appearance announces the coming of God in his wrath, the destruction of nations and the end of time.

III

When we review the entire course of Hayden's development, the importance of the poet as historian seems to lessen drastically over time. In his last two volumes of verse, only "Beginnings" immediately strikes us as aspiring to the largeness of historical vision of a "Full Moon" or the early explorations of the Afro-American past for which Hayden is chiefly known. What we feel is responsible for this change is not something so simple as the symbolist's displacement of the historian, but a growing preoccupation in the historian with ever smaller units of time. Having exhausted his examination of the problematic interactions of present and past, Hayden's historian is free to chronicle the mystery of change itself. Instead of feeling obliged to overcome the effects of change, he is more and more fascinated by single moments of metamorphosis. This is clearly the case in the poetry of *The Night-Blooming Cereus*. Standing before the "Arachne" of the black sculptor Richard Hunt, the poet is transfixed by the impenetrable mystery of the total change of essence he witnesses. At the same time his language manages to evoke Arachne's terror, it confesses, by the violent juxtaposition of concepts of motion and stasis, the human and the animal, birth and death, the singular incapacity of rational terms to represent adequately such an event:

> In goggling terror fleeing powerless to flee
> Arachne not yet arachnid and no longer woman
> in the moment's centrifuge of dying
> becoming.

The capacity of short-lived and seemingly trivial events to manifest truths of exceptional import is shown in "The Night-Blooming Cereus." The speaker initially anticipates the blooming of that flower with a casual disregard for the miracle it will actually be. He and his companion are, in effect, two decadent intellectuals whose interest in the "primitive" is really just a shallow trafficking in the exotic. For them the blossoming sanctions hedonistic indulgence: they will paint themselves and "dance / in honor of archaic mysteries." Yet so much more than they can possibly imagine depends on the appearance of that blossom. When the bud unfolds, the phenomenon of its transformation enlarges into the enigma of eternal re-currence, the riddle of the cyclical alternation of life and death. And the blasphemous are reduced to near speechlessness:

> Lunar presence
> foredoomed, already dying,
> it charged the room
> with plangency
>
> older than human
> cries, ancient as prayers
> invoking Osiris, Krishna,
> Tezcatlipoca.
>
> We spoke
> in whispers when
> we spoke
> at all.

Just as Hayden's historian's engrossment with the epochal modulates into an absorption with the momentary, there is a parallel shift of his focus away from the history of a people to the biographies of individuals, away from the public figures of the past to persons who are the poet's contemporaries. The boxer Tiger Flowers and the artist Betsy Graves Reyneau take the place of Nat Turner and Harriet Tubman. If the personages that engage him impress us as having little relation to the main currents of our history, they clearly arouse anxieties in him that nothing less than a total reconsideration of the nature of history itself can assuage. Just as Hayden's early historian is compelled to personalize the past he confronts, his later one is compelled to objectivize his own subjectivity. His private anguish never locks him into the sterile deadend of solipsism; it impels him outward into the world. "The Peacock Room," Hayden tells us, grew out of an intense emotional experience. A visit to that room designed by Whistler excited painful recollections of his dead friend Betsy Graves Reyneau, who had been given a party in the same room on her twelfth birthday. Contemplating the rival claims of art and life,

> Ars Longa   Which is crueller
> Vita Brevis   life or art?

the poet seeks shelter in Whistler's "lyric space," as he once did in the glow "of the lamp shaped like a rose" his "mother would light / . . . some nights to keep / Raw-Head-And-Bloody-Bones away." But he knows that the dreadful facts of the nightmare that is our history—"Hiroshima Watts My Lai"—scorn "the vision chambered in gold." The very title of the poem, however, has already hinted that his meditations will not issue into a simplistic espousal of art's advantages over life. The peacock is an ambiguous figure. The legendary incorruptibility of the bird's flesh has led to its adoption as a type of immortality and an image of the Resurrected Christ; but as the emblem of Pride, the root of all evil, the bird has always had ominous connotations in Christian culture. These intimations of evil remind the poet of the artist driven mad by Whistler's triumph, and the Peacock Room is transformed in his mind from sanctuary to chamber of horrors. The echoes of Stevens's "Domination of Black" and Poe's "Raven" heighten the poet's fears:

> With shadow cries
>
> the peacocks flutter down,
> their spread tails concealing her,
>   then folding, drooping to reveal
> her eyeless, old—Med School
> cadaver, flesh-object
>   pickled in formaldehyde,
> who was artist, compassionate,
> clear-eyed. Who was belovéd friend.
>   No more. No more.

The paradox of a lasting art that mocks man's fragility at the same time that it realizes his dream of immortality is resolved in the beatific, enigmatic smile of the Bodhisattva ("one whose being—sattva—is enlightenment—bodhi"):

> What is art?
> What is life?
>   What the Peacock Room?
> Rose-leaves and ashes drift
> its portals, gently spinning toward
>   a bronze Bodhisattva's ancient smile.

In a remarkable way, "Beginnings," the first poem of *Angle of Ascent*, re-enacts the course of the fruitful collaboration of Hayden's historian and symbolist. The historian summons up the essential facts of the poet's ancestry, and the symbolist immediately translates them into the terms of art:

> Plowdens, Finns,
> Sheffeys, Haydens,
> Westerfields.
>
> Pennsylvania gothic,
> Kentucky homespun,
> Virginia baroque.

As the poem moves forward in time, the ancestors are particularized. Joe Finn appears "to join Abe Lincoln's men" and "disappears into his name." Greatgrandma Easter lingers longer before the poet's gaze, and she is remembered not for the role she took in an historic conflict, but for her individual qualities: "She was more than six feet tall. At ninety could / still chop and tote firewood." The progression toward individuation that accompanies the poem's movement to the present—the sharpness of focus of the portrait of an ancestor is a direct function of that ancestor's nearness to the poet's own present—is paralleled by a growth in the poet's awareness of the figurative possibilities of language. As the historian's field of view contracts, the symbolist's artfulness becomes increasingly apparent. As we move from summaries of the entire lives of Joe Finn and Greatgrandma Easter to select moments in the lives of the poet's aunts, the symbolist's reveling in words for the beauty of their sound and rhythm becomes more evident:

> Melissabelle and Sarah Jane
> oh they took all the prizes one Hallowe'en.
> And we'll let the calico curtain fall
> on Pocahontas and the Corncob Queen
> dancing the figures the callers call—
> Sashay, ladies, promenade, all.

But when the poet himself finally appears, a curious—but, for Robert Hayden, characteristic—change occurs. The historian reasserts his centrality (the concluding piece is called "The Crystal Cave Elegy"), and the poem's steady flow toward life and the present is momentarily reversed in commemoration of the death of the miner Floyd Collins. The symbolist's increasing involvement in the resources of his art does not end in an autistic preoccupation with the poet's inner life but finally turns outward in prayer for the liberation of Collins. The timeless paradise of the imagination is invoked to release humanity from the limitations of time:

> Poor game loner
> trapped in the rock
> of Crystal Cave, as
> once in Kentucky coal-
> mine dark (I taste the
> darkness yet)
> my greenhorn dream of
> life. Alive down there
> in his grave. Open
> for him, blue door.

The province of the poet is neither the realist's moonscape of inert matter nor the romantic's starfire of pure spirit, but the middle kingdom of actual earth that unites the two. Robert Hayden's symbolist and historian long ago joined hands to seize this fertile territory as their own. Together they have kept it up very well.

Homage to Schubert the Poet

Irvin Ehrenpreis

The direction of David Schubert's best work is toward making poetry out of the inexpressible. Typically, the poet turns on himself as he tries to speak, and smiles at the effort to render attitudes so deeply ironical that the language must take one step back for every two steps forward. Schubert is allergic to clichés but feels challenged by the task of incorporating banalities into the life of the imagination.

A poem opens, "A ghastly ordeal it was." The words plainly fail to convey the emotion; but the reason is that they spring from the younger self, whose ordeal is the theme of the poem. They suggest the rawness of youth, and the mature poet replies with the subtler style of the accomplished writer: "In / Retrospect, I am no longer young."

Now analyzing his consciousness, the poet observes his younger self as if he were pondering a sexual attachment:

> Wise, sad, as unhappy as seeing
> Someone you love, with whom life has
> Brought suffering, or someone you
> Have nothing in common with, yet love,—
> Unable to speak a word.

The echo of "Gerontion" joins the fecklessness of the youth to the inadequacy of the poet's speech.

The poem is called, "No Title," being about the formation of the poet's character, which is of course still unformed. The younger self remains in the older, an object of sympathy but not a person that one can help. Inarticulately, the poet witnesses the pain he has not left behind. Try as he will, he cannot console the sad boy that he was.

From *Quarterly Review of Literature: David Schubert, Works and Days* (40th Anniversary Issue). © 1983 by *Quarterly Review of Literature*.

His genius, like the figure of the discus thrower, stays too, always ready to act, never acting. Maturity has brought a degree of knowledge. The suffering can therefore become the material of art. But the boy, out of touch, keeps his sadness—also like an unchanging Greek statue:

> I stood there on 42nd Street and
> Eighth Avenue. I stood there with two
> Nickels.

The memory of poverty recalls the insubstantiality of accomplishment. With his wiser and better fulfilled character, he yet remains, like all artists, ever on the brink of poverty: "How little space there is / Between success and nothing at all." Having echoed Eliot near the start, he echoes Shakespeare near the end. As if exorcising the ghost of youthful frustration, he contemplates the old (that is, the young) but also present self, like Lear unable to revive Cordelia:

> Never. Never. Never. Never. Never.
>   Shall I stand spellbound by the
> Reiteration's disaster?
>   No! What is
> Over is over.

Only, of course, it is not.

At the same time as language defeats Schubert, it is also his salvation. In a poem called "Corsage" he plays with the etymological pun of "pansy-pensee," and echoes Wallace Stevens. Once more, the gap between experience and expression is the theme. Asked by a young lady for an account of himself, the poet can only voice a cliché; for how could he possibly tell her of the savage nightmare that constituted his early years? Fortunately, she acts out his consolation, because she meets him a day later with an image of hope:

> The next day you wore a
> Corsage of pansies.
> Exultantly alive, serious scholars
> Of melancholy, brave and lionhearted
> With thoughtful thoughts.

So he changes what might be called his thoughtless (or unthinkable) thoughts, and allows the blossoms to absorb him, "These pansies, profoundest / Professors of the world's woes." The alliteration suggests the rich color of the flowers; and again "professor" suggests (by etymology) not only a scholar but a speaker aloud of the poet's sadness, to which the pansies give the adequate expression that his words (so he says) cannot. The poet too must transform bleak moods into seductive verse. His congenital gloom must give way to gladness.

The symbolist techniques which have kept Schubert's work from fading, depend on such a movement from despair to exultation. Those techniques make the poems obscure but alluring, and responsive to continual rereading. Behind the devices of art there is also a peculiar view of human development. According to this, childhood, painful and secretive, sets the boy or girl yearning for an exalted, colorful style of life such as one glimpses in fairy tales, in carnivals, and in those moments of unexpected pleasure that even a deprived youth encounters. But adulthood betrays the dreamer. Its tedium and disappointments provoke regrets over the passing of the hopeful years, delicious in retrospect because ultimate despair and disillusionment had not yet infused themselves into the poet's character.

"Kind Valentine" is a splendid accomplishment—compact, obscure, and dramatic. The poet seems to be presenting a girl in various stages of her short life, all seen together as one might scan one's entire existence at the moment of dying. Joanne as a sad child, then as a girl dangerously in love, next as a psychotic mourning the loss of her mysterious lover, and so as a suicide and at last as a corpse, all appear at the same time, because the poet shifts rapidly among the phases of a pathetic career.

The imagery is dense but not clotted. Joanne, herself a flower, seems vulnerable and brief in blooming. The white rose given her by the beloved fades significantly as she breathes on it; and the poem will close with an evocation of violets and forget-me-nots suggesting the devotion the lonely girl had for the lover who abandoned her. (They also recall Ophelia.)

In the lines which Schubert employs on Joanne as a child, she goes to bed and dreams of herself as the sleeping beauty. But in the course of the poem, Prince Charming wakens her from sleep only to drive her to self-destruction. Meeting the challenge of banality, the poet is careful to indicate his own remoteness from the commonplace desires and disappointments of Joanne. Yet his sympathy is never condescending. One suspects that he considers his own aspirations to be as childish in their way as those of Joanne. The end of the poem offers us a stunning combination of fellow-feeling and evocative imagery, rich patterns of sound, and unpretentious, exquisite language. The rhymes, like the images, bring out the conventionality of the girl's imagination. But the tone of the poet could not be more tender:

> Please, star-bright,
> First I see, while in the night
> A soft-voiced, like a tear, guitar—
> It calls a palm coast from afar.
> And oh, so far the stars were there
> For him to hang upon her hair
> Like the white rose he gave, white hot,
> While the low sobbing band—it wept
> Violets and forget-me-nots.

In other poems Schubert again draws an ironic parallel between the hackneyed or vulgar longings of ordinary people to escape from routine and the desire of the poet for high esthetic self-realization. The impossibility of achieving this supernal existence is suggested by a title, "When Apples on the Lilac"; for of course apples neither grow on lilacs nor mature when lilacs blossom. The same poem opens with a list of carnival attractions that inserts surprising invitations among the familiar brass band and coconut shy:

> DANCE WITH FRIENDS IN THE EVENING!
> WITH THE TRUNKLESS MAN IN THE MOON!
> SEDUCTIVE TUNES! IRRESISTIBLE ORCHESTRA! SAIL
> FOR THE BALI ISLES IN A DINNER PAIL!

Among the echoes of "The Owl and the Pussy-Cat" we suddenly find ourselves in the mind of a poet as he recalls those moments of childhood when the note of romance interrupted the drone of the ordinary world. In a brilliant image Schubert brings together the poem he is writing and the false promises of a boy's fantasy: "The paper airplane sinks, freighted with lies—"

The poem actually is a set of modulations declining from the cheerful invitations of the opening lines to a bitter allusion to Dante—the last words of *Paradiso*—at the close. (Triple rhymes suggest terza rima.)

> And pity like an adolescent cries
> —Crossing the street—self-conscious awkward tears
> For love! . . . Love that moved the stars
> Begs at the corner and a hag's face wears.

We remember that Schubert did his work during the Great Depression, and that his own suffering was not merely private but an element in the agony of a nation.

Schubert gives us his theory of the imagination in a poem of extraordinary power, "Midston House." Since he conceives of himself primarily as an embodiment of creative imagination, the poet must elevate common experience into emblems of the esthetic faculty at work. He must, Schubert says, take the humdrum of tedious routine and transform it into a luminous figure of creative power. At the same time the poem is a revelation of the inner self; it is a means of saying what could not otherwise be told about one's deepest feelings.

Not only does Schubert elaborate his symbolist theory in "Midston House," but he also puts it brilliantly to work. When he turns on the electric light in an unpleasant room (dull reality) at the beginning of the poem, he produces an artistic insight at the same time: the two senses of illumination operate together.

> What is needed is a technique
> Of conversation, I think, as I put on the
> Electric light.

The movement of poetry then must be in appearance the random movement of conversation—not, however, the narrow vocabulary of the surface "irritations which pile up" but rather the expression, "Metamorphosed, of what they are the / Metaphor of; / and their conversion into light."

In section two of the poem, Schubert finds himself on a bus, going to an appointment in a hotel; and he notices how unexciting the people seem, caught as they are by "the insurance of habit," which the poet must break through. Like the relaxed but drab citizens, he is not fulfilling his own promise of talent. In section three he asks,

> Yet how to transform
> The continual falling clouds of
> Energy, into light?

He hopes that the man who will meet him may know how to effect transformation. The poet sounds as if he has just lost a job that interfered with the composition of his poetry. The gloom and bitterness that the failure has fed reveal his uncertainty about his true vocation—the career of writing. The appointment seems to be for the discussion of a new job. The poet fears that the man—of "vital intelligence"—will not show up, even as he fears losing the inspiration that awakens his genius.

But the man does appear; the conversation is highly satisfactory; and the meeting even approaches, in effect, a religious experience, although the two men indelicately talk of the faults of a third, whose unworthiness the poet is afraid that he himself may share. This suspicion leads to a fresh insight:

> But the poem is just this
> Speaking of what cannot be said
> To the person I want to say it.

So the man of vital intelligence is like a messenger from the realm of the imagination, one of Rilke's angels.

Evidently, the poet secures the new position, which will support his creative talent and will also connect him with the man "Whose handshake was happiness." The future, consequently, is like a bus ride, taking him away from the cramped room, dark and lonely, of his deprived existence— the place where the poem began: "On the vehicle, Tomorrow, I will see / That man, whose handshake was happiness."

With such a view of art, the poet can define himself through an imaginative act of identification with just those persons who seem to lack color and originality. In the end, it is they, and the common things of their environment, that must be exalted. So the seasons of the year become symbols of the stages of poetic abundance and drought, against which appropriate figures—sailors, girls, a beggar—evoke the loss or triumph of inspiration. Emotional states and moral principles join the cycle. As a result, such articles as selfishness and a lovers' quarrel, or winter and a want of creative energy, can be associated by the poet. It is Schubert's task to transmute them.

In the poem, "The Meaning of Winter," the speaker is in a wintry phase; and consequently, he gives the job of imaginative transformation to a friend, who does the work of a muse. The friend's name is carefully unpoetic, as are the place names. But the images and language (reminiscent of Wallace Stevens) call up the realm of metaphor and art. In conveying his discontent, Schubert has indeed exalted its significance, even as his theory requires; for it is of course he who really supplies the poetry:

> Carolyn told me:

> "The winter wind on Amsterdam Avenue
> Behind St. Luke's Hospital, listens, halts.
> It is a maimed crippled beggar, wanting a
> Handout. The sailors talk of big
> Times. Then the winter wind begins.

> "The winter wind blusters like
> A base ingrate; has no patience.
> Muck tramples the green film of
> Girls in remembered frocks."

Eliot and Shakespeare (the song from *As You Like It*) are in the wind, as Stevens is beside the girls. But the fidelity to drabness, along with the power to make it shine like gold, is Schubert's own.

The point made in "Midston House," that a poem is "speaking of what cannot be said," to the person whom the poet wishes to hear it, recalls Schubert's fundamental theme, the inadequacy of language to convey the most important thoughts and feelings, or even the clash between word and meaning. Emotionally, we dare not speak out to those we love most. If we tried to do so, our speech would give a false impression of our intent.

But sometimes the words do succeed. If winter is the season of inadequate speech, the sound of sleighbells is the signal of poetry coming through. In "Victor Record Catalog," the poet discovers that he really likes a girl and that she likes him. But their feelings emerge in riddling sentences. Rather than tell us what he or she said, Schubert gives us a mystery—a speech that imaginatively illustrates the process of true affection, like poetry, rising from silence and dark language.

People speak "by contradiction," the poet says. So the poem is filled with contradictions. Outside, the weather is August heat. But the poet feels wintry and inarticulate. Outside, the Coast Guard is drilling for war. But the discovery of his affection makes the poet exude friendliness, and he imagines the girl as saying that all men are brothers. In her expression she looks "Alternately too severe and too / Gentle." But the poet thinks of her, in his closing words, as "the gayest person."

The central contradiction is between the intimacy of the pair's emotion and the remoteness of their apparent positions. The girl lives in a warren of offices; and the tortuousness of the building symbolizes her inaccessibility to plain speech. So also there is a myth at the center of the poem, whose obscurity defies us to reach the poet even as he has reached the girl.

To help us, the symbolist technique provides a parallelism of image and meaning which cuts across the contradictions between speech and emotion. If the girl's true character can only be approached through a tortuous route (by reversing the apparent sense of her language), we have also seen that in a correspondent image she lives off a passageway that is tortuous or, as Schubert says, "Kafkalike." He therefore imagines her as speaking in the manner of Kafka, telling a parable that indicates the relation between the poet and either herself or the reader.

In this enigmatic tale the two friends succeed in making a journey "under the four winds," or under aimless motion among transient relations. They pass the "enemy's chariot," or the threat of death; and they pass a river "where drown the attached," or the river of forgetfulness, which breaks up friendships. They survive because they are "glad," or rescue each other from despair. If the poem comes off, the author and reader make a similar journey together, achieving an esthetic design rather than random motion, and building a work that will last and not be forgotten; and they find gladness or pleasure in their cooperative accomplishment.

The analogy with music springs from the opening metaphor, that the feeling for the girl is like the sound of sleighbells in winter. Because the poet is poor, he must study a record catalog when he would like to be listening to Eugene Ormandy and the Philadelphia Orchestra. So also the wait until he may talk to the girl is like hunger for food, which conversation cannot satisfy. By negating the girl's meanings, he will transform her evasions into the cheering affection that he yearns for. He will be fed just as the reader should be nourished by the poem.

It is a mistake to concentrate too much attention on the sadness that pervades many of Schubert's poems. His humor is normally present, offering through wit and irony a gentle smile at the inability of the world to live up to his desires. Even in "Dissertation on the Detroit *Free Press*," which is an elegy for his mother, the poet starts with a restrained ironic wit that establishes a tolerable distance between the speaker and his grief. Telling of a wish to visit Detroit, where he had lived a child with his parents, Schubert quotes a condescending expression of the art critic Craven, whose tone he implicitly mocks:

> For my vacation, I thought like Silas
> Marner, being my own miser of the past,
> To revisit what Craven calls "the good
> People of Detroit." I went elsewhere.

The humor is delicate and at his own expense. The poet always seems aware of the contrast between his ambition and his accomplishment. (He also knows how much stronger his talent is than that of more obviously successful writers.) The difficult style itself has a comic aspect; for Schubert associated the imagination with light, and admired a lucid style at the very moment when he could only satisfy his expressive needs with obscure complexity. In a letter to Ben Belitt, he says, "I've thought of writing utter transparency of expression with terrific intensity—but that, I suppose, is a matter of a lifetime" (September 15, 1938).

In the masterly "Dissertation on the Detroit *Free Press*," Schubert's quiet smile provides a seductive accompaniment to the tender, self-deprecating pathos of his speeches to a dead mother. (Here the flowers are the verses:)

> I offer you a candle, old fashioned
> Fidelity, on your grave, O lonely dead,
> To whom unhappiness no longer makes a difference.
> These flowers, which I do not bear, I drop
> On your tombstone.

It may be apropos simply to mention here the refinement of Schubert's phrasing, the care with which he balances rhythms and sound patterns in lines like the following, on the train's motion—lines in which the opening and closing words are matched like the parallel tracks on which a train composes its sibilant murmur. (The poet says he is going to—)

> Spend seven hours watching cities
> Tossed away like memories, hustled
> So that I have to tell myself that this
> Tempus of existence, rather than a tempest
> Is life, with all these people I am
> Living through their lives.

Even when the steady tone of a poem is comic, Schubert maintains his care for expressive effects. In "The Mark," which is a humorous treatment of his sense of failure, the poet draws a contrast between the "B-" that God has given him and more interesting examination marks. Here is the *C*, with its aural and visual puns:

> Think of the sinuous bosom
> Of a C, which sees all and feigns
> Indifference! An open mind is a C, a good
> American, friendly, someone you can talk with.

Again in "BA (On the Same Theme)," he complains punningly and allusively about his lack of a research degree. (Notice the "wagging" effect of the sound patterns in the "BA" line, as the sheep becomes a dog; and the punning allusion to Virgil's "facilis descensus," or easy descent to hell; and yet again the Latin "ab" or "from":)

> I see my name baaing
> At me, like the blackest sheep of all.
> All my associates have a great many
> Degrees, BA wags after me
> Like the can on a beaten cur's tail. . . .
>   Who wants to be
> The facile descensus AB, from being
> To ineffable lowest depths. I tell you I'm
> In a black mood. As
> In the voices of grieving Euripides, woe
>   Is me.

But in truth "woe" is only a part of Schubert. Wit, pathos, and true imaginative genius are much more of him. It is time we saluted the poet as a rightful heir of Stevens, Eliot, and Crane.

Spoils of Joy:
The Poetry of Delmore Schwartz

R. K. Meiners

New Directions has brought out a new paperback edition of Schwartz's *Summer Knowledge,* a selection of his poems first published in 1959. While this is, consequently, not a new book, there are a number of reasons for considering it carefully. One is that although Schwartz was a fine poet there seems to be relatively little attention paid to him these days, and there is some danger that he may be lost sight of amidst the flashier reputations of his generation. A second is that, as I shall attempt to show, Schwartz's work displays some representative qualities which it is peculiarly important for us to consider *at this time.*

There are no real differences between this edition and the 1959 Doubleday edition, unless one looks at the jacket copy. One probably should be above calling attention to such matters, but I think there is an important point here. The 1959 edition's jacket only gave the usual skeletal summary of Schwartz's career, and in relatively undemonstrative terms spoke of him as an "accomplished and sensitive poet" and of his book as a "rich gathering of Mr. Schwartz's early poetry and a varied collection of his later verse." With the 1967 edition, matters are different. There we learn of Schwartz's death in 1966, and of the cruel turnings of his career; the misery of his mental illness, and the loneliness and isolation of his last years.

It is difficult to speak of these matters without being in the absurd position of condescending to Delmore Schwartz. Heaven knows that anyone with some small knowledge of literary fashion has heard enough condescension toward him already: the bad jokes about the brilliant Jewish boy who tried to make it with the *Partisan* crowd and the *Kenyon* crowd simultaneously (his book is dedicated to John Crowe Ransom *and* Dwight

From *The Southern Review* 7 (New Series), no. 1 (January 1971). © 1971 by R. K. Meiners.

Macdonald), the manner in which his poetry often echoed this or that fashionable writer, his compulsive intellectuality, painful anecdotes about his last, sad years. It is important that we should say now that no matter what stories one may have heard, or whatever merely derivative qualities any critic might find in his work, Delmore Schwartz was an astonishing poet and an extraordinary man.

But it is even more important that we should think of the implications of his work. In its unwitting way the jacket copy is for once correct. We are told that we cannot read Schwartz's poems without thinking of "the alienation of the poet from our society," and we are told to regard the life and work of Delmore Schwartz as if he were "some tormented figure in a myth." And perhaps we should, if it will help to bring some issues into sharp focus. There is the testimony of poem after poem by Schwartz that he often thought of himself in a similar light, and this is perhaps all the license we need for reminding ourselves that if Schwartz is indeed "some tormented figure in a myth," that myth must surely be our orthodox myth of the poet and of poetic consciousness.

Although it may sound pretentious to speak in this way, I submit that there *is* such a myth, and that one cannot talk sensibly about Delmore Schwartz without considering it. It was not Schwartz's myth, though he understood its import more than most writers. He had not simply culled it from Coleridge, Hölderlin, Nietzsche, Freud, Rimbaud, though he knew that all these and many other nineteenth-century masters participated in the myth and had helped to articulate it. The extraordinary thing is the extent to which the myth was realized in Schwartz's poetry. To a remarkable degree, the explicit subject of his poetry is the implicit subject of all modern poetry: the terrible difficulties of consciousness. Indeed, if we are to use traditional figures to describe the modern myth of poetry we must invoke both Prometheus and Orpheus, for they remind us that whether the goal is to raise consciousness to a supernal level or to descend into the depths of the unconscious, the cost is terrible.

We all know these things. The key turning in the lock in Eliot's Wasteland, the interior voyage of Stevens's Comedian: these and a thousand other instances are part of our obsession. And yet, although we know these things, I can convinced of the absolute necessity to give yet closer attention to them, for unless we do so we shall remain caught at a most stultifying and claustrophobic stage in the evolution of human consciousness, and the dangers attendant upon that possibility are grave.

I am deeply suspicious of any attempt to reduce complex spiritual matters to a diagrammatic level, but I think it might serve some purpose to borrow the example of Northrop Frye and introduce a "visual aid" at this point. Draw a horizontal line from X to Y. X may be labelled Memory; Y, Apocalypse (the limits of consciousness extended backward and forward in time, both poles dependent upon consciousness). This horizontal line is intersected at its midpoint by a perpendicular line AB. A is Apollo; B,

Dionysus (the two terms and much of their significance coming, of course, from Nietzsche). The intersection of the lines forms the center of two concentric circles, one much smaller than the other. The smaller circle may be called self-consciousness; the larger circle, with lines AB and XY as its diameters, may be called simply consciousness. Or, it may be clearer if the smaller circle is labelled consciousness proper and the larger, projected consciousness. The upper segment of the vertical line represents the Promethean movement of consciousness, and its goal is clairvoyance; the lower segment is the opposing Orphic movement, downward into the unconscious.

This is very crude; there is no way to make it command assent without exposition and argument. Nevertheless, there are a number of crucial points that must be made; they are essential to modern notions of poetic consciousness. The first is that it is *creative*. In terms of my diagram, the energy is generated in the smaller circle of self-consciousness (including the personal unconscious, the lower half of the circle), and moves outward. In other words, this is in opposition to earlier theories of inspiration, in which the poet's vision was given by the Muse, God—something other than his own being. The poet is now *creator*. He does not imitate the life of the universe; he draws life out of himself. To trace the implications of this would require a book at least as comprehensive as M. H. Abrams's *The Mirror and the Lamp*; or, better, Abrams supplemented by any of Owen Barfield's work, particularly *Saving the Appearances*. The second quality of modern notions of poetic consciousness is that it is *inescapable*. There is nothing which is not involved with consciousness. Even the *unconscious*, including Jung's collective unconscious, is defined in relation to the conscious, for it funnels into the individual consciousness. All is drawn within this closed sphere; my world is my creation: my glory and my prison. It is this quality which accounts for the ubiquity of such conceptions as those of repression on the one hand, and projection on the other. In terms of my diagram, once more, whether the mind seeks the way down, into the Dionysiac unconscious, or the way up, into Apollonian wisdom, its limits are still to be found within a closed circle. The major traditions of modern thought have so far failed to solve the problems inherent in the classical Kantian formulations that the very possibility of a shared world of consciousness in which we participate is all but unthinkable.

It is incumbent upon anyone who has entertained such speculations to demonstrate that he has not taken leave of his senses, that they have some bearing upon the poetry in question. Fortunately, this is not difficult. If one is going to speak of the poetry of Delmore Schwartz he must either resign himself to triviality or allow such questions their full place: Schwartz's poetry demands it. For the reader who may think that I have imputed too many of my own concerns to Schwartz, I suggest that there are not many alternatives open if one wishes to deal with poetry of this type:

ONCE AND FOR ALL

Once, when I was a boy
Apollo summoned me
To be apprenticed to the endless summer of light and
          consciousness,
And thus to become and be what poets often have been,
A shepherd of being, a riding master of being, holding the
          sun-god's horses, leading his sheep, training his
          eagles,
Directing the constellations to their stations, and to each
          grace of place.

But the goat-god, piping and dancing, speaking an unknown
          tongue or the language of the magician,
Sang from the darkness or rose from the underground,
          whence arise
Love and love's drunkenness, love and birth, love and
          death, death and rebirth
Which are the beginning of the phoenix festivals, the tragic
          plays in celebration of Dionysus,
And in mourning for his drunken and fallen princes, the
          singers and sinners, fallen because they are, in the
          end,
Drunken with pride, blinded by joy.

And I followed Dionysus, forgetting Apollo. I followed him
          far too long until I was wrong and chanted:
"One cannot serve both gods. One must choose to win and
          lose."
But I was wrong and when I knew how I was wrong I knew
What, in a way, I had known all along:
This was the new world, here I belonged, here I was wrong
          because
Here every tragedy has a happy ending, and any error may
          be
A fabulous discovery of America, of the opulence hidden in
          the dark depths and glittering heights of reality.

Although this is not quite Schwartz at his best, it is in many ways typical
of his later work: open, declarative, deliberately flat with loosely parallel
cadences, and without the trace of a "persona" (Schwartz almost always
speaks directly in his later work). It should serve to demonstrate that the
questions I have been raising are not arbitrarily imposed upon his poetry.
And if Schwartz's language sounds as if it were gathered from Nietzsche
and Freud, so much the better: he was always aware of all the precedents,
of the great men who had given names and shapes to his obsessions.

It is with the later poetry that I am most concerned. If there are still those who do not know Schwartz's early poetry, they should have the joy of discovering such poems as "In the Naked Bed, in Plato's Cave" or "The Heavy Bear Who Goes with Me" for themselves; they should also discover that the poetry Schwartz was writing in his early twenties will compare favorably with anything written at that time by his generation.

These early poems are collected in the first half of the book, to which Schwartz gave the retrospective general title, "The Dream of Knowledge." Considering the perspective from which Schwartz assembled the book, these poems must be viewed as preliminaries, records of painful groping toward the fullness of knowledge, the vision of plenitude that he attempted to obtain in the second half of the book, "Summer Knowledge." Nearly half of this first section is devoted to the long, pseudo-dramatic "Coriolanus and His Mother." It is hard to describe this work: five "acts" in loose blank verse and five prose interludes. Characters from Shakespeare's play go through the motions Schwartz prescribes for them, and the actions are viewed and commented on by other characters named Aristotle, Beethoven, Sigmund Freud, Karl Marx, and another unnamed Ghost (at one point it seems he may be Immanuel Kant, but in the end he seems to represent the one who knows that which is beyond the narrator's own restless erudition). It is probably misleading to use so impersonal a term as "narrator" even when discussing Schwartz's earlier poetry: his own experience was so intimately involved (a certain kind of reader will always raise the "aesthetic distance" objection when he encounters Schwartz). In any case, the narrator is split into the boy accompanied by ghosts watching the play, and the garrulous personage holding forth in the interludes, telling anecdotes about Fichte drinking a toast when his son said "I" for the first time (self-consciousness dawning), relating stories of a father and son named Schrecklichkeitunendlich and their brown pony named Ego, and so on. The work is a tour de force, and probably a failure, though certainly one of the most extraordinary failures I know. In an age where alienation (as the book jacket says) has come to be the accepted condition for the artist. "Coriolanus and His Mother" is something like the ultimate schizophrenic spin-out, though it is so long, and vacillates so much between the obvious and the excruciating, that much of its impact is dissipated. Nevertheless, it is clear why Schwartz wanted to include it, for its nightmarish intellectuality is the perfect opposite side of the coin to the vision he later sought. As the self-deprecating narrator says, speaking of the human individual, the hero of this psychodrama: "And he moves, because he must, and thus he is betrayed to the *unending agony of conscious being.* Thus he moves forward to what he has not yet been. Here his pain awaits him and here he is as yet nothing. The repetition of yesterday and the day before will never suffice, but he must create again and again from what has been the unheard-of future. The future of time which is nothing cannot be grasped by the repetition of what has been. *It is not enough. He must create what has never existed"* [italics mine]. I could ask for no better paradigm, nor better justification for saying that even though we "know" these things we had better do some hard thinking about them and ask whether this is indeed the only mode of being open to us, and whether to remain caught at this stage of consciousness would not be disastrous.

Schwartz himself was preoccupied with such matters, and I believe that he would have answered my last rhetorical question in the affirmative. For it seems clear to me that his later poems were devoted—sometimes awkwardly, always heroically—to the attempt to press onward through this stage. It cannot really be said that he succeeded, but these later poems nevertheless deserve the most careful attention. It would be difficult to think of an instance in which a poet was so deeply involved with the modern tradition and its prison of *self*-consciousness and made such a conscious attempt to extricate himself. At this stage of our development we can only hope to deal with the dilemmas of self-consciousness by becoming even more conscious, by attempting to see whether some of our standard dogmas about human consciousness are indeed *quite* true. Nothing can be gained by wishing things were not as they are, or by trying to "restore" more fixed notions of order, reason, etc.

I suggest that this is, at least in part, what Schwartz was about, though I do not suggest that he would have put it in these terms. I think that a reading of the poems in the last half of the book will quickly reveal certain words recurring time after time. Among these are *knowledge, mortality, reality*; but the really operative words are *consciousness* and *love*. The dangers and penalties of consciousness are, if anything, even more Schwartz's obsessive subject here than in the earlier work, but there is a marked difference, and that difference is marked by the coupling of *love* with the preoccupation with consciousness. It would be foolish to pin much of an argument on the recurrence of a single word, especially one so ambiguous as "love," and I do not do so. But its continual presence is one indication of an awareness of the possibility of an openness and freedom, in human relations and toward living nature, that was hardly noticeable in the early work.

The tone which is struck in "Summer Knowledge" is quite unlike anything in the first half of the book:

> Summer knowledge is green knowledge, country knowledge,
>   the knowledge of growing and the supple recognition
>   of the fullness and the fatness and the roundness of
>   ripeness.
> It is bird knowledge and the knowing that trees possess
>   when
> The sap ascends to the leaf and the flower and the fruit,
> Which the root never sees and the root believes in the
>   darkness

> and the ignorance of winter knowledge . . .
> For summer knowledge is the knowledge of death as birth,
> Of death as the soil of all abounding flowering flaring
>   rebirth.
> It is the knowledge of the truth of love and the truth of
>   growing:
>   it is the knowledge before and after knowledge:
> For, in a way, summer knowledge is not knowledge at all: it
>   is
>   second nature, first nature fulfilled, a new birth
>   and a new death for rebirth, soaring and rising out
>   of the flames of turning October, burning November,
>   the towering and falling fires, growing more and
>   more vivid and tall
> In the consummation and the annihilation of the blaze of
>   fall.

This is all, one may say, common enough; but if one says it one fairly shuts himself off from further discussion. One is tempted to such a reaction because one has been subjected to such a plethora of ready-made plastic mysticism, both literary and nonliterary. But I can detect very little if any of that merely fashionable quality in Schwartz: it has been won at too great a cost for that. There is in a sense nothing here that we have not heard—and probably been suspicious of—often enough before. For, as Schwartz wrote, in a sense this "is not knowledge at all." Certainly it is not "knowledge" that will fit into the straightjacketed conventions to which the Western mind has been accustoming itself for the past three centuries.

Even in the later poetry, however, the condition of "Summer Knowledge" remained more of an aspiration than an achievement. There is none of the certainty of vision that characterizes the great visionary poets. It was as if he had the memory of the ancient visionary wisdom of poetry, and the conviction that it was in that direction that one had to turn if the effects of the destructive myth of the isolation of consciousness were to be overcome, but little confidence in his ability to really talk that language. He was so complete a modern that the equation, to be conscious = to suffer, was for him a nearly unchallengeable formula. And so, any alternative view of consciousness he could conceive only negatively. In "Seurat's Sunday Afternoon along the Seine," a long poem which is one of the most impressive pieces in the book, he develops the matter quite clearly. He senses the effort of the impressionist to paint nature "in the light of the eye," as Owen Barfield has finely said; to concentrate on the mysteries of vision until they yield themselves up, and in so doing to transform consciousness itself:

> If you can look at any thing for long enough,
> You will rejoice in the miracle of love,

> You will possess and be blessed by the marvelous blinding
>   radiance of love, you will be radiance.
> Selfhood will possess and be possessed, as in the
>   consecration of marriage, the mastery of vocation, the
>   mystery of gift's mastery, the deathless relation of
>   parenthood and progeny.

Schwartz comes right up to the edge; he nearly says, if you will continue to look carefully and meditatively at the world, you will find consciousness becoming transformed into that imaginative vision which is not isolated, but at one with its object and all nature, but he cannot quite manage it. He seems aware of the possibility, but he can only conceive of a temporary cessation from suffering:

> The sun shines
> In soft glory
> Mankind finds
> The famous story
> Of peace and rest, released for a little while from the tides of
>   weekday tiredness, the grinding anxiousness
> Of daily weeklong lifelong fear and insecurity,
> The profound nervousness which in the depths of
>   consciousness
> Gnaws at the roots of the teeth of being so continually,
>   whether in sleep or wakefulness,
> We are hardly aware that it is there or that we might ever be
>   free
> Of its ache and torment, free and open to all experience.

I hope it will not sound condescending, as if I could make some claim to a mastery of experience which I certainly cannot, to say: poor Schwartz! He knew what was required, which direction to move, but he could not move himself. Here is the conclusion of the poem:

>   Far and near, close and far away
> Can we not not hear, if we but listen to what Flaubert tried
>   to say,
> Beholding a husband, wife and child on just such a day:
> *Ils sont dans le vrai!* They are with the truth, they have found
>   the way
> The kingdom of heaven on earth on Sunday summer day.
> Is it not clear and clearer? Can we not also hear
> The voice of Kafka, forever sad, in despair's sickness trying
>   to say:
> "Flaubert was right: *Ils sont dans le vrai!*
> Without forbears, without marriage, without heirs,
> Yet with a wild longing for forbears, marriage, and heirs:

> They all stretch out their hands to me: but they are too far
> away!"

The long cadences wind themselves up into the compulsive rhyme of these last eleven lines, as if the very pattern of Schwartz's words on the page— quite apart from the typical reference to Kafka—were testimony of his ability to see freedom on the one hand, and the closed compulsive repetitiveness of self-consciousness on the other, but could find no mode in which man could be both conscious *and* free.

We have come to the place where even the phrase "confessional poetry" is common enough, and the experience of witnessing the most intimate terms of the poet's life with the attendant spiritual anguish arouses no particular surprise (or the poet may be presenting a close enough fictive approximation; the point is not the closeness of the experience to autobiography, but that the poet adapts the convention of self-revelation). I do not mean to make animadversions on the work of other poets, nor to suggest that Schwartz was a *better* poet than those who later worked in this manner. I do mean to say that, whether the *man* was growing sicker or not, the *poet* was becoming more aware of the toll exacted by this mode of life and thought and that poetry which intends to merely reveal it. That Schwartz was at least approaching the confessional manner as early as the 1930s the early poem "Prothalamion" will make clear:

> Now I must betray myself. . . .
>
> I will forget the speech my mother made
> In a restaurant, trapping my father there
> At dinner with his whore. Her spoken rage
> Struck down the child of seven years
> With shame for all three. . . .
>
> For thus it is that I betray myself,
> Passing the terror of childhood at second hand
> Through nervous, learned fingertips.
> At thirteen when a little girl died,
> I walked for three weeks neither alive nor dead,
> And could not understand and still cannot
> The adult blind to the nearness of the dead,
> Or carefully ignorant of their own death. . . .
>
> But this is fantastic and pitiful,
> And no one comes, none will, we are alone,
> And what is possible is my own voice,
> Speaking its wish, despite its lasting fear.

This may seem tame enough when compared with, for example, Sylvia Plath's "Tulips" or Lowell's "Skunk Hour." But Schwartz had been there. He was the poet who had written "Do they whisper behind my back? Do they speak / Of my clumsiness? Do they laugh at me, / mimicking my gestures, retailing my shame?"

The remarkable thing is not that Schwartz was unable to get out of the dilemma of consciousness = suffering; the remarkable thing is rather that he came so far; that, considering his presuppositions, he understood as much about the destructiveness of those views as he did. As I have said, he never found a way out for himself, but he was reaching for the way out more deliberately than most poets ever manage to command. In "I Did Not Know the Spoils of Joy" he wrote, partly in play, but mostly in a spirit of exorcism:

> I did not know the truth of joy:
> I thought that life was passed in pain. . . .
>
> And when I followed where sleep fled
> I woke amid the mixing dream:
> My self or others hurt my head,
> I heard the frigid Furies scream.
>
> Yet when I fled from this estate,
> I drove the quickest car to bliss:
> With drunken fools I struck at fate,
> Charmed, by the falls of consciousness. . . .
>
> Illusion and madness dim the years:
> Mere parodies of hope, at best,
> And yet, through all these mounting fears,
> How I am glad that I exist!

In his later work Schwartz knew at least several things, in at least one portion of his being. He knew that the myth of the poet as sufferer was, if partly true nevertheless more wrong. He knew that to make consciousness an explicitly suffering state was wrong, but that the reverse, the flight into the Dionysiac attractions of the Unconscious was not necessarily less wrong. The "love" and "joy" which appear so often in the later work were not conditions he could claim to have reached, but he knew they *must* be attainable. The awareness of the beauty of growth, the loveliness of life, illuminates all the darkness which is always as close to Schwartz as his very name. He reaches toward something like a Goethean vision of a beautiful life permeating all our experience, a vision which denies the separation of an inner and an outer world, which mocks the notion of consciousness as a something which sits inside the box of the skull, sadly insulated from everything "out there":

> All through the brilliant blue and gold afternoon
> All space was blossoming: immense and stately against the
>   blue heights

The sailing, summer-swollen milky and mounting clouds:
      colossal blossoms,
And the dark statues of the trees on the blue and green
      ground, flowing. And every solid thing
Moved as in bloom, leafing, opening wing upon wing to the
      sun's overwhelming lightning!
And every solid sight was a great green drum, throbbing
      and pulsing in the growing vividness of the greenness
      darkening
So that the litter and ripple of the river was excited by the
      advent and descent of light upon its slow flowing:
The river was opulence, radiance, sparkle, and shine, a
      rippling radiance dancing light's dances;
And the birds flew, soared, darted, perched, perched and
      whistled, dipped or ascended
Like a ballet of black flutes, an erratic and scattered
      metamorphosis of the villages of stillness into the
      variety of flying:
The birds were as a transformation of trunk and branch and
      twig into the elation which is the energy's celebration
      and consummation!

He does not really need the injunction which he issues to himself in the rest of this poem, to remember that winter and death follow this abundance of life: that awareness he always carried. The marvelous thing is the confidence that rebirth and new life will follow, and that there is an unutterable beauty in consciousness accompanying all the terror. I know that I repeat myself, and that this wisdom, if that is what it is, is as old as our history. But nearly all of us have forgotten it, or if we "know" it, we know it only as a series of footnotes to certain eccentrics about whom it may be very well to *write:* but who can *believe* these things? We have very nearly thought and written ourselves into a corner, and we have come even closer to saying that the corner is inescapable. And when, as poets, we believe that we have no choice, that this is the way life is and the way we *must* think and write in the late twentieth century ("after such knowledge, what forgiveness?") we sound singularly like those who say, but in *this* world we must be strong because of our enemies, we must develop new weapons and new chemicals, we have no choice. Which is nonsense. There are still choices open. We cannot cease to be conscious, but we *can* change the mode of our consciousness, and realize that an isolated *self*-consciousness, set off in a tension against all the world, is not only not inevitable but a calamitous falsehood. It is right to be scornful of those—if they still exist—who are unaware of suffering, of the pain attendant upon much of life, and the monstrous evils in our society, but in the midst of this awareness we must also learn that if these evils are ever to be overcome, it will only be through the sense of the larger life in which we all participate.

I WAKEN TO A CALLING

I waken to a calling,
A calling from somewhere down, from a great height,
Calling out of pleasure and happiness,
And out of darkness, like a new light,
A delicate ascending voice,
Which seems forever rising, never falling
Telling all of us to rejoice,
To delight in the darkness and the light,
Commanding all consciousness forever to rejoice!

To obey that command and to learn that sort of joy is not easy. It does not simply fall by accident into one's lap. One must *change* one's life, and to do so requires effort.

How to Read Berryman's
Dream Songs

Edward Mendelson

Anyone who writes about *The Dream Songs* puts himself in a dangerous position. The poem's landscape resembles in some places a minefield where an explanatory footstep triggers explosions of warning and invective, bursting in the face not only of critics but of all readers. Berryman's mildest warning to his expositors is both a simple renunciation and a complex, tragic claim:

> These Songs are not meant to be understood, you
> understand.
> They are only meant to terrify & comfort.

Henry (Henry Pussycat, Henry House, Mr Bones, Berryman's verbal stand-in, the poem's agonist) maintains that the "ultimate structure" of the Songs is inaccessible to critical analysis, that the Songs lack the regular articulated structure that informs "cliffhangers and old serials," that his "large work . . . will appear, / and baffle everybody." One response to bafflement seems to have little chance of success, considering its source:

> When the mind dies it exudes rich critical prose,
> especially about Henry. . . .

Henry knows the etiology of lit. crit., so "back on down boys; don't express yourself," he warns. "His foes are like footnotes" ("comic relief,—absurd"). The structure of the Songs does not articulate deep inside the poem where criticism could rout it out, but is "according to his [Henry's] nature": the skeleton of the poems is "Mr Bones" himself.

Berryman's ludditisms (there are dozens of them) against the critical

From *American Poetry since 1960: Some Critical Perspectives*, edited by Robert B. Shaw. © 1973 by Edward Mendelson. Carcanet Press, 1973.

act amount to an elliptical statement about the poem's organization, its way of being. Unlike most of the recent verse that gets filed away in one's memory under the heading "confessional," Berryman's poem invents a form and language assertively its own, an achievement possible only because Berryman wrestled successfully the master voices of Hopkins, Auden, Cummings and Pound. He also has a strategy of his own, one which looks at first like the familiar confessional self-justification ("Miserable wicked me, / How interesting I am," Auden parodied in another context) but is in fact far more complicated. The title *The Dream Songs* asserts the subjectivity of the poem's occasions: dreams are events absolutely inaccessible to shared or common experience. But neither are they events subject to the organizing power of the dreamer himself. The poem claims to derive from mental activity at a place so deep in the poet's self that the self is no longer in control. Berryman makes an explicit disclaimer of responsibility in a forenote to the completed work: "Many opinions and errors in the Songs are to be referred not to the character Henry, still less to the author, but to the title of the work." This is to say, the Songs are not what they appear to be, a transparently autobiographical series of dramatic monologues (trespassed by other voices now and then), but a verbal corporation whose members are uncontrolled responses to—and translations from—the world of experience, and whose rules are flexible and mostly hidden.

Yet the poems are not only dreams but "Songs," and they are always patterned and often musical. Berryman suggested the solution to the paradox of the title *The Dream Songs* in an interview: "Henry? He is a very good friend of mine. I feel entirely sympathetic to him. He doesn't enjoy my advantages of supervision; he just has vision." *Entirely sympathetic*: Berryman is too shrewd not to mean this in its fullest sense, that Berryman's feelings and Henry's are precisely the same. *My advantages of supervision*: though the statements in the poem are in Henry's voice, the Apollonian will to pattern and outline is the poet's own. The portion of the Songs which is the most regular in form and meter, most grave in language, is the Opus Posthumous series, written after Henry's "death" (in the center of the poem) when he is most subject to supervision by the living. And an arithmetical precision surrounds the Songs, though Henry keeps mum about it: seventy-seven Songs in the first volume, *77 Dream Songs* (1964); 77×5 in the completed 385 Songs; fourteen $(7+7)$ in the Op. Posth. series that opens the second volume, *His Toy, His Dream, His Rest* (1968); seven epigraphs; seven books in all. And the title of the second volume comes from a source no less formal and playfully sedate than the Fitzwilliam Virginal Book, where three songs may be found in sequence with the titles "A Toy," "Giles Farnaby's Dreame," and "His Rest." (The connection was noted by Professor Edith Borroff of Eastern Michigan University, to whom my thanks.)

The Songs have a formal frame, and, despite dozens of variations, each Song is built upon a regular pattern of three six-line stanzas, rhymed variously, with the number of feet in each line varying around 5–5–3–5–5–3. Berryman said that the Songs are not individual poems but "parts" of a single poem. As for the structure of that single poem, Berryman allowed in another interview that there is a "plot" to the work, but "its plot is the personality of Henry as he moves on in the world." After sixty years of *The Cantos*, readers are more or less accustomed to poems organized in the autobiographic-picaresque mode, but Berryman's Songs, unlike the Cantos, have a recognizable beginning, middle, and end. A poem may be autobiographical, and Henry's public experiences are the same as Berryman's, but before personal experience can fit into a literary form it must endure a cataclysmic transformation. Berryman wrote that one problem involved in a long poem is "the construction of a world, rather than the reliance upon one existent which is available to a small poem"—and this is an invitation to a phenomenological rather than structural reading of the Songs.

This issue deserves further definition. Everything in a poem that makes its world different from that of life is derived ultimately from the *closure* of art, its beginning and middle and end. In life no one has any clear sense of one's beginning, nor, after the fact, can one have any sense at all of one's end. (In a late Canto Pound put it simply: "No man can see his own end.") One can close one's life, as Berryman did, but one cannot look up at the clock afterwards and begin something new. In an age that worships process and fragmentation, tentativeness and aporia, even the most deliberately fragmented works of literature, even the last shavings of *The Cantos*, still imply the existence of larger closed structures which they are fragments *of*. Though Henry "moves on in the world," and, at the end of the first volume of the Songs, is explicitly "making ready to move on," the whole poem is finished and sealed. (There are, to be sure, miscellaneous Songs outside the main work, but these have the role that Wordsworth hopes to assign his minor poems in relation to his projected masterwork *The Recluse*: "little cells, oratories, and sepulchral recesses" attendant on the central edifice.) The world of *The Dream Songs*, the world that is "according to [Henry's] nature," depends *from* the kinds of events that happen there, the verbal events that translate the dream.

Don Quixote met a prisoner who had written his own story, *La Vida de Ginés de Pasamonte*. "Is it finished yet?" asked Don Quixote. "How can it be finished," answered Ginés, "when my life isn't." Berryman's special kind of transformation of extended personal experience into finished forms is probably his most important achievement, a model of method, if not a model of what to do with a method. At a time when most "confessional" verse tends to the dreary anecdote told in formless chat, Berryman's enterprise towards an idiosyncratically appropriate language, in an appropriate form, is courageous and rare. He said that "we need a poetry that gives up everything—all kinds of traditional forms—and yet remains rich." To make such poetry involves a long and risky effort, and Berryman certainly did not develop his style at all once. His earliest work, written in what he dismissed as "several fumbling years," was written "in what it's convenient to call 'period style,' the Anglo-American style of the 1930s, with no voice of my own, learning from middle and later Yeats and from . . . W. H. Auden." But although Berryman managed it well, the voice of the "period style" was insufficient for his purposes. In one early poem, for example, he begins by out-Audening Auden:

> The statue, tolerant through years of weather,
> Spares the untidy Sunday throng its look,
> Spares shopgirls knowledge of the fatal pallor
> Under their evening colour,
> Spares homosexuals, the crippled, the alone,
> Extravagrant perception of their failure;
> Looks only, cynical, across them all
> To the delightful Avenue and its lights.

The voice is Auden's but the heart is absent. Yet Berryman does not want to maintain this clinically hard detachment, and he reaches at the end of the poem a tone quite different, a tone which is the poem's real object:

> the dark apartment where one summer
> Night an insignificant dreamer,
> Defeated occupant, will close his eyes
> Mercifully on the expensive drama
> Wherein he wasted so much skill, such faith,
> And salvaged less than the intolerable statue.

Insignificant dreamer . . . wasted so much skill, such faith. The ironic depreciation hides the twin giants, self-aggrandizement and self-pity. Berryman wants to fit himself into the poem, but the voice won't let him do it until the last lines, and even then only with a strained tone and forced bitterness. The early poems are always assured and learned, always excellently sleek examples of their kind, but they never quite land successfully in the fields of egocentricity over which they so longingly hover.

Berryman devised various strategies for making his personal statements, but during the 1940s, at least, most of these strategies were limited to dramatic indirection. Some of the best poems in his second book, *The Dispossessed* (1948, including most of his first book, 1942, titled *Poems*—of course), are the "Nervous Songs," spoken by "the demented priest," "a professor," "the captain," "the young Hawaiian," "the tortured girl," "the man forsaken and obsessed," and so forth. Each poem is a complete dramatic lyric in itself, but together they coalesce into the different aspects of a single "personality," one dissociated and tense, but still ultimately complete and whole. This unification is of course never stated, only implied: each "Nervous Song" speaks for a different kind of "nerve." In *Berryman's Sonnets*, written apparently in 1946 and published when they came of age twenty-one years later, a love affair provides the occasion for a sonnet sequence in which aggressively modern clotted syntax and eclectic diction depend heavily upon Petrarchan form and convention: through Sidney by Hopkins. Here, as in the later poems of *The Dispossessed*, Berryman began to twist received syntax in his first experiments towards the language of *The Dream Songs*, but his essentially traditional forms (for some short poems he even borrowed terza rima) still restricted the force of the idiovocal statements he was trying to learn to make.

With *Homage to Mistress Bradstreet* (1956) Berryman first successfully fused his by now perfected syntax into a thoroughly personal form and subject. This remarkable poem, probably the most consistently successful that Berryman ever wrote, has a narrative "plot" which may be described briefly. The poet imagines the body of Anne Bradstreet, and "summons" her from the centuries; she speaks her history, which through one of Berryman's best imaginative leaps, turns out to be a grimly witty narrative of modern, almost suburban isolation and detachment, set in Puritan New England; Berryman and Anne, each to the other a ghostly presence, speak a dialogue, and each *almost* takes the other for a lover. Anne escapes the (to her) temptation offered by the twentieth-century voice, and asserts her seventeenth-century independence. Berryman's voice returns to the poem only after Anne's death. The structural device through which Berryman first creates Anne Bradstreet, then is thrown off by his own creation, might appear to be a conventionally modernist sleight-of-hand, a familiar form of play with the status of appearances, but Berryman summons a vast emotional universe of personal loss and assertion to the device, and succeeds in rendering it as deeply moving as it is artificial. The tortured syntax, here as earlier borrowed from Hopkins but rendered insistently secular, finally enjoys a wide enough range of situations to render into its language. Berryman moves easily from the grave to the comic, as in the arrangements for Anne's marriage, her resigned loss of sensual "bliss" to religious severity:

> vanity & the follies of youth took hold of me;
> then the pox blasted, when the Lord returned.
> That year for my sorry face
> so-much-older Simon burned,
> so Father smiled, with love. Their will be done.
> He to me ill lingeringly, learning to shun
> a bliss, a lightning blood
> vouchsafed, what did seem life. I kissed his Mystery.

Or the astonishingly persuasive rendering of her first childbirth:

> No. No. Yes! everything down
> hardens I press with horrible joy down
> my back cracks like a wrist
> shame I am voiding oh behind it is too late

hide me forever I work thrust I must free
now I all muscles & bone concentrate
what is living from dying?
Simon I must leave you so untidy
Monster you are killing me Be sure
I'll have you later Women do endure
I can *can* no longer
and it passes the wretched trap whelming and I am me

drencht & powerful, I did it with my body!
One proud tug greens Heaven. Marvellous,
unforbidding Majesty.
Swell, imperious bells. I fly.

(There is little that is quite as intense and various as this in all of English poetry.) And finally, Berryman's meditation after Anne's funeral:

Headstones stagger under great draughts of time
after heads pass out, and their world must reel
speechless, blind in the end
about its chilling star, thrift tuft,
whin-cushion—nothing. Already with the wounded flying
dark air fills, I am a closet of secrets dying.

O all your ages at the mercy of my loves
together lie at once, forever or
so long as I happen.
In the rain of pain & departure, still
Love has no body and presides the sun,
and elfs from silence melody. I run.
Hover, utter, still,
a sourcing   whom my lost candle like the firefly loves.

(The phrase "Love . . . presides the sun" recalls the final line of the *Paradiso*, "L'amor che muove il sole e il altre stelle," and suddenly deepens Berryman's conversation with the dead.)

The lost and isolated voice of the poem gains force through its reduplication in the seventeenth and twentieth centuries, but Berryman was not satisfied. *The Dream Songs* resume his quest for a single voice, but the quest is not completed or resolved until the middle of the work. In *77 Dream Songs* Henry "has a friend, never named, who addresses him as Mr Bones and variants thereof," and usually engages Henry in the midst of one of his bursts of blackface or burnt-cork monologue—another distancing pose which Berryman managed to give up before too long.

You may be right Friend Bones.
Indeed you is. Dey flyin ober de world,
de pilots, ober ofays. Bit by bit

our immemorial moans

brown down to all dere moans. I flees that, sah.

What is characteristically Berryman's in this sort of passage is not the distancing dialect so much as the sudden shift to a vaguely "high" style in "our immemorial moans," which, in addition to the effect of the dialect, distances the Song doubly. Berryman is always ready to walk along the dangerous cliffs of self-indulgence ("O ho alas alas / When will indifference come, I moan & rave"), but only by taking risks can he achieve the mutual conciliation of the colloquial and the formal which the Songs propose, bend to the breaking point again and again, and finally ratify and consummate.

The risks of Berryman's style are great (rhymes on "O" or "pal" have little merit, unless some lies in their nose-thumbing insouciance towards The Tradition), but the risks of his subject are greater. Although there is no lyric or narrative stance available in literature that is more tedious than the Wild Old Wicked Man, Berryman persists in delighting in it. Leaving aside for a moment the "plot" of the poem, one can approach it usefully according to Berryman's own suggestions. In the interview where he denied the presence of an "ulterior structure," he indicated that what is most important in the poem's organization is the *kind of event* that happens in any of its various territories: "Some of the Songs are in alphabetical order [117–122, for example, allowing an obvious inversion of the first two phrases of 118; and so much for narrative pattern]; but, mostly, they just belong to areas of hope and fear that Henry is going through at a given time." The primary event in the Songs is of course the dream, yet what ordinary language knows as dreams are imitated rarely. Abrupt endings, sudden shifts in referent and style (recalling to its source the technique named by MacNeice the "dream parataxis"), fantasies of sexual power and weakness, all refer obliquely to dreams, but Berryman uses the word "dream" in a wider sense. Disputing Freud, he writes in a late Song that "a dream is a panorama / of the whole mental life." This statement is a revision of the romantic conception of the dream—a conception elevated by Freud from poetic assertion to scientific dogma—which is premised on the belief that dreams are messages from the psychic interior. When Berryman elevates his domestic miseries and petty wrongs into the material of secondary epic—without, apparently, it ever occurring to him that the subject might not deserve so much paper and type—he adopts a standard romantic convention, but does so partly in order to invert it. Berryman's most characteristic literary *manner* is that of a Wordsworth *in extremis* ("Wordsworth, thou form almost divine, cried Henry"), aware of the real pain in the world: his poems intimations of mortality, tranquillity (at best) recollected in emotion; his great work not a preparation for future effort, but a record of loss, a Postlude, or the decay of the poet's world. But instead of listening, resolving, communing, Henry acts, and his most characteristic *action* is scrambling or stumbling up to proceed again, after one more defeat, the death of one more friend, one more hollow and temporary pleasure. Henry's dreams give no comfort. Freud suggested that dreams are the guardians of sleep. Not Henry's dreams:

> I can't go into the meaning of the dream
> except to say a sense of total LOSS
> afflicted me thereof:
> an absolute disappearance of continuity & love
> and children away at school, the weight of the cross,
> and everything is what it seems.

Everything is what it seems: the loss is real; no romance or celebration can remedy it. Berryman's stance refuses the private luxuries of the romantic vision, a privacy he finds in its most limiting form in Wallace Stevens. The Song "So Long? Stevens" brilliantly demolishes this extreme version of romantic self-consciousness:

> He lifted up, among the actuaries,
> a grandee crow. Ah ha & he crowed good.
>
> What was it missing, then, at the man's heart
> so that he does not wound? It is our kind
> to wound, as well as utter
>
> a fact of happy world. That metaphysics
> he hefted up until we could not breathe
> the physics.

Berryman's dreams, for all their irresponsibility, are responsive, openly conscious as well as self-conscious, or so Berryman claims. Again from an interview: "What is wrong with poetry now is that poets won't take on observation, dealing with what is sent into individuals from the universe. It would seem to be that the job of the poet, if I may speak of such a ridiculous thing, is to handle the signs, to field them as in baseball."

So much does Berryman claim for his art. But do the events in the dreams or in their Songs stand up to the claim? Berryman's notion of "what is sent into individuals from the universe" is necessarily determined by his idea of the "universe" itself. *Homage to Mistress Bradstreet* is among other things an historical narrative, yet its central statements are "about" isolation and love. Anne Bradstreet seems at times an historical convenience. She is not a Yeatsian "mask" but a *projection*. In *The Dream Songs* the poem's universe is that of a man at the extremes of noisy passion and unhappiness, but also, alas, when considered outside his world of private eros and thanatos, *l'hommme moyen social*. Berryman and Lowell admire each other enthusiastically in print, but their phenomenal worlds are vastly different: where Lowell takes everything in the *polis* for his subject, Berryman's social commentary—except where the subject is at least marginally "literary," as in the trials of Soviet poets—is nearly as crazy as the later Yeats, and much less sonorous. "I'd like to write political poems, but aside from *Formal Elegy* [which hovers somewhere near John Kennedy], I've never been moved to do so." (Actually this is not quite true: *Poems* and *The Dispossessed* include some political verses reading like watered Auden. And Berryman once described the early "Winter Landscape" as a poem which indicates "what is necessary to be said—but which the poet refuses to say—about a violent world." This borders on the sophistic, but Berryman's refusal to talk about that which he cannot talk about is finally an honorable one. Graves's subject matter is no wider than Berryman's, but Graves decorously writes lyrics while Berryman raises problems for himself by exploding his discontents into epic.)

What is sent into Henry from the universe falls mostly under the vivid scarlet rubrics of death, survival, love, and fame. To the right and left of him fall so many poets; so many deaths seek him out:

> I'm cross with god who has wrecked this generation.
> First he seized Ted, then Richard, Randall, and now
>   Delmore.
> In between he gorged on Sylvia Plath.

Roethke, Blackmur, Jarrell, Schwartz, Plath—Berryman's staying power seems so much more strained, his survival so difficult, compared with the losses that surround him. Not that he is himself exempt. The very first Song in the whole work marvels at Henry's persistence after a "departure" from felicity and coherence, a departure that the line following relates elliptically to the Fall:

> All the world like a woolen lover
> once did seem on Henry's side.
> Then came a departure.
> Thereafter nothing fell out as it might or ought.
> I don't see how Henry, pried
> open for all the world to see, survived.

And throughout the first volume Henry refuses to wake, or is mutilated, blinded, or stalled:

> They sandpapered his plumpest home. (So capsize.)
> They took away his crotch.

And

> —What happen then, Mr Bones?
> —I had a most marvellous   piece of luck. I died.

(This ends Book I.) And

> I am obliged to perform in complete darkness
> operations of great delicacy
> on my self.
> —Mr Bones, you terrifies me.
> No wonder they don't pay you. Will you die?
> —My
>   friend, I succeeded. Later.

And when he isn't dying, Henry spends much of his time in hospital, immobilized.

The second volume of the Songs, *His Toy, His Dream, His Rest*, begins with Henry's "posthumous" works, when "Good nature is over" and he lies in "a *nice* pit":

> I am breaking up
> and Henry now has come to a full stop—
> vanisht his vision, if there was, & fold
> him over himself quietly.

The grave is not without its consolations, however, and when Henry's responsibilities become an issue at law, "this august court will entertain the plea / Not Guilty by reason of death." Though Henry's trial is interrupted by the news that he "may be returning to life / adult & difficult," no one need worry. After he has been dug up, and has "muttered for a double rum / waving the mikes away," two weeks later he returns to the graveyard, desperate to get back underground:

> insomnia-plagued, with a shovel
> digging like mad, Lazarus with a plan
> to get his own back, a plan, a stratagem
> no newsman will unravel.

In the next book, the metaphor of Henry's death translates itself, reasonably enough, into a long stay in hospital, and a more or less ordinary narrative resumes. By book 6 it is not Henry who is elegized but Delmore Schwartz who is granted a long series of elegiac Songs before Berryman sets him "free of my love," in the conventional end-of-elegy hope that he may "recover & be whole."

Henry's own elegies also end with consolation. Set against his reiterated, battological dyings are his movings-on ("recoveries" is too strong a word), which are figuratively the "movement" of the poem. The areas of hope and fear in which Henry finds himself have their geographical analogues—from India, where "his migrant heart" hurts at the thought of stability and repeated Spring, to Japan, where in the permanence of a temple he remembers that "Elsewhere occurs . . . loss," and finally, amazingly "in love with life / which has produced this wreck," to Ireland, the site of the seventh and longest book of the Songs. Always Henry is surprised at his own resilience:

> it is a wonder that, with in each hand
> one of his own mad books and all,
> ancient fires for eyes, his head full
> & his heart full, he's making ready to move on.

Moving on is his epic impetus. With no Ithaca or Penelope (or dozens of them, which means the same thing), no historical destiny or Roman Imperium, no Beatrice or St. Francis to draw him onwards, his straitened private energy must suffice.

Whether or not it *does* suffice for almost four hundred Songs is open to question, and one suspects, as one nears the end of the poem, that energy-scrambling-for-a-system-to-act-in is a theme pathetically at variance with the scale of the whole enterprise. Berryman suspects this also, and Henry's energy does have contexts, although they seem more and more narrow as the poem proceeds. Part way through *His Toy, His Dream, His Rest* the interlocutor and friend who addresses Henry as Mr Bones drops almost entirely from sight, and Henry is left to speak alone. Berryman finally achieves the single voice he worked towards for thirty years, but one might be dismayed by the uses to which he applies it. (Although so assertively single a voice can only, perhaps, be assertively single-minded.) Henry's chief interests, especially in the later Songs when the elegiac note has faded, are two, and the poem stutters over them almost incessantly: Henry's delight in, and difficulties with, (1) fame and (2) women. His response to publicity seems rather out of proportion, as if the occasional notice granted a very good minor poet by media that glut themselves on "celebrity" could give that poet the public currency of a Yeats, or even a Churchill. What fame he does have, and the grateful attention of his friends, fully justify a supple and active response like this one:

> he staked his claim upon obscurity:
> a prayer to be left alone
> escaped him sometimes or for a middle zone
> where he could be & become both unknown & known
> listening & not.

("Obscurity" is of course both "difficulty of interpretation" and "lack of recognition.") But a Song that begins by musing, "Fan-mail from foreign countries, is that fame?" and continues through a catalogue of awards and interviews, to end with the throwaway line, "A lone letter from a young man: that is fame"—can only sound hollow and mawkish. (It is just conceivable, though unlikely, that this is self-parody. But Berryman *likes* the subject too much for that.)

Nor does the unedifying spectacle of Henry's relations with women have much to recommend it. Early in the book Berryman manages some fine dramatic absurdity:

> Filling her compact & delicious body
> with chicken páprika, she glanced at me
> twice.
> Fainting with interest, I hungered back
> and only the fact of her husband & four other people
> kept me from springing on her.

And later he sounds disingenuous at finding the situation reversed:

> a Belfast man
> last night made a pass at my wife: Henry, who had passed
>   out,
> was horrified
> to hear this news when he woke.

But usually he is much nastier than this, and seems to realize it fairly well— which does not improve the situation. The women of *The Dream Songs* are divided roughly into two familiar classes: those he went to bed with, and those he did not. The former find themselves dismissed with an epithet ("whereon he lay / the famous daughter"), the latter idealized and trans- figured, their names prefixed by "Lady." In neither case does there seem to be much participation ("Women serve my turn"—*Homage to Mistress Bradstreet*). In both the relation is with another human being as object, whether debased or idolized, which is why "He was always in love with the wrong woman," and why, for all his sexual energy and success, he finds sex degrading: "Them lady poets must not marry," and Berryman thinks one of those ladies is even "too noble-O" for sexual experience.

Death is the heaviest burden, drawing the Songs constantly to earth. Survival, moving on, is the essential form taken by the poem's energy. The objects of that energy become the title of Berryman's next book, *Love and Fame:* and in reference both to that book and to the Songs, the first term in the title seems euphemistic, the second hyperbolic. (Berryman himself may have seen the title in an ironic light, as its possible literary source, Pope's "Eloisa to Abelard," bears a reminder of defeat: "Lost in a convent's solitary gloom . . . There dy'd the best of passions, Love and Fame.") The deepest goal of Henry's energy, its ultimate use, is the familiar lowest common denominator, power. "Love" in Berryman's poetry stands for the exercise of sexual power, or the worship of sexual power in idealized women. His use of fame is best described by Elias Canetti:

> Fame is not fastidious about the lips which spread it. So long as there are mouths to reiterate the one name, it does not matter whose they are. The fact that to the seeker after fame they are indistinguishable from each other and are all counted as equal

shows that this passion has its origin in the experience of crowd manipulation.

(*Crowds and Power*)

Berryman writes often that he prefers the praise of his friends to the baying of the crowd, but taking into consideration all his references to fame, the use of this passage does not appear unjust.

But Berryman is no naif. His power-plays are not simply subject matter for his poem, but are enacted in the poem itself. Berryman is smart enough to realize that he presents himself in the least prepossessing manner he can imagine: his personal offensiveness is not accidental but entirely deliberate, for what he wants from his readers is their critical approval despite their personal disapproval, their assent despite their awareness of what they are assenting *to*. What Berryman hopes to enjoy is not the power to delight or enchant, but the power to control those who are both conscious and unwilling.

American poets have never been able to consider themselves part of a clerisy or of any comfortably well-defined class, and for that reason have always been far more concerned with power than their European contemporaries. Berryman's generation of poets seems to have been more obsessed with the attainment and use of power than any other in America, and its obsession proved costly. Jarrell, Shapiro, Lowell, Roethke (of whom Berryman said "He was interested in love and money; and if he had found a combination of them in something else, he would have dedicated himself to it instead of poetry"), Berryman himself—all tried or still try to exert more control than words ever made possible over people, politics, the literary pecking-order, and time which no one controls.

Yet no matter how irritating or boring or murky the Songs can be on occasion, they remain the most courageous and interesting poetic experiment of their decade. When they succeed, when they open into something rich and strange, no other poem in their historical neighborhood can equal them. Few who have written on Berryman have been able to avoid quoting one in particular of the early Songs entire, and there is no reason to buck the trend:

> There sat down, once, a thing on Henry's heart
> só heavy, if he had a hundred years
> & more, & weeping, sleepless, in all them time
> Henry could not make good.
> Starts again always in Henry's ears
> the little cough somewhere, an odour, a chime.
>
> And there is another thing he has in mind
> like a grave Sienese face a thousand years
> would fail to blur the still profiled reproach of. Ghastly,
> with open eyes, he attends, blind.

All the bells say: too late. This is not for tears;
thinking.

But never did Henry, as he thought he did,
end anyone and hacks her body up
and hide the pieces, where they may be found.
He knows: he went over everyone, & nobody's missing.
Often he reckons, in the dawn, them up.
Nobody is ever missing.

This Song, number 29, exemplifies in an unusually clear and regular manner
the paratactic method by which almost all the Songs are organized. The
first sestet describes an experience in intensely private terms; the "thing"
is on Henry's heart, the cough "in Henry's ears." In the second sestet he
notices or remembers the world outside, and does so through a metaphor
("a grave Sienese face") whose vehicle at least is publicly accessible, although the tenor is only an unspecified guilty "reproach." Rather than
locating sound "in Henry's ears," it is the bells, outside, that speak; and
although blind, Henry at least "attends." Finally, in the last sestet, he
acknowledges almost in defeat the social world of others, all those who
persist in surviving despite his dreams of violence (the cause of the "reproach" is now identified), who remind him that the thing on his heart is
only private. This neat enactment of Husserlian epistemology (awareness
of self, things, others) recurs throughout *The Dream Songs*, but often in
reverse order—with the awareness of others narrowing down to awareness
of self—or in some other variant pattern. And this paratactic method informs the relations between Songs as well as within them. The two final
Songs provide perhaps the best example. In the first Henry stands over
his father's grave, initially with restrained anger, then in stagy fury:

> I sit upon this dreadful banker's grave
> who shot his heart out in a Florida dawn
> O ho alas alas
> When will indifference come, I moan & rave
> I'd like to scrabble till I got right down
> away down under the grass
>
> and ax the casket open ha.

The poem is bloody with death and separations. But the very last Song
subsumes the death of one man into the cycle of seasons, where no endings
are final:

> My daughter's heavier. Light leaves are flying.
> Everywhere in enormous numbers turkeys will be dying
> and other birds, and all their wings.
> They never greatly flew. Did they wish to?
> I should know. Off away somewhere once I knew
> such things.

> Or good Ralph Hodgson back then did, or does.
> The man is dead whom Eliot praised. My praise
> follows and flows too late.
> Fall is grievy, brisk. Tears behind the eyes
> almost fall. Fall comes to us as a prize
> to rouse us toward our fate.

The dead father in the previous Song balances the growing, "heavier" daughter in this one. Henry's rage against his father is transmuted into praise for the dead poet, his obsession with the past metamorphosed into concern for his daughter and her (implied) future, his destruction of his father's casket transfigured into his calm respect for the permanence of his house, also wooden:

> My house is made of wood and it's made well,
> unlike us. My house is older than Henry;
> that's fairly old.

And the Songs close heart-rendingly with a meditation and plaint on the incoherence of the world, the dualism that divides soul from flesh and so from all "things," the discontinuity that makes Henry scold his child, "heavy" and a "thing," but loved:

> If there were a middle   ground between things and the soul
> or if the sky resembled more the sea,
> I wouldn't have to scold
>
>   my heavy daughter.

And at the same moment that it closes, the poem thrusts itself out of its frame into the undefined future.

Love and Fame (1970), which lies outside the range of this survey, continues Berryman's development of a personal voice. He drops the Henry-doppelgänger and speaks autobiographically and directly in his own name. The title of one poem, " 'Regents' Professor Berryman's Crack on Race," would have been impossibly direct only a few years earlier, but with directness came a dangerous facility and self-importance. The book makes pleasant reading, but the struggles of *The Dream Songs* have diminished to chat. Berryman's last book, *Delusions, etc.*, indicates that the mad-lyric mode was Berryman's mainstay to the end, intensely personal, slightly desperate, persistent in its survivals, its paradoxes, and its celebrations.

Finally the survivals gave out. Most of this essay had been written when the news came that the body of John Berryman had been found on the bank of the Mississippi River near the campus of the University of Minnesota. Berryman had walked to the railing of a bridge, waved to a passerby, and stepped off. Whatever the pressures and necessities may have been to which Berryman finally yielded, we probably have no right to know them. But his wave of farewell, so unlikely in those circumstances, was a thoroughly public gesture: Henry's last.

John Berryman:
Near the Top a Bad Turn Dared

Diane Ackerman

In a natural way, John Berryman is oblique, private, elliptical. We seem to overhear him. Locked in a verbal spasm, he has trouble, often enough, in getting out or across, and an essential part of his performance is a rheumatism of the sensibility, in which the grammar is so knotted up that his poems evince the difficulty of getting them written at all. Beginning, he seems not quite to know what is nagging at him; finished, he has allowed into the poem various accidents, concomitants, and ricochets. As A. Alvarez observes, "you either love or loathe" his jagged, high-strung outbursts. One of the most ego-ridden poets, he makes authoritative rhetoric out of the nervous tic, and an original voice as well. It is almost out of the question to confuse lines by Berryman with those of any other poet, though like a celebrant magpie he echoes dozens of poets from Pound and Stevens to Hopkins and Cummings. His "grammaticisms" alone would identify him, I suppose: his wrenchings or mutilations of grammar are not those of others. In fact, nearly everything about him is manneristic and, at times, he seems almost like an involuntary exercise in the manner of poet as idiosyncratic paradigm. A hard nut to crack, he is a poet fully qualified for exegesis and often badly in need of it.

My purpose here is not to look at him in the round, but to consider certain tendencies in *Homage to Mistress Bradstreet* and *Delusions, Etc.* There were times when Berryman verged on the metaphysical mind, although never sustainedly; it seems to have haunted him, the possibility of getting into such a frame of mind (and reference) flickers in his work like morganatic fire. It shows up in *Dream Songs*, I think, in the persona of intervening Mr. Bones, the death-figure who puts awkward questions at the wrong mo-

From *Parnassus: Poetry in Review* 7, no. 2 (Spring/Summer 1979). © 1980 by Poetry in Review Foundation.

ments only to answer them himself in a weird combination of black lingo and uncouth blues. Henry, the poet figure whose interior biography the Songs jerkily reveal, owns Mr. Bones and, presumably, goes on owning him until Mr. Bones owns him, which is when the Songs end, as they did in 1972. But I don't think it would be right to regard *Dream Songs* as metaphysical: a big pack of cards having to do with travel, children, politics, liquor, sex, theology, other poets, they impose on us voluptuously, but their drift is social. The wit is, too, and of course the bizarre tone—full of jangling self-interruptions that generate even further useful disturbances— might almost qualify him as an inheritor from Donne and Cowley. But to do so would be merely to make of him a superficial metaphysical, the essence of *Dream Songs*, in my view, being that he cannot break out of his bag of skin. True, he writes, "We are using our skins for wallpaper and we cannot win," which implies that the outside world keeps on coming through or that the self keeps leaking out; but in the end this is more like a problem with the plumbing. The poet is unhappy because he cannot forget himself. Henry is upset because he can't escape the poet who doubles as Mr. Bones. The entire sequence is an almost spastic search for a self, and it's not a self blurred through transcendental overlap with rocks and stars and trees, it's a self blurred by its own chemistry. If Berryman reaches out in these short poems, it's to bring himself back, not to steal a magic from the universe at large. Psychologically of enormous interest, especially for devotees of Berryman *in toto*, they are actually a bit short—in voracious interest, in intuited vastness, in empathetic penetration—compared with certain other works, to which I must now turn.

Homage to Mistress Bradstreet is an imaginary portrait almost in the manner of Walter Pater; indeed, Berryman's real-life alias has more fictional range than does the invented, arbitrary one of Henry. The answer, I think, is that, down the track, there was something precise and vivid to aim at, whereas Henry is too much Berryman himself to have edges. The one poem is a monument, the other a potpourri of broken images. Not that *Homage* isn't a poem of voices; it is, and these include the poet's own, as the first of the appended notes informs us: "The poem is about the woman, but this exordium is spoken by the poet, his voice modulating in stanza 4, line 8 [4.8] into hers." In fact, vocally, it is a polyphonic tour de force, sometimes achieving the uncanny effect of what has been presented serially becoming simultaneous: the voice lingers in one's ear and overshoots the next voice that comes along. Most impressive of all, the rhythm of Anne Bradstreet's mind comes boldly through, not only from Berryman's study of her own *Meditations* and his occasional use of phrases from them (some of which she had culled from the Scriptures), but also from his almost involuntary impersonations, which leave her mental gait on the silent white space around the poem like an oral signature. Adroit, subtle, tight, *Homage*—if it were nothing more—is an astonishing feat of invasive homage; her mind breathes again and, courtesy of the later poet, makes new images galore:

> Drydust in God's eye the aquavivid skin
> of Simon snoring lit with fountaining dawn
> when my eyes unlid, sad.
> John Cotton shines on Boston's sin—
> I ám drawn, in pieties that seem
> the weary drizzle of an unremembered dream.
> Women have gone mad
> At twenty-one. Ambition mines, atrocious, in.

To begin with, it is hard to parse, even retrospectively, and the first three lines in particular. Very well, then, the reader concludes: fall back on something else—an asyntactical reading, as if the lines were in Chinese, and all of a sudden "lit" emerges as the verb, not a past participle. The gain, I think, is the suggestión (which you're not obliged to cancel even after the verb has revealed itself) that she assimilates phenomena to herself through constantly expanding appositions: "Drydust" = "skin" = "sad." She might be concluding that "Drydust" is "sad," as perhaps the encrustations of an after-weeping are; we wake up, with "sleep" in our eyes, as if we have been weeping all night, and this doesn't have to go by the board when we reach the second conclusion, via grammar, that Simon's skin is dry. My point is that, through grammar or "grammaticism," Berryman offers optional readings which, rather than providing us with alternative insights into Anne herself, multiply her world instead, attuning us to things she may not be aware of, but which the intruding poet has supervised. And the motions thus implied, on our part complied with, not only turns the duo Bradstreet-Berryman into the Marcus Aurelius of Massachusetts, but also provides the poem with almost supernatural auspices that enter her occasional use of an acute accent on a word ("ám" in the above) and turn the whole thing ontological. The implication is that she might *not* be "drawn" and, if not drawn, might not even exist. Her death keeps her company throughout, and the intrusive other poet—both ventriloquist and dummy—uses her as proxy for his own process of getting used to such a *null* idea.

Four stanzas further on, the ontological clamp makes her scream, and the blurt-rhythms enact a moment of biology that seems to her very much between life and death.

> So squeezed, wince you I scream? I love you & hate
> off with you. Ages! *Useless.* Below my waist
> he has me in Hell's vise.
> Stalling. He let go. Come back: brace
> me somewhere. No. No. Yes! everything down
> hardens I press with horrible joy down
> my back cracks like a wrist
> shame I am voiding oh behind it is too late.

This is vivid empathy of course; how many male poets have gone so alertly, so keenly, to the core of a female experience? Pain, relish, and disgust come together here to make a shocking, though far from sensationlist whole. The odd thing, as so often in Berryman, is that the means to this effect feels also like the means to something bigger that looms just beyond the stanza's edge. It's not just a woman, a woman poet, it's a human being in a fit of being tweaked by body chemistry, if you like by the matrix of all human life. The apparatus, the cadences, the sheer drops, the psychodramatic speaking of the unspoken in response to the unspeakable, all betoken the sense of being *put upon* by the universe; only—this qualifier will reappear apropos of Berryman—he never quite takes it to the limit to say, for example, the stuff that stars are made of is giving her hell, just as having to *be* was hell for him. All the physical sensations are there, the dizzying lapse from pain's peak, but tilted downward, as it were, away from the domain of the mystic to that of the doctor or midwife. He, too, contracts.

Further on the poem's nature (and caliber), as the epitome of a certain kind of sensation, becomes even clearer when Berryman introduces

> faintings black, rigour, chilling, brown
> parching, back, brain burning, the grey pocks
> itch, a manic stench
> of pustules snapping, pain floods the palm,
> sleepless, or a red shaft with a dreadful start
> rides at the chapel, like a slipping heart.
> My soul strains in one qualm.

This is the iconography of panic, the physical equivalent of a pandemonium which Berryman excels at conveying without, however, getting quite past it into an imaginative survey of its sources. Somehow he stays with the physical end of the stick that is divine or cosmic. And when he has her exclaim

> I see the cruel spread Wings black with saints!

or

> torture me, Father, lest not I be thine!

he himself is on the edge of something he can't altogether manage. I mean faith or vision; he wants something beyond either, and he isn't prepared to deal in either as a means to that end. The result is that he gets next to nothing, although accumulating by the score states of mind of almost terrifying jagged intensity. In the following, for instance, what is clear is his vicarious flailing:

> I'll—I'll—
> I am closed & coming. Somewhere! I defile
> wide as a cloud, in a cloud,
> unfit, desirous, glad—even the singings veil.

The ardor of the would-be recipient is undeniable, but it ends feeding on itself, masticating its own convoluted texture. If ever a poem sat on the edge of an abyss, *Homage* does: it teeters, wobbles, falls apart, invites some cosmic power to rend it further, rends itself, comes provisionally together again, and comes to a dead stop with "a sourcing whom my lost candle like the firefly loves." It is no accident that he puts a double space between "a sourcing" and "whom": in that gap languishes the ghost of a missed connection which the relative pronoun disguises as "whom" while really implying whatever might have gone into the space. And it is no accident that the note to stanza 35 refers us to "cliffhangers" right after a note, concerning 33, on rapture of the deep (*"Délires des grandes profondeurs"*).

I have said enough, I hope, to establish Berryman, in this long poem at least, as the master of the ceremonies of homelessness. Not at home in the universe, he isn't located anywhere else. Unable to sift from cosmic phenomena the one he wants (maybe a personal intervention in his life by a caring God?), he transcribes the froth of wanting. In other words, he uses Anne Bradstreet to delineate the bitter-sweet, thwarted transcendence of a non-believer who asks only: Why should all this emotional ferment lead to nowhere, have no point? He aspires to a metaphysical habit in almost purely emotional terms without the least reaching out into the cosmic evidence. Or, if he does so, he does it allusively with an incurious nod: "The fireflies and the stars our only light." If you scrutinize the early and later poems together with *Homage*, you find a characteristic motion of his mind made plain: into gaps he keeps on finding, he stuffs not answers—or epiphanies, visions, saliences—but big fat badges of ruinous emotion:

> Your fears,
> Fidelity, and dandelions grown
> As big as elephants, your morning lust
> Can neither name nor control. No time for shame,
> Whippoorwill calling, excrement falling, time
> Rushes like a madman forward. Nothing can be known.

Nor measured, says Heisenberg. Nor whistled, says Wittgenstein. But that's too easy—what can be known, and know it we do, is how he feels being thus adrift, unhoused, not so much "ill" at ease as *terminally* ill at ease. At times he expresses it with lucid control:

> What I am looking for (*I am*) may be
> Happening in the gaps of what I know.

That is almost definitive. It will never be untrue of him. Images of ruin abound, from the voluntary of his Demented Priest who says "Someone interferes / Everywhere with me" to that of the Young Hawaiian who swims alone ("Whom Nangganangga smashed to pieces on / The road to Paradise") and the Professor who envisions meeting his refractory class ("in Upper Hell / Convulsed, foaming immortal blood."). Numerous personae act out his uneasiness, his sense of doomed velleity. The bridegroom extends his hand and places it in the womb, for lack of anything more ambitious to do. The tortured girl can no longer remember what her torturers want her to say. Again and again Berryman confronts himself with giving the mind something really worth doing or "the sick brain estop." His position, if that isn't too stern a word for it, is that the mind is redundant, existing only to invent problems it can never solve. In the end we cannot help ourselves, and that wan line in "Not To Live" takes on the force of an etymological reminder:

> a flux of a free & dying adjutant.

Adjūtāre means to assist or aid, which seems to be the one thing we cannot do for ourselves, "free" as we might be, even "dying" as we are.

Small wonder, then, that Berryman becomes the poet of metaphysical desolation, overloaded with feelings that don't belong anywhere. What becomes his forte is the desolating image in which fright, jitters, nightmare, and general ontological vertigo get the reader on the raw and rake the flesh:

> With a bannister he laid a blue bone bare
> A tongue tore hard but one boot in a groin
> Sank like a drift   A double fist of hair
> Like feather members that will not rejoin
>
> Flat slams below there but I blew my drag
> Against my ash and strained.

Piled-up stresses evince his stress. The violence violates an old decorum of having something to say; all he has "to say" is how he feels, and he feels lousy because he has no idea of what he wants, except it's what he doesn't have. A famous, nerve-numbing, drum-beating line does the work of many:

> Near the top a bad turn some dare. Well,
> The horse swerves and screams, his eyes pop.

Such is his compression of panic, and Berryman never loses the ability to produce (perhaps after Hopkins) lines that embody an almost unidentifiable terror, which is perhaps in the long run all this poet ever had.

Twenty years separate *Delusions, Etc.* from *Homage.* The imagery has widened out, especially the cosmic sort, from references to "the Local Group" (of galaxies, that is), the Hale reflector, Wolf-Rayet stars (which are *extremely* hot ones), to God as "Corpuscle-Donor," "pergalactic Intellect," and such novelties as collapsars and the expanding universe:

> Finite & unbounded
> the massive spirals absolutely fly
>
> distinctly apart, by math and *observation*,
> current math, this morning's telescopes
> & inference.

But the references come out of duty, not enthusiasm. Many of the poems in *Delusions, Etc.* add up to what he slyly calls "Opus Dei," otherwise to be described as

> (a layman's winter mockup, wherein moreover
> the Offices are not within one day said
> but thro' their hours at intervals
> over many weeks—such being the World).

Agile, suave in the extreme ("my heart skips a beat / actuellement"), full of cultural and historical allusions, the poems are monuments to a failed religious attitude. As much dares as entreaties, as much acts of defiance as calls for help, they more or less ask the Creator why the hell he hasn't come yet and gotten John Berryman, whose untidy, cussed, bad-mouth waiting is getting on John's overwrought nerves. In the wake of Auden's clinical and public-school "Sir," Berryman comes up with a miscellany of vocatives, from "Your Benevolence," "Thou hard," "Dear," to "You," "innegligent Father," "Sway omnicompetent," and others; but, although he works dismally hard at his new-found vocation of convert-disciple-prodigal unbeliever—he only keeps running headlong into the old panic which no flip "Okay" is going to mitigate. Shuddering and quaking, he says:

> High noon has me in pitchblack, so in hope out

and

> Shift!   Shift!
> Frantic I cast about abroad
> for avenues of out: Who really this this?
> Can all be lost, then?

and

> Dust in my sore mouth, this deafening wind,
> frightful space   down from all sides, I'm pale
> I faint for some soft & solid & sudden way out

which confirm him as a poet of unsignifying pain, whose yearning is as metaphysical as Herbert's, say, whose images are as dishevelled as those of Cowley and Carew, but whose mind just cannot shed ego and hitch an atomic or molecular or electromagnetic lift along one of the avenues of out. It is a sad spectacle, an even sadder sound, when he recites the physique of *Angst*. That is what he does from his beginning to his end and he has few competitors for his demoralized post. Perhaps no one else has done this narrow, yet inescapable thing quite so vividly, knowing that at the end of the line (end of the life-line) there is only sensuous escapism:

> O PARAKEETS & avocets, O immortelles
> & ibis, scarlet under that stunning sun,
> deliciously & tired I come
> toward you in orbit, Trinidad!

or something unspeakably bleak (and literally so):

> I don't think I will sing

> any more just now;
> or ever. I must start
> to sit with a blind brow
> above an empty heart.

Neither putting parakeets in upper case, as if to make them even bigger and more special (a superspecies), nor telegraphing "or ever" with a semi-colon that slows everything to an almost permanent halt anyway, changes the basic hurt. Berryman may not have cut through to the *x* for unknown that he craved and coveted with all his being; the increasing scope of his references has more a look of trophy-hunting than that of awed immersion; he never achieved what a *Newsweek* reviewer incredibly gifted him with (an "austere, level voice . . . so quiet it's sometimes hard to hear him"!); but it is impossible not to recognize the gibbering convulsions of his need. I think of him as a naturally metaphysical spirit, but one unable to sense the wonder that accompanies what he thought the *insult*, the *snub*, behind the nomenclature, almost as if the Local Group—never mind its inclusion of the Milky Way system, the Andromeda and Triangulum Spirals, the Magellanic Clouds, the two dwarf systems in Sculptor and Fornax, and maybe even two objects in Perseus called Maffei 1 and 2—were something from which he'd been shut out. That is the least we can say about him, though; the best is that he somehow mustered the courage to face ontological precipices dared by only a few.

Randall Jarrell:
The Man Who Painted Bulls

Mary Kinzie

We learned from you so much about so many things
But never what we were; and yet you made us that.

Randall Jarrell is the bridge between the great Freudian poetry of the twenties and thirties (especially that of Allen Tate and W. H. Auden) and the definitive movement in American poetry since the war, confessionalism (Lowell, Schwartz, Roethke, Berryman, and later Snodgrass, Plath, and Sexton). In order to give Jarrell his due as a poet, one need only reread Allen Tate knowing that Jarrell would write after him. In this light, Tate can seem as class-conscious, time-bound, predictable, and outmoded as Tennyson. Or compare Robert Lowell with Jarrell, and he sounds in *Mills of the Kavanaughs* aimlessly mad (as if imitating Dylan Thomas), and in *Life Studies* and *For the Union Dead* a bit like a Browning character on the slats.

In other words, the way in which Randall Jarrell acts as watershed or eponym tends to make both his forebears and his successors (not to mention his contemporaries) sound traditional. Surely this is proof, or partial proof, of Jarrell's peculiarity, his originality in absorbing his evident influences. But it is the kind of rescue, the kind of proof, that has motivated too few critics to return to Jarrell for his own sake, namely, for the sake of what he did that was never to be copied. As he admitted, he identified himself, in a way no one else ever quite has, "with something something's wrong with, with something human." I know of no other writer in our period who could write of war, technology, military nerves, the common soldier or pilot, so that these things appear mystical: not lovely, but secret. He is, in addition, one of the great psychologists of childhood and dream. And after Pound and Eliot and before Berryman, Jarrell is the great twentieth-century master of the dramatic monologue. Nor, finally, do I know of any other writer who could, at his best, so inundate his characters with the

From *The Southern Review* 16, no. 4 (October 1980). © 1980, 1987 by Mary Kinzie.

commonest kinds of objects to form their immediate world, yet present them as more than the sum of these things.

As an experiment, compare the disembodied quality of the disadvantaged in Jarrell with the treatment of the poor we get in that Thomas Hobbes of verse, William Carlos Williams. As soon as one puts the two realms side by side, bizarre things happen, and the paralysis we are so struck by in a Jarrell poem like "Lady Bates" seems paradisiacal next to that in *Paterson*. And at the same time, next to Williams, that arch-poet of bare things and bare places, Jarrell appears to have come from no place. Without Whitman's rhetorical exuberance, being from no place could not mean, for Jarrell, being from everyplace. He was simply somebody who didn't fit anywhere in particular but pretty well everywhere in general. Williams *fit* in New Jersey, he chose it and suffered it, even though his deliberate classlessness would seem prima facie the opposite of, say, Robert Lowell's identification with New England aristocracy. Again: in Jarrell's light, both Lowell and Williams seem more *placed* than they otherwise would.

When asked what strikes them first and last about Jarrell's poetry, many writers have answered and I would concur: his heart, his sentiment, even his sentimentality. *He was*, critics, admirers, eulogists say, *so*—something; so fair, so soft, so tender; or so mean, so unyielding, so brave, so cruel—*that he could not . . .* (whatever it was they wanted him to have done). The adjectives in the second group, of course, apply to his criticism; those in the first to his poetry. Jarrell seemed to many to have split his imagination in two, reserving for the poetry the gentler emotions while plying the critical reviews with his dazzling and rebarbative genius. It is on account of his powerful visibility as a critic that so many writers have divided over his poetry. He has been a principal case for the exercise of polemic. About what other writer has there been ranged so much dismay, so much misgiving, so much regret? Is it, moreover, any accident that Jarrell did for magazine writing after the war what T. S. Eliot did for literary criticism before it? Or that Jarrell gave to *his* critics the weapon by which, not to slay him, but to ignore him?

In the ideal *History of Taste* that someone will write for our period, a small and interesting appendix will be affixed to explain the unfortunate way Jarrell's writing of criticism, or the writing of the often obstreperous *kind* of criticism he wrote, clouded judgment of his poems not only on the part of those he irritated but also among those who knew the criticism better than they knew the poetry—or who responded to it more readily. (Many of us have been wont to take arguments about art more seriously than we take art. By a nice irony, Jarrell himself frequently wrote *essays* on this problem.) And in this *History of Taste*, in addition to a history of the ways in which Randall Jarrell's criticism not only described but perhaps partially created the conditions under which poetry like his own could be dismissed (that is, because his principles of praise and blame were eccentric, evaluative, and uncodified), we would have to be given another history:

of the extent to which, after the publication of *The Seven-League Crutches* in 1951, Jarrell could be said to have substituted the writing of prose for the writing of poetry. Might the chroniclers then side here with Robert Boyers, who wrote in *Modern Occasions* in 1972 that Jarrell's choice of poetry as a medium throughout his career appeared arbitrary: "Frequently we have the sense that he might well have written in some other medium and done as well, said as much, moved us as deeply"? Certainly the criticism, the novel *Pictures from an Institution* (1954), the children's tales, and the translations of Goethe (all of *Faust*, part 1), Rilke, Chekhov, Mörike, Grimm, Radauskas, and Corbière, were other mediums through which he moved, and moved us.

But the work of the poet does not appear to me to blend with the tones and concerns of the prose-writer—that strong surface gaiety that can suddenly rise to exuberance, that broad but limiting urbanity—until *The Woman at the Washington Zoo* (1960). And even in this volume, half of which is translations, and where we find, among others, the long, garrulous, and unsuccessful poem "The End of the Rainbow" (an attempt to reproduce his successes in "The Night before the Night before Christmas"), we also find some of Jarrell's most stunning work: the title poem, the marvelous sinister Donatello poem, "The Elementary Scene," "Windows," "Aging," and "A Ghost, a Real Ghost." I would argue that, however his prose may have deflected his or our interest away from his poetry, and however different the voices of Jarrell in his great scornful epistles and in his many touching poems about childhood, the fortunes of Jarrell's genius are perhaps more complex than a simple split between genres, or than the application of different kinds of energy or intellect to different forms of disclosure. Like all half-truths, this one can get us over the subject, not into it.

All poets, artists, and thinkers are hobbled by their temperaments, by their opinions. It is when their opinions, these automatic predilections, balance most precariously over certain kinds of issues in the imagination that we can look at the result and say: this was a representative mind. (With regard to the increasing amounts of prose in his poetry, the hobbling by one's temperament can become a kind of stylistic fate, one no longer precarious because of the ideas, but standardized and a bit hopeless of solution.) I will label the two sides of Jarrell's automatic or tempermental predicament in this shorthand form: he was a negative thinker, tending to nihilism, about the way of the world, who nevertheless had a huge reservoir of nostalgia, melancholy, wistfulness, and pity that he displayed toward the categorically innocent individual. In the most fatuous numerical form, one might say that this point of view resulted in the judgment that the collective was evil, the negligible integer good. I will also label his truly representative result, the peculiar form Jarrell's defense against these irreconcilables took, as a narcissism out of which was drawn an inordinate sympathy for others. I would like to discuss some of the ways these warring opposites appear in the poems, and explain my reasons for thinking that his poetry gives us one of those extraordinary simplifying ideas that represent us to ourselves.

Jarrell was, I believe, one of those narcissistic poets to whom, as to Wordsworth and Arnold in their periods, we owe one of the most important of the modern age's definitions of the self. For Jarrell, the self is what comes into being without our help, without our notice, and without our having been, at any point, able to alter what we have become:

> That is what happens to everyone.
> At first you get bigger, you know more,
> Then something goes wrong.
> You are, and you say: I am—
> And you were . . . I've been too long.

This is a paradoxical attitude for a good Freudian to hold, although commensurate with Freud's thought as I will try to show later, and equally paradoxical for a poet as characteristically attuned to children and to his own childhood as Jarrell was. With respect to childhood, in fact, Jarrell had the uncanny ability to think himself back to states of mind, attitudes of hope, dread, and tremulous expectancy that the combative passages of adolescence arrange to hide from most of us:

> We wept so? How well we all forget!
> One taste of memory (like Fafnir's blood)
> Makes all their language sensible, one's ears
> Burn with the child's peculiar gift for pain.

This ability to *think back* was so highly defined—Jarrell's self as a child so distant from and hence identical with his later self—that he was able to extend the principle to the minds of others. He was able to relinquish himself to those monologists who are aging, misplaced, bewildered, dying; to become those speakers caught in the dark wood of a fairy tale or dream; to mime those voices audible among the dead.

Now neither Wordsworth nor Arnold was especially good at this kind of transfer of allegiance from their own to the lives and minds of others. The scholar-gypsy and Empedocles were counters for Arnold's ego and desire, just as the leech-gatherer and the old Cumberland beggar, half-erased transparencies that they were, were agreeable places for Wordsworth to project himself upon the landscape. It is part of Jarrell's great difference from them, and part of his suitability to his period, that his concept of self does not allow for projection; the self is not continuous. Jarrell cannot rehearse the *changes of state* from infant to child, child to adolescent, adolescent to adult. He can only record the sense of confusion *within a state* that has no clue as to how to get itself changed. This is the source of the trapped, bewildered pathos on the part of the child questioning the adult world, the sense of loss of the mature being looking back on the child, and of the dead looking back on the living. Often, Jarrell will insist that the two are one, the man the child, the living the dead.

Among so many pairs of opposites in the poems—men vs. children, living vs. dead, bad vs. good, the masses vs. the human soul—there is one recurring mediating state: the dream. It is this uncertain threshold to which Jarrell the poet tried to hold himself, sometimes unsteadily or too vaguely, sometimes tipping over into rivers of mythic blood (*Orestes at Tauris*, "Che Faro Senza Euridice," "The Märchen"), sometimes falling into Freudian bathos ("A Little Poem") or the Audenesque variant ("The Iceberg," "Love, in Its Separate Being"), and sometimes dwelling too obsessively on detail ("The End of the Rainbow," the longer of the two poems entitled "Hope"). But even in poems I would call failed or strained, the main business is dream-work, which translates the experience of the childhood self into the language of the adult. Not that the poetry is literally the product, as some poetry can appear to be, of dreams the author may actually have had; Jarrell's program is a deliberate dreaming-back, a relatively conscious act. It is further significant that the realm of early years to which his poetic dreams recur is principally the period of latency, not the earlier precognitive period. It is as if the two great periods of libidinal and aggressive energy, infancy and adolescence, had been erased by their very violence, and what remained were the states among which Jarrell holds his dialogue, childhood and maturity, two periods of achieved quiescence that do not know their real histories or their real names:

> Today, the child lies wet and warm
> In his big mother; tomorrow, too, is dumb,
> The dry skull of the cold tomb. "Between?"
> Between I suffered.
>   ("The Difficult Resolution")

Some of the characteristic exclamations and insistent questions in Jarrell's poems derive from this sketch of the matched states of mutually exclusive consciousness, as if each version, child and adult, of the self-in-arrest were asking about its dark, forgotten, torrential years, suspecting that there is a link, a point of passage, all the while it is unable to prove anything. The terminal convalescent in "The Long Vacation" in *Blood for a Stranger* (called "A Utopian Journey" in *Collected Poems*) asks of his experience, *"But what was it? What am I?"* In the dream of "The Night before the Night before Christmas" the girl's little brother learns that he is dying. He replies, "I didn't know," indicating a touching acceptance, while the girl whose dream it is cries out her unaccepting "I don't know, I don't know, I don't know!" The sick child in bed in "A Quilt Pattern" discovers, or nearly discovers, strange truths in his feverish hallucinations; he almost knows that the true witch is the gingerbread house:

>   the house of bread
> Calls to him in its slow singing voice:
> "Feed, feed! Are you fat now?
> Hold out your finger."
> The boy holds out the bone of the finger.
> It moves, but the house says, "No, you don't know.
> Eat a little longer."
> The taste of the house
> Is the taste of his—
>   "I don't know,"
> Thinks the boy, "No, I don't know!"

In Jarrell, one might say, the self defines itself by its desire to be unlike the eternal rule, the law of the masses, the voice that says, You too will die and be unimportant, or, Your very unimportance is the equivalent of your death. But still the self hopes to escape the law of large numbers, the force of history's evidence, by being—itself. Some early poems of Jarrell's close on the irrevocable fact of this bleak knowledge:

> I see at last that all the knowledge
>
> I wrung from the darkness—that the darkness flung me—
> Is worthless as ignorance: nothing comes from nothing,
> The darkness from the darkness. Pain comes from the
>   darkness
> And we call it wisdom. It is pain.
>
>   ("90 North")

But increasingly throughout his poetic career Jarrell inserts the strange keynote following the characters' recognition that pain outstrips knowledge, and this keynote is the tenacious belief in *something*, something else, something more, something one hasn't thought of yet that must nevertheless be there, something that will make a more human sense out of this human discomfort. Often these assertions of the necessary existence of the saving residue are called, simply, "something":

>   *Say again*
> Say the voices, *say again*
> *That life is—what it is not;*
> *That, somewhere, there is—something, something;*
> *That we are waiting; that we are waiting.*

What I find chilling about those lines is the fact that they are spoken by people who have died. As the dead implore in "The Survivor among Graves," so Jarrell's characters persistently ask that life be—*what it is not*. But when his people try the statement out, and turn "Life is life" into "Life is not life," "it sounds the same." The simple contrary, the insertion of the negative into one's belief, makes very little difference:

> In the great world everything is just the same
> Or just the opposite, we found (we never went).
>   ("The Märchen")

This perverse, affronted, ambiguous mood, in which to say *Life is life* amounts to the same thing as saying *It isn't,* is part of Jarrell's flat style, the undercurrent of nihilism that runs through the verse. In the original version of "The Memoirs of Glückel of Hameln" in *Blood for a Stranger,* Jarrell addresses the memoirist with the dismissive conclusion that about him

> there is none to care.
> Glückel, Glückel, you tell indifferently
> To ears indifferent with Necessity
> The torments and obsessions of our life:
> Your pain seems only the useless echo
> Of all the evil we already know.

In a poem he did not publish, Jarrell makes the same sort of heavily careless statement: "Life is—why, life: / It is what all our evils have in common." Such statements are part of Jarrell's melancholy determinism, especially evident in the first three volumes, according to which nothing the individual does will make a difference to the States who are conducting the war with *his* life. "The Wide Prospect" in *Little Friend, Little Friend* is an apt example of the Jarrell allegory of Trade fed by the bodies of living men. In the same volume, guns practice against the thin body of a soldier "pinned against the light." A tormented life is nothing more than the fly caught in "the lying amber of the histories." "The Difficult Resolution" exhorts us to realize that we have no way to exercise the will except in realizing that we cannot exercise it. The warrior dressed in an ancient name to fight modern war in "Siegfried" chants over and over to himself that "It happens as it does because it does." The great thinkers of the dawn of the scientific age, Bruno, Galileo, and Newton, have at least taught us how "to understand but not to change." The world tells the dead child that it "will not be missed." What is left to us in this dreary program is but the "bare dilemma of the beast—to go on being."

But something rather remarkable happens when the poet's ire is directed, not against the modern State at war, not against the tawdry laws of destiny, not against the evil mass, but against the mechanisms of unavoidable suffering in the individual soul. The same logical structure is also present in the world of highly eccentric and highly self-absorbed individuals with whom we have come to identify Jarrell's best poetry. This structure is that of the logical contrary made into a tautology, one that makes changing and not changing the same thing. Just as Siegfried implores everything to "be the way it was. Let me not matter . . . Let me be what I was," the woman at the Washington Zoo cries to the god she sees behind the vulture,

"You know what I was, / You see what I am: change me, change me!" The state wished for in either case is that of the infinite, integral world of the past.

A phenomenon related to that of changing and not changing—a dilemma that resolves itself into the *tertium quid* of desire to be a child again, to be what one was—is the easy transitive relation between the world and the human being. It is not only in derisory poems like "A Girl in a Library" that Jarrell is moved to say, of the confrontation of the individual with reality, that "they look alike already," but in the more mysterious confrontation of the soul with its deathly double in "Hohensalzburg: Fantastic Variations on a Theme of Romantic Character" (a title that is, to say the least, a bit defensive), where the homely German ghosts transform the clumsy wanderer-through-the-wood into chandeliers and china roses: "these German ghosts . . . only change / Men into things, things into things." Even in the poems where we find what is certainly Jarrell's prescription for the highest human art, say a poem like "The Old and the New Masters," which was meant as a penultimate answer to the view of art Jarrell considered most despicable, namely, Auden's in "Musée des Beaux Arts," each thing takes on a signal majesty—not only in contributing to the whole (the old organic argument), but in settling once and for all the place of the negligible small object in the plan of God as we can still perceive it in the fallen world. Under this paradigm, the place of all celebrants in Georges de La Tour's *St. Sebastian Mourned by St. Irene* is that of beings who watch, and are, "the one thing in the world." Although the topic is not quite so elevated in the poem that follows in *The Lost World*, "Field and Forest," the same transitive sympathy occurs between the forests-that-were before the farmer cleared them and the fields-that-are, and Jarrell makes clear that the same transitive overflow informs the farmer's guilty recognition that his boyhood self and the fox he watched from his young, credulous, observant life so many years ago are the same double being (no longer in harmony but accuser and accused); thus the sad irony in "The trees can't tell the two of them apart."

Taken to a further extreme, the principle of interchangeability between the human observer and the observed world results in a like interchangeability between the very feeling of being and the items from which the person derives that feeling so that even in the very early poem "The Christmas Roses," the dying woman, the poles of whose thought are her coming death and the master leaver whom she loves, knows that if he touches her she will not die. Similarly, after the long rehearsal of all the details in Dürer's engraving of the knight, death, and the devil, the poet can affirm that the being of the knight defines itself in despite of the exhaustively catalogued qualities of his two companions: "A man's look completes itself." The intention of the human beings is equated by Jarrell with the intention of the world. Because they have the world within them, these figures become it and, after a fashion, do not need it.

Given a slightly different twist, this notion of the self-sufficiency of the intent consciousness allows Jarrell to make a long, scathing judgment of Donatello's vain adolescent David, the bronze statue of the indifferent, callow young victor which, by putting between itself and the world "a shining / Line of delimitation," becomes a thing entire and apart: "The body mirrors itself." Although the bronze David is viewed from a perspective that is not merely celebratory but critical, while the poems on Dürer and de La Tour are written in a mood more closely affirmative both of the artist and the subject, I think one can see how the tendency toward definition of the self in the transport of high aesthetic moments resembles the selves defined in moments of extremity, as in "The Christmas Roses" or "Burning the Letters." One comes down in the end to mere being. Gertrude Johnson, the novelist in *Pictures from an Institution* (1954), is brought to her knees by the question she asks herself: *"Am I—was she what?"* and then Jarrell writes that the question turned into *"Am I? Am I?"* His final lines describing the Dürer knight read:

> The face is its own face—*a man does what he must*—
> And the body underneath it says: *I am.*

In light of the recessive claim, the small *I am*, it would be a marvelous solution to all the problems Jarrell has raised if it were still possible to watch with reverence a great miracle, to become thereby the miracle. But "The Old and the New Masters" is about a vision in that other time when everything, even art, was better. The more apt definition of the youth in the landscape is to be found in the first poem of *The Seven-League Crutches*, "The Orient Express." The vivid, brief tableaux one sees from the train window appear, says Jarrell, almost as they would to a child. By day, it's all right, "but at evening . . . a questioning / Precariousness comes over everything." The precariousness is not the imminent dissolution of the real into the unreal, but the awful reverse, as the sick child to whom the narrator looks back observes the few "things from a primer" about his room, then

> Outside the window
> There were the chairs and tables of the world. . . .
> I saw that the world
> That had seemed to me the plain
> Gray mask of all that was strange
> Behind it—of all that *was*—was all.

No mask hiding mysteries, the world is the dreary front—and back, and interior—of all that it is and has to offer. The people with their lives and real gestures beyond the train window, like the fields on which they are silhouetted, and the paths one can see leading to a wood all full of lives, and the train

Passing, after all unchangeable
And not now ever to stop, like a heart—

It is like any other work of art.
It is and never can be changed.
Behind everything there is always
The unknown unwanted life.

Something extraordinary happens to the condensation of this poem after the syntactic break. The tempo shifts to a swifter and more inexorable kind of utterance, and the last four lines raise as many questions as they solve. Was this series of scenes through a train window a work of art then? Was the scene beyond the child's sickbed one also? Is it the prime talent of art to be and not be changed? Is it the fact that "it" is art that makes it shelter "the unknown unwanted life?" Or is it because "it" is like any other thing that the unwanted and somehow one-dimensional life resides behind it? Does Jarrell mean that art is window dressing for the unmysterious world we all sooner or later learn is there?

If we go a bit beyond the terms set by the poem in "The Orient Express," these questions will not be difficult to answer. Let us rephrase them, in fact, so that it is neither art nor even memory that constitutes the "it" that "never can be changed," but rather the self. The rapidly changing scenes out the train window, says the long simile of the poem, are like the solidly unchanging things in the child's bedroom, which at a crucial moment of insight and growth are compared to the things in the greater world beyond: "the chairs and tables of the world." At some moment, random as far as any direct cause could be discerned by the subject, yet known and recorded by thinkers like Freud and Piaget, the world fixes itself in the subject's attention in such a way as to make everything at once solid and coherent, and *unto itself*. The experience of selfhood is couched in terms of the retreat of the nurturing world to the outside, the other, although of course the real result is the individual's sense of separate being. This produces the angry melancholy of the Jarrell poem: those scenes are unmade, unwanted by *me*. Even here, needless to say, there is a rapid transitive interchange between the observing self and the observed world, so that in proportion as the obstinate exterior scene is unwanted, the self perceives his own unwantedness, his own dispensability for some other observer, not least of all, finally, for himself.

Before discussing the companion poem to "The Orient Express," a poem paired with it both in *The Seven-League Crutches* (1951) and *Selected Poems* (1955), namely "A Game at Salzburg," I would like to suggest very briefly the early poems one would look to in order to trace this experience of the separation of the young self from the solid world, and of the self's first insight into its own integral separateness. In *Blood for a Stranger* (1942) Jarrell treats the coming of the self to the self as a polarity between love for the world and a sense of betrayal by it. "A Little Poem" and "Love, in

Its Separate Being . . . '' give us two variants on the theme of betrayal; in the former, a child has been usurped by the arrival of an interloper, another child, to whom he speaks while the other is still in the womb; in the second poem the child is betrayed by the forces of history. In a third poem, ''Fear,'' Jarrell articulates this abused estrangement of the child by suggesting that the little girl here is caught and compromised by being a cipher in the dreams of the adult world, and in a grim forecast of the willful retreat of the chairs and tables of the world in ''The Orient Express,'' the child is encouraged by the statues, those substitute adults, to ''be like us, absolute.''

''The Iceberg'' and ''90 North'' are children's adventure dreams of Arctic exploration and skin diving in which the outcome of the exuberant voyages is a fierce despair. The iceberg is a symbol of Necessity in a poem where even air and water are malevolent. In ''90 North,'' when the child decides (as the strange arbitrary power-shifts of dreams permit him to do) to leave the North Pole and go home,

> Turn as I please, my step is to the south.
> The world—my world spins on this final point
> Of cold and wretchedness: all lines, all winds
> End in this whirlpool I at last discover.
>
> And it is meaningless.

Although this voyage to the north had meaning for him as a child, now the speaker sees that (as we quoted earlier) the knowledge he thought he had gained was worthless, and that the pain he wrung from the darkness and called wisdom was really only pain.

On the other side of the picture we find ambiguous, painful dream poems in which love for the world and the state of being loved by it—the self's adventuresomeness rewarded—are emotions that the dream keeps curiously blocked or inflexible. In ''The Lost Love'' a dead woman (the mother as lover) returns to caress the dreaming child; when the child responds, something fearful is suggested: ''When I touched you / My hand was cold.'' ''The Skaters'' is the early apotheosis of the adventure poem and of the category of poems like ''Fear,'' which are broodings on hidden losses when the self and the world dream together. But ''The Skaters,'' like ''The Lost Love,'' is also a poem of yearning that nearly becomes passion, a passion repressed by the eeriness of the rhythms of the dream; ''How long we pled our love / How thorough our embrace!'' is followed by the two lovers' rout into

> The abyss where my deaf limbs forget
> The cold mouth's dumb assent;
> The skaters like swallows flicker
> Around us in the long descent.

The original love of the child and the mother finds its place here, in the pleading and thorough embraces of stanza six, just as the mother returns to the child in "The Lost Love"—and in many later poems ("2nd Air Force," where the mother, perhaps to his infinite aggravation, visits her son in basic training; "Mother, Said the Child," the first of the many *Kindertotenlieder* Jarrell was to write, among them "Come to the Stones . . . ," "Protocols," and "The State," in the same volume of which we are now speaking, *Little Friend, Little Friend*, 1945).

Many intonations are given to the central theme of the child's family struggle, which is also the struggle to import the flexibility and childish sense of adventure into the world of action without being haunted by sexuality. The escape to dream in "The Skaters" is linked to the poems in which the child escapes yet further from his life and makes his family pay yet more dearly for his loss. The schoolboy's fantasy of his own disappearance in "A Story" in *Blood for a Stranger* (1942) is written in the same ingenuous, sorrowing mood as the later laments of those who are actually dead in *Little Friend, Little Friend* and in *Losses* (1948), "Lady Bates," "Jews at Haifa," and "In the Camp There Was One Alive." When these songs of dead children in *Losses* are compared to the living child's bereavement at the loss of his father after his parents' divorce in "A Child of Courts" in the same volume (called "The Prince" in *Collected Poems*), it is clear what equivalences have been enforced between the living and the dead. The child construes loss not as the absence of the good but as the presence of the good turned into the bad, into the dead. The child lies in an agony of fear, shrinking up like his pet rabbit, when he hears the father's hand like a rabbit's paws scraping at the dirt. Then, in a majestic act of courage and forgiveness, the boy "inch[es] my cold hand out to his cold hand." In the third stanza, after nothing has grasped his heroically offered hand, the boy throws his "furs" off, then hears a sentry calling.

> I start to weep because—because there are no ghosts;
> A man dies like a rabbit, for a use.
> What will they pay me, when I die, to die?

The transfer in the child's reason from the retreat of the parent to his own retreat in death is made here by the sudden additional knowledge, or recollection, that the child is grown, asleep in a barracks in wartime, that they have all long since really died, father, rabbit, many military cronies, many millions of Europeans, and that the smaller deaths were to be followed by the greater ones. Across the chasm of guilt abruptly opened as the child turns—before his eyes as well as ours—into a grown man, the speaker has no opportunity to enact the desired retribution: to make *them* pay for their "deaths" by dying himself. When he does die, it will be for a small use, as a rabbit dies for a use, as a soldier dies in his numbers.

Losses contains several other poems in which a child wakes up in the war. The recuperating dreamers here all bear a strong resemblance to the child of courts. The prisoner with a pet rabbit in "Stalag Luft" dreams an adventure dream about being an Indian brave ("The dappled mustangs graze / By the quills of the milky leggings"). The wounded pilot in "A Field Hospital" translates the remembered sound of an air battle into the report of a hunter's gun:

> "The great drake
> Flutters to the icy lake—
> The shotguns stammer in my head.
> I lie in my own bed,"
> He whispers, "dreaming"; and he thinks to wake.
> The old mistake.

The wounded men of "A Ward in the States" dream that they are still in the Pacific wishing they were home. And the wounded man in "In the Ward: The Sacred Wood" creates a more complex relation between the child's creation by things outside him and his desire, or even ability, to "unmake" that which made him:

> The trees rise to me from the world
> That made me, I call to the grove
> That stretches inch on inch without one God:
> "I have unmade you now; but I must die."

In *Losses* we also find two of Jarrell's most famous war poems, "The Dead Wingman" and "Pilots, Man Your Planes," the latter a record of a long air engagement between American and Japanese planes that ends in the destruction of the aircraft carrier. These two poems, realistic rather than hallucinatory, both end in a way curiously complementary to the dreams: the pilots fall asleep. The one

> Knows, knows at last; he yawns the chattering yawn
> Of effort and anguish, of hurt hating helplessness—
> Yawns sobbingly, his head falls back, he sleeps.

The other, failing in his search for his wingman, keeps on

> Gliding above the cities' shells, a stubborn eye
> Among the embers of the nations, achingly
> Tracing the circles of that worn, unchanging *No*—
> The lives' long war, lost war—the pilot sleeps.

Clearly, these are the responses of utterly weary bodies; but equally clearly, the yawn "of effort and anguish, of hurt hating helplessness" makes the pilots kin to the helplessly dreaming wounded in the book, to the speaking dead who cannot yet bear to leave the earth, to the lives from which men try to wake ("the old mistake").

I began by claiming that Jarrell's influence on modern poetry derives from his definition of the self as something that got to be the way it is without the human's conscious ability to control what he would become, or even to record the process of becoming. The dream seemed to me to be the mediating state in which Jarrell's children discover or combat the discovery of what they are becoming, and where his grown-ups become children by forgetting the same knowledge, or courting an earlier, less lethal form of it. Jarrell is a poet who proceeds in shadow language, as if to say the truth in a dream released him from the guilt of revealing it. The characteristic pleas, *Let me be what I was, Let nothing matter, Change me, change me!* resemble the characteristic questions, *But what was it, what am I?* and the brilliant exclamations, *I don't know, I don't know!* as well as the repeated assertion of belief in *Something, something,* because they all rehearse, after their fashions, the principles of avoidance and incredulity in the developing life. Thus the urgency on the part of things to turn into things, and on the part of men to turn into things or to share with things the bare property described in the statements *These are,* or *I am,* are solutions with a double edge. On the one hand, to feel that one *is* makes one the center of a reverently circumscribed world; but on the other hand, one shares that simple, dull, and unqualified being with everything that lies beyond, sometimes only a short distance away, just as unknown, but also unwanted. In discussing "The Orient Express," and with a view toward returning to it and to its companion poem "A Game at Salzburg," I suggested that the dark pattern of being—life as what all our evils have in common, or the knowledge of our unimportance and the simultaneous knowledge of our death—was always balanced in Jarrell by the contrary impulse to affirmation, the light pattern, the unutterable love; that both the light and dark patterns were adumbrated in the dream poem, and that the alternations beween them illustrated the child's recurrent "family tragedy." It may have sounded casuist (although I do not think it is) to uphold a poem like "The Skaters" as a crucial scene in the family tragedy by virtue of its "happy ending"; that is, the flexible hope of the dreaming child is protected by the dream both from himself (his desire) and from his companion (the world). ("The Skaters" belongs to that plaintive group of Jarrell poems that treat of yearning in the human soul; I hope to place "The Black Swan" beside it in a moment.) The sadder or more vicious counterparts to "The Skaters" in the child's family album, the little-child-lost poems, "The Child of Courts," and the *Kindertotenlieder,* are still visible in the background when we come to the large group of war poems in *Little Friend, Little Friend* and *Losses.*

One of the most remarkable features of Jarrell's style is his application of an essentially descriptive, cataloguing turn of mind, not to nature descriptions or to the households where his people find themselves (we see very little in a sure photographic sense), but to the psychological traits and the life-histories of his personae. When, as is the case in "Lady Bates," "The End of the Rainbow," or "The Next Day," a person's life is reputed to have been bound up with things, blackberries and washtubs, tubes of paint, grocery bags, we find out through those lists of things a bit about where and how these people lived. But the emphasis is on the wavering habits of selection, a sort of neurosis of choice, whereby the suburban matron, the old lady who paints watercolors in Laguna Beach, and the wife and mother visited by the eland in *"Seele im Raum,"* take from the real world only what is nearest for reflection in their inner worlds. At the same time, Jarrell is so anxious that we *know* the people he speaks of that he is not always judicious in letting them select. The reason may be that Jarrell needed to discover people through their things, even to discover his own thought through its accidental or contingent counters, for he uses the same catalogue system when he writes of his own childhood in "Children's Arms," "A Night with Lions," "A Street off Sunset," and "Thinking of the Lost World." Jarrell might have been speaking of this habit of desultory obsessiveness when he wrote, in "Children's Arms," that in his

> Talk with the world, in which it tells me what I know
> And I tell it, "I know"—how strange that I
> Know nothing, and yet it tells me what I know!

The most successful of the long life-portraits that Jarrell drew is "The Night before the Night before Christmas" in *The Seven-League Crutches* (1951). The young girl here is presented differently, with much more sympathy than is "A Girl in a Library." We know more about the Christmas girl because she thinks more deeply about things than the Phys. Ed. major with glasses and braids and the legs of a Valkyrie. She is, in addition, more full of pathos because she is surrounded by pathos: her little brother is perhaps dying, her mother is dead, the squirrel that she and her brother had fed in the park has gone away, her father is a distant and, one suspects, harried Rotarian with peppy slogans on his office wall. The young girl has a social conscience that she imposes somewhat stubbornly on friends and family; she is wrapping a copy of Engels for a Christmas gift, and her mind is full of workers' slogans, an enlightened atheism, Value, Power, ponies in the mines. But she is also full of cosmetics and angora socks and vaguely romantic yearnings. And, finally, her world is also haunted by the residual talismans of a childhood she assumes she has left behind, the fairy tales on her bookshelf, the covering presence of the spirits of animals, the story of Hansel and Gretel, the dream of a galaxy webbed with the icy eyelashes of the squirrel.

The point of the poem, when we reach the end of its thirteen pages, *cannot* have been a life study or a grotesque (in Sherwood Anderson's sense). What is the point then? Simply that we assent to the realization that "they are all there together"? That is part of it. The rest is that we're brought through the long emotional crescendo of the last five pages of the poem, not just to a sympathy with the essential being of the girl—her knowledge that her brother is dying, that she and he are suspended in an ambiguous universe together, and that she cannot help any of it—but to a manifestation of Jarrell's victory over his own limitations. Although he restricts the portrait to what he considers truest about the young girl, limiting himself to a narrative instead of a full-fledged dramatic monologue, we do not feel he has either falsified or condescended to her. For the poet knows that the girl only plays with Marxism the way most middle-class Americans do, making it sentimental at a safe distance; he also knows that, even among those who play with moral and political structures they needn't adopt, there is a craving for the good that is shown in understanding. The great crisis of sympathy in Jarrell's portrait here comes about when the sister "grows up" into her essential childlikeness. The two things that matter are her sick brother and the fact that Friedrich Engels (in German the name means angel) represents a snowy presence, a Father Christmas, with no feast to celebrate: "There is not one thing that knows / It is almost Christmas." The poem's closing rush of sentiment, so characteristic of Jarrell's work, is thus a true "arrival" for this girl, and a much less cloying image than the one of her brother being sent down into the capitalists' mines: "She feels, in her hand, her brother's hand. / She is crying." We hear in these closing lines a muted reference to a more powerful plot in the poem, although Jarrell doesn't press the point but rather allows the long associative struggles of the sister to bring this last small clue to the surface; she had earlier seen how, "At the side of the shepherds Hansel / Stands hand in hand with Gretel."

The pull of the fairy tale is particularly strong in *The Seven-League Crutches*, doubtless Jarrell's best book. The parable of the two children who are turned into birds in "The Black Swan" presents the love of a girl for her sister, who has been turned into a black swan, as a willingness to follow the changed one into death. Both Sister Bernetta Quinn and Suzanne Ferguson have traced the fairy tale sources in many of the poems. But no one in speaking of Jarrell's Grimm fixation has explained it as devastatingly as Karl Shapiro:

> Germany is the preconscious of Europe, almost all—no, all—her geniuses are maniacs, Germany itself is a maniac, the bright dangerous offspring of the Western soul.

But I don't know that anyone in talking about Jarrell's use of Grimm has indicated the persistent divergence of the poet from the spirit of these tales. Jarrell has imposed something closer to Hans Christian Andersen's conception of final metamorphosis, immutable change, upon the essentially restorable world of the Brothers Grimm. The maimings in the *Märchen* are fierce, bloody, and gratuitous, but in the end, really, no harm will come. The severed head is restored to the body, the hands that were cut off are put back, the bear turns back into the prince, the blind see, the foul are cleansed. But though there is less bloodshed in the Andersen stories about the little mermaid, the red shoes, the snow queen, and little Inger, the girl who stepped on bread in order not to dirty her fine new clothes, the maimings and changes of state, when they do come, horrify the more because they are more endless, more final. Consider the many long years during which little Inger must stand like a caryatid in the peristyle of hell until her heart is softened by her mother's tears. At last Inger is allowed to become a sparrow who gathers crumbs for the other birds to expiate her wastefulness. But she is never turned back into a girl, whereas the seven swans or seven ravens into which a witch has transformed the princess's seven brothers in several Grimm tales are allowed to return to human shape after several years of their sister's silence, and finally they are all human again, and they can all speak, and they have not grown in the meantime very much older. In Jarrell's "Black Swan" the little sister wants to expiate some sin—perhaps that she has a "bad sister," as a child in "A Quilt Pattern" has a "Good Me" and a "Bad Me"—but the form of expiation is union with her sister, so that love and longing are indistinguishable from remorse and complicity. The poem tells us (and the little sister knows this too) that the transformations into swans are only happening in a dream,

> But the swan my sister called, "Sleep at last, little sister,"
> And stroked all night, with a black wing, my wings.

In other words, the poem tells us that its experience is not real, but in a way it then retracts: we get no comfort from the proviso that it's only a dream. The little girl whose sister was turned into a swan, who yearned toward her in the center of the lake where she, too, was transformed into one, keeps on being a swan stroked by the black wings of the other. Although it is true, as Jarrell writes at the end of "The Märchen," that the tales are allegories of the human heart, and that the exercise of power in forming and delivering the wishes one is allowed to make is a version of the desire *to change, to change!*, the spirit of this and other poems of Jarrell's tell us that the change we wish for is never the one that visits us.

More and more in the later poems in *The Woman at the Washington Zoo* (1960) and *The Lost World* (1965), the world of the great fantasies, in which tales like "Hansel and Gretel" had figured, contracts. Consider the use of the tale in "A Quilt Pattern":

> Here a thousand stones
> Of the trail home shine from their strings
> Like just-brushed, just-lost teeth.
> All the birds of the forest
> Sit brooding, stuffed with crumbs.
> But at home, far, far away
> The white moon shines from the stones of the chimney,
> His white cat eats up his white pigeon

and in "The Elementary Scene" from *The Woman at the Washington Zoo:*

> Looking back in my mind I can see
> The white sun like a tin plate
> Over the wooden turning of the weeds;
> The street jerking—a wet swing—
> To end by the wall the children sang.

It is interesting that "The Elementary Scene" rejects the child's point of view to speak from the adult's: "I float above the small limbs like their dream: / I, I, the future that mends everything." Another poem from *The Woman at the Washington Zoo*, "A Ghost, a Real Ghost," in which the present time is just as dreary, dead, and removed, contains an equally harrowing formulation of the principle we have already found at work in so many of the poems: "The child is hopeful and unhappy in a world / Whose future is his recourse." But there is no future in this poem, only mourning:

> The first night I looked into the mirror
> And saw the room empty, I could not believe
>
> That it was possible to keep existing
> In such pain: I have existed.
>
> . . . .
> Am I dead? A ghost, a real ghost
> Has no need to die: what is he except
> A being without access to the universe
> That he has not yet managed to forget?

It is as if the girl in "The Night before . . . Christmas" were speaking from the other side of maturity; as if the sister turned into a swan were addressing the world she loved from the vantage of her paralyzed, disenfranchised doom.

Jarrell had earlier written of the stubborn duality of the unwanted world and the unknown unwanted self in "The Orient Express." In "A Game at Salzburg" he lets the world speak its parallel poem of yearning toward humankind, for in proportion as the self and the world had only their flat contours in common in the one poem, in "A Game at Salzburg" they have in common their compatible need of the other in order to be:

> the sun comes out, and the sky
> Is for an instant the first rain-washed blue
> Of becoming: and my look falls
> Through circling leaves, through the statues'
> Broken, encircling arms
> To the lives of the withered grass,
> To the drops the sun drinks up like dew.
>
> In anguish, in expectant acceptance
> The world whispers: *Hier bin i'*.

One hears in this splendidly modulated poem even the rhymes that aren't there. By virtue of the sing-song game of the Austrian children earlier in the poem (*Hier bin i'*, *Da bist du*), and the appearance here of the word "dew" in the third from the last line, we "hear" the speaker's response to this innocent, breathless, confidently quiet chant of the new risen world, *Da bist du*, Yes, there you are. In his note to the poem in *Selected Poems* Jarrell wrote, "If there could be a conversation between the world and God, this would be it." Coming after the morose final stanza of "The Orient Express" ("Behind everything there is always / The unknown unwanted life"), the gentle hide-and-seek of Jarrell with the universe in "A Game at Salzburg" is welcome and revealing. I suspect that we hear the two poems' closing statements as complements, neither of which is hard to resolve with the lines about the ghost who cannot touch the very world he cannot forget, or with the lines about the fighter pilot at the end of "Pilots, Man Your Planes": "He yawns the chattering yawn / Of effort and anguish, of hurt hating helplessness." Compare "In anguish, in expectant acceptance / The world whispers: *Hier bin i'*." Even if the outcomes of the war poem and the Salzburg poem are different, the direction of the language, the accumulation of the descriptive prepositional phrases that take all the weight of the emotion while the verbs retreat from motion, are very like.

As a description of how Jarrell's imagination functions in the presence of his most tender and beleaguered subjects, these remarks about the expansion of the qualitative markers and the simultaneous retreat of the formative ones (prepositions and adjectives gaining strength over verbs) may provide a useful model for the way Jarrell's methods in the earliest poems extend to his work as a whole. The qualities of things, his attentiveness to moods and feelings and secondary characteristics, are magnified, while the motion and strength of the world shrink to a small point. One of the most telling illustrations of such a method becoming a fate of style, a *Weltanschauung*, occurs in *The Animal Family* (1965), which is not only Jarrell's best children's book and the site of Maurice Sendak's wisest collaboration with Jarrell, but also a work that can risk comparison with *Pictures from an Institution* (for example, with the passage near the end of the novel where Constance is trying to read "The Juniper Tree" in German and breaks into tears because the story is so touching and her life is so good and she perceives herself to be so stupid and so blessed). In the following excerpt from *The Animal Family*, what I would draw to your attention is the way the world seems, here at the close of this marvelous allegory of childhood, to have become dimmer, smaller, somehow weaker, yet how the heart is nevertheless moved to respond, *Da bist du*, once again:

> The meadow was no different for the mermaid's tears or the hunter's knowledge; warm and soft and smelling of flowers, it ran out to the sunny beach, green to the shadowy forest, and the hunter and the mermaid sat there in it. Below them the white-on-green

of the waves was lined along the white shore—out beyond, the green sea got bluer and bluer until at last it came to the far-off blue of the island. There were small seals on the seal rocks, and the little gray spot out above the waves was a big blue-and-white osprey waiting for fish. But no fish came, and it hung there motionless. Everything lay underneath them like something made for them; things got smaller and smaller in the distance, but managed, somehow, to fill the whole world. . . . The lynx started down through the meadow, and the hunter stood outside the door, half-listening to the story the mermaid was making up, and half-looking at—

He didn't know what he was looking at. He stretched with his front legs, like the lynx: that is, he held out his arms and tightened his muscles and reached out as far as he could reach, for nothing. The lynx was already small in the distance. . . . The boy looked and saw him and said laughing, "That's where he found ME!"

The hunter was looking at . . . he didn't know what he was looking at. The world. The things that get smaller and smaller and yet seemed to fill the whole world. How characteristic is that break in the telling. One becomes the things one sees: a point of substance as well as a point of style. Like the speaker of "A Man Meets a Woman in the Street," Jarrell believes about his hunter and his mermaid that they were "so different from each other that it seemed to them, finally, that they were exactly alike." And like the Salzburg peasants under siege in Gottfried Rosenbaum's parable of the artist in *Pictures from an Institution*, who kept painting new markings on their one remaining steer and leading it along the ramparts to convince the enemy that they had an endless supply of food, Jarrell was touchingly ingenious in the face he put on sameness.

Randall Jarrell was very much a poet of the homely horrors, for at the back of every transcendent impulse he saw the doom of common disappointment crouching in its lean and idle way behind the bolster. In his brilliant essay on Jarrell's ideology, as much a tour de force as Jarrell's essays on the stages in Auden's, Jerome Mazzaro (*Salmagundi*, Fall 1971) suggests that Jarrell was done in by happiness, and that to have been comforted and forgiven was equivalent to having been bereft of every defense against his own accepting world: "The mechanisms by which one's self has been defined, once withered away by forgiveness, leave one nothing by which to define self—a fear implicit in any real skepticism and here expressed 'in happiness.' " Jarrell's imagination followed Freud, dwelling not on illness but rather on what Freud supposed to be our common condition, human suffering and yearning. I therefore do not intend to make Jarrell seem neurotic when I maintain that he wrote about being trapped in the state of being that never changes: the child under the thumb of mortality, the adult who cannot yet manage to forget the loved earth. More work, of a more scholarly kind, should be devoted to Jarrell's image of the self that "float[s] above the small limbs like their dream" and to his deep impression on the poetic world of the mid-century above which he hovered, condemning, accepting, helpless, unable to leave:

> We learned from you so much about so many things
> But never what we were; and yet you made us that.
> We found in you the knowledge for a life
> But not the will to use it in our lives
> That were always, somehow, so different from the books'.
> We learned from you to understand, but not to change.
> ("The Carnegie Library, Juvenile Division,"
> *Little Friend, Little Friend*, 1945)

Weldon Kees:
The Ghost of American Poetry

Charles Baxter

Long curtains blow into an empty room. Fully-dressed, clay-faced "vaca-tioners" sit in beach chairs (seen distantly, and from the side), casting enormous shadows behind them. In a beat-up car, a teenaged couple out in the middle of nowhere arouse one another until both are frantic. These classic images of repression were not born in the American 1950s and they did not die there, but they stick to that decade as if they were keys to a particular style, or part of the era's Victorian mental furniture. Lacking flappers, a world war, or a depression, the fifties sometimes had the effect of throwing everyone back into the arms of the self, an especially tedious regression when the body simultaneously gets treated as a shell, a taxicab to take the mind from place to place. Confessional poetry is born in cir-cumstances like these, in part out of sheer boredom. A confession suggests sin, and sin implies evil, which then justifies the writing of poetry. Poets start to stage their own private McCarthy hearings. So it may be with some surprise that a reader encounters the work of Weldon Kees, who started publishing poetry in 1937 and who committed suicide or disappeared in 1955. If it is possible to talk about poems "resonating with emptiness," then his work resonates with emptiness on every line, like the sound of a hammer in an underground garage; but through a devious strategy, his poems escape confession and the need for atonement. In so doing, they manage to speak without self-pity; they grow luminous in their impersonal bitterness. In a general climate of boredom, they sound depths and grow passionate about what they deny.

As Donald Justice has noted in his preface to the one collected edition of Kees's work, "Kees is one of the bitterest poets in history." It was Kees's

From *A Book of Rereadings in Recent American Poetry*, edited by Greg Kuzma. © 1979 by Greg Kuzma. Best Cellar Press, 1979.

special talent to discover how to write passionately, and not just ironically, about this bitterness. To do this, he became a specialist. Happiness, love, and joy he simply ignores, either because he has no interest in them, or because he can't treat them. His techniques are limited as well: his style is rather flat, almost prosy, totally unsuited for flights of pure rhetoric but easily adapted to narrative, at which he excels. The combination of mood and style give his work an obsessive focus, making him the kind of writer who (as Auden said of Nathanael West) "knows everything about one disease and nothing about any other." Kees knew about several different diseases, but it is still a fact that he writes almost exclusively (as West did) about disability. What happens in his work, as a consequence, is that the poems sometimes turn against themselves: so remorseless is the revulsion in them that they become, spiritually, very pure. They make repression seem erotic. Concentrated and fixed, they resemble a lighthouse that can shine in only one direction.

The subjects that can fit inside such a style are the products of repression: the feeling that one is an object, never a subject (an animal used for experiments); the necessity for lowering one's expectations until they pass zero and enter the negative column; the inappropriateness of childhood for what happens later; the illness of nostalgia; and always in the background, the feeling that the "I" is not there, never has been, but may be watching from a distance.

> The mirror from Mexico, stuck to the wall,
> Reflects nothing at all. The glass is black.
> Robinson alone provides the image Robinsonian.
>
> Which is all of the room—walls, curtains,
> Shelves, bed, the tinted photograph of Robinson's first wife,
> Rugs, vases, panatellas in a humidor.
> They would fill the room if Robinson came in.
>
> The pages in the books are blank,
> The books that Robinson has read.

This is not just alienation, but a special kind of perception. In it, even the smallest objects are seen as if for the first time, though they carry no sense of freshness, but rather of oddity or outright hostility. Kees's world is thus one of sickening novelty, where nothing ever becomes familiar or comforting. Objects refuse to be enmeshed in human concerns. So does consciousness generally. A man under such circumstances will say, "The memories I happen to have are not mine, but someone else's. I don't know where my ideas come from, but they don't come from me." This may sound like classic paranoid thinking, but actually it is only to the degree that both the world and consciousness have been radically impersonalized; there is no "enemy." To create friends and enemies the individual has to have a knowledge of where the self is, and in Kees's poetry no one has such a sense. One's own self is as alien as anyone else's. "I" is as much an enemy as "you"; this being the case, one no longer has appropriate language to express the situation, which is quickly perceived as a travesty of logic and a crime besides.

> Consider the clues: the potato masher in a vase,
> The torn photograph of a Wesleyan basketball team,
> Scattered with check stubs in the hall;
> The unsent fan letter to Shirley Temple,
> The Hoover button on the lapel of the deceased,
> The note: To be killed this way is quite all right with me."
>
> Small wonder that the case remains unsolved,
> Or that the sleuth, Le Roux, is now incurably insane.

The cross-cultural feeling of de-personalization in the 1940s and 1950s is raised in Kees to a metaphor of being itself. This enables him to shock both himself and his audience with anti-poems that begin in reverie, progress through the degradation of conventions, and end in a razor slash over the skin of the "poetic." As in "For My Daughter":

> Looking into my daughter's eyes I read
> Beneath the innocence of morning flesh
> Concealed, hintings of death she does not heed.
> Coldest of winds have blown this hair, and mesh
> Of seaweed snarled these miniatures of hands;
> The night's slow poison, tolerant and bland,
> Has moved her blood. Parched years that I have seen
> That may be hers appear: foul, lingering
> Death in certain war, the slim legs green.
> Or, fed on hate, she relishes the sting
> Of others' agony; perhaps the cruel
> Bride of a syphilitic or a fool.
> These speculations sour in the sun.
> I have no daughter. I desire none.

This early poem, so elegant in its ruthlessness as a vicious anti-sonnet, creates a very neat double-bind: it seems at first to be praising a daughter, then to be attacking her, then to be attacking itself (with the daughter, at this point, eradicated). We know nothing about the daughter except that her absence opens a hole in the speaker and in the poem's last line. The history of poetry is somehow being violated in order to make this poem work; it is a kind of trick on conventional reader response. Kees understood a good deal about such verbal double-binds, having spent time with Gregory Bateson's psychology-of-information group (one of his poems is dedicated to Bateson, the author of *Steps to an Ecology of Mind*). Knowing about double-binds doesn't necessarily ease them, any more than being a polyglot of creativity does—besides his poetry and behavioral studies, in which he co-authored *Nonverbal Communication* with Jurgen Rausch, he was an abstract expressionist painter, a musician, a short story writer and essayist, and a film maker. He was clearly at home in no art. This quality of homelessness, of the inability to feel at rest anywhere is a constant in his poetry.

> —Sleep. But there is no sleep. Far down on Lexington,
> A siren moans and dies. A drunk is sobbing
> In the hall. Upstairs, an organ record
> Of a Baptist hymn comes on. Past one o'clock.
> It is the time of seconal, of loss, of
> Heartbeats of a clock, enormous, by your bed,
> Of noises in the walls,
> Of one more drink.—

This sense of dispossession is most acute with reference to the past; there is no means to retrieve it. It controls but is absent, like a god in whom one no longer believes. To have a good memory cuts two ways, since one can remember innocence without enjoying it, as innocence is not enjoyed when it *is* possessed because it has nothing with which to know itself.

> The porchlight coming on again,
> Early November, the dead leaves
> Raked in piles, the wicker swing
> Creaking. Across the lots
> A phonograph is playing *Ja-Da*.
>
> An orange moon. I see the lives
> Of neighbors, mapped and marred
> Like all the wars ahead, and R.
> Insane, B. with his throat cut,
> Fifteen years from now, in Omaha.
>
> I did not know them then.
> My airedale scratches at the door.

Kees's attitude toward the past colors much of his work: the speaker in many of his poems wishes to return to the blithesome emptiness of his youth, knowing that he cannot and that such a wish has a way of emptying the present of most of its potential. Another double-bind, seemingly, this one breeding the image of the ghost, an impressive and important figure in his poetry. For the ghost is a spirit dispossessed by both the past and his body, by the physical world. As in the last lines of "Return of the Ghost":

> And now the nights begin. Your absence breeds
> A longer silence through the rooms. We haunt ourselves.
> There is a shutter, pounding in the mind,

Old spiderwebs that drift behind the eyes,
A moaning in the heart that warns insistently.
—Old ghost, friend of this house, remain!
What is there now to prod us toward
The past, our ruinous nostalgias?

The gallery of characters Kees presents, no matter what their station happens to be, all have this ghost-like quality, a vaguely ectoplasmic nature like couples at shopping centers. When their pasts do not haunt them, their bodies do, so that many of the poems are set in hospitals, sickrooms, or institutions devoted to one or another kind of imprisonment. As the work continues through *The Fall of the Magicians* (1947) and *Poems 1947–1954*, the bitterness and sense of dispossession turns almost into resignation, as in the conclusion of "Saratoga Ending."

I reach for a cigarette and my fingers
Touch a tongue depressor that I use
As a bookmark; and all I know
Is the touch of this wood in the darkness, remembering
The warmth of one bright summer half a life ago—
A blue sky and a blinding sun, the face
Of one long dead who, high above the shore,
Looked down on waves across the sand, on rows of yellow
     jars
In which the lemon trees were ripening.

The despondency of tone results in a characteristically flattened language, which nevertheless creates with great delicacy and precision the sense of a wholly isolated spiritual condition. While he does share with many other American poets this tone of the outcast, he regularly de-realizes the isolated self as well, so that even the artifical in his poems is robbed of its artificiality, and in an eerie way becomes genuine. In one of his longest poems, "A Distance from the Sea," one of the apostles of Jesus explains how a raft was rigged up under the waves to give the impression of water-walking. Such fakery is necessary because

      if you want a miracle, you have to work for it,
Lay your plans carefully and keep one jump
Ahead of the crowd. To report a miracle
Is a pleasure unalloyed; but staging one requires
Tact, imagination, a special knack for the job
Not everyone possesses.

But in the haunting conclusion to this poem, the speaker thinks back on the fakery, and in a curious moment of suspension the theater of the false turns real.

The days get longer. It was a long time ago.

Nothing will be the same as once it was,
I tell myself. —It's dark here on the peak, and keeps on
        getting darker.
It seems I am experiencing a kind of ecstasy.
Was it sunlight on the waves that day? The night comes
        down.
And now the water seems remote, unreal, and perhaps it is.

The almost pathological repetition of the qualifiers ("I tell myself . . . " "seems . . . " "kind of . . . " "seems . . . " "perhaps") reinforces the man-made nature of this ecstasy. The miracle was a fake, and now, additionally de-realized in memory, it comes back as a ghost to haunt its perpetrator. But in the mental world Kees describes it is better to fake a spectacle than to be shut up with the emptiness of the ordinary, where, if you want stones, even stones will be denied.

        Although the woods were full,
        And past the track
        The heavy boughs were bent

        Down to my knees with fruit
        Ripe for a still life, I had meant
        My trip as a search for stones.

        But the beach was bare
        Except for the drying bones
        Of a fish, shells, and old wool

        Shirt, a rubber boot.
        A strip of lemon rind.
        They were not what I had in mind:

        It was merely stones.
        Well, the days are full.
        This day at least is spent.

        Much cry and little wool:
        I have come back
        As empty-handed as I went.

    In this poem and in several others the reader may note the prevalence of lists, long lists of unrelated objects that sit on the surface of perception, inert. At first this device seems to be a pick-up from Eliot, whose river in *The Waste Land* bears no "empty bottles, sandwich papers, / Silk handker-chiefs, cardboard boxes, cigarette ends" and so on. Eliot's trash heap, however, emerges in a somewhat allegorical condition as the evidence of the leftovers (and waste) of western civilization; they are contextualized to suggest how history has taken a wrong turn. This is exactly what Kees's lists will not do. That is, they may be pieces of evidence (as in "Crime Club"), but what they suggest cannot be known. The poems speak again and again of epistemological bewilderment, of the effort to gather data for a conclusion that is never reached. To this degree, every object loses its force as an object (and whatever physical integrity it may have had) and turns into information instead. If all experience is just information, then the explosion of pure data trivializes or swamps discrete facts, and, in its assault on the individual, makes the mind a mechanism for processing, not understanding. The man who says, "I am de-centered everywhere" will confront a world that wants to fill up his emptiness with its totally mean- ingless plenitude. Emptiness does not result in a lack of feelings; such a person will feel buried, suffocated.

This poetry constitutes a kind of ethnography, an ethnography of va- cancy, where the collection of materials is more-or-less random. The non- identity of the self cannot ground anything and loses its boundaries in multiplicity, in counting and naming. If this is a nightmare of forlorn em- piricism, it is also a peculiar variety of mysticism, the sort that goes on for too long and leaves the individual, undifferentiated among objects, still trying to get back to himself. Therefore the lists: in a pretense to control objects they only emphasize the lack of connection between themselves and the observer. The poems, at one level, fly apart in linguistic parataxis. This may have a certain surrealistic quality at first, but the unconscious seems to have no hand in their ordering, though a psychoanalyst would probably deny it; what yokes the objects together is only a neutral eye, forced to see them. They are funny because they are arbitrary, in the way that heaps of junk are sometimes funny, but that is because we see the incongruity, thanks to our own comfortable sense of order. If we can locate this experience that Kees writes about it would be in Sartre rather than Eliot, and the sickened detachment of Roquentin.

The self, lacking a substantial ego and a world to which it can refer, can speak only of ecstasy in its absence. In "A Distance from the Sea" the miracle is both in the past, and faked: remembering it, the speaker may feel it is genuine only because he no longer has it. This joy-by-proxy is the only joy one knows. Such poetry tends, however, to rob itself of oxygen. It is so articulate in creating and depicting the difficulties of a lost identity and a de-realized world that, within its own context, it has no room to turn. When writers create a full feeling of nothingness as Kees did, the force of the poetry keeps them from developing. Of all styles, Kees's is the one that, taken on its own terms, precludes growth or change of any kind. In its directness it details a paralytic condition and moves only toward more paralysis.

> Nothing is left
> But the desire to be something you are not—
> To have been wholly evil or less evil than you were,
> To have returned exactly as you left
> Before the preparations for this darkness were arranged.
> To find the lips to say, "At least it was a life."

Roethke could write, "I know the purity of pure despair," but he knew other purities as well, and in fact anticipated that particular line with the subjective apocalypse of "The day's on fire!" There is always some sense with Roethke that despair provides a radical glimpse into the mechanics of both the self and God, so that, no matter how ugly the derangement may at times get, such de-centering of the ego involves heroism and subsequent applause. In Kees's world no one claps. The machine just gradually runs down. In the late work this lethargy, these calls from the depression's pit, seem unmistakeable, and the despair has no nobility.

> Here where I built my life ten years ago,
> The day breaks gray and cold;
> And brown surf, muddying the shore,
> Deposits fish-head, sewage, rusted tin.
> Children and men break bottles on the stones.
> Beyond the lighthouse, black against the sky,
> Two gulls are circling where the woods begin.

If a poet draws upon the source that Kees drank from, then the possibility of satisfaction is endlessly deferred. Nothingness begins to corrode the work, and the poet who sees it coming may either give up poetry (Hofmmansthal, Rimbaud), commit suicide, or try to become another kind of poet. Kees was of a generation that, by and large, chose the second course. To his void Kees was dyingly loyal, and so was his work.

Kees was so much a man of parts that, in some quarters, he is known as a psychologist by professionals who are unaware that he wrote poetry; perhaps there are painters who know of his canvases and nothing else. He was no martyr to art; that particular contemporary mythology does not suit him at all, and in fact the pleasures of the imagination are among the few he acknowledges:

> Then grass upon those lawns again!—and dogs
> In fashion twenty years ago, the streets mysterious
> Through summer shade, the marvelous worlds
> Within the world, each opening like a hand
> And promising a constant course.

"The marvelous worlds / Within the world, each opening like a hand" is a beautiful phrase, and, in the context of Kees's entire work, an almost unbearably sad one. For in the last lines of this poem, the speaker sees himself, through the imagination, as "a fool with smiles," leading to the last, collapsing image of "And snow is raging, raging, in a darker world." The imagination, too, is peopled with ghosts, and like any ghostworld containing a treasure it retreats upon being approached. It therefore seems luminous, almost incandescent, precisely because it can never be entered or possessed. A similar line, in Bellow's *Henderson The Rain King* ("That stone, too, was a world of its own, or more like a single world, world within world, in a dreaming series") takes part in the apprehension of the luminous, but Kees's imagination is of the sort that de-substantializes whatever it treats, so that in a peculiar way the poetic representation meant to give meaning to a world of anomalies simply contaminates it further with more unreality. In America, the home of the assembly line and interchangeable parts, however, this variety of imagination finds a subject it was born to treat: that is, Kees's objects all tend to be *duplicates*, object-doubles for originals that have either disappeared or deteriorated. An object becomes real in such a culture not through its use but by virtue of how many times it can be reproduced. Even objects, Kees writes, yearn to conform, to escape attention and the pain of singularity; even objects want to be ghosts. In "Travels in North America" one sees a parade of likenesses.

> And sometimes, shivering in St. Paul or baking in Alaska
> The sudden sense that you have seen it all before:
> The man who took your ticket at the Gem in Council Bluffs
> Performed a similar function for you at the Shreveport
>   Tivoli.
> Joe's Lunch appears again, town after town, next door
> To Larry's Shoe Repair, adjoining, inescapably, the Acme
>   Doughnut Shop.
> Main, First, and Market fuse together.
> Bert and Lena run the laundromat. John Foster, D.D.S.,
> Has offices above the City Bank.—At three or four
> On winter afternoons, when school is letting out
> And rows of children pass you, near the firehouse,
> This sense is keenest, piercing as the wind
> That sweeps you toward the frosted door of your hotel
> And past the portly hatted traveler with moist cigar
> Who turns his paper as you brush against the rubber
>   plant.
> You have forgotten singularities.

And yet in this ghostworld of duplication there is a mystery; never directly exposed in the poems and never exactly named, it nonetheless seems to emerge time and again, usually figured as a sound, a mere tone, that has traveled a great distance and still says nothing. This sound is not music or language. But Kees's poems end with this sound as if the words had done all they could, and the product of the words was a melancholy noise.

> The block was bare. The Venus
> Bathed in blue fluorescent light,
> Stared toward the river. As I hurried West,
> The lights across the bay were coming on.
> The boats moved silently and the low whistles blew.

This sound moves the poem away from the self, toward another source that is impersonal, inhuman, and which is usually associated with the sea. In one poem Kees calls it "The Bunyip":

> Feathered and gray, about the size
> Of a full-grown calf, its long neck
> Budded with an emu's head, covered
>
> With fur. The voice (reportedly) is like
> A thousand booming drums. It puzzled aborigines
> Long before the white man came.
>
> It lives in the sea. Its names
> Are musical: Tumbata, Bunyip,
> Kanjaprati, Melagi. From its back
>
> A plume of water spouts, the terror of
> The womenfolk of fishermen.
> It crosses oceans into inland waters,
>
> Crying sometimes, after dark, that it is not
> Extinct, imaginary, or a myth—
> Its feathers ruffled, and its voice
>
> Not like a thousand drums at all,
> But muffled, dwindling, hard to hear these nights
> Like far-off foghorns that the wind throws back.

But Kees heard it, and his poems, particularly the late ones, attempt to surround this tonality in order to make it more articulate. In the cover photograph for *The Collected Poems* he stands, cigarette in mouth, by the waters as if he were listening for it. It is that sound that his poems leave in mind after the words have finished doing what they do; they are poems of the anti-sirens, of self-effacement, and of emptiness that seems to beg the self to stop pretending that it contains an identity, that it knows how to separate itself from what is not. They are poems in which, bit by bit, the speaker gives himself up to the depths and explains, as he does, how it happened:

> Journeys are ways of marking out a distance
> Or of dealing with the past, however ineffectually,
> Or ways of searching for some new enclosure in this space
> Between the oceans.

Here is Milpitas,
California, filling stations and a Ford
Assembly plant. Here are the washboard roads
Of Wellfleet, on the Cape, and summer light and dust.
And here, now textured like a blotter, like the going years
And difficult to see, is where you are, and where I am,
And where the oceans cover us.

Robert Lowell: The Life of Allegory

Anthony Hecht

Writing of what we may call (if we disregard the early, privately printed, limited edition of *Land of Unlikeness*) Lowell's second book, *The Mills of the Kavanaughs*, [Ian] Hamilton remarks, "It is immediately noticeable . . . that the book is a clamor of distraught, near-hysterical first-person speech, and that almost always the speaker is a woman. The men in the book are usually under attack. Thus, the rhetoric of 'Thanksgiving's Over' and of large sections of the title poem, can, not too fancifully, be heard as a fusing of two rhetorics—the enraged, erupting aggression of *Lord Weary* somehow loosened and given new spitefulness by echoes of letters Lowell had been getting—throughout 1947—from Jean Stafford, and echoes too (we might reasonably speculate) of the 'adder-tongued' invective that she used to pour into their quarrels."

As a description of the poem "Thanksgiving's Over" this is seriously off course and regrettable; and I am not concerned here with questions of biographical or autobiographical veracity, nor with the genesis or sources of Lowell's work. Instead, I want to indicate what strikes me, and furthermore, I would like to claim, must have struck Lowell himself, as a remarkable, over-arching design to his poetry, a thematic recapitulation or recurrence that resonates from the early work to the very latest with hollow and mordant overtones. It expresses itself, early and late, as a domestic drama of a bitter and terrifying kind, and early exhibits itself in "Thanksgiving's Over." The poem bears a headnote which reads,

> Thanksgiving night, 1942: a room on Third Avenue. Michael dreams of his wife, a German-American Catholic, who leapt from a window before she died in a sanatorium. The church is the Franciscan church on 31st Street.

From *Obbligati: Essays in Criticism.* © 1986 by Anthony Hecht. Atheneum, 1986.

Though the note says "Michael dreams" in the present tense, the whole poem is retrospectively cast in the past, giving it the sinister effect of a nightmare that cannot be exorcized or forgotten.

THANKSGIVING'S OVER

Thanksgiving night: Third Avenue was dead;
My fowl was soupbones. Fathoms overhead,
Snow warred on the El's world in the blank snow.
"Michael," she whispered, "just a year ago,
Even the shoreleave from the *Normandie*
Were weary of Thanksgiving; but they'd stop
And lift their hats. I watched their arctics drop
Below the birdstoup of the Anthony
And Child who guarded our sodality
For lay-Franciscans, Michael, till I heard
The birds inside me, and I knew the Third
Person possessed me, for I was the bird
Of Paradise, the parrot whose absurd
Garblings are glory. *Cherry ripe, ripe, ripe . . .* "

Winter had come on horseback, and the snow,
Hostile and unattended, wrapped my feet
In sheepskins. Where I'd stumble from the street,
A red cement Saint Francis fed a row
Of toga'd boys with birds beneath a Child.
His candles flamed in tumblers, and He smiled.
"Romans!" she whispered, "look, these overblown
And bootless Brothers tell us we must go
Barefooted through the snow where birds recite:
Come unto us, our burden's light—light, light,
This burden that our marriage turned to stone!
O Michael, must we join the deaf and dumb
Breadline for children? Sit and listen." So
I sat. I counted to ten thousand, wound
My cowhorn beads from Dublin on my thumb,
And ground them. *Miserere?* Not a sound.

There is enormous drama here, and a complication of settings in time. Michael as dreamer or meditator sets the scene, but even as he does so it is in retrospect, and chiefly in order to allow the remoter voice of his now dead wife to recall something still further in the past. She speaks reminiscently, and, on the whole, reverently, though perhaps somewhat insanely with regard to her possession by the Holy Ghost, and with only a passing touch of bitterness or recrimination when mentioning "This burden that our marriage turned to stone!" though what is presented on the one hand

as a touching and innocent piety is ironically undermined by an allusion
to a Flaubert tale of credulous simplicity. Here the dead woman says,

> I heard
> The birds inside me, and I knew the Third
> Person possessed me, for I was the bird
> Of Paradise, the parrot whose absurd
> Garblings are glory. *Cherry ripe, ripe, ripe. . . .*

This confusion of parrot and Paraclete seems grotesquely to recall a similar
confusion regarding a stuffed bird, a parrot, in Flaubert's *Un Coeur Simple*
and to remind us that the word *simple* is honorific in a religious context
but contemptuous in a worldly one. The cry (*Cherry ripe, ripe ripe*) is a well-
known London street cry (weirdly echoed later in "our burden's light—
light, light") which is also, in this poem, a bird cry, an especially apt
conflation to suit Saint Francis among the slums and gutters of Manhattan.
Most of the poem is given to the patient, enduring, suffering voice of the
dead woman, who concludes with a question and a plea:

> O Michael, must we join the deaf and dumb
> Breadline for children? Sit and listen.

That request to Michael by his dead wife is not a request to listen to her.
It is a plea to listen to the divine voice.

> So
> I sat. I counted to ten thousand, wound
> My cowhorn beads from Dublin on my thumb,
> And ground them. *Miserere?* Not a sound.

Divinity does not vouchsafe its voice to him, offers no mercy. And the only
things that linger in the silence are the defunct syllables of anguish by a
defunct wife. Though not explicitly accusatory, they are the words of one
driven to madness and suicide, and they are also the words of one who
can hear a divinity which to her husband is dumb. And possibly deaf. The
poem leaves us wondering whether it is God or Michael who is unhearing.
That muteness, that blank communicative silence would reappear just as
accusingly in poems Lowell wrote near the end of his career.

They are unrhymed sonnets, like the poem about Thomas More [in
Notebook 1970], and they appear, side by side, bearing the same title, in the
volume called *For Lizzie and Harriet*. The poems are called "No Hearing,"
and they concern themselves with the pain and blankness that attends the
end of love and marriage. Their common title seems worth a moment's
consideration, not only because it bears upon that silence with which
"Thanksgiving's Over" concludes, but because it appears twice as a refrain
in George Herbert's penitential poem, "Deniall." In considering the possibility of some connection, I mentioned the matter to the critic David
Kalstone, who replied as follows: "I think you're absolutely right about the

Lowell poems. It isn't beyond him to repeat the title because it occurs twice in the Herbert poem. The 'silent universe our auditor' is, I suspect, an accidental glance at the 'silent ears' of 'Deniall.' But most of all it's the tone, the quoted, intervening voices . . . 'Skunk Hour' revisited in a more moving key. . . . Cal knew Herbert very well. First on his own and then because Herbert was such a favorite of Elizabeth Bishop's. When EB left Castine [Lowell's home in Maine] after a troubled visit to the Lowells in 1957, Cal gave her a two-volume family Herbert which had belonged to RTSL I [i.e., Lowell's grandfather]. 'Skunk Hour' [dedicated to Elizabeth Bishop] was written within a few weeks."

I want to quote the Herbert poem for its beauty and its relevance.

DENIALL

When my devotions could not pierce
  Thy silent eares;
Then was my heart broken, as was my verse:
  My breast was full of fears
   And disorder:

My bent thoughts, like a brittle bow,
  Did flie asunder:
Each took his way; some would to pleasures go,
  Some to the wars and thunder
   Of alarms.

As good go anywhere, they say,
  As to benumme
Both knees and heart, in crying night and day,
  Come, come my God, O come,
   But no hearing.

O that thou shouldst give dust a tongue
  To crie to thee,
And then not heare it crying! all day long
  My heart was in my knee,
   But no hearing.

Therefore my soul lay out of sight,
  Untun'd, unstrung:
My feeble spirit, unable to look right,
  Like a nipt blossome, hung
   Discontented.

O cheer and tune my heartlesse breast,
  Deferre no time;
That so thy favours granting my request,
  They and my mind may chime,
   And mend my ryme.

The blankness of life, the bleak, heedless, unresponsive silence—these, in Lowell's poems, are not relieved by even the possibility of prayer, and the disorder and dissolution of which they tell is worldly, secular, and irreparable. I have time here to attend only to one of them.

NO HEARING

Belief in God is an inclination to listen,
but as we grow older and our freedom hardens,
we hardly even want to hear ourselves . . .
the silent universe our auditor—
I am to myself, and my trouble sings.
The Penobscot silvers to Bangor, the annual V
of geese beats above the moonborne bay—
their flight is too certain. Dante found this path
even before his first young leaves turned green;
exile gave seniority to his youth. . . .
White clapboards, black window, white clapboards,
    black window, white clapboards—
my house is empty. In our yard, the grass straggles. . . .
I stand face to face with lost Love—my breath
is life, the rough, the smooth, the bright, the drear.

This is a dense and rich poem about impoverishment, and its first line ("Belief in God is an inclination to listen") connects it intimately and directly with "Thanksgiving's Over" from a much earlier period in the poet's career. The poet here is able to acknowledge that "our freedom hardens" us, and is itself imprisoning and isolating: "we hardly even want to hear ourselves . . . / the silent universe our auditor—" And then comes a line that appears in the text in italics: "*I am to myself, and my trouble sings.*" The line is at least a spiritual echo of details in "Skunk Hour" ("I hear / my ill-spirit sob in each blood cell") but rendered conspicuous by being italicized, the line appears to declare itself a quotation, or at least an allusion to some text outside Lowell's own corpus. I freely acknowledge that he may be quoting something I don't know and can't identify, but I'm prepared to make a wild guess nevertheless, and my guess is that this line is a parodic inversion of the refrain as it first appears in the first stanza of Spenser's "Epithalamion": "So I unto myselfe alone will sing, / The woods shall to me answer and my Eccho ring." Here, in Lowell's poem, which is the opposite of the marriage hymn Spenser composed for his own blissful marriage to Elizabeth Boyle, we have a line which is the reverse and negation of Spenser's, a grim and bitter finale: "I am to myself, and my trouble sings." The Penobscot River, the migrating geese, have their destinations and destinies, about which they have little or no choice. Dante's destiny, which involved his passage through Hell, was marked out for him when, at the age of nine, he fell in love with the only woman he would ever love, the Beatrice who would someday guide him to Paradise. Neither Dante, the river nor the geese are as free as Lowell is, but they move to ends which are not only ordained but desirable. In contrast, Lowell sees his life and his future spelled out in black and white: "White clapboards, black window, white clapboards, black window, white clapboards—" a litany that ends with "my house is empty." And the poem ends with the same absence, the same solitariness that was dramatized in "Thanksgiving's Over." Here the poet says: "I stand face to face with lost Love—my breath / is life, the rough, the smooth, the bright, the drear. The poem becomes a small allegory at the end. Breath is indeed life for us all, but for Lowell it is also the allegory of the harsh, irreconcilable inconsistencies of life; the poor, run-of-the-mill, everday infernos and paradisos that possess us like the random motions of atoms; the ordinary man's secular (rather than divine) comedy, which, unredeemed and unremarked by God, and played out beneath a heaven that is both deaf and dumb, seems for that very reason more like tragedy than comedy.

In one of his longest letters, composed on and off between February 14 and May 3, and written to George and Georgiana, his brother and sister-in-law, in 1819, John Keats remarked:

> A Man's life of any worth is a continual allegory—and very few eyes can see the Mystery of his life—a life like the scriptures, figurative—which such people can no more make out than they can the hebrew Bible. Lord Byron cuts a figure—but he is not figurative—Shakespeare led a life of Allegory; his works are the comments on it.

If I began with a deceptively easy comparison of Lowell with Byron, I hope you will allow me to amend that judgment, and to assert that if it is no more plausible to compare him with Shakespeare, he is, first of all, clearly and singularly, Robert Lowell—which, as a poet, is not a bad thing to be; and that through his constant moral and artistic endeavor to situate himself in the midst of our representative modern crises, both personal and political, he has led, for us—as it were, in our behalf—a life of Allegory; and his works are comments on it.

History's Autobiography:
Robert Lowell

Alfred Corn

Dante's praise is that he dared to write his autobiography in colossal cipher, or into universality.
> —RALPH WALDO EMERSON, *"The Poet"*

Like most poets of stature, Robert Lowell takes his lead from several traditions. The early modernists just before him had done so. They absorbed continental symbolism into a late nineteenth-century American tradition that had already (through Emerson, Poe, and Whitman) influenced French poets from Baudelaire to Mallarmé and Laforgue. This Franco-American hybrid was made to sort with late Victorian poetry, especially Browning; to answer as best it could to the rise of positivism and scientism; to look for values in Freud and Jung; and to strike back at the modern age with the help of Dada and surrealist poetics. Surrealism is a late form of symbolism, given a scientific base by Freud, a political theory by Marx, and a style of outrage by Dada. If symbolism was a sort of *prélude* for the Word, scored for flute, harp, and fountain, surrealist poetry was a café-concert vaudeville, accompanied by organ-grinder, biplane, and X ray.

The American modernists used surrealism each in a different way. Pound was the least affected by it, adopting just one of its techniques, radical juxtaposition; but he is much more interested in *continuities* across time and space than the provocative surrealist discontinuity. Stevens was drawn to some of the dadaist elements in surrealism—its jarring humor, its fantasy, its French—but he judged the unconscious to be inadequate for poetry, and social revolution undesirable. Williams liked the inclusiveness and unpredictability of surrealism—its Americanness, in short—but was more interested in daylight than in dreams. Eliot is probably the most convinced surrealist of these early innovators. The Eliot of *The Waste Land* and *The Hollow Men* is, squarely, a surrealist, Dante and the English Renaissance notwithstanding.

By the time Lowell began writing mature poems, most of the surrealists

From *The Metamorphoses of Metaphor*. © 1987 by Alfred Corn. Viking Penguin, 1987.

had lost interest in revolution. Moreover, Eliot had declared himself to be classicist, Catholic, and royalist, for once without apparent irony. His classicism meant, in practice, a still more pronounced reliance on the English tradition, and a giving over of surrealism in favor of its root form, symbolism. *Ash Wednesday* and *The Four Quartets* are symbolist, not surrealist poems. Several of the younger modernists were to follow Eliot's lead, if not in politics, then in religion and poetics. Auden's conversion to Christianity was perhaps the most discussed, but there were others, in some instances a simple renewal of faiths inactive since childhood. Robert Lowell, brought up as a lukewarm Episcopalian, became a "firebreathing Catholic C.O.," confirmed into the Roman church and marrying the Catholic Jean Stafford almost at the same moment. Eventually and reluctantly, Allen Tate was to join the new faithful. One could say that among the poets of the 1940s, Catholicism constituted something of a freemasonry, a movable cell or sodality under the benign supervision of Jacques Maritain. A spirit of the catacombs made itself felt among these converts, who stood in ardent, sometimes firebreathing opposition to the prevailing paganism around them, which they saw as responsible for the disorder of contemporary society.

Lowell became a Roman Catholic modernist, inscribing himself in a multiple tradition. His modernism emphasized the Catholic and surrealist strains, in a way that can only have struck writers of conventional religious poetry as strange, not to say grotesque. Poems in *Lands of Unlikeness* name the Virgin a "hoyden" and Christ a "Drunkard," with no conscious will toward blasphemy. As for politics, Lowell liked to write about kings and to recall the kingship of Jesus, but he kept close to the left-liberal convictions that most American intellectuals had espoused in the thirties, without, to be sure, ever becoming a Stalinist. His politics were part of a program of historical consciousness. Eliot had urged such consciousness on all his disciples long before—though it is more literary than political history that preoccupied the author of "Tradition and the Individual Talent." Lowell adds to Eliot a consuming interest in nonliterary fact, from the present as well as the past. (Some of the same impulse can be noted in the "tape-recorded" bits of popular speech in *The Waste Land*, but much more prominently in the documentary texture of Williams's poetry.)

In Eliot's sensibility there were at work some of the forces of his Puritan heritage, its unremitting concern with the fallenness of human life, and a particular squeamishness concerning the body. In Lowell the Puritan legacy becomes even more pronounced. He could be expected to have negative feelings about the Bay Colonists from whom he and Eliot were descended, but to excoriate them as he did was dubious proof being safely beyond their influence. Besides, the antihierarchical Congregationalist spirit could be felt as a valuable democratic tradition in American history, admirable even to those with no family connections to the New England Puritans. Also, some tenets of Calvinist theology prefigure and perhaps partly account for Lowell's devout interest in history. For the believer in predestination, every event on earth, small or great, is an expression of the divine will; it is capable of being deciphered if interrogated long enough. History is a factual allegory, not incompatible with newspapers and bookkeeping. Or so Cotton Mather argued in *Magnalia,* a detailed account of the flowering of Puritan religion in the New World, intended for the edification of Calvinist readers the world over. It showed how Providence had in one instance worked its design in human history, a pattern that was both earthly and divine. To be a practicing Puritan is to be a practical allegorist of human life.

Puritanism has its dark side: a constant dwelling on sin and damnation that sometimes resembles relish of them; an antipathy to Nature, especially to the body and appetitive pleasure. The Pauline and Calvinist quarrel with the material world was only intensified by specific conditions in the Bay Colony, where the natural environment, anything but pastoral, proved a deadly adversary. Something like a state of siege was the norm, lending extra vehemence to forces of repression in a small society that attempted, in any case, to approximate the absolutism of a theocracy. In this atmosphere of stricture and tension, outbreaks of irrationality could be counted on to appear, and so they did, both in the public and private realms. Witch hunts were perhaps the most horrible manifestation, but there were also chronic waves of revivalism and hysterical religiosity, in some ways comparable to the "born again" movements of our own day. The alert historical sense of Puritanism and its democratic premises were bound directly to a strain of repression, hysteria, and madness that contributed some violent chapters to American history.

Robert Lowell falls heir to the savage aspects of Puritanism as well as to its benign elements, though surely without intending to do so. It is not so much a matter of genes as simply having been reared in the old Bostonian milieu by parents who preserved good and bad traits from their ancestors and passed them on with no second thoughts. "91 Revere Street," Lowell's memoir about his childhood, has been read as a sort of prose *Prelude* that describes the making of a poet; it is also a case study in the origins of mental illness. For the misfortune of mania-depression, there was only one consolation. The "madness of art" was presumably connected to madness per se, and, if surrealism had expanded the notion of what was intelligible, then Lowell's own psychic constitution might not be an insuperable disadvantage. Oneiric and violent imagery was never far from Lowell's consciousness, but surrealist esthetics taught him that this material could be used for art and in some sense be redeemed.

As a modernist, Lowell inherited not only the irrationality of surrealism but also an enthusiasm for myth, which is also a vehicle of the irrational but one given structure by the logic of narrative. For Lowell, as for most artists, the single most important myth was the Orpheus story in all its variants. Its essential structure involves a descent into the underworld of death and then a restoration to life with added powers of understanding or skill. This framework underlies narratives as disparate as the Virgilian account of Aeneas's descent into Hades to consult the dead; Dante's *Inferno*; the Christian Passion, Descent into Hell, and Resurrection; and—in contemporary terms—any submersion in sleep, the unconscious, or even madness, with a subsequent reemergence into light, consciousness and a renewal of imaginative power. Lowell made constant reference to classical myth during his first phase as a poet, and it remained a potent force in his writing throughout his career, sometimes openly and sometimes covertly. The most extended use of myth in his early phase came in *The Mills of the Kavanaughs*, constructed on the model of the story of Persephone, which is a female variant of the Orpheus myth. Later works follow the contour of the myth usually without directly naming it. The most characteristic moment in Lowell's poetry is going to sleep—or waking after a long sleep. Poems like "Falling Asleep over the Aeneid" and "The Lesson" show the author as he begins the Orphic descent; and more than a dozen other works depict him waking at sunrise to a painful lucidity that keeps, nonetheless, a low-level hangover of dream as part of the emotional tenor of the poem. (Among these poems, consider "Waking in the Blue," "Man and Wife," and "Ulysses and Circe.")

The several strains that went into the formation of Lowell's poetics and style—symbolism, historical consciousness, Puritanism, surrealism, Roman Catholicism, progressive politics, the documentary impulse—are by turns antithetical and reinforcing, and of course all of them had to be accommodated to the personal condition of mental illness. The story of Lowell's career is the record of changing emphases among these constitutive strains. Eventually the Roman Catholicism of early Lowell was abandoned—leaving behind some indelible marks—and the Williamsesque documentary impulse was given much greater prominence. There was, also, one final shift that had been only barely foreshadowed at the beginning— an involvement with American Romanticism as derived from Emerson.

Historical consciousness seems to be active in Lowell throughout his career, but even in his early phase it often took the form of documented autobiography. It is not easy for us now to revive the qualms and hesitations of poets in the early 1940s who wished to treat autobiographical subjects. They had to resolve for themselves Eliot's strictures in behalf of "impersonality." Was writing about oneself an exercise in vanity or futility? Perhaps it wasn't if one could show that personal experience was *representative* (which is not necessarily to say exemplary). Lowell felt he could write about himself if he stood for something more general than himself, at the level of myth or historical dialectic.

"Rebellion" is among the most explicitly autobiographical poems in early Lowell. Its subject—Lowell's knocking his father down—has an immediate scandalous interest, but Lowell was not satisfied with that. From the details of the poem we can see that it is his father's *house*, with its heirlooms and "chimney flintlock," as much as any person that is being brought down in this act of rebellion. Lowell labors to make this act represent a larger historical pattern: he stands for a principle of social change, militantly opposed to the oppressive traditions associated with his family— mercantilism or capitalism, land-grabbing, and military violence. Well enough: but this covers only the first six pentameter lines of the poem. Several shorter lines follow, most of them in trimeter, then a pentameter couplet, some more short lines and a concluding pentameter. This second half of the poem describes a dream that follows the reported incident.

> Last night the moon was full;
> I dreamed the dead
> Caught at my knees and fell:
> And it was well
> With me, my father. Then
> Behemoth and Leviathan
> Devoured our mighty merchants. None could arm
> Or put to sea. O father, on my farm
> I added field to field
> And I have sealed
> An everlasting pact
> With Dives to contract
> The world that spreads in pain;
> But the world spread
> When the clubbed flintlock broke my father's brain.

Here is the Orphic descent into the irrational dream world, a recapitulation of what has already occurred in daylight. The shorter lines (notice the metrical "pun") outline Lowell's "pact" or "contract" to alleviate suffering in a world of pain. But the world of pain swells to full proportions again in the concluding pentameter, which recalls the poet's violence toward his own father and his tendentious use of the ancient heirloom weapon presented earlier as part of an ensemble symbolizing historical injustice. The poem's representative rebellion is seen as having been accomplished at the cost of violence, indeed, family violence—of adding to the universal sum of pain. This is the dilemma of the Christian revolutionary. Significant social change can come only at the cost of violence and suffering, in which the Christian can, in conscience, have no part. "Rebellion" also gives insight into some of the sources of Lowell's mental illness: the problem of actualized Oedipal aggression, guilt, and a need to return to an unconscious state in order to confront that guilt.

The idea that one's personal experience derives from larger patterns of history and economics is good Marxist doctrine and was shared by most intellectuals of the late thirties and early forties. That the unfolding of one's own life has a mythic and religious dimension is as old as human culture; but this belief had been discarded along with Christianity by the intellectuals of the second half of the nineteenth century. It returned in some of the secular but spiritual propositions of psychoanalysis and anthropology and was then brought under the Christian rubric with Eliot's and other modernists' conversion to Catholicism. Lowell gives the impression of having always remained at least theist, even after abandoning Roman Catholic faith in the early 1950s. (According to his wishes, his funeral offices were said at the Episcopal Church of the Advent in Boston.)

Whereas Eliot's reliance on Greek and Roman classical mythology was never large, not even as extensive as his debt to Dante, Lowell was from the first saturated with it. At Kenyon, he majored in classics and took his degree summa cum laude. His mentor Tate was a near example of Latinity in poetry, and of course the mixture of classical and Christian elements had impressive earlier precedents. It is the structural basis for the *Commedia*, and it is intrinsic to Milton's poetry as well as to much Neoclassical poetry in the seventeenth and eighteenth centuries. The same blending determined the structure and substance of *Ulysses*, which still somehow remained secular and was the modernists' favorite novel. *Ulysses* also incorporated personal and autobiographical matter and for that as well could serve as a model for the kind of poetry Lowell was to develop. Lowell's invocation of mythic or Christian perspectives always had, directly or indirectly, a bearing on the mere facts of his life. The notion that Eternity is in love with the works of Time can be applied in many ways. For Lowell, the Eternity of myth (pagan or Christian) has at last married Time (or history), and their child is Poetry (mythic autobiography)—"one life, one writing," as a later poem puts it. We can see why the early Lowell is entirely at home with Roman Catholicism, which, ideally, welds together the historical and mythic dimensions. Catholicism asserts on one hand that divine purpose is at work in historical evolution and on the other that there is an eternal dimension to experience that never changes, a dimension figured in the mass and in the succession of sacred seasons in the church calendar.

Life Studies marks the point in Lowell's poetry when classical and Christian references begin to retreat in favor of "mere" historical and autobiographical fact. "Beyond the Alps," the first poem in the volume, announces Lowell's renunciation of Roman Catholicism and in part tries to account for it. A parenthetical note after the title sets the poem "On the train from Rome to Paris. 1950, the year Pius XII defined the dogma of Mary's bodily assumption." We should not assume that it was solely the promulgation of a new dogma that led to Lowell's disaffection with the Roman church. For one thing, 1950 was the year of his father's death, as a poem placed farther on in the volume mentions. This event, given the burden of guilt and confusion that Lowell's father represented, can only have come as a release to Lowell. The bolstering structures of Christian myth would then be needed commensurately less by the survivor.

At another level, the text of the poem makes it implicitly clear that for Lowell Roman Catholicism had become too provincial a system of belief to answer to the modern world and its record of violence and horror. So far from being the infallible spokesman on earth for Godhead, the pope is simply another mortal (who shaves each morning under the watchful gaze of his pet songbird). The papacy was unable or unwilling to halt the rise of Fascism; it must bear the guilt. And since, unlike individual popes or fathers, the papacy cannot die, Lowell sees his task as one of discreditation, by implied argument and overt satire. Moreover, when the poet turns his attention to the legacy of classical myth, it is found to be of not much more use than religion. Lowell conflates the cultural summit reached in ancient Greece with the Alps of the then-unscalable Everest. "There were no tickets for that altitude," not for moderns caught in the cultural disintegrations of post–World War global society. Lowell goes a step farther: he presents a negative version of Athena or Minerva, goddess of wisdom and military skill. She is "pure mind and murder at the scything prow— / Minerva, the miscarriage of the brain." This immaterial virgin, whose Parthenon is an unscalable mountain, offers no help to mid–twentieth-century citizens. Meanwhile it has been the fault of the pope to take the very human, physical figure of Mary and transform her into a purely mythic, otherworldly goddess. This is a metaphoric way of summing up the failure of the Church to keep its historical dimension alive and active. Lowell sees it as retreating into pure myth and immateriality, and hence irrelevant to him and the modern condition. But his is no joyful deconversion. "Much against my will," Lowell says, "I left the City of God where it belongs."

The Church belongs "beyond the Alps," a local, cisalpine Italian cult. The contemporary world, on the other hand, was born in Paris, city of enlightenment, revolution, and art. Between the second and third sonnets that make up this poem, night comes on and the poem's speaker falls asleep. When "Beyond the Alps" was first printed in *Partisan Review,* an extra sonnet stanza at this point described a dream of the narrator. (Lowell reprinted the poem in *For the Union Dead,* with the missing stanza restored.) The "dream" is a quasi-surrealist ramble in which the dreamer comes to speak in the voice of the author of *Metamorphoses.* In *Life Studies'*s shorter version, the dream sonnet is replaced by ellipsis, and the poem goes directly to the poet's awakening—"kicking in my berth," as he puts it. An overnight trip to Paris has been metaphorically transformed into the Orphic descent and rebirth to waking reality, as the City of Lights hoves into view: "Paris, our black classic, breaking up / like killer kings on an Etruscan cup." Lowell's ambivalent feelings toward the new secular order is manifest here. If Paris is a "classic," it is also black. If it is like a cup (and not a chalice), still the image painted on it is of Etruscan "killer kings." The Etruscans were, of course, the first to use the emblem of the *faces* adopted by Mussolini. In the official version of Roman history, the last Etruscan reign ended with Tarquinius Superbus, the father of the Tarquin of Shakespeare's *Rape of Lucrece.* In the legend, the elder Tarquin murdered his father-in-law so as to be proclaimed king. This deed, and the rape of Lucrece, so enraged the

Roman people that Superbus in turn was assassinated, the monarchy scrapped, and the Roman Republic founded. To invoke him at the conclusion of the poem is to remind us of the burden of historical violence continuous from classical times to the present, which the Pax Romana sought to counteract. To give up hope in the personal and historical effectiveness of the Church is to be abandoned to history. The remainder of *Life Studies* is a working out of the implications, positive and negative, of this new, secular set of conditions.

The negative themes of *Life Studies*—apart from wars, murder, and tyrannical rulers—include the persistence of Victorian repressiveness, incarceration (of criminals or the insane), the "woe that is in marriage," death, the disorder of modern life, sexual maladjustments, and mental illness. By the mid-1950s, Lowell had come to recognize that manic episodes would almost certainly be chronic with him. If there could be no lasting cure for this ailment, perhaps some compensation for it could be found in applying his condition to the external world, seeing his illness as a truthful representation of that world. Madness might be felt as more than a private calamity, indeed, a symptom of universal madness in modern society. (I leave aside the question of whether seeing one's private condition as *representative* contains in itself a strain of madness.) As for Lowell's returns to health, did they betoken a recovery for society as well? Perhaps: if Lowell could survive a confrontation with misery and insanity, others might as well, in however small or great numbers. Lowell saw himself as going haltingly on, hand in hand with modern civilization, never certain when the next setback would come. His cures were temporary, chapters in a tale of patience and endurance. One sees that the temptation to suicide was great for him, yet he managed to outwit it, as though he had decided not to end his own life until the world's life came to an end, as was always possible after the development of nuclear armaments. Since Lowell equated his life as an artist with his life per se, work was a redemptive task for him; he kept to it constantly, turning his hand to translation and other literary tasks when subjects for poems were lacking. Part of the heroism to be found in Lowell's example is the heroism of work.

Apart from the labors of the artist, there are other forces that Lowell set into motion against the drift toward madness and suicide. From the evidence of the poetry alone, one can point to three qualities that Lowell associates with health: the drive toward prose; humor; and physicality, animal well-being. *Life Studies* marks an important thematic shift in Lowell's work, and it embodies as well a formal change for him, the use of a free-verse poetics. In poetry, he looked to the examples of Williams and Elizabeth Bishop but also adapted some of the virtues of prose writers like Flaubert and Chekhov—their careful observation and unheightened presentation—to his purposes. The volume includes a long prose memoir, "91 Revere Street," a title as factual as the texture of the memoir itself. Actually the very factuality of the piece is part of its humor; seldom has satire been based on circumstantial evidence so minutely detailed. The young Lowell comes in for ridicule as much as anyone else, but there is no hint of self-flagellation. Prose rhythms, conversational tone, humor, a constant recurrence to fact—these can all be used as counterforces to the hypnotic meter of poetry, its heightened diction and presentment, its swelling emotions, the undertow toward fantasy and dream. When poetry seemed like a mild or not so mild form of hallucination, the chronically ill poet might look to the prosaic elements in verbal art as a steadying antidote, turning to the prescriptions of, say, Chekhov so as to bolster the reality principle. Beyond that, the cultural spokesman in Lowell allows *Life Studies* to register the extent to which he felt that the peculiar qualities of poetry had been supplanted by prose strategies in contemporary writing. A decline in the prestige of religious myth will necessarily bring along with it a decline in the prestige of poetic form: among the things Lowell finds beyond the Alps is free verse. Even though it is poetry he continues to write, not prose fiction or nonfiction, the relationship of his poetry to prose is always strong after *Life Studies*. And we recall, incidentally, that all three women to whom Lowell was married were prose writers.

The careful plotting of *Life Studies*, with its many significant leitmotifs and balanced pairings, its color themes and its echoes, can persuade us that a poetry based on prose need not lose richness and complexity. The book is awash in factual detail, but the wonder is just how much Lowell makes his details cooperate and signify. Objects apparently modest and empty of signification are often found, on closer inspection, to have subterranean connections with a larger system of meaning. The ingenuity with which Lowell draws out these themes may remind us of paranoid fantasy, and if so perhaps we can see it as one more example of Lowell's turning a personal flaw into a poetic strength. Has anyone looked closely, for instance, at *Life Studies*'s garbage cans? In "91 Revere Street" we are told that the narrator's father painted the label "R. T. S. Lowell—U.S.N." on his family's personal receptacles. No explicit comment is made in the memoir; perhaps it is an amusingly pathetic detail put in for the humor. But when the poet (in "Memories of West Street and Lepke") mentions seeing a man scavenging the garbage can behind his house on "hardly passionate Marlborough Street," we begin to wonder. Finally, when Lowell concludes "Skunk Hour" with the image of a mother skunk plundering a garbage pail to find sustenance for herself and her kittens, we know the poet is up to something.

Eliot's *Waste Land* was a landscape of "stony rubbish," a "heap of broken images," or an "Unreal City," where crowds of humanity are felt to be simply one more disposable waste product—but where, also, fragments can be shored against the ruin of self and society. The junk pile interested Stevens, too, who viewed modern consciousness as a "Man on the Dump," thought rooting among discarded images and "mattresses of the dead" to find some wherewithal for continuing life. Lowell's response to the scrapheap of history is to follow the skunk's lead, to dig into the garbage of experience, personal and historical, no matter how miscellaneous or ugly, and to wring sustenance from it. The Etruscan cup of "Beyond the Alps" (as J. D. McClatchy has pointed out) is replaced by a cup of sour cream in the last poem of *Life Studies*. The mother skunk jabs her head into it, feeds, and "will not scare." The skunk's fearlessness, her rich animality, are presented as saving qualities in a world of disorder and madness. And she is female. The refreshing and commonsense qualities of women rank very high for Lowell. The ability to appreciate physical life he associated with Elizabeth Bishop, to whom the poem is dedicated. In any case, the warm, mammalian version of womanhood is seen as a positive counterpart to cold goddess figures, statuary or immaterial, like Minerva, "pure mind and murder," "the miscarriage of the brain."

After *Life Studies*, Lowell published *Imitations*, a collection of translations from many languages and periods. Lowell seems to have anticipated the criticism it would receive for the "inaccuracy" of his renderings—he does not call the book *Selected Translations*. In effect he has made new Lowell poems at the instigation of the originals, an approach as old as the English Renaissance. "Imitation," as opposed to strict translation, is of course a way of making the fixity and otherness of non-English poetry from the past susceptible to time and change, of, so to speak, taking an art work out of the Louvre and bringing it into one's own house. In Lowell's case, this kind of translation amounts to colonizing other literary traditions with personal contemporaneity, appropriating them to an expanded notion of the self. *Imitations* contains in germ the scope and intention behind Lowell's "epic," *History*, which took the whole of Western culture, its political as well as its literary record, as Lowell's province.

Several more steps, though, were needed before Lowell arrived at the threshold of this grand project. The title poem of *For the Union Dead* inaugurates that more active role Lowell was to take in American politics of the 1960s. As a citizen and a poet, Lowell was to strike blows, first, in favor of the Civil Rights movement and then against United States involvement in the Vietnam war. The record of private and public life found in *Near the Ocean* and *Notebook 1967–1968* by turns stuns and leaves us indifferent, as Lowell succeeds well or poorly in the task of welding the two realms into a convincing poetry. Political activism brought Lowell a fame or notoriety outside the purely literary realm. People who had never read so much as a word of his poetry came to recognize the participant in the 1967 march on the Pentagon and the campaign supporter of Eugene McCarthy. The distractions that went with political activism seem to have been outweighed, in Lowell's case, by the pleasure of making history—and from history, literature. Lowell said it was the Pentagon march that inspired him to take up writing *Notebook 1967–1968*. The expanded and revised *Notebook* came out in 1970, to be followed by yet a third redaction, which was larger still and moreover had calved with two attendant volumes (*For Lizzie and*

Harriet and *The Dolphin*) made up of poems pruned from the earlier *Notebook*. This startling literary event (the books all appeared in 1973) brings us to the final phase, or next-to-final phase, in Lowell's career. *History* embodies Lowell's sense of what he had accomplished from the beginning of his career up to that time.

History and the *Notebooks* that led up to it mark another stylistic shift in Lowell, a new adaption of surrealism to his purposes. American poetry at large in the sixties had turned toward surrealism, of a Latin American rather than a French variety, and the sensitive barometer of Lowell's attention to actuality had registered this change. In his "Afterthought" to the first *Notebook*, he said, "I lean heavily to the rational, but am devoted to surrealism." The difference between heavy leaning and devotion is like the contrast between the reality principle and aspiration. The *Notebooks* are suffused with an irrationality of a peculiar Lowellian variety, whose roots go all the way back to his early work. In the revised *Notebook*, he was to change his "Afterthought" in several particulars, substituting the word "unrealism" for "surrealism." He thereby recognizes the differences between his own mode and that of the other American surrealists. This telling difference, moreover, is epitomized in a word from the vocabulary of Wallace Stevens, philsopher-poet of the realized "unreal." By the late 1960s, Lowell had become interested again in the American Romantic tradition, the one that runs from Emerson, through Whitman, Dickinson, Crane, and Stevens. Of course the interest in Crane and Emerson has been present from the beginning of Lowell's career. There is a poem to Emerson in *Land of Unlikeness*, and he is the leading light of "Concord" in Lowell's next book. Lowell had inherited Crane through inclination and the example of Allen Tate. Although the poem to Crane in *Life Studies* gives an aberrant portrait of Crane, it still testifies to a deep fascination with him. Whitman, Lowell more than once singled out as America's "best poet." And Lowell had admired Stevens as early as the publication of *Transport to Summer*, which he reviewed for *The Nation* in 1947, calling Stevens "one of the best poets of the past half-century." Emerson and Whitman had been generally in discredit with Lowell's mentors (Tate and Ransom) when he began writing. The Eliotic-aristocratic-Agrarian poets saw Emerson as having contributed to the paganism, optimism, and market mentality that had all but wrecked the American experiment, and they considered Whitman's ideals of democracy indiscriminate and unrealistic. But so multiple, so Protean a figure as Lowell could still draw on a potential relationship to the central American Romantics, and this tradition was activated within him as strongly as it could ever be in *History*.

Lowell's book is a startling literary realization of Emerson's views on the proper stance that his ideally self-reliant representative man should take toward history. Consider these statements from the essay "History": "There is one mind common to all men. Every man is an inlet to the same and to all of the same." "Man is explicable by nothing less than all his history." "Each new fact in [individual man's] private experience flashes a light on what great bodies of men have done, and the crises of his life refer to national crises." "The student is to read history actively and not passively; to esteem his own life the text, and books the commentary." "All history becomes subjective; in other words, there is properly no history, only biography."

History might just as well been called *The Lowelliad*, though of course that would have put off readers. Lowell was content to suggest that for all its range of reference, it is still "his story"—and hence so much more than that. One can substitute the author's name for the word "History," which opens the first line of the sequence's opening poem: [Lowell] has to live with what was here," and go on to substitute "I" for "we": "Clutching and close to fumbling all [I] had— / it is so dull and gruesome how [I] die, / unlike writing, life never finishes." In fact, by the end of the poem, pronouns are changed to singular in the text: "my eyes, my mouth, between them a skull's no-nose— / O there's a terrifying innocence in my face."

These opening pages labor, as David Kalstone has observed, to make the characteristically Lowellian moment of awakening fuse with the dawn of human consciousness. The fourth poem of the sequence, titled "Dawn," brings in "Adam and Eve, adventuring from the ache / of the first sleep" to enhance Lowell's perception of how he feels waking next to his wife, "early Sunday morning in New York— / the sun on high burning, and most care dead." The sequence passes through several Biblical subjects (Cain and Abel, King David), intermingling them with personal observations and appropriations. The sixteenth sonnet (a translation of Valery's "Hélène," first published in *Imitations*) introduces the Hellenic tradition, rich with monuments Lowell claims as his own. Still, we cannot avoid a moment of shock when we see a statement belonging to Lowell's mother (as recorded in "91 Revere Street") ascribed, in the twenty-first sonnet, to Clytemnestra. "I usually / manage to make myself pretty comfortable," is the conclusion to a long speech not found in the earlier prose work but, even so, entirely consonant with what we know about Mrs. Lowell. "Clytemnestra 1" is followed by sonnets "Clytemnestra 2" and "Clytemnestra 3," these two hewing much closer to the original mythic subject. We can, however, no longer read them "innocently"; each detail is sifted and weighed for autobiographical and psychological meaning.

A "stereoscopic" reading of *History* yields the most coherent understanding of Lowell's autobiographical epic, so long as the component strands remain in balance. Curious overlaps appear. Of the two sections devoted to Caligula, the first is a distant version of Baudelaire's "Spleen," translated line for line by Lowell a decade earlier but now cut down to sonnet size and attributed to the mad Roman emperor. The second Caligula section is also a reduced and reworded version of an earlier poem (from *For the Union Dead*), in which Lowell reflects on the monstrous historical figure childhood schoolmates had likened him to—indeed, going so far as to nickname him "Cal." (This was the name he was familiarly called by the rest of his life.)

History first makes an overwhelming impression of inclusiveness, but, after that has subsided, we can observe just how little of its field it draws upon. Aside from the Far East's being utterly disregarded, we note that Western history up to the twentieth century takes up only the first half of the book. The remainder corresponds roughly with Lowell's own lifespan from 1917 to the late 1960s. Taking a census of the first half shows that more subjects are drawn from French history and culture than from English or American. Napoleon receives more attention than Washington and Jefferson combined. Literature counts as much as political history; a sonnet of Baudelaire weighs as heavily in the sum total as the entire career of Mohammed. Also, despite the abundant erudition, mistakes now and then creep in—as when Lowell conflates the seventeenth-century French poet Malherbe with the eighteenth-century *encyclopédiste* Malesherbes ("Malesherbes, l'Homme de Lettres"). Closing the book, anyone not hushed by erudition into uncritical reverence will surely feel much more the idiosyncrasy of the sequence than its universality. But of course Lowell intended a personal, Emersonian "epic," not a general one.

To treat the *Notebooks* and their culmination in *History* as Lowell's *Leaves of Grass* asks us not only to see the development of a personal epic, but also to follow on the track of another intention. Just as any writer has a personal history—his autobiography—a body of work has its history, too—the developing contour of a career. The *Notebook–History* trio stands, among other things, for Lowell's changing sense of what he had achieved in poetry, under the influence of three temporal forces: modern political events; his own life story (marriages, displacements, work, fatherhood, aging, fame); and, finally, the deployment and evolution of his own talents as a poet as they unfolded in the shifting climate of American literature. Even the first *Notebook* revisits themes from earlier Lowell. The second *Notebook* revisits these revisitings; and *History* returns again to this twice-spaded soil. In all three cases, the reworkings amount to a continuous reevaluation by Lowell of the shape and meaning of his own career. He seems to have been trying to embody in his work a metaphysical fable about Time and Writing. Time has made him one more reader of his poetry and so, inevitably, into a reviser of it.

The actual specific terms of this rewriting will some day be worked out in close detail. Most critics have declined the challenge of *History*. The "unrealism" or hallucinatory impressionism of Lowell's compositional habits in the sequence do of course put obstacles in the path of understanding. Yet that very inwardness, knotty and recalcitrant, is inseparable from the power of *History;* and an important question is whether eventual decipherment will render the sequence less arresting and provocative or add range and meaning to it.

History did not put the final seal on Lowell's achievement. In 1976 a

Selected Poems appeared, with poems taken from all his books up to and including *History* and the companion volumes published in 1973. This selection (which involved a few revisions) amounts to yet another assessment by Lowell of the shape and meaning of his career—which comes to seem like the literary equivalent of a "mobile," with constantly shifting relationships between its parts. Lowell saw life as "pure flux," and he wanted poetry to come as close to life as is consistent with artistic order. The extremely elaborate relationship of his writings to *themselves* adds a new quality of unfixity to a work already complex and diverse. Lowell's last book, *Day by Day* (1977), was much simpler in style than its recent forerunners; and in it autobiography and classical myth again came forward as chief structural elements. Was Lowell entering a new stylistic phase? The book may have been the first step in a return from the Emersonian "Orphism" of *History*. As matters stand, *Day by Day* comes only as a coda to the rest of Lowell's work, not really changing our sense of what he had accomplished. Or at least not yet: unlike life, writing and reading never finish.

Robert Lowell died in 1977. He is buried in Dunbarton, New Hampshire, among the gray headstones of his Stark, Winslow, and Lowell relatives, a "suave Venetian Christ" in quiet surveillance over all. Lowell's own monument, in pink marble, bears the inscription, "The immortal is scraped unconsenting from the mortal." A characteristic reversal of graveyard sentiment, this is a good summary of Lowell's work as well as his life. His whole effort as a poet was bent toward welding these irreconcilables into one poetry—eternizing the transitory *and* making sure that gray eternity was kept in the pink of health and life.

Frank O'Hara: Glistening Torsos, Sandwiches, and Coca-Cola

Thomas Meyer

Since the last war the United States has had a certain number of poets die young and unexpectedly, leaving behind them a body of work that begs for immediate evaluation in terms of authentic greatness. The directness and quality of impact these poets had on their own and a budding generation allows them, once dead, to contend for the title of unsung, overlooked Major Figure. It is hard to tell how much of this ambience was their presence and how much the poems themselves. And that makes us uneasy, as does the life not lived out, especially when there was definitely a spark of promise evident. Alas, greatness or the "major" is quixotic, never anything like its last appearance, try as we may to predict its next. That does not stop us in our need to proclaim genius, or even to cry humbug in the constant battle against our fear that nothing ever amounts to anything, so why bother. But asking whether X or Y were geniuses we run up against the "minor" and near-great, more comfortable, less problematic judgments to make. All the same, we're uneasy. Especially when faced with previous misses and faux pas; it is always good to remember that before the Great War (1914) Mozart was considered a delightful entertainer by the discerning ears of London, no more than a Gottschalk or Satie.

Indeed, it is that much harder to say anything about an interrupted and unexpectedly terminated life's work, the work from under which all further life has been yanked. Marjorie Perloff begins her *Frank O'Hara: Poet among Painters* by peeling back a sad and tangled legend, rightly convinced the poems themselves stand on their own considerable merit without need of a "tragic, early death," the subsequent glamorization of which has served only to unsettle an already flighty critical attention. I agree, yet have myself

From *Parnassus: Poetry in Review* 6, no. 1 (Fall/Winter 1977). © 1978 by Poetry in Review Foundation.

talked to a close reader of American poetry who knew nothing about O'Hara's death or its circumstances. To have heard of, or read O'Hara, it seemed, meant also knowing he was run down by a beach taxi on Fire Island . . . not so, we no longer know who knows what, common knowledge just isn't.

However intricate the underpinning gender arrangements, we are still convinced the opposite of all that is authentic, expressive, and profound remains the light, quick, casual though deft gesture. And when considering greatness the absolute enemy is camp, best exemplified by the urban, loose, and high-living male homosexual. In O'Hara's case we are faced with imagining a poetry that deliberately does not exhibit those smooth, monolithic surfaces of the profound and well-wrought, while being neither incomplete nor flawed in its author's eyes. This isn't to say the work is a mess, uneven in ways we put down to incompetence or lack of talent and discipline. From among the choices the poet could make, he allowed himself not to work an area while still including it, letting it be, wanting it the way it was, as is. Until we are convined by encountering not a single but several successful instances of anything new, contrary, and unfamiliar, it all remains talk. Then too the material O'Hara worked with looks too often on first glance chi-chi, dizzy, piss elegant, and faggoty. Or else his poems seem adolescent, their exuberance and excitement made embarrassing by what appears a lack of emotional maturity. Too many "Oh's" and "Ah's," "Gee's" and "Whee's," and more than a fair share of exclamation points. O'Hara was far more interested in dealing with emotional honesty than the emotions per se. The qualities of emotion he wrote about, and from, are the hardest to admit: breathlessness, excitement, anticipation and expectation. To be open and honest about them is almost a form of intimacy; these feelings usually find expression within the privacy of adult relationship, the pet names and shared pidgins. I don't mean we automatically cringe whenever we see someone unable to contain his coltishness, just that even in our New American Poetry, this isn't what we expect in a poem. Poems can now be about anything, well almost anything, a phrase like "It's heaven!" still raises an eyebrow or two, making one question, if not the sincerity, then the intention. Though *"It's heaven!"* occurs twice in O'Hara's "At the Old Place," and as camp and silly as that poem is, not one note of cynicism creeps in. Dancing the lindy with Button, or being wrapped in Ashes's arms that night at that gay bar was heaven, absolute heaven.

In the scattered statements O'Hara made about his poetry he often displayed a petulance that seems flip, contrary to the passionate devotion and joie de vivre his best lyrics celebrate. As Marjorie Perloff points out, poetry in the Fifties was so openly a matter of manifestoes, declarations, and factions that it was out of irritation as much as aesthetic concern that O'Hara framed his "Personism: A Manifesto." In a letter to the Paterson Society, he refers to his statement in *The New American Poetry* as "even more mistaken, pompous, and quite untrue, as compared to the manifesto. But it is also, like the manifesto, a diary of a particular day." He honors the mood of depression surrounding the statement when he wrote it. It is indicative that when asked for a statement about his art, O'Hara has only his feelings and their particularity with which to respond. Probably all any of us has, though we're slow allowing them voice over what we think are our intentions. As though how we felt had nothing to do with what we meant. Perloff takes great pains to show her reader the depth of concern beneath his bitchiness. She is eager as well to prove O'Hara developed a considerable, conventional poetic technique he then ignored. Posterity needs no convincing, though it still remains important for us mortals to know Picasso could draw a lady looking in a mirror that looked like a lady looking in a mirror—if he wanted to. So too we want to know there's a heart behind a statement like:

> I don't think of fame or posterity (as Keats so grandly and genuinely did), nor do I care about clarifying experience for anyone or bettering (other than accidentally) anyone's state or social relation, nor am I for any particular technical development in the American language simply because I find it necessary. What is happening to me, allowing for lies and exaggerations which I try to avoid, goes into my poems. I don't think my experiences are clarified or made beautiful for myself or anyone else; they are just there in whatever form I can find them. What is clear to me in my work is probably obscure to others, and vice versa. My formal "stance" is found at the crossroads where what I know and can't get meets what is left of that I know and can bear without hatred. I dislike a great deal of contemporary poetry—all of the past you read is usually quite great—but it is a useful thorn to have in one's side.
>
> ("Statement for *The New American Poetry*")

Although they are hardly silenced, the drum-beating, thesis-nailing broadcasts of movements tend to drown out those quieter voices the single heart proclaims its needs with. It's worth noting that O'Hara came out of the McCarthy era, and like John Cage or the entire beatnik involvement with Zen, the distrust of the public and demand for honesty often sound self-gratified when they were, in fact, a form of necessary self-protection. I don't think noise as noise irritated him so much, the pomposity of it, as did the way these campaigns in poetry's name failed to notice poetry was more complicated and detailed than any manifesto could do justice to.

> It may be that poetry makes life's nebulous events tangible to me and restores their detail; or conversely, that poetry brings forth the intangible quality of incidents which are all too concrete and circumstantial. Or each on specific occasions, or both all the time.
>
> ("Statement for *The New American Poetry*")

Perhaps emotions aren't after all the stuff of poetry, its profundity and sublimity, perhaps all we can do in a poem is make a structure about emotions; circumscribe rather than define, if the heart is to be present at all. Even the vague can yield accurate particulars. An articulate process doesn't always create articulated form. In the twentieth century, we've had to confess, care and exactitude can result in as much confusion as it does order.

Now that Grey Fox Press, under Donald Allen's editorship, has brought out Frank O'Hara's *Early Writing* and *Poems Retrieved* his corpus feels solidly there, available. In 1971 when *The Collected Poems* appeared there were those who'd known O'Hara and how he worked who were convinced Knopf's handsome five hundred pages couldn't be anything like a complete collected poems. Quite right, the Grey Fox books make available half again as much text as the Knopf, three hundred fifty new pages. I'd recommend anyone interested in O'Hara read both these recent books rather than the *Collected,* or even the later (1974), ample *Selected.* In one swoop they leave a Loie Fuller silk dragon trailing after them in the air. Reading the *Collected* though is to live a life. What won't emerge if you read O'Hara as I suggest is a definite sense of his being on the verge of something else or new when he died. The poems after "Biotherm" are each beats of a fluttering, impatient heart; he seems ready for something not quite ready for him. On first reading, Marjorie Perloff's account of O'Hara's last year was extremely moving. But going back, I was let down. Superb as her fourth chapter is, and the beginning of the fifth, they depend upon the flux of events for their emotional coloring, in very much the same manner as the *Collected* depends upon a complete, rather than selective, reading for its impact. More an observation and less a criticism, this. I like it that she calls the book *Frank O'Hara: Poet among Painters* in homage, is it, to Francis Steegmuller's *Appollinaire, Poet among Painters?* O'Hara and Apollinaire are linked in a way that would have pleased the *poète américain* very much.

A couple of poems seem to haunt the book, working like silent motives; "A Step Away from Them" and "Why I Am Not a Painter" come first to mind. Throughout, the analogies to painting are extremely useful, especially her picking out O'Hara's idea that the poem has a surface comparable, say, to a painting's, a deKooning's. And while Perloff's explications of individual poems often seem like hoop-jumping, the recapitulation of her own comments on "Music" against the broader context of O'Hara's entire work strikes me as one of the cleanest available summaries of certain new or recent poetic concerns. As she demonstrates in the section called "Reshaping the Genres," Mauna Loa that his output was, O'Hara meant it when he said in "Biotherm," "I am guarding it from mess and measure."

Mess and measure? Well, begin with the vexing notion or idea of detail and accuracy which characterizes all that is post-Georgian about American verse. When is it important the sandwich in a poem be liverwurst *qua* liverwurst and when could it be egg salad or ham as long as it's definitely nominated one or the other? This rather strange consideration crops up all over O'Hara's poems. How is it the specific creates an interchangeability that undercuts our trust in specificity as the very quality of uniqueness? Is this a side-effect of technology? Somewhere a fine line can be drawn between the hand-made and the machine-made, a distinction that depends upon intuition and the actual feel an object has. Though it flattened much like a steam-roller when it began, the Machine Age has gone on to delineate a myriad of previously unseen differences in every day things. Take a simple example. Some kinds of cornmeal breads cannot be cooked in either gas or electric ovens but require the even, surrounding, constant heat of a woodstove. Mayonnaise made in a blender is not mayonnaise made by hand, and when this point is argued the contention, albeit hidden, is usually over whether one is better than the other, rather than about their inherent differences. Once you know how to make a mayonnaise by hand, it's as fool-proof as a blender's. It takes longer, is harder work, uses more egg, can use more oil, and on and on until it's completely impossible to tell if the craft versus technology issue's main controversy is over Time, Quality, or Quantity.

In a note comparing O'Hara's use of a plane tree in "Memorial Day 1950" to Robert Lowell's "As a Plane Tree by Water," Perloff remarks, "The plane tree, used as a central symbol by Lowell, is simply an item in the Cambridge landscape for O'Hara—another tree would do." Exactly. This is a very disturbing and unnerving modus operandi. Especially for those in Pound's camp, those for whom each word, much less each image, is charged with selectivity to the point of being psychologically overdetermined. Not to mention the still widely held trust in poetry as a confirmation of those values and authenticity we associate with what is special and unique. (Overlooking momentarily poetry's ability to divert and entertain or aptly express consensual sentiments, i.e., the greeting card—those capacities, along with the didactic, belong now to television, that is if there ever was a poetic tribal encyclopedia, a romance post-modern poets have been given to, I think, because of the diffidence and scorn with which America has regarded all the non-entertainment arts, poetry in particular.)

Dada, that's where this disjunction of intention and content creeps into poems. Surrealism takes things a bit farther by widening the growing gap between the poem and what the poem is about. The hard to define, but unmistakable human capacity for caring makes our caring a specific and unique act bestowing both uniqueness and specificity upon its object. How can we trust a poem that doesn't care if a tree is an elm, not a lime? The implication, of course, is that our own identity is only as strong as our capacity to discern identities outside ourselves. Therefore, not-caring in any form gets conflated with the facelessness and soullessness plaguing our late, modern world.

The role of that "I"—that agent of identity—Marjorie Perloff notices

in a poem like O'Hara's "Music," "is to respond rather than to confess—
to observe, to watch, to be attentive to things." *Je est un autre*, Rimbaud
observed, "I is somebody other." The act of attention is as complicated,
unique, and personal as what we attend and importantly, it is *us* at that
moment. We can care about how we exercise perception as much as we
do about the perceptions themselves, not to mention what is perceived. In
this sense we do have, since the nineteenth century, a psychological art
which must take into consideration the subject as well as its object. The
machine's uniform, mass-production processes obliterate the irregularities
and unevenness that stimulate those perceptions our bodies delight in
endlessly. The riot of perception is a primal fantasy: deprived of it the *I*
can only go inward, slowly identifying with its unfed, graying memory.
Sensory deprivation leads to psychic depletion, soullessness. Rilke in a
letter dated November 13, 1925, writes:

> To our grandparents, a "house," a "well," a familiar steeple, even
> their own clothes, their cloak *still* meant infintely more, were in-
> finitely more intimate—almost everything a vessel in which they
> found something human already there, and added to its human
> store. Now there are intruding, from America, empty indifferent
> things, sham things, *dummies of life* . . . A house, as the Americans
> understand it, an American apple or a winestock from over there,
> have *nothing* in common with the house, the fruit, the grape into
> which the hope and thoughtfulness of our forefathers had entered.
>
> *(Briefe aus Muzot)*

What we feel can be made palpable, as available as a house, a chair, and
be recalled like a place or mislaid wallet. "In Memory of My Feelings"
(O'Hara had something akin to genius when it came to titles) suggests a
detachment and reification that puts emotion on a par with the most trivial
everyday occurrences. O'Hara remains a poet who insists on letting it all
in, on regarding everything he takes time to notice as worth the attention
spent. He honors his weakest feelings along with his strongest and most
noble. Compare him to Charles Olson in this respect. On the simplest level
both deal with their own material, Olson with, say, the Pleistocene and
O'Hara with his feelings. His. All of Olson's fire and data are just as much
Olson's as the feelings, moods, and fluctuations pervading O'Hara's poems
are specifically O'Hara's. Our hearts can be just as much a fact outside
ourselves as the cultivation of wild grasses.

Still, we cannot live without a sense of intimacy or inseparability in
our lives. The lack of an immediate presence involved in observing and
noticing is made up for by what is done with these observations. The
mastery associated with craft supplies that kind of feel for the material
which is an appreciation, not an identification with it. "For sentiment is
always intruding on form," O'Hara writes in "To Hell with It." That is no
heartless bon mot, it is the observation of a man who aches to do something
with what he feels. But how?

The familiar must become unfamiliar, or indirect, at least, not certain of itself:

> To name an object is to destroy three-quarters of our pleasure in a poem—the joy of guessing, step by step. The ideal is to suggest the object. We derive the most from the mystery that constitutes the symbol when we evoke the object step by step in order to portray a state of mind. Or, the other way round, when we choose an object and derive a state of mind from it by a sequence of decipherings.

"A state of mind," Mallarmé insists, details of a particular mood: the poem is a withholding, an implication bent upon regaining for us the mystery of not-knowing, rather than an explication. "The contemplation of objects, the image that rises out of the reverie the objects provoke—those are the song." The poem's raison d'être is hidden inside or under the words' sense. We know only a little of what we intimate is present. Mallarmé gave the poem an inside and an outside which then resulted in a "surface," an aspect of the poem which begged for penetration. It is Apollinaire who literally "surfaces" from the oceanic depths of symbolism to begin working the newly observed outer skin of the poem. Composition becomes an admitted act, not an invisible armature or the divine intervention of Muses. For example, André Billy recalls "Les Fenêtres" was composed in a café on Rue Danou when Apollinaire suddenly remembered he'd forgotten to write a preface for a catalogue of Robert Delaunay's paintings which was due that very day. So he, Billy, and Dupuy, also present, started batting around words, or the words batted about were randomly recorded by the poet. However, Delaunay and wife Sonia remember the poem's being composed otherwise. It was a meal Apollinaire had with them, oursins were served, and indeed oursins or the word "oursin" is there in the poem, along with two tan shoes, a curtain, and a window, all clearly placing it in their studio which was dominated by a window. Whatever the true history of "Les Fenêtres," it's interesting that a poem having nothing to do with sea urchins (oursins) has sea urchins in it because of the circumstances of its composition, a vermouth or a dinner. A surface means certain definite areas can be observed separately and on their own without affecting similar, nearby surfaces. Sea urchins could be changed to liverwurst sandwiches without causing the least ripple anywhere else in the poem.

That the poem is an event, that it happens and is not just suddenly, pop, there like a box of corn flakes on the grocer's shelf or the Ten Commandments when the smoke blew away, wouldn't have been a possibility had Mallarmé not perfected invisible composition. The symbolist method became almost a form of addressing subject matter. Mallarmé treats writing a poem like a beautiful and dangerously impulsive woman. He is careful, meticulous, and always respectfully formal lest anything offend, scaring her off. Subsequently Mallarmé's surfaces are transparent, politely unobtrusive (things like his *Les Loisirs de la Poste* take the lid off most theories based on casual reference to earlier work, even though they remain occasional in the purest sense.) Writing, that is, composing the poem, exists as a noiseless facility whose process is to produce that illusion the reader witnesses; nothing must be given away, everything finished, no rough edges to betray the means used.

Mallarmé took full advantage of the compositional act, producing enigmatic, mysterious poems that nearly disappear on the page or seem read through rime-frosted panes. Enigmatic and mysterious as they may become, the allusions, references, hints, and names in an O'Hara poem create the opposite effect: a constant, shifting sense that the poet's relationship to all this stuff on the poem's surface is always one of immediacy, if not intimacy. What greater joy in an O'Hara poem than to name and tell, be it place, person, day, the joy of not guessing, but being told who, when, or where—everything spelled out. He was no *fumiste*. Americans produce poems which strain to become objects, poems that are spatial, linear only when they can go in lines straight as interstates. Big flat prairies of detail.

It is this notion of surface that O'Hara inherited from Mallarmé via Apollinaire, coming as it did through Dada and surrealism on the way. Maybe unwittingly, but looking back, it seems Dada pried the art-work momentarily out of the strait-jacket of genre. It may never be possible, but Dada made it seem as though you could take a thing for what it essentially was. It wouldn't quite work in America; this buoyant wit had to be aimed at a bourgeoisie as stodgy and self-satisfied as Zurich's or Vienna's. Americans were still awfully hard-working, incapable of fuss, bluster, and outrage when it came to art, though they aped such sentiments with the Armory show. Dada emptied meaning from poems.

In surrealism a rearrangement took place of those relationships once assumed to exist between the object and its image or description. Paintings or poems starting out as *this* could wind up *that*, sometimes nothing like whatever inspired them or triggered their inceptions. Cubism is probably a better description of the fundamental processes involved. Surrealist poetry came closest to cubist painting when it maintained a definite even surface, avoiding those depths a symbolist poem might hint at by innuendo. But it isn't until we Americans discover abstract expressionism that we can understand the dynamics of surfaces such as those.

Let me quote the first stanza of Apollinaire's early poem, "Vae Soli":

> Hélas s'en sont venus à la male heure
> Diogène le chien avec Onan
> Le grimoire est femme lascive et pleure
> De chaud désire avec toi maintenant.

Without that second line, it would be hard to tell this model symbolist poem was about masturbation: Diogenes masturbated in public with no more shame than a dog and Onan spilled his seed carelessly. Or change that second line to read something like, *Socrate le chat avec Nebuchodonosor*, and the poem's surface undergoes distortion. By covering up the "source" of the poem (masturbation) I can give the poem an outside skin or covering, in this case obscuring its inside, i.e., the poem's occasion. Having established this surface I could begin to work on it. As surrealist I probably would have started an arabesque: Wise Men and their totem animals in procession with Ancient Kings. The cubist might begin looking at the Hebrew and classical edges and then butt lines and planes of text dealing with biblical or Greek matters up against them. Abstract expressionism, at least for its natives, solved these compositional problems with intuition; you learned how to feel your way through the process upon its surface; your aim was to keep it alive, untrapped, almost the opposite of the cubist notion of flattening, then finishing off each surface. Cubism delighted in the diversity of elements entering its compositional field; abstract expressionism concentrated much more on the diversity of approaches offered by whatever got you going. Had I kept up the distortion of that line in "Vae Soli" following any or all the approaches I'm discussing, no telling where that poem would have ended or what, if anything, it would be like when I finished, *other than itself*. Ah, there it is, the great ontological bedrock of postmodernism: the arts in America, poetry no exception, have ached so passionately to be themselves, to represent no tradition, not even that of their materials. We now have literary paintings and visual poems, pieces of music that are soundless—the other day I heard a dance on the radio done by a group who perform for the blind.

Let's stop, sit down and order a very cold *vin blanc* with a dash of cassis. I've been an intrepid sight-seer, guide in one hand, reader in tow with the other, dashing all over O'Hara as though he were Manchester, Bourge, or Washington, D.C. The very abundance of his poetry makes a topological metaphor apt and its completely urbane cast will bide none other than the city, one with a definite European quality. Frank O'Hara is rather like Toronto. We've just come out of the Nineteenth/Early Twentieth-Century French district, time to take our bearings. Forgive my meandering, beginning with the hesitancy I first had encountering the emotional façade, fine example of vernacular building—the use of the commonest, most typical materials, forms, and decorations of the period. Here and there, more and more evidence of what architects call *slang* with its nonstandard structures, spontaneous construction, arbitrary and often ephemeral materials. What's behind all this? The poet's valid desire to create a new surface, to indicate by working it a long neglected or never imagined area of a poem (to break my metaphor). The raciness and dazzle of O'Hara take on resonance, I hope, if given a place in time, when he is seen as rightful heir to Apollinaire and Mallarmé. Still experimentation is a weak excuse for poetry; surfaces little more than glazing when there is nothing to spread them over, no matter how much working they invite.

I must take pains not to *intend* anything but the work itself, to let the work take shape as it comes (as the best of Anaïs Nin does, despite her self-imposed difficulties) and develop into an entity

without interruptions or stumble-posts; I must think only of and
for the emergent work and not allow messages or ideas as such
to displace the validity of the work with their sham importance
and subtle derangement of emphasis. The social novel is a scrap-
book, the thesis novel a pamphlet.

That is an entry from Frank O'Hara's journal, made on October 26, 1948.
The day before he had noted: "So often the direct way of doing a thing is
ruinous; try to grab the trout and it always gets away." These are quoted
from *Early Writing*. O'Hara's commitment to poetry wasn't literary but
literal, a passionate conscription of the heart. It is instructive to reflect on
how shy he was presenting himself to the world as a poet. To the public
at large he was a curator of modern art, as well as its critic. He served God
and not Mammon. His insouciance, weakness as well as strength, along
with his seriousness amidst all the throw away, slang aesthetic, always had
at heart a devotion to the poem he couldn't help writing and to poetry.
"Poetry is the highest art, everything else, however gratifying . . . moving
and grand, is less demanding, more indulgent, more casual, more gratuitous, more instantly apprehensible, which I assume is not exactly what
we are after," he wrote Bill Berkson, in August 1962.

It is that kind of poet who cannot help being a poet, who is helplessly
enslaved to his craft, who writes the fresh, previously unknown sort of
poem. The two Grey Fox titles rounding out the corpus, *Early Writing* and
Poems Retrieved, help but don't reveal clearly how O'Hara did this, or better
yet, how it happened to him. He was from the start, we see, accomplished,
by no means brilliant, but extremely graceful executing complex though
unlabored poems. Influenced or not by Sitwell's *Façade*, "Military Band"
in *Early Writing* sets lines to popular dance measures. He appears to be
past-master of the lean though supple surreal poem, with its sexy touches
and occasional breathiness:

> As the ship pulls out
> of the rind-strewn harbor
> stevedores dock-loll
> tired after labor;
>
> a go-away basket
> gunned with champagne
> summons the salt wind's
> gull, white champion!
>
> and grey hills fall
> apart like thighs.

This first section of "Sea Changes" is by far the best of the three: those
compound images, *rind-strewn*, *dock-loll*, *go-away*, let the rhymes escape like

smoke rings, *harbor/labor* and *champagne/champion*, just as the archness of an exclamation like "white champion!" is turned into an eerie cut-out set next to the final stanza, "and grey hills fall / apart like thighs," where the coyness of the first two becomes a sudden sensual fantasy just as flirtation gives way to passion.

Both books make clear that early on O'Hara's gift was for lyric. He was a serious and devout lover of music who abandoned a promising career as pianist and composer to write poetry; the technical ground was laid firmly. Though it is his longer poems ("Oranges," "Easter," "Second Avenue" in particular of earlier things) where his liveliest and most ambitious side shows up. Like most such non-narrative poems since the *Cantos*, they involve the reader's physiology almost as much as his reading temperament. That numbing task of scanning page upon page, sustaining a blurred but determined eye, lets the text flow mechanically over us: part boredom and part bathing, baptism by total immersion. Yet, there is nothing like that moment when light breaks through the chink a few lines make. A stanza, a section, maybe the whole thing begins to add up and the poem begins to cohere. Two such regions opened up O'Hara's work for me. The first came in his "Ode on Causality" (a fine, fine poem, I hasten to add):

> to be layed at all! romanticized, elaborated, fucked, sung,
>   put to "rest"
> is worse than the mild apprehension of a Buddhist type
>   caught halfway up
> the tea-rose trellis with his sickle banging on the Monk's lead
>   window, moon
> not our moon
>   unless the tea exude a little gas and poisonous
>   fact
> to reach the spleen and give it a dreamless twinge that love's
>   love's near
>
>   the bang of alertness, loneliness, position that prehends
>   experience.

The second gestalt happened about here in "In Memory of My Feelings" and went on through the closing fifth section of that equally fine poem:

>   Grace
> to be born and live as variously as possible. The conception
> of the masque barely suggests the sordid identifications.
> I am a Hittite in love with a horse. I don't know what
>   blood's
> in me I feel like an African prince, I am a girl walking
>   downstairs
> in a red pleated dress with heels I am a champion taking a
>   fall

I am a jockey with sprained ass-hole I am the light mist
                              in which a face appears
and it is another face of blonde I am a baboon eating a
        banana
I am a dictator looking at his wife I am a doctor eating a
        child
I am a child smelling his father's underwear I am an Indian
sleeping on a scalp
                    and my pony is stamping in the birches,
and I've just caught sight of the *Niña,* the *Pinta* and the
        Santa Maria.
                    What land is this, so free?

In these passages, in both their contexts, the shiny details are piled up with
the fervor of a magpie, and at that very moment when the next bobble or
image would become another tiresome addition, O'Hara releases the tension. Bland phrases like "worse than the mild apprehension" introduce
those contortions of fantasy (a monk caught climbing a trellis to a lover's
window) that finally resolve themselves in another, equally colorless bit of
rhetorical huff, "position that prehends experience." The words themselves, their fragmentary phrases and details (i.e., the lead window and
tea-rose trellis) convince us the manic effect is artful, so too the flatness.
That cascade of imaginary identities in the second quotation would remain
no more than a list if it weren't for the last, that of the Indian. The narrative
touches (a pony stamping in the birches, sleeping on a scalp) make us
pause over this image, as though the rest had all been like dressing up in
the attic. "Grace / to be born and live as variously as possible" as a proposition opening the stanza has been demonstrated and resolved by finding,
at last, the freest possible identity to assume. An Indian, the noble savage
watching in his freedom the impending end to all his variousness. The
irony here is lightly done, though the *Niña, Pinta* and *Santa Maria* with
their innocent, geography class notion of history provide a poignant, rather
than stinging contrast.

When O'Hara died at forty his work had paused. The quick, effortless
surfaces of his short lyrics were attempting to cover the big hulking ex-
panses of longer poems like "Biotherm." Clearly he's already achieved an
impressive, personal poetic form all his own, free of any references but his
daily life, with whose seemingly inconsequential details he could create
poems like "The Day Lady Died." What he still ached for from a poem
needed a larger scale, more room, and a bigger slice of life. The success of
his lyrics as lyrics began to obscure for him what he wanted. And what
was that?

To set out on a voyage of discovery there is no need to choose,
with the help of rules—even the rules of taste—a fact labelled
sublime. An everyday fact can serve: the dropping of a handker-

chief can be for the poet the lever with which he will lift the universe. We all know about Newton's apple and what it did for that scientist, who can well be called a poet. That is why the poet of today scorns no event in nature. He seeks to make discoveries in the vastest, the most ungraspable snytheses—crowds, nebulae, oceans, nations—as well as in what are seemingly the simplest facts—a hand fumbling in a pocket, a match lighted by friction, animal cries, the smell of gardens after rain, birth of a flame on a hearth. Poets are not interested in the beautiful alone.

O'Hara, whether we have begun to feel his effect or not, inoculated American poetry with Apollinaire's spirit, and it looks like it could still take, protecting us from a deadly academic lifelessness on one hand and the current sterile, dry intellectualization of art on the other. But we can't be too quick to judge, though it seems we are at a crossroads similar to French poetry's when Apollinaire delivered his lecture "L'Esprit nouveau et les poètes" in November 1917 at the Théâtre de Vieux Colombier.

Thus we may hope for an inconceivably rich freedom as concerns the content and the means of art. Today poets are serving their apprenticeship in this encyclopedic freedom. In the realm of inspiration, their freedom need be no more restricted than that of a daily newspaper, which on a single sheet touches on the most diverse subjects and tours the most distant countries. Why should the poet not enjoy a freedom at least equal to this? In the era of the telephone, wireless, and aviation, why should he be confined to narrower space?

American poetry hasn't, however, struggled under the iron hand of an Academy like that weighing down early twentieth-century French literature. We are, all the same, a freedom-hungry nation seeking the wide open spaces and that "encyclopedic freedom" Apollinaire mentions in order to "live as variously as possible," in O'Hara's words.

"Hitherto, modern poetry has not matched the rapidity and simplicity with which we habitually evoke, each time with a single word, entities as complex as crowds, nations, or the universe." The synthesis Apollinaire anticipated, O'Hara brought our modern world a bit nearer. As an American he was a bit more wary of "the formidable beings called machines," acquainted with their processes and those boringly accurate and unending surfaces Rilke deplored. In fact, almost the entire artistic intelligence of the last seventy-five years has waged a campaign to alert us to the pitfalls of technology, the kind of products it turns out, the market those products create, and the consumers they make of us. Unwarned, man risks becoming plastic, vacuum-formed simulacra, zombies, our planet filling with those pod-people from Walter Wanger's *The Invasion of the Body Snatchers*. In spite of the *K-Marts* and *Pizza Huts*, I am optimistic because of efforts like those

of O'Hara's "to force oneself to 'see' in new ways, to *defamiliarize* the object
. . . one way of avoiding boredom, of keeping oneself and one's reader
'more keenly interested,' is to create a poetic structure that is always changing, shifting, becoming."

Evenness of surface was the fear Formica struck in abstract expressionist's hearts. But until the *Cantos,* we hadn't seen what an uneven surface
might look like in a poem. (I'm sure Pound had no intention of creating a
poetic equivalent to "painterly.") That is just what poetry apparently
needed, a limbering up and looseness, upon whose first appearances we
see only the *vertige* of details; implications rather than possible explications.

O'Hara was not alone in this attempt to push American poetry into a
new freedom. Charles Olson is a fine partner and contrast, though his work
finally has intellectual sources which eclipse his attempt at creating a future
for man's imagination. So it seems; and like Olson's, O'Hara's work anticipated more than it accomplished, making him as much precursor as influence. Or that is only the way we have of dealing with these poets whose
work embeds itself in the "belief that high art has a communicability far
superior in scope and strength to any form of human behavior."

Frank O'Hara was heroic in his ceaseless effort to keep his lines absolutely fresh and honest. Anyone who writes poems will tell you how
hard that is. The sheer difficulty of doing so is why would-be poets abandon
the craft. All I have tried to say about him has been an attempt to explain
how and what he did in this attempt to keep his poems alive.

> It seems they were all cheated of some marvellous
>   experience
> which is not going to go wasted on me which is why I'm
>   telling you about it
>   ("Having a Coke with You")

could be O'Hara's aesthetic, writ in gold upon the heavens to outshine all
the neon, engine exhaust, and inattention. As early as 1898 Gertrude Stein,
summarizing her half of a series of tests she had given fellow students,
wrote:

> In these descriptions it will be readily observed that habits of at-
> tention are reflexes of the complete character of the individual.

It is in our individual attentions that O'Hara seeks to restore to us our
possible completeness and character. He would refresh us and does, not
only with that work of his we have, but also with the future he gave to
the work of a next generation of poets.

Anne Sexton: "Some Tribal Female Who Is Known But Forbidden"

Richard Howard

There are some areas of experience in modern life, Theodore Roethke has said, that simply cannot be rendered by either the formal lyric or straight prose. We must realize—and who could have enforced the realization upon us better than Roethke—that the writer in "freer forms" must have an even greater fidelity to his subject matter or his substance than the poet who has the support of form—of received form. He must be imaginatively "right," his rhythm must move as the mind moves, or he is lost. "On the simplest level, something must happen in this kind of poem." By which Roethke meant, I am certain, that it is not enough to report something happening in your life merely—it must be made to happen in your poem. You must begin somewhere, though, generally with your life, above all with your life when it seems to you to welter in a particular exemplary status. Such is Anne Sexton's case, and she has begun indeed with the report of her case:

> Oh! Honor and relish the facts!
> Do not think of the intense sensation
> I have as I tell you this
> but think only.

In fact, she has reported more than anyone else—anyone else who has set out to write poems—has ever cared or dared, and thereby she has gained, perhaps at the expense of her poetry, a kind of sacerdotal stature, the elevation of a priestess celebrating mysteries which are no less mysterious for having been conducted in all the hard glare of the marketplace and with all the explicitness mere print can afford.

From *Alone with America: Essays on the Art of Poetry in the United States Since 1950.* © 1980 by Richard Howard. Atheneum, 1980.

Anne Sexton is the true Massachusetts heiress of little Pearl, who as the procession of the Worthies passes by asks Hester Prynne if one man in it is the same minister who kissed her by the brook. "Hold thy peace, dear little Pearl," whispers her mother. "We must not always talk in the marketplace of what happens to us in the forest." Like the sibylline, often insufferable Pearl, Anne Sexton *does* speak of such things, and in such places, and it makes her, again like Pearl, both more and less than a mere "person," something beyond a "character"; it makes her, rather, what we call a *figure*, the form of a tragic function. If you are wearing not only your heart on your sleeve, your liver on your lapel and the other organs affixed to various articles of your attire, but also a whole alphabet in scarlet on your breast, then your poetry must bear with losing the notion of *private parts* altogether and with gaining a certain publicity that has nothing to do with the personal. Further, if you regard, as Anne Sexton does, the poem as "a lie that tells the truth" (it was Cocteau who first spoke of himself this way), then you face the corresponding peril that the truth you tell will become a lie: "there is no translating that ocean" as Miss Sexton says. And it will become a lie because you have not taken enough care to "make something happen"—in short, to lie in the way poems must lie, by devising that imaginative rightness which Roethke located primarily in rhythm, but which has everything to do as well with the consecution of images, the shape language makes as it is deposited on the reader's mind, the transactions between beginnings and endings, the *devices*—no less—of art.

"Even one alone verse sometimes makes a perfect poem," Ben Jonson declared, and so much praise (it is the kind of praise that leaves out of the reckoning a great deal of waste, a great deal of botched work) it will be easy, and what is more it will be necessary, to give Anne Sexton; like the preposterous sprite whose "demon-offspring" impulses she resumes, this poet is likely, *at any moment*, to say those oracular, outrageous things we least can bear but most require:

> Fee-fi-fo-fum
> Now I'm borrowed
> Now I'm numb.

It is when she speaks beyond the moment, speaks as it were consecutively that Anne Sexton finds herself in difficulties; if we are concerned with the poem as it grows from one verse to the next, enlarging itself by means of itself, like a growing pearl, the real one (Hawthorne's, for all he tells us, never grew up), then we must discover an Anne Sexton dead set, by her third book of poems, against any such process. Hers is the truth that cancels poetry, and her career as an artist an excruciating trajectory of self-destruction, so that it is by her failures in her own enterprise that she succeeds, and by her successes as an artist that she fails herself.

In 1960 Miss Sexton's first collection of poems, *To Bedlam and Part Way Back*, was published with an epigraph from a letter of Schopenhauer to

Goethe echoing Hester Prynne's reproof: "Most of us carry in our heart the Jocasta who begs Oedipus for God's sake not to inquire further." The poems begin right there in Bedlam, unacclimated, unexplained, and take shape, apparently, as a therapeutic project—the very ingenuity of their shape, indeed, has something of the basket-weaver's patience about it, it is the work of a *patient*. The very first, addressed to the doctor "who walks from breakfast to madness," refers to the speaker and the other inmates as "magic talking to itself, / noisy and alone." Only gradually are we given a hint of the circumstances that brought her there, circumstances it will be Sexton's life work to adumbrate until the shadows fall indeed over her entire existence as a poet—here we simply start out in the asylum, where "my night mind / saw such strange happenings." The poet is in her own dark forest:

> I am afraid of course
> to look—this inward look that society scorns—
> Still, I search these woods and find nothing worse
> than myself, caught between the grapes and the thorns.

She is even, like Daphne, her own tree:

> I live in my wooden legs and O
> my green green hands . . .
> I am a fist of my unease
> as I spill toward the stars in the empty years.
> I build the air with the crown of honor; it keys
> my out of time and luckless appetite.
> You gave me honor too soon, Apollo.
> There is no one left who understands
> how I wait
> here in my wooden legs and O
> my green green hands.

That strikes the proper note of the priestess: it is the voice of a woman defiled by the very life she would expose, and whose knowledge has been granted by her defilement and is thereby partial, momentary and changing: "caught between a shape and a shape and then returned to me."

In these first poems, Anne Sexton has already mastered not only an idiosyncratic stanza, but a verse paragraph whose characteristic diction has, in Robert Lowell's choppy wake, restored to our poetry not only the lyric of self-dramatization which had hidden out in the novel for so long, but an unmistakable notation of events—not witty but always *grinçant*, and without more music than mere accuracy affords:

> It is a summer evening.
> The yellow moths sag
> against the locked screens
> and the faded curtains

> suck over the window sills
> and from another building
> a goat calls in his dreams.
> This is the TV parlor
> in the best ward at Bedlam.
> The night nurse is passing
> out the evening pills.
> She walks on two erasers,
> padding by us one by one.

The line break at "passing," the intermittent rhyme and the rhythmic subtlety, particularly in the last two lines, suggest the gifts employed here (Flaubert himself would have been pleased with that second sentence), even or especially when the matter is "given" so unbearably that no further gifts can, in short, matter:

> because we mind by instinct,
> like bees caught in the wrong hive,
> we are the circle of the crazy ladies
> who sit in the lounge of the mental house
> and smile.

There is, demonstrably, a care in these first poems for the poem's *making*; invariably it is Sexton's practice to use rhyme to bind the poem, irregularly invoked, abandoned when inconvenient, psychologically convincing. It is the rhyme introduced into English verse by Arnold, refined by Eliot, and roughed up here by Miss Sexton, who seeks to recover for poetry the expressive resources of chaos and is not to be coerced, "in that narrow diary of her mind," to any spurious regularity:

> Today is made of yesterday, each time I steal
> toward rites I do not know, waiting for the lost
> ingredient, as if salt or money or even lust
> would keep us calm and prove us whole at last.

She conducts her funneling and furious tour of the wards, in this collection, so that the final third of the book is focussed on the purely private horrors: on the separation from individual impulse that leaves us

> too alien to know
> our sameness and how our sameness survives;

and on the terrible demands, nonetheless, of the ego imprisoned in the woman's wanting body:

> My dear, it was a time,
> butchered from time,
> that we must tell of quickly
> before we lose the sound of our own
> mouths calling mine, mine, mine.

The last three poems, "For John, Who Begs Me Not to Enquire Further," "The Double Image" and "The Division of Parts" are specifically concerned with a disengagement from the sacred world of madness and a weary return to sanity, or at least to a version of secular (bourgeois) life which must seem sane for being so bleak. The painful poems to the estranged daughter, to the mother dying of cancer, and about the two suicide attempts (Sexton is more than half in love with easeful death; as her envying poem to Sylvia Plath insists, she is altogether enamored of a difficult one) are an exorcism, a caveat and a mustering of forces; to the daughter is assigned the disabused confession:

> I, who was never quite sure
> about being a girl, needed another
> life, another image to remind me.
> And this was my worst guilt; you could not cure
> nor soothe it. I made you to find me.

And to the mother, an outraged voice with whom Sexton is to wrestle in almost every poem, a deferred reconciliation:

> You come, a brave ghost, to fix
> in my mind without praise
> or paradise
> to make me your inheritor.

While to herself the entire book stands as a valorization of the present, a way of facing up to a perishable existence, all transgressions acknowledged and even embraced—were they not the source of ecstasy?—and of recognizing the daily extinctions that make suicide not undesirable but unnecessary:

> Today the yellow leaves
> go queer. You ask me where they go. I say today believed
> in itself, or else it fell.

"Her first book, especially the best poems, spills into the second and somehow adds to it," Robert Lowell said when *All My Pretty Ones* was published in 1962: the title comes, of course, from the "one fell swoop" passage in *Macbeth*, in which the operative phrase, for Miss Sexton's retrospective purposes, quite defines the volume's enterprise:

> I cannot but remember such things were,
> That were most precious to me.

There is also an inner epigraph, parallel to the remark from Schopenhauer in the first collection, this time from a letter of Kafka's, to the effect that "a book should serve as the ax for the frozen sea within us." Thus the therapeutic requirement is still served, along with the memorial function, by these poems which, as Lowell remarked, pursue what Anne Sexton has always had in view, "the tongue's wrangle, the world's pottage, the rat's star," the minimal furniture, too, of a life confined but also privileged by madness, disease, death and violence to "spells and fetishes":

> I cannot promise very much.
> I give you the images I know.

Such knowledge has afforded the poet a certain abundance, and if the harshness of her concern makes us wonder with her "how anything fragile survives," there is in *All My Pretty Ones* an intimation of survival that is the more powerful, not the less, for its obsessive mortality. "Nothing is sure. No one. I wait in doubt," Anne Sexton confesses after surgery, "my stomach laced up like a football / for the game." Attending to herself between the periods when those other attendants must take over, she continues to catalogue the ills not only the flesh is heir to, but the mind and the body politic as well, always convulsively yet with a vividness generally associated with a more sanguine view:

> Outside the bittersweet turns orange.
> Before she died my mother and I picked these fat
> branches, finding orange nipples
> on the gray wire strands.
> We weeded the forest, curing trees like cripples.

It is strong stuff and invariably brought to a devastating close—by postponed rhymes, or by pruning down the stanza to the simplest terminal phrase, standing alone as a line: "my son," or "I wish I were dead"—the cadences of agony, loss and division. What a relief when the design works against the poet's distemper, as in "The Abortion" and "The Operation," instead of surrendering—condescending, really—to that awfulness of it all. Such titles suggest Sexton's preoccupations, but not the lucid obstruction to sentimentality which her firm control, at her best, of the stanza and her fine colloquial diction set up. I cannot guess what another generation—before or after our own—might make of such incisions as this, from "Housewife":

> Men enter by force, drawn back like Jonah
> into their fleshy mothers.
> A woman *is* her mother.
> That's the main thing.

But abjuring incantation of any obvious kind for statement, choosing truth and taking the always discreditable consequences does not, for all that, mean that Anne Sexton has given over the oracular role, the Pythian occasion. Once she is on the tripod, it does not matter that images are extinguished, metaphors dissipated, words harrowed. What is left is a poem which utter necessity seems to have reduced to absence and which, nonetheless, is acknowledged in such absence as the image—the final image—of an absolute plenitude. Though nothing is smooth or caressing here—it

is a rough magic indeed that Sexton, unlike Prospero, refuses to abjure—
it is still "The Black Art" she practices, as in the poem of that name:

> A woman who writes feels too much,
> those trances and portents!
> As if cycles and children and islands
> weren't enough; as if mourners and gossips
> and vegetables were never enough.
> She thinks she can warn the stars.

By 1966, Miss Sexton had completed another book of poems, with the almost expected, certainly self-parodying title *Live or Die*—from Bellow's *Herzog*, and the quote goes on, in what I take to be an exacerbated self-adjuration: "But don't poison everything"—and also written a full-length, theater-of-the-mind play called *Tell Me Your Answer True*. It is not surprising, after the tremendous series of intimacies to which she has made us a party, to find now in any one poem not only a case-history versified into its most painful crises, the analects of continuing dissolution ("life enlarges, life takes aim"), but also accounts of drug addiction, the bloody accidents of children, the death by cancer of at least one parent, and certainly the disappearance of God ("need is not belief"). A lessening of attention to what happens in the poem, as Roethke prophesied, has obliged Sexton to move into it every kind of event that can compel *our* shocked attention, if not our assent, to that other world, the world where "I am the target." The poet's attitude toward her art is defined, I think, by the fact that many of the speeches in her garishly articulated psychodrama are the word-for-word texts of poems from the third collection, written out as prose and simply *uttered*, always by Daisy, the self-exploring heroine who is "tired of the gender of things":

> Dreams came into the ring
> like third-string fighters . . .
> each one a bad bet
> who might win
> because there was no other.
>
> I stared at them
> concentrating on the abyss,
> the way one looks down into a rock quarry . . .
>
> You taught me
> to believe in dreams,
> thus I was the dredger.
>
> I have come back
> but disorder is not what it was.
> I have lost the trick of it!

> I stand at this old window
> complaining . . .
> allowing myself the wasted life.
>
> This is madness
> but a kind of hunger.

However effective, and ultimately reductive, such utterance may sound within the play, the mere fact that it is set down there as merely spoken prose suggests what Sexton's entire career—"submerged in my own past / and my own madness"—has imposed upon her talent: the priestess's commitment to survival at the expense of artifice or appearance:

> To be occupied or conquered is nothing—
> to remain is all!

and again, from the final "affirmative" poem, "Live":

> Even so,
> I kept right on going on,
> a sort of human statement,
> lugging myself as if
> I were a sawed-off body
> in the trunk

a hostage to the perpetuation of the self, even if it is in "the domain of silence, / the kingdom of the crazy and the sleeper." So assured, in these poems which won her a Pulitzer Prize, and in the ones to come after, is Anne Sexton of her hieratic position ("Everyone has left me / except my muse *that good nurse*") that she can afford, literally, to say anything and know that for all the dross it will be, in some way, a poem. "I am an identical being," she proclaims, and it might indeed be the sibyl talking, confident that what is said has its virulent, its vatic status because *she says it*, out of the welter of love, "that red disease," and of death, "an old belonging"—

> I am your daughter, your sweetmeat,
> your priest, your mouth and your bird
> and I will tell you all stories
> until I am laid away forever,
> a thin gray banner.

Sylvia Plath: "And I Have No Face, I Have Wanted to Efface Myself"

Richard Howard

The first review I ever wrote of a book of poems was of *her* first book of poems, that breviary of estrangement (the rhymes are all slant, the end-stop avoided like a reproach), *The Colossus* (1961; all the poems in it were completed by 1959), and in my account

> her eye is sharp and her wits responsive to what she sees. She
> prefers, though, to make you *hear* what she sees, the texture of
> her language affording a kind of analogue for the experience she
> presents. . . . Event is reproduced in the aural imagery: "a racket
> of echoes tacking in crooks from the black town . . . gave way to
> fields and the incessant seethe of grasses." Once in a while this
> concern for texture as the dramatization of experience blurs the
> poem's movement, but in most cases what catches in the ear is
> governed, checked, and we grasp what it is she wishes us to know
> because of the way we hear it

my *audition*, then, of these well-behaved, shapely poems by a *summa cum laude* graduate of Smith who had worked as a guest editor of Mademoiselle and won a Fulbright to Newnham, the wife of Ted Hughes and the mother of two children, I missed a lot—I had no premonition of what was coming. Perhaps I glimpsed, though, what was *going*, what was being discarded, or stepped over, or fended off; for once I had identified the girl who speaks in "The Manor Garden":

> The fountains are dry and the roses over.
> Incense of death. Your day approaches . . .
> Hours of blankness. Some hard stars

From *Alone with America*. © 1980 by Richard Howard. Atheneum, 1980.

> Already yellow the heavens . . .
> The small birds converge, converge

as an Oracle at the world's funneling center, as the Lady of Situations who acknowledged herself the victorious victim of paralysis, the world round about locked in a process of corresponding necrosis ("the crow *settles* her garments"):

> Sylvia Plath's burden is, throughout, the disaster inscribed within the surface of landscape (if she is a "nature poet" it is not because she runs ahead down the path and holds out her hand: she makes us push through the weeds with her every step of the way, and occasionally snaps a bramble back in the most unladylike manner:
>
>> Grub-white mulberries redden among leaves.
>> I'll go out and sit in white like they do,
>> Doing nothing. July's juice rounds their nubs . . .
>> Berries redden. A body of whiteness
>> Rots, and smells of rot under its headstone
>> Though the body walk out in clean linen);
>
> her poems, though there are no people in them, are instinct with Presences, which best arrive of themselves through the accurate evocation of their site. She has a genius for the *genius loci*

once I saw that much, once I saw that the spirit of place, for her, was *her* spirit in *that* place: "mist-shrouded sun focussing all the white and silent distances that poured from every point of the compass, hill after pale hill, to stall at my feet," why then I could see more—my notice ended so:

> The last poem in *The Colossus*, "The Stones," is what I take to be a new departure. Here there is more than the Pythoness' expectancy as she broods over a broken landscape: here is a vividly human voice, speaking from "the city of spare parts, the city where men are mended." I look forward to hearing more about that.

And indeed I was—we all were—to hear a great deal more about that, more in her novel or narrative of renewal *The Bell Jar* (1963), where the same note is struck that *I* had been so struck by in "Stones":

> There ought, I thought, to be a ritual for being born
> twice—patched, retreaded and approved for the road,

and more in her second, posthumous book of poems *Ariel* (1965—Sylvia Plath took her life, or rather left us her death, in 1963) as well as in the uncollected poems to be found, along with some valuable studies of her work, in the "Womanly Issue" of *Tri-Quarterly* (no. 7, Fall 1966).

Of course when I spoke of "The Stones" as a departure, I did not intend the word in all the drastic sense it has come to have in Sylvia Plath's case. Still, the valedictory was there, and the words certainly drastic:

> I entered
> The stomach of indifference, the wordless cupboard.
> The mother of pestles diminished me.
> I became a still pebble.

The conflict, or at least the confrontation between what I should designate the lithic impulse—the desire, the need to reduce the demands of life to the unquestioning acceptance of a stone, "taciturn and separate . . . in a quarry of silences"—and the impulse to live on, accommodating the rewards as well as the wrecks of existence so that "the vase, reconstructed, houses / the elusive rose": such was the dilemma I glimpsed as a departure at the end of *The Colossus*, and whatever it was I missed then of the true bent, or actually the breach, of Sylvia Plath, what I *did* make out is interestingly ratified by Ted Hughes's notes on the order of her poems:

> "The Stones" was the last poem she wrote in America. The immediate source of it was a series of poems she began as a deliberate exercise in experimental improvisation on set themes. She had never in her life improvised. The powers that compelled her to write so slowly had always been stronger than she was. But quite suddenly she found herself free to let herself drop, rather than inch over bridges of concepts.

Yet now that we have the whole thing together, the two books of poems and the novel—their interdisciplinary relevance, by the way, is suggested by conferring, as the old books used to say, such a quotation as this from the novel:

> Wherever I sat . . . I would be sitting under the same glass bell jar, stewing in my own sour air and listening to the old brag of my heart. I am, I am, I am

with these lines from "Suicide off Egg Rock":

> Sun struck the water like a damnation.
> No pit of shadow to crawl into,
> And his blood beating the old tattoo
> I am, I am, I am

—now that we can see Sylvia Plath's life, as she kept meaning us to, from the vantage of her death, we must not make too great a disjunction between the "conceptual" and the "immanent," the bridged and the engulfed in her utterance. It was all one effort—as Hughes says perfectly: "she faced a task in herself, and her poetry is the record of her progress in the task. . . . The poems are chapters in a mythology"—and it was all one quest, as

Sylvia Plath says imperfectly (that is, with the abiding awareness of imperfection), in an uncollected poem:

>   With luck I shall
>   Patch together a content
>   Of sorts. Miracles occur,
>   If you care to call these spasmodic
>   Tricks of radiance miracles.

Her entire body of work can be understood best as a transaction—out of silence, into the dark—with otherness: call it death, or The Stone, or as she came to call it, "stasis in darkness" ("Ariel"), "great Stasis" ("Years"), in the first book such negotiations taking the form of a dialogue ("your voices lay siege . . . promising sure harborage"), which is to say *taking a form;* while in the later poems she is speaking from a point of identification with stasis which is complete, resolved, irreversible ("the cold dead center / where spilt lives congeal and stiffen to history")—she is on the other side, within the Deathly Paradise, so that it is the triumph of her final style to make expression and extinction indivisible ("I like black statements"). Which is why A. L. Alvarez says that her poems read as if they were written posthumously, for the very source of Sylvia Plath's creative energy was her self-destructiveness.

We say that a particularized self is original—not in the paltry sense of being new, but in the deeper sense of being old: original in the sense which deals with origins—when that self acknowledges it begins somewhere and lives its own life and, being as we also say individual, lives no other life, which is to say, dies:

>   It is Adam's side,
>   this earth I rise from, and I in agony.
>   I cannot undo myself . . .
>
>   It is so small
>   The place I am getting to, why are there these obstacles—
>   The body of this woman . . .
>   An animal
>   Insane for the destination.

In the experience of the original individual self, then, it is true as Freud says that the aim of all life is death; the effort of the mortal self is to reduce stimuli to an equilibrium, to cancel out tension, to return to the inanimate condition. The urge to restore an earlier state of things:

>   What I want back is what I was
>   Before the bed, before the knife,
>   Before the brooch-pin and the salve
>   Fixed me in this parenthesis; . . .
>   A place, a time gone out of mind

to impose, indeed, a *statics,* is indeed an expression of the *conservative* nature of organic life, of the inertia inherent in it ("my bones hold a stillness"). These urges toward homeostasis, these impulses to cancel out, to level off ("how she longed for winter then! / scrupulously austere in its order / of white and black / ice and rock"), to "stall"—*stalling* indeed is one of Sylvia Plath's favorite words: "distances that poured from every point of the compass to *stall* at my feet"; "desolation, *stalled* in paint, spares the little country in the corner"; "hammers hoisted, wheels *stalled*"; another favorite is *stilled,* as in "these *stilled* suburbs," "air *stilled,* silvered," "I became a *still* pebble"; both words being derived, like the series clustering round the Latin *stolidus,* from an earlier root meaning "to be rigid"—all these yearnings toward deadlock, then, are indeed beyond the pleasure principle; they tend rather to that great kingdom of alienation, of *otherness* we call ecstasy (standing outside oneself) which is not a matter of moving around but of being encircled, of being the center of an orbit, of being transfigured, *standing still:*

> till there you stood,
> Fixed vortex on the far
> Tip, riveting stones, air,
> All of it, together.

Not movement but ecstasy, then; not pleasure but—joy. We shall best realize the goal and the gain of Sylvia Plath's poetry if we reckon with Joy as Nietzsche accounts for it:

> All that suffers wants to live, longing for what is farther, higher, brighter. "I want heirs"—thus speaks all that suffers; "I want children, I do not want *myself.*"
> Joy it is that wants *itself*—the ring's will strives in it. . . .
> Joy, however, does not want heirs, or children—joy wants itself, wants eternity, wants everything eternally the same.

And we shall best recognize the vestal responsibilities of the woman occupied by such joy if we invoke the demonstrated responsibilities of other women—such heroic initiates as Pauline Réage and Doris Lessing; it is in the cause of a sacramental joy that *Histoire d'O* and *To Room Nineteen* survey the entire sweep of a spiritual evolution, an ascesis whose inevitable conclusion—after everything else has been endured—is the body's destruction. With a like submission, a like dedication:

> My heart under your foot, sister of a stone . . .
> Father, bridegroom, in this Easter egg
> Under the coronal of sugar roses
> The queen bee marries the winter of your year.

Sylvia Plath enters upon her apprenticeship to otherness, to ecstasy; more ceremonious than Lessing, more ingenuous than Réage, but like them prepared to obey a tragic ontogeny ("I am ready for enormity"), she sloughs off—we see her divest herself of—mere personality like the cloud

> that distils a mirror to reflect its own slow
> Effacement at the wind's hand,

in order to achieve the ecstatic identity conferred by Joy. Throughout her first book, there are recorded many impediments to this nuptial occasion. Often the very instances which are meant to provide the means, the measures of acceding to stillness refuse to enter into a dialogue with the postulant. Though she submits herself to the ordeal, the process refuses to *take*, and the would-be victim is left with only the impenetrable surface of existence:

> Sun's brass, the moon's steely patinas,
> The leaden slag of the world.

On other more fortunate occasions, the initiation proceeds, through trials by trituration, drowning, petrifaction, calcination, all manner of murderous espousals:

> Stars grinding, crumb by crumb,
> Our own grist down to its bony face.

But even when the universal processes are willing to do their part, some unready revulsion in the bride-apparent spoils everything, and as so often in *The Colossus*, the spell breaks:

> The whole landscape
> Loomed absolute as the antique world was
> Once, in its earliest sway . . .
> Enough to snuff the quick
> Of her small heat out, but before the weight
> Of stones and hills of stones could break
> Her down to mere quartz grit in that stony light
> She turned back.

There is darkness ("my hours are married to shadow"), there is silence ("I saw their mouths going up and down without a sound, as if they were sitting on the deck of a departing ship, stranding me in the middle of a huge silence"), there is stupefaction ("the no-color void . . . in some secret part of her, that long, blind, doorless and windowless corridor of pain was waiting to open up and shut her in again")—all the conditions, one might assume, for the wedding between the self—"the profane grail, the dreaming skull"—and the system, between the victim and the vortex. But no— joy cannot be willed, it can only be surrendered to, gained when it has been given over:

> I tire, imagining white Niagaras
> Build up from a rock root, as fountains build
> Against the weighty image of their fall.

That is why the poems in this first book, as the quotations from the novel, are all confessions of failure, records of estrangement, even boasts of betrayal: "in this province of the stuck record," Sylvia Plath laments, she is excluded from that true stillness which is at the center ("it seemed / a sly world's hinges had swung / shut against me. All held still"—all, that is, except her own awareness, circling even yet in the stream of mere animal perpetuation,

> The stream that hustles us
> Neither nourishes nor heals).

The exhaustion before its term of the lithic impulse, as I have called it, the impoverishment of the effort to escape effort ("the stars are no nearer . . . and all things sink / into a soft caul of forgetfulness. . . . This is not death, it is something safer") is the worry of *The Colossus*, and we may take the aporia of the title poem as the correct centerpiece of these poems that implore the broken earth for rest:

> I shall never get you put together entirely,
> Pieced, glued, and properly jointed . . .
> Thirty years now I have labored
> To dredge the silt from your throat.
> I am none the wiser.

Landscape and weather have failed her, have refused to take her into their stony certainty ("clearly the genius of plenitude," she observes wryly, "houses himself elsewhere"), and in two poems of supplication, the most poignant in this first book, Sylvia Plath apostrophizes the Rock Maidens— the Mothers, the Sisters, the Fates, the Muses, the Lorelei: her names are many for the Medusa-figures that will release her from the bonds of life ("my mendings itch") into the barrow of death ("by day, only the topsoil heaves. / Down there one is alone"). In the first of these, "The Disquieting Muses," she acknowledges the gradual take-over of her being by these "muses unhired by you, dear mother . . . these three ladies nodding by night around my bed, / Mouthless, eyeless, with stitched bald head." The changeable earth is stanza by stanza renounced, the mortal mother is occulted, "and I faced my travelling companions." A little guilty still, as the last two lines suggest, her loyalties to life dividing her a little from the nodal peace she seeks, Sylvia Plath accounts for her situation, says plainly enough (though I for one failed to hear her) where she is, fixed fast:

> Day now, night now, at head, side, feet,
> They stand their vigil in gowns of stone,
> Faces blank as the day I was born,
> Their shadows long in the setting sun
> That never brightens or goes down.
> And this is the kingdom you bore me to,
> Mother, mother. But no frown of mine
> Will betray the company I keep.

And in the second poem of petition, "The Lorelei" (which in my first review I took for mere stage properties, though now I see—she has helped me, made me see—the *auto sacramental* which employed such devices, ritual objects in the passion of achieved death), the prayer goes up to the overpowering yet elusive forces for which she is not, palpably, ready—"it is no night to drown in." Except for John Ashbery's early poem "Illustration," I know of nothing that echoes farther into that undiscovered country of suicide felt to be as yet unearned, unmerited. Deterred, recalled, Sylvia Plath pleads to make the journey for which she is unready ("all the gods know is destinations"), though so eager:

> Your voices lay siege. You lodge
> On the pitched reefs of nightmare,
>
> Promising sure harborage;
> By day, descant from borders
> Of hebetude, from the ledge
>
> Also of high windows. Worse
> Even than your maddening
> Song, your silence. At the source
>
> Of your ice-hearted calling—
> Drunkenness of the great depths.
> O river, I see drifting
>
> Deep in your flux of silver
> Those great goddesses of peace.
> Stone, stone, ferry me down there.

So much has been said about *Ariel*, and its success—or at least its cessation—has been so vividly acknowledged, that it would be politic to agree with Sylvia Plath, or with Ted Hughes's account of her, in dismissing everything prior to "The Stones" as juvenilia, produced in the days before she became herself. But as I hope I have shown, it was not herself she became, but totally Other, so that she (or the poems—it is all one now) looked back on "herself" as not yet having become anything at all. The poems we know were written first in *Ariel* still admit an uncertainty:

> I am exhausted, I am exhausted—
> Pillar of white in a blackout of knives

—but one soon to be resolved. "Your first gift," she says to death in "The Rival," "is making stone out of everything." And in most of these poems, we have the sense that the fierce calm sisters apostrophized in "The Lorelei" have done their work for her, and that she has come to that place to which she asked to be ferried: the last poem in the book, "Words," is that poem of Nietzschean Joy which dispenses with heirs, with children, which wants itself, wants eternity, wants everything eternally the same:

> Words dry and riderless,
> The indefatigable hoof-taps.
> While
> From the bottom of the pool, fixed stars
> Govern a life.

No longer a postulant, she has been accepted in that "country far away as health," and we may take all these terrible *statements* as the spousal-verses of the marriage arranged so long ago: "the soul is a bride / in a still place." There is no pathos in the accents of these final poems, only a certain pride, the pride of an utter and ultimate surrender (like the pride of O, naked and chained in her owl mask, as she asks Sir Stephen for death); "Tulips," for example, is a poem of total purification—not even the rhythms any longer resist the run of utterance from what Sylvia Plath called her "silent center":

> My body is a pebble . . . they tend it as water
> Tends to the pebbles it must run over, smoothing them
>   gently . . .
> I am a nun now, I've never been so pure.
> I didn't want any flowers, I only wanted
> To lie with my hands turned up and be utterly empty.
> How free it is, you have no idea how free—
> The peacefulness is so big it dazes you,
> And it asks nothing . . .
> It is what the dead close on, finally.

Deliver me from the body of this death! is the great sacramental cry of our culture, and in these unquestioning last poems of Sylvia Plath's, it is to death that the words are addressed, and what she is delivered of, as of a child, is the world itself, to which, in her mystical marriage, she has given birth:

> Let it not come by the mail, finger by finger.
> Let it not come by word of mouth, I should be sixty
> By the time the whole of it was delivered, and too numb
>   to use it.
> Only let down the veil, the veil, the veil . . .
> There would be a nobility then, there would be a birthday.
> And the knife not carve, but enter
> Pure and clean as the cry of a baby,
> And the universe slide from my side.

Biographical Notes

Louise Bogan (1897–1970) was born in Livermore Falls, Maine. She grew up in New England and entered Boston University in 1915. A year later, however, she left school and married Curt Alexander, an Army career man. In 1917, they moved to the Panama Canal Zone, where their daughter was born. Two of Bogan's poems, "Betrothed," and "The Young Wife," were published that year in the magazine *Others*. In 1918, she returned to the United States with her daughter; her marriage broke up soon afterward. Bogan continued to write and she held a number of jobs, including work at various branches of the New York Public Library. In 1924, she began writing book reviews and accepted the managing editorship of *The Measure*. In 1931, close to a nervous breakdown, she entered the New York Neurological Institute. Her recovery was speedy, and a month later she resumed her normal life. Two years later, Bogan received a Guggenheim Fellowship for writing abroad, went to Europe, and, on her return, had another brief breakdown. From 1948 through 1968, Bogan taught at seven different universities ranging from the University of Washington to New York University. She continued to write poetry and criticism, and she made several collaborative translations: Goethe's *Elective Affinities* with Elizabeth Mayer, poems by Paul Valéry with May Sarton, and *The Journals of Jules Renard* with Elizabeth Roget. Bogan also continued to receive awards: she won the Bollingen Prize in 1955, a $5,000 prize from The American Academy of Poets in 1959, the Senior Creative Arts Award from Brandeis in 1962, and a $10,000 prize from the National Endowment for the Arts. She died February 4, 1970.

Bogan's books of poetry include *Body of This Death* (1923), *Dark Summer* (1929), *The Sleeping Fury* (1937), *Poems and New Poems* (1941), and *The Blue Estuaries* (1969). She also published *Selected Criticism* (1955) and *A Poet's Alphabet: Reflections on the Literary Art and Vocation* (1970).

Melvin Beaunorus Tolson (1900–1966) was born in Moberly, Missouri. His mother, Leah (Hurt) Tolson, was part Creek Indian and wrote verse; his father, A. A. Tolson, was an itinerant Methodist minister who had taught himself Latin, Hebrew, and Greek. As a child, he displayed unusual talent as a painter, but at twelve he turned to verse. Attending ward schools in Iowa, he published his first poem in an Iowa newspaper in 1914. The family moved to Kansas City in 1917, and Tolson became senior class poet in high school. After studying briefly at Fisk University, he matriculated at Lincoln University, where he received his B.A. with honors in 1923. He found a teaching position at Wiley College, in Marshall, Texas, where he taught a wide range of subjects and coached several sports. At Wiley, he wrote several plays and a considerable amount of verse. In 1939, his poem "Dark Symphony" won a nationwide competition sponsored as part of the Negro American Exposition in Chicago. In 1947, he was appointed Professor of Creative Literature at Langston University, Langston, Oklahoma, where he also served as director of the university's Dust Bowl Theatre, and where he was to serve four terms as mayor of the city of Langston. The same year, Tolson was named Poet Laureate of Liberia and composed for that country's centennial his *Libretto for the Republic of Liberia*, published in book form in 1953. In 1952, he received *Poetry*'s Bess Hopkin Award. In 1954, the Liberian president awarded Tolson the Order of the Star of Africa. In 1965, Tolson published the first volume of *Harlem Gallery*, a large-scale work intended to be a history of blacks in America, and on which he had been at work for more than twenty years but never lived to complete. Tolson retired from Langston University in 1965 and was appointed the first Avalon Professor of the Humanities at Tuskegee Institute in Alabama. Despite repeated operations for cancer, he lectured throughout the United States. He died in 1966, survived by his wife, Ruth (Southall) Tolson, and his four children.

Tolson's chief works were *Rendezvous with America* (1944), *Libretto for the Republic of Liberia* (1953), *The Curator* (Book I of *Harlem Gallery*) (1965). His plays and dramatic adaptations include *Black No More* (1952), *The Fire in the Flint* (1952), and *Black Boy* (1963).

Arthur Yvor Winters (1900–1968) was born in Chicago to Harry and Faith Ahnfeldt Winters. The poet's father was a stockbroker. The family moved to Pasadena for several years, returning to Chicago when Arthur was a teenager. In high school he adopted a serious interest in contemporary poetry, reading magazines like *Poetry* and the *Little Review* and acquiring books for what became an outstanding collection in the field. At the University of Chicago, he was active in the poetry club with Harriet Monroe, who later published his early poems in *Poetry*. Tuberculosis interrupted Winter's education, and he withdrew to a sanitarium in Santa Fe for three years. There he read and wrote, corresponding with Monroe, Marianne Moore, Hart Crane, and Allen Tate. Moore, a librarian, mailed him books from the New York Public Library. Released from the sanitarium, he taught school locally. He took a B.A. and an M.A. in Romance Languages at Colorado and taught at the University of Idaho at Moscow. He married the novelist Jean Stafford, with whom he had two children. In 1928, he started studying for his Ph.D. in English at Stanford and retired from teaching there in 1966. Winters was an extraordinarily professional scholar who grounded himself in systematic study of the Classical, early Romance, Renaissance and modern European, English and American languages and literatures. A steady worker, he published about twenty books of poems and criticism. He was especially associated with the imprint of his friend Alan Swallow. A dedicated teacher, he published the work of his students in his magazine *Gyroscope* and in two poetry anthologies. He also exerted his influence as Western editor of *Hound and Horn*. Janet Lewis, J.V. Cunningham, Ann Stanford, and Thom Gunn are four of the poets and scholars tied closely to Winters by debts of affection. A public-spirited man, he headed civil defense in Los Altos during World War II. When a local man was falsely imprisoned, Winters spent two years freeing him, taking the issue to the national press. He was the recipient of the Bollingen Prize, two Guggenheim Fellowships, grants from the National Institute of Arts and Letters and from the National Endowment for the Arts, and Brandeis's creative arts award. He died in 1968 of throat cancer.

Winters's books of poems include *The Immobile Wind* (1921), *The Magpie's Shadow* (1922), *The Bare Hills* (1927), *The Early Poems* (1966), *The Proof* (1930), *Before Disaster* (1934), *Poems* (1940), *The Giant Weapon* (1943), and the *Collected Poems* (1952, rev. ed. 1960). His books of criticism include *Primitivism and Decadence* (1937), *Maule Curse* (1938), *The Anatomy of Nonsense* (1943), *Edward Arlington Robinson* (1946), *In Defense of Reason* (1947), *The Function of Criticism: Problems and Exercises* (1957), *Forms of Discovery* (1967), and the posthumous *Uncollected Essays* (1973).

Edwin Orr Denby (1903–83) was born in Tientsin, China, where his father was the American consul. In 1908, his family moved to Vienna where Edwin received his first schooling and also attended his first ballet, which had unusual significance for the young Denby, who later became a leading critic of dance. Edwin was subsequently educated at Hotchkiss Preparatory School and Harvard, from which he took no degree. Instead, he traveled through Europe from 1927 to 1935, studying dance and theater and writing poetry. When he returned to the United States in 1935, he settled in New York and began writing librettos and articles on dance, his chief source of income. Although a quiet and retiring man, or to use the poet's own words, "white-haired, ferrety, feminine," Denby was nevertheless well known among the New York School of Artists, which included the poets Frank O'Hara, Kenneth Koch, and John Ashbery and the painters Larry Rivers and Fairfield Porter. His modesty prevented him from ever considering his poetry with any seriousness, and his work remained largely unknown until after his death by suicide in 1983.

Denby's collections of poetry include *In Public, In Private* (1948), *Mediterranean Cities* (1956), *Snoring in New York* (1974), *Collected Poems* (1975), and *Complete Poems* (1986). He is the author of two novels, *Mrs. W's Sandwich* (1972) and *Scream in a Cave* (1973), numerous works on dance, three librettos, and translations.

Richard Palmer Blackmur (1904–65) was born in Springfield, Massachusetts. After high school, he began his career as a critic by his own authority and published poems and reviews in the *Dial, Poetry,* and the *Saturday Review of Literature*. While in Cambridge, he became an editor of *Hound and Horn,* Harvard student Lincoln Kirstein's extraordinary review. Blackmur made his name by publishing in that journal a series of essays on Cummings, Yeats, Stevens, Crane, and especially T. S. Eliot. After marrying Helen Dickson, he published his first collection of criticism, *The Double Agent* (1936), then his first book of poems, *From Jordan's Delight* (1937). A Guggenheim grant started him on a long study of Henry Adams, collected posthumously. Allen Tate brought Blackmur to Princeton to assist him in the creative writing program. He remained at the university, first at the Institute for Advanced Study and finally as a professor in the department of English. He died in 1965.

Blackmur's books of poems include *From Jordan's Delight* (1937), *The Second World* (1942), *The Good European and Other Poems* (1947), and the posthumous *Poems of R. P. Blackmur* (1977). The books of criticism include *The Double Agent* (1936), *The Expense of Greatness* (1940), *Language as Gesture* and *Form and Value in Modern Poetry* (both 1952), *The Lion and the Honeycomb* (1955), *Eleven Essays in the European Novel* (1964), and the posthumous *Primer of Ignorance* (1967) and *Henry Adams* (1980).

Richard Ghormley Eberhart (1904–) was born in Minnesota. The year after his high school graduation, Eberhart's mother died and his father lost a considerable fortune in two swift business reverses. Richard was educated at Minnesota, Dartmouth, Cambridge, and Harvard. He punctuated this career with work in a department store, in a slaughterhouse, at sea, and as a tutor, once to the children of the King of Siam. He published poetry steadily from his college years onward. At Dartmouth he earned the attention of Robert Frost, and while in Chicago, that of Harriet Monroe. He was a contemporary of C. P. Snow and William Empson at Cambridge, and he worked closely with F. R. Leavis and I. A. Richards. At Harvard, he met George Kittredge, Irving Babbit, Alfred North Whitehead, and T. S. Eliot. His education perhaps displayed too broadly his independent mind, and Eberhart did not receive a university appointment until he was forty-eight. He taught at St. Mark's School, where Robert Lowell was his pupil, and then the Cambridge School. He married Helen Elizabeth Butcher and entered the Navy to train aerial gunners for the duration of the Second World War. While stationed near San Francisco, he became friendly with Kenneth Rexroth and his circle. After his discharge, Eberhart joined the Butcher Polish Company, his wife's family business. For six years, he turned down attractive teaching offers but maintained his literary career and hosted poets who visited Harvard. He left the business for a series of brief academic appointments: He filled in for Roethke at Seattle, taught a semester at the University of Connecticut, and a year each at Wheaton, Coe College, and Princeton. He has taught at Dartmouth since 1961. A gregarious poet, hosting and promoting his fellows and contributing to magazines and public events, Eberhart has won a variety of prizes, and was Consultant in Poetry to the Library of Congress. He has a son and daughter.

Eberhart's books of poems include *A Bravery of Earth* (1930), *Reading the Spirit* (1936), *Song and Idea* (1940), *Poems, New and Selected* (1944), *Burr Oaks* (1947), *Brotherhood of Men* (1949), *An Herb Basket* (1950), *Selected Poems* (1951), *Undercliff: Poems 1946–1953* (1953), *Great Praises* (1957), *Collected Poems 1930–1960* (1960), *The Quarry* (1964), *Selected Poems 1930–1965* (1965), *Thirty One Sonnets* (1967), *Shifts of Being* (1968), *Fields of Grace* (1972), *Poems to Poets* (1976), *Collected Poems* (1976), and *Ways of Light* (1980). Other books include *The Collected Verse Plays* (1962), *Selected Prose* (1978), and *Of Poetry and Poets* (1978).

Louis Zukofsky (1904–78) was born on Manhattan's Lower East Side. His parents were immigrant Russian Jews. Zukofsky was a lifelong New Yorker, attending Columbia and teaching at Polytechnic Institute, Brooklyn. Mark Van Doren remembered Zukofsky as a true poet. Zukofsky was known to dedicated readers by poems in small magazines and privately printed booklets of lyrics and essays but made his career outside the public curriculum of honors and appointments. He married Celia Thaew in 1929. Celia collaborated on the translations of Catullus and composed musical settings for her husband's poems. The couple had one son, Paul.

Zukofsky's principal work was his *"A"* (1979), passages of which appeared earlier as *"A" 1–12* (1959) and *"A" 13–21* (1969). It is a record of both his personal experiences and the historical events of his time, and an anthology of ingenious analogues to his favorite poems and musical compositions. His lyrics are collected in *All the Collected Short Poems, 1923–1958* (1965) and *All the Collected Short Poems 1956–1964* (1966). With Celia, he translated the works of *Catullus* (1969) into English that closely mimics the sound and rhythm of the Latin. Zukofsky edited *Poetry 37* (February 1931), titled *An "Objectivists" Anthology*. His collections of essays include *Le Style Apollinaire* (1934), *A Test of Poetry* (1948), *Bottom: On Shakespeare* (1963), *Prepositions* (1967), and *The Gas Age* (1969). He also wrote *Autobiography* (1970) and the novels *It Was* (1961), revised as *Ferdinand* (1970), and *Little; for Careenagers* (1970).

Stanley Jasspon Kunitz (1905–) was born in Worcester, Massachusetts, to a woman recently widowed by the suicide of her husband, a fellow Jewish immigrant from Russia. Kunitz moved to a YMCA at fifteen, working as a cub reporter for the Worcester *Telegram*. He earned an A.B. summa cum laude and an A.M. at Harvard. The English department refused him a teaching post because he was a Jew. He returned to the *Telegram* to report on the trial of Sacco and Vanzetti, whose cause possessed him. After the execution, he traveled to New York to find a publisher for Vanzetti's letters. He found instead a job with the H. W. Wilson Co., a reference publisher. He founded and edited the house organ, and produced several series of biographical dictionaries of authors. They remain a standard source. He married Helen Pearce, divorced seven years later, and then married Eleanor Evans. Drafted in 1943 as a thirty-eight year old conscientious objector, he underwent basic training three times. His editorial skills led to a post in Washington, D.C., where he refused a commission. He had published widely in magazines, won the Oscar Blumenthal Prize, and published a first book well before the war, but the service interrupted this career. After his discharge, he published a second book and took a Guggenheim Fellowship. Theodore Roethke, suffering a breakdown while teaching at Bennington, insisted upon Kunitz as his replacement. Kunitz began a series of teaching appointments, fellowships, grants, and residencies. Since 1967, he has been affiliated with Columbia. He has been Consultant in Poetry to the Library of Congress and judged the Yale Younger Poets competition for eight years. His continuing publications have brought him a steady stream of other honors and responsibilities. He still edits his reference works and now translates Russian poetry. He divorced his second wife, with whom he has a daughter, in 1958 to marry Elise Asher.

Kunitz's books of poems include *Intellectual Things* (1930), *Passport to the War* (1944), *Selected Poems 1928–1958* (1958), *The Testing-Tree* (1970), *The Poems of Stanley Kunitz, 1928–1978* (1979), and *The Wellfleet Whale and Companion Poems* (1983). His translations, done with collaborators, include *Antiworlds and the Fifth Ace* (1967) by Andrei Voznesensky, *The Poems of Anna Akhmatova* (1973) by Max Hayward, and *Orchard Lamps* (1978) by Ivan Drach.

Theodore Roethke (1908–63) was born in Saginaw, Michigan. His grandfather, chief forester to Bismarck's sister, had immigrated there from Prussia to grow produce with his son Carl and his son Otto, the poet's father. The brothers expanded into the nursery business, turning the family home into a compound of greenhouses. Carl killed himself and Otto died of cancer when Theodore was fifteen. Roethke earned a degree at Michigan, studied at Harvard, and then began a teaching career. Subject to mania, depression, and heavy drinking, Roethke did not hold any post for long. He taught at Lafayette, Michigan State, Pennsylvania State (where he also coached tennis), Bennington, and Breadloaf; all appointments were punctuated by hospital stays. His habits were tolerated at the University of Washington, and he settled in Seattle. Roethke won two Guggenheim and two Ford Fellowships, a Fulbright Lectureship, a summer at Yaddo, the National Book Award, the Bollingen Prize, and another National Book Award after his death. In 1953, he married a woman who had been his student at Bennington, Beatrice O'Connell. He died suddenly of a coronary occlusion while swimming in his pool.

Roethke's books of poems include *Open House* (1941), *The Lost Son* (1948), *Praise to the End!* (1951), *The Waking: Poems 1933–1953* (1953), *Words for the Wind* (1958), and *I Am! Says the Lamb* (1961). *Sequence, Sometimes Metaphysical* (1963), *The Far Field* (1964), and *The Collected Poems of Theodore Roethke* (1966) appeared posthumously. *On The Poet and His Craft* (1965) collects essays and lectures, *Selected Letters* (1972) gives correspondence, and *Straw for the Fire* (1972) draws from the notebooks.

Charles Olson (1910–70) was born in Worcester, Massachusetts. His father, a letter carrier, was from Sweden, and his mother was a local Irish-American. Young Olson's success in high school debates started him on a series of scholarships. He took bachelor's and master's degrees from Wesleyan and studied at Yale as an Olin Fellow. His master's thesis on Melville's growth led immediately to original researches recovering the novelist's library. Olson taught two years at Clark before entering Harvard as one of the first students in American studies. The doctoral thesis he never submitted won him a Guggenheim, and he left Harvard. He never published his study in its scholarly form, revising it into *Call Me Ishmael* (1947), a very personal work that both T. S. Eliot and F. O. Matthiessen, Olson's Melville teacher, refused to publish. He began work as publicity director for the American Civil Liberties Union. Later, he worked for the Foreign Language Information Service of the Common Council for American Unity, and then the Office of War Information, speaking for minorities. He was offered the directorship of the Foreign Nationalities Division of the Democratic National Committee, but abandoned his career suddenly to spend the winter of 1944 in Key West. He published an essay in defense of Ezra Pound, "This Is Yeats Speaking," in *Partisan Review,* and poems in magazines like *Harper's* and *Atlantic Monthly.* After meeting repeatedly with Pound in St. Elizabeth's, he attended the first meetings of what became the United Nations and won a second Guggenheim to study the interaction of racial groups in the settlement of the American West. He never completed the project. Olson plunged into poetry entirely when Josef Albers invited him to give some talks at Black Mountain College. Albers extended the invitation to a year's lectureship, then to a summer theater program. Olson left Black Mountain armed with a theory of poetic practice. He published a manifesto, "Projective Verse," and began promoting his ideas among his acquaintances. He spent six months near the Yucatan. Students invited him back to Black

Mountain College, where his return provoked a struggle among the faculty. Olson emerged as rector of the college. He remained for five years, ultimately executing the dissolution of the college and supervising the liquidation of its assets. He moved to Gloucester, Massachusetts, where he had summered as a child. He often left, but Gloucester was his base for the remainder of his life, the focus of his attention, and the subject of his lifework, *The Maximus Poems*. He attended conferences in the West, taught two years at Buffalo, and spent five months in England researching Gloucester's history. Olson had just started to teach at the University of Connecticut when he entered a hospital, dying of cancer. He never married. Among his students were a number of influential poets and energetic promoters of poetry, including Robert Creeley and Jonathan Williams.

Olson's books of poems include *To Corrado Cagli* (1947), *Y and X* (1950), *Letter for Melville* (1951), *This* (1952), *In Cold Hell, In Thicket* (1953), *O'Ryan 2 4 6 8 10* (1958), *The Distances* (1960), *O'Ryan 1 2 3 4 5 6 7 8 9 10* (1965), and the collection *Archaeologist of Morning* (1970). Olson's epic is found in *The Maximus Poems 1–10* (1953), *The Maximus Poems 11–22* (1956), *The Maximus Poems* (1960), *Maximus from Dogtown I* (1961), and *The Maximus Poems IV, V VI* (1968). His other writings include *Letters for Origin* (1969), the letters he wrote Cid Corman on how to edit his magazine, and *The Mayan Letters* (1953) to Robert Creeley about the lessons of anthropology to the poet. *A Bibliography on America for Ed Dorn* (1964) is another personal exhortation. The more public writings include *Call Me Ishmael: a Study of Melville* (1947), *Projective Verse* (1959), *The Human Universe and Other Essays* (1964), *Reading at Berkeley* (1968), *Causal Mythology* (1969), *The Special View of History* (1970), and *Poetry and Truth: The Beloit Lectures and Poems* (1971). Creeley edited *Selected Writings* (1967).

Elizabeth Bishop (1911–79) was born in Worcester, Massachusetts. Her father died eight months after her birth, and her mother was hospitalized for mental disorders several times in Bishop's very early life, and then from 1916 until her death in 1934. She grew up in the homes of various relatives: with her mother's parents in Nova Scotia, with her father's parents in Worcester, and finally with her Aunt Maud in Boston. In 1934, during her senior year at Vassar, Bishop met Marianne Moore, and the two poets became very close friends. Bishop's first poems were published in 1935 in an anthology entitled *Trial Balances*. In 1947, she received a Guggenheim Fellowship. Other awards followed, from Bryn Mawr and the American Academy of Arts and Letters, and Bishop decided in 1951 to use some of her prize money to travel in South America and through the Strait of Magellan. She came to a halt in Brazil because of illness but, after she recovered, decided to stay there. For the next twenty-three years she lived with her friend Lota Constenat de Macedo Soares in Rio de Janeiro and Ouro Prêto, Brazil. Bishop won the 1956 Pulitzer Prize, a *Partisan Review* Fellowship, an Amy Lowell Traveling Fellowship, and a National Book Award. In the fall of 1970, she began a yearly one-semester appointment at Harvard, and when Lota died, Bishop moved to Boston. In 1976, she received the Neustadt International Prize for Literature, and three years later she died.

Bishop published three collections of verse during her lifetime: *North & South* (1946), *Questions of Travel* (1965), and *Geography III* (1976). *The Complete Poems* and *The Complete Prose* followed posthumously.

J. V. Cunningham (1911–85) was born in Cumberland, Maryland. He was educated at St. Mary's College and Stanford, from which he took his Ph.D. in 1945. In 1937, he married the poet Barbara Gibbs, whom he later divorced. He also married Dolora Gallagher and Jessie Campbell. Cunningham maintained appointments at the University of Hawaii and the University of Chicago, among others. He was Professor of English at Brandeis University. Cunningham was twice a Guggenheim Fellow and recipient of a National Institute of Arts and Letters grant. He died in 1985.

Cunningham's collections of verse include *The Helmsman* (1942), *The Judge Is Fury* (1947), and *The Exclusions of a Rhyme* (1960), among others. His critical works include *Woe or Wonder*:

The Emotional Effect of Shakespearean Tragedy (1951) and *Tradition and Poetic Structure* (1960). His *Collected Poems* and *Collected Essays* appeared in 1971 and 1974, respectively.

William Oliver Everson (Brother Antoninus) (1912–) was born in Sacramento, California, to Louis Waldemar Everson, a musician, and Francelia Marie Herber, and spent his child-hood in the small town of Selma, California. Although raised a Christian Scientist, Everson became an agnostic as an adolescent. He was educated at Fresno State College, where he was introduced to the work of Robinson Jeffers, whose work had a profoundly religious effect on him. He dropped out of college to "go back to the land," become a poet, and get married. Everson was a conscientious objector during World War II and spent three-and-one-half years in work camps in Oregon. While there, he co-founded the Untide Press, one of the few experimental presses of the war period. Everson moved from Oregon to San Francisco and fell in with the group of anarchists and poets that formed around Kenneth Rexroth. He was married, for the second time, to Mary Fabilli, through whom he was introduced to Christianity. He entered the Roman Catholic Church in 1949. After a year on a Guggenheim Fellowship, Everson joined the Catholic worker movement in the slums of Oakland, during which time he decided to become a monk. Everson joined the Dominicans in 1951 as Brother Antoninus. He dropped out of the literary scene for seven years, returning in the late fifties and allying himself with the Beats of the San Francisco Renaissance. In 1969, Everson left the Dominicans, married Susanna Rickson, and moved with her and her son to Stinson Beach in northern San Francisco. In 1971, he became poet in residence at Kresge College, University of California at Santa Cruz.

Everson's books of poetry include *War Elegies* (1944), *Triptych for the Living* (1951), *The Year's Declension* (1961), and *Man-Fate: The Swan Song of Brother Antoninus* (1974). His poetry written as Brother Antoninus includes *A Fragment for the Birth of God* (1958), *The Rose of Solitude* (1964), *A Canticle to the Waterbirds* (1968), *Who Is She That Looketh Forth as the Morning* (1972), and one recording, *The Savagery of Love* (1968). He has also edited a number of books by Robinson Jeffers.

Robert Hayden (1913–80) was born in Detroit. The family lived in the East Side ghetto called Paradise Valley, near the street St. Antoine, an artery of the high black culture of the time. He won a scholarship to Detroit City College, now Wayne State University. As an under-graduate he played the role of the voodoo priest in *Drums of Haiti* before the playwright, Langston Hughes. After college Hayden researched local black history for the Federal Writ-er's Project. He reviewed drama and music for the *Michigan Chronicle*. After he married Erma Inez Morris, they lived briefly in New York while she studied piano at Julliard. He did graduate work at the Universiy of Michigan under W. H. Auden where he won the university's Hopwood Award. He stayed on at Ann Arbor for two years as a teaching fellow. While there, the Haydens became Baha'i, maintaining this creed all of their lives. Hayden also served as poetry editor to the Baha'i journal, *World Order*. He taught twenty years at Fisk University in segregated Nashville and then returned to the University of Michigan. At Fisk he founded the Counterpoise publishing series for nonpolemic black poets and served as consultant to Scott, Foresman publishers. His own books were brought out by a small press in London. Though anthologized by Langston Hughes and Arno Bontemps, Hayden came to national attention only with the publication of his *Selected Poems* (1966). He won a Rosenwald Fellowship and a Ford Foundation grant. Hayden was visiting poet and professor at the Universities of Louisville, Washington, and Connecticut, and Denison College, and a staff member at Breadloaf. In 1976, he became Consultant in Poetry to the Library of Congress. He won the grand prize in poetry at the First World Festival of the Negro Arts in Dakar. Brown, Grand Valley State, Wayne State, and Benedict awarded him honorary degrees. He was a Fellow of the Academy of American Poets and member of the American Academy and Institute of Arts and Letters. Hayden died in Ann Arbor in 1980.

Hayden's publications include *Heart-Shape in the Dust* (1940), *Figure of Time* (1955), *A Ballad of Remembrance* (1962), *Words in the Mourning Time* (1970), and *American Journal* (1978).

David Schubert (1913–46) was born in New York City, of Russian parentage. Extreme poverty made it necessary for Schubert's father to work at a variety of jobs, often away from the family. In 1928, Schubert's mother died, leaving the children to be raised by a number of different relatives. After attending Boy's High School in Brooklyn, Schubert entered Amherst, from which he was twice expelled for absenteeism. It was at Amherst, however, that Schubert began writing poems seriously. There he met Robert Frost, who recognized his talent and took an interest in him, often lending him money. Indigence was to be a lifelong problem for Schubert. In 1934, he moved to New York City and worked at odd jobs. He met Judith Kranes, and the two were married the following year. In 1935, Schubert enrolled at CCNY and attended classes. Despite financial worries, this was a period of great productivity for Schubert, and his poems appeared in *Poetry, the Nation, Partisan Review,* and *Yale Review.* In 1939, he spent time at Yaddo. Whether due to the stress of constant economic hardship or the coming to the fore of more deeply seated problems, by 1940 Schubert began to have psychological problems. He entered psychoanalysis, but his mental condition declined rapidly. He became manic-depressive and withdrawn and had to be hospitalized full time by 1943. His situation worsened until the spring of 1946, when he died of tuberculosis.

Schubert published two volumes of poetry, *The Simple Scale* (1941) and *Initial A* (1961). His collected works appeared in the *Quarterly Review of Literature's* fortieth anniversary issue (1983).

Delmore David Schwartz (1913–66) was born in Brooklyn to Harry and Rose Nathan Schwartz. The poet graduated from high school in Manhattan, where his family relocated. After a year at the University of Wisconsin, he returned and took a bachelor's degree from New York University in 1935. He continued his study of philosophy at Harvard, leaving with high grades but no advanced degree. Once back in New York, Schwartz began publishing poetry, fiction, and reviews in magazines. The following year he married a high school friend, Gertrude Buckman. He wintered at Yaddo, spent a summer on a Guggenheim Fellowship, and in the fall of 1940 began a seven-year appointment at Harvard, teaching composition and advanced writing. In 1943, he became an editor of *Partisan Review*, an association he maintained for twelve years. Schwartz divorced his first wife and married Elizabeth Pollet. The two moved to New York and then to rural New Jersey. He became Visiting Lecturer at Princeton, Kenyon, Indiana, and Chicago, as well as Consultant to the Ford Foundation and to New Directions publishers. Schwartz received the 1959 Bollingen Prize and the 1960 Shelley Memorial Prize. He died of a heart attack in 1966, estranged from family and friends by personal problems and mental illness.

Schwartz's books include *In Dreams Begin Responsibilities* (1938), a translation of Rimbaud's *A Season in Hell* (1939), *Shenandoah* (1941), *Genesis* (1943), *Vaudeville for a Princess* (1950), and *Summer Knowledge* (1959), among others. Schwartz is also said to be the model for Saul Bellow's Von Humboldt Fleisher in *Humboldt's Gift.*

John Allyn McAlpin Berryman (1914–72) was born John Allyn Smith in McAlester, Oklahoma. His father was a banker and his mother a schoolteacher. John was the first of two sons. When he was ten, the four moved to Tampa, Florida. Two years later, his father killed himself. The boy's mother married a Wall Street banker, John Angus McAlpin Berryman and young John was educated at South Kent School, Columbia, and Clare College, Cambridge. At Columbia Berryman was a cherished student of the poet Mark Van Doren. Berryman remained in the academy, winning many fellowships and teaching as a visiting professor at several universities. He taught writing and lectured in the humanities. His longest associations were with Princeton and the University of Minnesota, where he was

Regent's Professor. He committed suicide by leaping from a bridge high over the Mississippi onto the frozen riverbank. He left three wives, two daughters, and a son.

Berryman was an active literary critic but published only one book-length study, *Stephen Crane*, a critical biography. He edited Thomas Nashe's *Unfortunate Traveller*, wrote an introduction to Matthew Gregory Lewis's *The Monk*, and collaborated with Allen Tate and Ralph Ross on *The Arts of Reading*. His books of poetry include *Poems* (1942), *The Dispossessed* (1948), *Homage to Mistress Bradstreet* (1956), *His Thought Made Pockets and the Plane Buckt* (1958), *77 Dream Songs* (1964), *His Toy, His Dream, His Rest* (1968), *Berryman's Sonnets* (1967), *Short Poems* (1967), *The Dream Songs* (1969), and *Love and Fame* (1970). Berryman left a great deal of manuscript. *Delusions, Etc.* (1972) and *Henry's Fate* (1977) gather late poems and unpublished "Dream Songs." *The Freedom of the Poet* (1976) collects stories and essays, and *Recovery* (1973) is an imcomplete novel based on the poet's own experience as an alcholic.

Randall Jackson Jarrell (1914–65) was born in Nashville, Tennessee. As a child he posed for the bas-relief of Ganymede on his hometown's replica of the Parthenon. When his parents separated, Jarrell was cared for by his grandparents in Hollywood, California. He returned to Nashville for high school and stayed to attend Vanderbilt. There he was a prized student of John Crowe Ransom and Donald Davison. While writing his master's thesis on A. E. Housman, Jarrell became an instructor at Kenyon College, rooming for a while with Robert Lowell. Jarrell next taught at Austin, and he married a colleague, Mackie Langham. He spent the war years in the army as an instructor in celestial navigation. Thereafter, he held brief appointments at colleges all over the country. He was literary editor of the *Nation*, won two Guggenheim Fellowships, was Consultant in Poetry at the Library of Congress, and judged the Bollingen Award and the National Book Award. He divorced and married Mary Eloise von Schrader. Jarrell had been full professor at the Women's College of the University of North Carolina, Greensboro, for seven years when he was hospitalized for four months with a breakdown. On a trip back home, he was struck and killed by a car while walking.

Jarrell's books of poems include *Blood for a Stranger* (1942), *Little Friend, Little Friend* (1945), *Losses* (1948), *The Seven-League Crutches* (1951), *Selected Poems* (1955), *The Woman at the Washington Zoo* (1960), *The Lost World* (1965), the posthumous *Complete Poems* (1969), and the incomplete drafts of *Jerome* (1970). His collected criticism includes *Poetry and the Age* (1953), *A Sad Heart at the Supermarket* (1962), *The Third Book of Criticism* (1969), and *Kipling, Auden, & Co.* (1980). Jarrell worked hard to promote deserving literature, translating *Part One of Goethe's Faust* (1973) and Chekov's *The Three Sisters* for a 1964 production, and editing *The Best Short Stories of Rudyard Kipling* (1961), two other Kipling collections, and *Six Russian Short Novels* (1963). His children's books, *The Bat-Poet* (1964), *The Gingerbread Rabbit* (1964), and *The Animal Family* (1965), also sprang from his deep concerns. Jarrell published one novel, *Pictures from an Institution* (1954), set among the faculty of a women's college.

Weldon Kees (1914–55) was born in Beatrice, Nebraska, to John and Sarah Green Kees. After high school, he attended Doane College, the University of Missouri, and the University of Nebraska. His stories had already begun appearing in magazines, especially his teacher Lowry Charles Wemberly's *Prairie Schooner*. After graduation, Kees found work with the Federal Writer's Project in Lincoln. He married Ann Swan and moved with her to Denver. Kees worked in the public library there, taking another bachelor's degree in library science. He swiftly succeeded in anything he turned his hand to. He became director of the Bibliographical Center of Research, Rocky Mountain Region. When he turned to poetry, his work appeared in *Partisan Review* and *Kenyon Review*. In 1943, he moved to New York. He wrote briefly for *Time's* book review section and for four years wrote scripts for Paramount newsreels. He had now published two books of poems and won *Poetry's* Oscar Blumenthal Award. Kees reviewed books for the New York newspapers and consulted to publishers, replacing Clement Greenberg as the *Nation's* art critic. While still writing poetry, he had turned to abstract expressionist painting as well, mounting several one-man shows. He left New York for San Francisco in 1951. There he made films for the University of California, illustrating various psychiatric concepts, and collaborated with a psychiatrist on a book about nonverbal communication. Kees was also a jazz pianist and lectured on jazz. His marriage ended in divorce. Kees has not been seen since 1955. He had talked both of suicide and of starting a new life in Mexico. His empty car was found near the Golden Gate Bridge.

Kees's books of poems include *The Last Man* (1943), *The Fall of the Magicians* (1947), *Poems 1947–1954* (1954), and the posthumous *The Collected Poems of Weldon Kees* (1960, rev. ed. 1972). His stories were collected posthumously in *The Ceremony and Other Stories* (1983). He authored *Nonverbal Communication: Notes on the Visual Perception of Human Nature* (1955) with Jurgen Ruesch. He made the film *Three Families* (1952) with Gregory Bateson, illustrating the anthropologist's double-blind theory of the genesis of schizophrenia. Kees's own film is *Hotel Apex* (1952), and he scored James Broughton's *Adventures of Jimmy*.

Robert Traill Spence Lowell, Jr. (1917–77) was born in Boston to R. T. S. and Charlotte Winslow Lowell. Richard Eberhardt taught him in his senior year at St. Mark's. Lowell started college at Harvard but transferred to Kenyon College, where he studied with John Crowe Ransom. He spent the summer between schools in a tent on Allen Tate's and Caroline Gordon's lawn, writing poetry. At college, he became friends with Randall Jarrell and the short story writer Peter Taylor. In 1940, Lowell graduated summa cum laude in classics, converted to Catholicism, and married the novelist Jean Stafford. He stayed on at Kenyon a year to teach English while he studied at Louisiana State University with Cleanth Brooks and Robert Penn Warren. He went to work in New York for the Catholic publishing firm Sheed & Ward, but left with his wife to spend a year with the Tates in a mountain cottage. When war broke out, he tried to enlist in the navy, then to went to jail as a conscientious objector. He served five months of a year-and-a-day sentence to protest Allied aerial bombing of civilians. In 1944, his first book, *Land of Unlikeness*, appeared in a small edition. His second book, *Lord Weary's Castle* (1946), won the Pulitzer Prize. The next year he was Consultant in Poetry to the Library of Congress, and the following year he was a Guggenheim Fellow. While in Washington, he made the acquaintance of Ezra Pound. Lowell later served on the committee that awarded the poet the first Bollingen Prize. He divorced Jean Stafford and traveled in Italy with his new wife, Elizabeth Hardwick. The two raised one daughter. In 1949, Lowell suffered the first of the manic breakdowns that were to punctuate the rest of his life. He taught at Iowa (where his students included W. D. Snodgrass), Indiana, and the University of Cincinnati. On the death of his mother in 1954, he brought his family to Boston. He taught five years at Boston University, where his students included Anne Sexton, Sylvia Plath, and George Starbuck. *Life Studies* (1959) won the National Book Award, and *Imitations* (1961) won the Bollingen Prize. He moved to New York and began a series of theatrical projects: among them, a translation of Racine's *Phedre*, an operatic Kaddish with Leonard Bernstein, an Oresteia for the Lincoln Center. Only two, *The Old Glory* (1965), a collection of shorts mounted in New York, and *Prometheus Bound* (1969), done at the Yale Drama School (where he was writer in residence), were produced. He took a lifetime appointment at Harvard. He continued to publish books of poems. He publicly refused an invitation to the Johnson White House in order to protest the war in Viet Nam, marched with thousands on the Pentagon, and campaigned for the candidate Eugene McCarthy. He taught for a year in England. In 1972, he divorced to marry the British novelist Caroline Blackwood, by whom he already had an infant son. He died in New York in 1977. His funeral was in Boston, and Lowell was buried in the family's New Hampshire plot.

Lowell's books of poems include *Land of Unlikeness* (1944), *Lord Weary's Castle* (1946), *Poems: 1938–1949* (1950), *The Mills of the Kavanaughs* (1951), *Life Studies* (1959), *Imitations* (1961), *For the Union Dead* (1964), *The Old Glory: Selected Poems* (1965), *Near the Ocean* (1967), *Notebook 1967–68* (1969, rev. ed. 1970), *The Voyage* (1969), *History* (1973), *The Dolphin* (1973), *For Lizzie and Harriet* (1973), *Selected Poems* (1976), and *Day by Day* (1977).

Francis Russell O'Hara (1926–66) was born in Baltimore to Russell and Katherine Broderick O'Hara. Within a year, the family moved to Grafton, Massachusetts. Russell O'Hara managed three farms and a farm equipment dealership. The poet attended a parochial high school in a nearby town and studied piano at the New England Conservatory. He served at sea in the wartime navy as a sonarman on the destroyer Nicholas. Another of his military duties included the shore patrol in San Francisco, where his beat was the bars and nightclubs. At Harvard, he studied music and English literature, and at Michigan, he took a master's degree in comparative literature. While there, he won the frequently prescient Hopwood Award for poetry. O'Hara moved to New York, where he started work at the Museum of Modern Art's information desk. He became an art reviewer and was important to the critical reception of the Action Painters and the New York School. He left MOMA to write for *Art News* but returned to assist in preparing traveling shows. He made a career at the museum, becoming Assistant, then Associate Curator. All this time, he published poetry frequently, usually in small magazines and exotic editions. A large selection of his verse in Donald Hall's *New American Poetry* brought many readers to his commerical press books. O'Hara's association with John Ashbery, starting at Harvard with a shared interest in contemporary continental composers and extending into poetry and painters and a New York lifestyle, is just one example of his wide circle of intense friendships in the arts. The poet was also a playwright, once a Ford Foundation Fellow at Cambridge's Poet's Theater, with plays produced by the avant-garde Living Theatre and the Writer's Stage Theatre. As curator, he wrote many catalogs. He died on a summer morning in 1966, hit the night before by a dune buggy on the beach at Fire Island.

Books of poems published during the poet's lifetime include *A City Winter and Other Poems* (1952), *Meditations in an Emergency* (1957), *Lunch Poems* (1964), and *Love Poems (Tentative Title)* (1965). Collaborations with artists include *Stones* (1958) with Larry Rivers, and *Odes* (1960) with Mike Goldberg. He wrote the study *Jackson Pollock* (1959), and his catalogs include *The New Spanish Painting and Sculpture* (1960), *Robert Motherwell* (1965), *David Smith*, and *Nakian* (both 1966). The posthumous *The Collected Poems of Frank O'Hara* (1971), *Early Writing*, and *Poems Retrieved* (both 1977), along with *Selected Plays* (1978) make available the work O'Hara left unpublished.

Anne Sexton (1928–74) was born in Newton, Massachusetts to Mayflower ancestry. She interrupted her finishing at the Garland School to elope to North Carolina with Kayo (Alfred Muller Sexton). The couple moved to Cochituate, Massachusetts, where Sexton won a scholarship to a modeling course. When Kayo entered the navy, Sexton followed him to Baltimore and back, then to San Francisco, modeling for the Hart Agency and working in a bookstore during the interlude in Boston. In 1953, the Sextons bought a home near Newton, just after the birth of Anne's first daughter. Within the year, came the first hospitalization for emotional disturbance, closely followed by the death of Anne's confidante, her great-aunt. Released from the hospital, Sexton had another daughter, only to return to the mental hospital within six months. Her children were sent to relatives and Sexton attempted suicide. She had been under the care of Dr. Martha Brunner-Orne, who was succeeded by her son Martin. Armed with the results of diagnostic tests, he convinced Anne to enroll in John Holmes's poetry workshop at the Boston Center for Adult Education. Sexton's classwork was soon published in *The New Yorker*, *Harper's Magazine*, and *The Saturday Review*. Sexton and Maxine Kumin met in the class. Together with George Starbuck they continued to work with Holmes until that poet's death. The two women collaborated on each other's poetry daily by phone for the rest of Sexton's life. They wrote five children's books together. The two were appointed independent scholars of poetry at Radcliffe, teaching there and at Harvard. Sexton had previously studied with W. D. Snodgrass and Robert Lowell. She conducted workshops under many auspices, and eventually held a full professorship at Boston University and a chair in literature at Colgate. She won prizes, grants, fellowships, and degrees; judged, consulted, sat on boards; and traveled as an honorary representative.

She started a rock group and toured with it, and she wrote a play and saw it produced at a prestigous off-Broadway house. Under psychiatric care all of her adult life, she was hospitalized two more times. She attempted to commit suicide twice more, succeeding at the third attempt.

Sexton's books of poems include *To Bedlam and Part Way Back* (1960), *All My Pretty Ones* (1962), *Selected Poems* (1964), *Live or Die* (1966), *Poems* (1968), *Love Poems* (1969), *Transformations* (1972), *The Book of Folly* (1974), *The Death Notebooks* (1974), and *The Awful Rowing toward God* (1975). The posthumous collections include *45 Mercy Street* (1976), *Words for Cr. Y.* (1978), and *The Complete Poems* (1981).

Sylvia Plath (1932–63) was born in Boston. Her father died when she was eight years old. In August 1950, just before she entered Smith College, her short story "And Summer Will Not Come Again" appeared in *Seventeen* magazine. A poem, "Bitter Strawberries," was also published in the *Christian Science Monitor*. These small successes were followed by more short stories and reviews in *Seventeen* and a prizewinning story published in *Mademoiselle*. At the end of her sophomore year, Plath won a guest editorship on the staff of *Mademoiselle* and for the month of June 1952, lived in New York in what seemed a fashionable whirl of celebrities. The month culminated in the publication of an article, an editorial piece, and a poem. Later that summer, after her return home, Plath attempted to commit suicide. She was rescued, however, and after several months of hospitalization and treatment, she returned to Smith and completed her degree with honors. Funded by a Fulbright Fellowship, she began a program of studies at Cambridge, and she continued to publish poems. She also met and married the British poet Ted Hughes in 1956. A year later the couple moved to the United States, Plath to teach at Smith, and Hughes at the University of Massachusetts. After a year of teaching, the two poets moved to Boston to try to live on the earnings from their writings. In December 1959, Ted Hughes and Sylvia Plath returned to England; the following April their daughter, Frieda, was born. In 1961, Plath received a Saxton Fellowship, and in 1962, a son, Nicholas, was born. That same year, Sylvia Plath finished a radio play entitled *Three Women: A Monologue for Three Voices* and discovered that her husband was having an affair. The dissolution of their marriage was explosive and catapulted Plath into a deep depression. She and the children moved to London and lived in a tiny apartment during the winter of 1962–1963. On the morning of February 11, 1963, Sylvia Plath committed suicide by inhaling gas from her oven.

Although almost all of her work appeared posthumously, Plath saw the publication of a volume of poetry *The Colossus* (1961) and a novel *The Bell Jar* (1963) under the pseudonym Victoria Lucas. *Ariel* appeared in 1963, and *The Collected Poems*, edited by Ted Hughes, won the Pulitzer Prize in 1981.

Contributors

HAROLD BLOOM, Sterling Professor of the Humanities at Yale University, is the author of *The Anxiety of Influence*, *Poetry and Repression*, and many other volumes of literary criticism. His forthcoming study, *Freud: Transference and Authority*, attempts a full-scale reading of all of Freud's major writings. A MacArthur Prize Fellow, he is general editor of five series of literary criticism published by Chelsea House. During 1987–88, he was appointed Charles Eliot Norton Professor of Poetry at Harvard University.

SANDRA COOKSON writes on American poetry.

ROBERT M. FARNSWORTH teaches English at the University of Missouri. His own book of poems is *Three or Four Hills & a Cloud*. He has edited a collection of Melvin B. Tolson's newspaper columns, *Caviar and Cabbage*, and collected, with David Ray, *Richard Wright: Impressions and Perspectives*.

ROBERT HASS teaches English at St. Mary's College in California. Author of *Twentieth Century Pleasures: Essays on Poetry*, his own books of poems are *Field Guide* and *Praise*. He has translated Czeslaw Milosz's *The Rising of the Sun*, and, with Robert Pinsky, Milosz's *The Separate Notebooks*.

LINCOLN KIRSTEIN is author of the unique and enduring *Rhymes of a PFC* and of the historical romance *Flesh Is Heir*. His many books on the dance include *The Classic Ballet* and *Thirty Years: The New York City Ballet*.

RUSSELL FRASER is author of *A Mingled Yarn: The Life of R. P. Blackmur* as well as *The Three Romes*, *The War against Poetry*, *The Dark Ages and the Age of Gold*, and *The Language of Adam: On the Limits and Systems of Discourse*.

RICHARD K. CROSS, Professor of English at the University of North Carolina, Chapel Hill, is editor of the *Oxford Book of Light Verse* and author of *Malcolm Lowry: A Preface to His Fiction*.

371

WILLIAM HARMON teaches English at the University of North Carolina at Chapel Hill. He is author of criticism, *Time in Ezra Pound's Work,* and of poetry, including *Legion: Civic Choruses* and *Treasury Holiday.*

ROBERT WEISBERG writes on American poetry.

CHARLES MOLESWORTH teaches at Queens College. His books include *Common Elegies, The Fierce Embrace: A Study of Contemporary Poetry, Words to That Effect,* and *Gary Snyder's Vision: Poetry and the Real Work.*

JAMES APPLEWHITE is Director of the Institute of the Arts at Duke University, where he teaches in the Department of English. He is author of several volumes of poetry and has received writing fellowships from the National Endowment for the Arts and the Guggenheim Foundation.

SHERMAN PAUL is Professor of English at the University of Iowa. His books include *The Shores of America: Thoreau's Inward Exploration,* as well as studies of Emerson, Charles Olson, Hart Crane, and Edmund Wilson.

CALVIN BEDIENT, Professor of English at UCLA, is author of *In the Heart's Last Kingdom: Robert Penn Warren's Major Poetry.*

BONNIE COSTELLO teaches English at Boston University and is author of *Marianne Moore, Imaginary Possessions.*

DAVID BROMWICH, Associate Professor of English at Princeton University, is the author of *Hazlitt: The Mind of the Critic* and of many essays on contemporary poetry.

JACK HILL writes on American poetry.

PAUL A. LACEY writes on American poetry.

WILBURN WILLIAMS, JR., took a doctorate at Yale in American Studies with his thesis *The Desolate Servitude of Language: A Reading of the Poetry of Melvin B. Tolson.*

IRVIN EHRENPREIS was Professor of English at the University of Virginia. His criticism includes *Acts of Implication: Suggestion and Covert Meaning in the Works of Dryden, Swift, Pope, and Austen* and *Literary Meaning and Augustan Values.*

R. K. MEINERS teaches English at Michigan State University. He is author of *Everything to Be Endured: An Essay on Robert Lowell and Modern Poetry* and *Poems: Journeying Back to the World.*

EDWARD MENDELSON is Professor of English at Columbia University. He is the author of several studies on W. H. Auden and is the literary executor of the Auden estate.

DIANE ACKERMAN is Assistant Professor of English at the University of

Pittsburgh and a poet. Her books include *Planets, Wife of Light*, and *On Extended Wings*.

MARY KINZIE teaches English at Northwestern University. She is editor, with Elliott Anderson, of *The Little Magazine in American: A Modern Documentary History* and author of *The Threshold of the Year: Poems*.

CHARLES BAXTER teaches English at Wayne State University. He is author of *The South Dakota Guidebook* and the collection *Harmony of the World Stories*. His poetry includes *Chameleon* and *Through the Safety Net*.

ANTHONY HECHT teaches in the Department of Rhetoric and Poetry at the University of Rochester, and is author of the recent *Obbligati: Essays in Criticism*. His many distinguished books of poems include *Venetian Vespers* and *Millions of Strange Shadows*, and, with John Hollander, *Jiggery-Pokery: A Compendium of Double Dactyls*.

ALFRED CORN, poet and literary critic, has taught poetry at Columbia, Yale, and other universities. He is the author of four books of poetry: *All Roads at Once, A Call in the Midst of the Crowd, The Various Light*, and *Notes from a Child of Paradise*.

THOMAS MEYER writes on American poetry.

RICHARD HOWARD is widely acclaimed as poet, critic, and translator. His best-known books are *Untitled Subjects*, a collection of his own poetry, and *Alone with America*, which gathers his essays on contemporary American poetry.

Bibliography

GENERAL

Bloom, Harold. *Figures of Capable Imagination.* New York: Seabury, 1976.

Breslin, James E. B. *From Modern to Contemporary: American Poetry, 1945–1965.* Chicago: University of Chicago Press, 1984.

Butterfield, R. W. (Herbie). *Modern American Poetry.* Totowa, N.J.: Barnes & Noble, 1984.

Castro, Michael. *Interpreting the Indian: Twentieth Century Poets and the Native American.* Albuquerque: University of New Mexico Press, 1983.

Davie, Donald. *Trying to Explain.* Ann Arbor: University of Michigan Press, 1979.

Gilbert, Sandra, and Susan Gubar. *Shakespeare's Sisters: Feminist Essays on Women Poets.* Bloomington: Indiana University Press, 1979.

Hass, Robert. *Twentieth Century Pleasures.* New York: Ecco, 1984.

Hallberg, Robert Von. *American Poetry and Culture 1945–1980.* Cambridge: Harvard University Press, 1985.

Hecht, Anthony. *Obbligati: Essays in Criticism.* New York: Atheneum, 1986.

Kostelanetz, Richard, ed. *The Avant-Garde Tradition in American Literature.* Buffalo, N.Y.: Prometheus, 1982.

Kuzma, Greg, ed. *A Book of Rereadings in Recent American Poetry.* Lincoln, Neb.: Pebble & Best Cellar, 1979.

McClure, Michael. *Scratching the Beat Surface.* San Francisco: North Point, 1982.

Mariani, Paul. *A Usable Past: Essays on Modern and Contemporary Poetry.* Amherst: University of Massachusetts Press, 1984.

Molesworth, Charles. *The Fierce Embrace: A Study of Contemporary American Poetry.* Columbia: University of Missouri Press, 1979.

Smith, Dave. *Local Assays on Contemporary American Poetry.* Chicago: University of Illinois Press, 1985.

375

Vendler, Helen. *Part of Nature, Part of Us.* Cambridge: Harvard University Press, 1980.

LOUISE BOGAN

Bowles, Gloria. "Louise Bogan: To Be (Or Not to Be?) Woman Poet." *Women's Studies* 5 (1976): 131–35.

Collins, Martha. *Critical Essays on Louise Bogan.* Boston: G. K. Hall, 1984.

Kinzie, Mary. "Two Lives." *American Poetry Review* 10, no. 2 (1981): 20–21.

Moore, Patrick. "Symbol, Mask, and Meter in the Poetry of Louise Bogan." *Women and Literature* 1 (1980): 67–80.

Morris, Harry. "Poets and Critics, Critics and Poets." *Sewanee Review* 80 (1969): 627–32.

Perlmutter, Elizabeth P. "A Doll's Heart: The Girl in the Poetry of Edna St. Vincent Millay and Louise Bogan." *Twentieth Century Literature* 23 (1977): 157–79.

Peterson, Douglas L. "The Poetry of Louise Bogan." *Southern Review* 19, no. 1 (1983): 73–87.

Ramsey, Paul. "Louise Bogan." *Iowa Review* 1, no. 3 (1970): 116–24.

Ridgeway, Jaqueline. "The Necessity of Form to the Poetry of Louise Bogan." *Women's Studies Quarterly* 5 (1976): 137–49.

Ridgeway, Jaqueline. *Louise Bogan.* Boston: Twayne, 1984.

Smith, William Jay. *Louise Bogan: A Woman's Words.* Washington, D.C.: Library of Congress, 1971.

Swafford, Russell Anne, and Paul Ramsey. "The Influence of Sara Teasdale on Louise Bogan." *CEA Critic:* An Official Journal of the College English Association 41, no. 4 (1979): 7–12.

MELVIN B.TOLSON

Basler, Roy P. "The Heart of Blackness: M. B. Tolson's Poetry." *New Letters* 39, no. 3 (1973): 63–76.

Cansler, Ronald L. "The White and Non-White Dichotomy of Melvin B. Tolson's Poetry." *Negro American Literature Forum* 7 (1973): 115–18.

Flasch, Joy. *Melvin B. Tolson.* New York: Twayne, 1972.

Hansell, William H. "Three Artists in Melvin B. Tolson's *Harlem Gallery.*" *Black American Literature Forum* 18, no. 3 (1984): 122–27.

Russell, Mariann. "Ghetto Laughter: A Note on Tolson's Style." *Obsidian* 5, nos. 1–2 (1979): 7–16.

Schroeder, Patricia R. "Point and Counterpoint in *Harlem Gallery.*" *CLA Journal* 27 (1983): 152–68.

Tolson, M. B. "The Foreground of Negro Poetry." *Kansas Quarterly* 7, no. 3 (1975): 30–35.

———. "Quotes or Unquotes on Poetry." *Kansas Quarterly* 7, no. 3 (1975): 36–38.

Walcott, Ronald. "Some Notes on the Blues, Style and Space: Ellison, Gordone, and Tolson." *Black World* 22, no. 2 (1972): 4–29.

YVOR WINTERS

Davie, Donald. "Introduction." In *The Collected Poems of Yvor Winters*. Chicago: Swallow, 1978: 1–8.
————. "Winters and Leavis: Memories and Reflections." *Southern Review* 87 (1979): 608–18.
Davis, Dick. *Wisdom and Wilderness: The Achievement of Yvor Winters*. Athens: University of Georgia Press, 1983.
Issacs, Elizabeth. *An Introduction to the Poetry of Yvor Winters*. Athens: Ohio University Press, 1981.
Levin, David. "Yvor Winters at Stanford." *Virginia Quarterly Review* 54 (1978): 454–73.
Parkinson, Thomas. "The Untranslatable Poetry of Yvor Winters." *Georgia Review* 34 (1980): 671–77.
Peterson, Douglas L. "Yvor Winters' 'By the Road to the Airbase.' " *Southern Review* 15 (1979): 567–74.
Powell, Grosvenor E. "Yvor Winters' Greek Allegories." *Southern Review* 14 (1978): 262–80.
————. *Language as Being in the Poetry of Yvor Winters*. Baton Rouge: Louisiana State University, 1980.
————. "Solipsism and the Absolute in Yvor Winters' Poetry." *Compass* 1 (1977): 44–59.
Stanford, Donald E. *Revolution and Convention in the Poetry of Ezra Pound, T. S. Eliot, Wallace Stevens, Edward Arlington Robinson and Yvor Winters*. Newark: University of Delaware Press, 1983: 191–244.
University of Denver Quarterly 10, no. 3 (1975). "Yvor Winters special issue."

EDWIN DENBY

Dickerson, George. "Essences and Sentiments." *New York Times Book Review*, 2 November 1986, 28.
O'Hara, Frank. "The Poetry of Edwin Denby." In *Collected Poems* by Edwin Denby. New York: Full Court, 1975: 175–78.

R. P. BLACKMUR

Boyers, Robert. *Richard Palmer Blackmur, Poet-Critic: Toward a View of Poetic Objects*. Columbia: University of Missouri Press, 1980.
Pannick, Gerald J. *Richard Palmer Blackmur*. Boston: Twayne, 1981.
Wellek, Rene. "R. P. Blackmur Re-Examined." *Southern Review* 7 (1971): 825–45.

RICHARD EBERHART

Engel, Bernard. *Richard Eberhart*. New York: Twayne, 1971.

Fein, Richard J. "The Cultivation of Paradox: The War Poetry of Richard Eberhart." *Ball State University Forum* 10, no. 2 (1969): 56–64.

Gordon, Lois. "Richard Eberhart: Romantic Poet and Love Child." In *The Fifties : Fiction, Poetry, and Drama*, edited by Warren French, 187–97. Deland, Florida: Everet/Edwards, 1970.

Hoffman, Daniel. "Hunting a Master Image: The Poetry of Richard Eberhart." In *The Sounder Few: Essays from the Hollins Critic*, edited by R. H. W. Dillard, 61–82. Athens: University of Georgia Press, 1971.

Mills, Ralph J. "In the Fields of Imagination." *Parnassus* 1, no. 2 (1973): 211–24.

———. *Richard Eberhart*. Minneapolis: University of Minnesota Press, 1966.

Perkins, David. "Auden and Eberhart: Collected Poems." *Southern Review* 13 (1977): 728–38.

Roache, Joel E. *Richard Eberhart: The Progress of an American Poet*. New York: Oxford University Press, 1977.

LOUIS ZUKOFSKY

Ahearn, Barry. *Zukofsky's "A": An Introduction*. Berkeley: University of California Press, 1983.

Carruth, Hayden. "The Only Way to Get There from Here." *Journal of Modern Literature* 4 (1974): 88–90.

Corman, Cid. *The Transfigured Prose*. Orono: University of Maine Press, 1978.

Cox, Kenneth. "Louis Zukofsky." *Agenda* 16, no. 2 (1978): 11–13.

Hatlen, Burton. "Art and/as Labor: Some Dialectical Patterns in 'A'-1 through 'A'-10." *Contemporary Literature* 25 (1984): 205–34.

———. "Zukofsky, Wittgenstein, and the Poetics of Absence." *Sagetrieb* 1, no. 1 (Spring 1982): 63–93.

Heller, Michael. "The Poetry of Louis Zukofsky: To *Draw Speech*." *Origin* 1 (1983): 44–55.

Kenner, Hugh. "Bottom on Zukofsky." *MLN* 90 (1975): 921–22.

Paideuma 7, no. 3 (1978). "Louis Zukofsky special issue."

Sylvester, William. "Creeley, Duncan, Zukofsky 1968 — Melody Moves the Light." *Sagetrieb* 2, no. 1 (Spring 1983): 97–104.

Taggart, John. "Louis Zukofsky: 'Songs of Degrees.' " *Credences* 1, nos. 2–3 (1981–1982): 122–49.

Terrell, Carroll F., ed. *Louis Zukofsky, Man and Poet*. Orono, Maine: National Poetry Foundation, 1979.

Yannella, Phillip R. "On Louis Zukofsky." *Journal of Modern Literature* 4 (1974): 74–87.

Zukofsky, Celia, Hugh Seidman, Allen Ginsberg, and Robert Creeley. "A Commemorative Evening for Louis Zukofsky." *The American Poetry Review* 9, no. 1 (1982): 22–27.

STANLEY KUNITZ

Boyers, Robert. "Imagine Wrestling an Angel: An Interview with Stanley Kunitz." *Salmagundi* 22–23 (1973): 71–83.

Davis, Cynthia A. "Stanley Kunitz and the Transubstantial Word." *The Literary Review* 24, no. 3 (1981): 413–26.

———. "An Interview with Stanley Kunitz." *Contemporary Literature* 15 (1974): 1–14.

———. "Stanley Kunitz' 'The Testing Tree.' " *Contemporary Poetry* 8, no. 1 (1975): 43–46.

Henault, Marie. *Stanley Kunitz*. Boston: Twayne, 1980.

Moss, Stanley. "The Darkness of the Self." *Times Literary Supplement*, 30 May 1980, 621.

Orr, Gregory. "On: *The Poems of Stanley Kunitz (1928–1978)*." *American Poetry Review* 9, no. 4 (1980): 36–41.

———. *Stanley Kunitz: An Introduction to the Poetry*. New York: Columbia University Press, 1985.

Perloff, Marjorie G. "The Testing of Stanley Kunitz." *Iowa Review* 3, no. 1 (1972): 93–103.

Ryan, Michael. "An Interview with Stanley Kunitz." *Iowa Review* 5, no. 2 (1974): 76–85.

THEODORE ROETHKE

Bowers, Neal. *Theodore Roethke: The Journey from I to Otherwise*. Columbia: University of Missouri Press, 1982.

Bowers, Susan R. "The Explorers' Rose: Theodore Roethke's Mystical Symbol." *Contemporary Poetry* 13 (1979): 41–49.

Gardner, Thomas. "North American Sequence: Theodore Roethke and the Contemporary American Long Poem." *Essays in Literature* 11, no. 2 (1984): 237–52.

Heyen, William. "The Yeats Influence: Roethke's Formal Lyrics of the Fifties." *John Berryman Studies* 3, no. 4 (1977): 17–63.

LaBelle, Jenijoy. "Martyr to a Motion Not His Own: Theodore Roethke's Love Poems." *Ball State University Forum* 16, no. 2 (1975): 71–75.

———. "Out of the Cradle Endlessly Robbing: Whitman, Eliot, and Theodore Roethke." *Walt Whitman Review* 22 (1976): 75–84.

———. *The Echoing Wood of Theodore Roethke*. Princeton: Princeton University Press, 1976.

Lecourt, Jean-Phillipe. "Deconstruction and Reconstruction: Langage et Violence chez Theodore Roethke." In *Le Discours de la Violence dans la Culture Americain*, edited by Regis Durand. Lilles: Publishers de l'Universite de Lille III, 1979: 139–66.

Liberthson, Daniel. *The Quest for Being: Theodore Roethke, W.S. Merwin, and Ted Hughes*. New York: Gordon, 1977.

Nadel, Alan. "Roethke, Wilbur, and the Vision of the Child: Romantic and

Augustan in Modern Verse." *The Lion & The Unicorn* 2, no.1 (1978): 94–113.

Parini, Jay. *Theodore Roethke, An American Romantic*. Amherst: University of Massachusetts Press, 1979.

———. "Theodore Roethke: An American Romantic." *Texas Quarterly* 21, no. 4 (1978): 99–114.

———. "Theodore Roethke: The Poetics of Expression." *Ball State University Forum* 21, no. 1 (1980): 5–11.

Pinsker, Sanford. "An Urge to Wrestle/A Need to Dance: The Poetry of Theodore Roethke." *The College English Association Critic* 41, no. 4 (1979): 12–17.

Spanier, Sandra Whipple. "The Unity of the Greenhouse Sequence: Roethke's Portrait of the Artist." *Contemporary Poetry* 12 (1979): 53–60.

Vanderbilt, Kermit. "Theodore Roethke as a Northwest Poet." In *Northwest Perspectives: Essays on the Culture of the Pacific Northwest*, edited by Edwin R. Bingham and Glen A. Love. Seattle: University of Washington Press, 1979: 186–216.

Williams, Harry. *"The Edge Is What I Have": Theodore Roethke and After*. Lewisburg, Pa.: Bucknell University Press, 1977.

Wolff, George. *Theodore Roethke*. Boston: Twayne, 1981.

CHARLES OLSON

Aiken, William. "The Olson Poetics: Some Effects." *Contemporary Poetry* 3 (1978): 62–80.

Barua, Dikbakar. "One and Many: The Paradox of 'Methodology' in Charles Olson's *Maximus*." *Massachusetts Studies in English* 9, no. 1 (1983): 1–21.

Bernstein, Michael A. *The Tale of the Tribe: Ezra Pound and the Modern Verse Epic*. Princeton: Princeton University Press, 1980.

Bove, Paul A. *Destructive Poetics: Heidegger and Modern American Poety*. New York: Columbia University Press, 1980.

Butterick, George F. *A Guide to the Maximus Poems of Charles Olson*. Berkeley: University of California Press, 1978.

———. "Charles Olson and the Post-Modern Advance." *Iowa Review* 11, no. 4 (1980): 4–27.

Christensen, Paul. *Charles Olson: Call Him Ishmael*. Austin: University of Texas Press, 1979.

Creeley, Robert. " 'An Image of Man': Working Notes on Charles Olson's Concept of Person." *Iowa Review* 11, no. 4 (1980): 29–43.

Davidson, Michael. "Archaeologist of Morning: Charles Olson, Edward Dorn, and Historical Method." *English Literary History* 47 (1980): 158–79.

Dawson, Fielding. "On Olson, with references to GD." *Sagetrieb* 1, no. 1 (1982): 125–32.

Eggers, Philip. "Old Mother Smith: The Offshore Hero of Charles Olson's Counter-Epic." *Contemporary Poetry* 5 (1982): 30–44.

Golding, Alan. "Charles Olson's Metrical Thicket: Toward a Theory of Free-Verse Prosody." *Language and Style* 14 (1981): 64–78.

Hogg, Robert. "Okeanus Rages." *Sagetrieb* 3, no. 1 (1984): 89–104.

Hutchinson, George. "The Pleistocene in the Projective: Some of Olson's Sources." *American Literature* 54 (1982): 81–96.

Knapp, James F. "The Undivided World of Pleistocene Eden: Charles Olson's *Maximus*." *Cithara* 19, no. 2 (1980): 55–65.

Paul, Sherman. *Olson's Push: Olson, Black Mountain, and Recent American Poetry*. Baton Rouge: Louisiana State University Press, 1978.

Wong, Shelley. "Unfinished Business: The Writing of 'Tyrian Businesses.' " *Sagetrieb* 3, no. 3 (1984): 91–106.

ELIZABETH BISHOP

Bloom, Harold. "The Necessity of Misreading." *Georgia Review* 29 (1975): 267–88.

Bromwich, David. "Verse Chronicle." *Hudson Review* 30 (1977): 279–92.

———. "The Retreat from Romanticism." *Times Literary Supplement*, 8 July 1977, 831.

Estess, Sybil P. "The Delicate Art of Map Making." *Southern Review* 13 (1977): 705–27.

———. "Shelters for 'What is Within': Meditation and Epiphany in the Poetry of Elizabeth Bishop." *Modern Poetry Studies* 8 (1977): 50–60

Goldensohn, Lorrie. "Elizabeth Bishop's Originality." *American Poetry Review* 7, no. 2 (1978): 18–22.

Hollander, John. "Elizabeth Bishop's Mappings of Life." *Parnassus* 5 (1977): 359–66.

Liebowitz, Herbert. "The Elegant Maps of Elizabeth Bishop." *The New York Times Book Review* 126, 6 February 1977, 7

Merrill, James. "Elizabeth Bishop, 1911–1979." *The New York Review of Books* 26, 6 December 1979, 6

Perloff, Marjorie. "The Course of a Particular." *Modern Poetry Studies* 8 (1977): 177–92.

Pinsky, Robert. "Elizabeth Bishop, 1911–1979." *The New Republic* 181, 10 November 1979, 32

———. "The Idiom of a Self: Elizabeth Bishop and Wordsworth." *American Poetry Review* 9 (1980): 6–8.

Schwartz, Lloyd. "Elizabeth Bishop, 1911–1979." *The Boston Phoenix* (October 16, 1979).

———. "One Art: The Poetry of Elizabeth Bishop, 1971–1976." *Ploughshares* 3 (1977): 30–52.

Schwartz, Lloyd, and Sybil P. Estess, eds. *Elizabeth Bishop and Her Art*. Ann Arbor: University of Michigan Press, 1983.

Shore, Jane. "Elizabeth Bishop: The Art of Changing Your Mind." *Ploughshares* 5 (1979): 178–91.

Spiegelman, Willard. "Elizabeth Bishop's 'Natural Heroism.' " *Centennial Review* 22 (1978): 28–44.

J. V. CUNNINGHAM

Barth, R. L. "The Vacancies of Need: Particularities in J. V. Cunningham's 'To What Strangers, What Welcome.' " *Southern Review* 18 (1982): 286–98.

Baxter, John. "The Province of Plain Style." *Compass* 3 (1978): 15–37.

Carruth, Hayden. "A Location of J. V. Cunningham." *Michigan Quarterly Review* 11 (1972): 75–83.

Kay, Frances W. "The Writer as Desolation: J. V. Cunningham's 'To What Strangers, What Welcome.' " *Southern Review* 11 (1975): 820–24.

Oliver, Raymond. " 'The Scholar Is a Mere Conservative': The Criticism of J. V. Cunningham." *Southern Review* 15 (1979): 545–59.

Pinsky, Robert. "Two Examples of Poetic Discursiveness." *Chicago Review* 27, no. 2 (1975): 133–41.

Ramanan, Mohan G. "A Learned Grace: The Poetry of J. V. Cunningham." *International Journal of American Studies* 14, no. 1 (1984): 77–87.

Shapiro, Alan. " 'Far Lamps at': The Poetry of J. V. Cunningham." *Critical Inquiry* 9 (1983): 611–29.

Stall, Landon. "The Trivial, the Vulgar and Exalted: The Poems of J. V. Cunningham." *Southern Review* 9 (1973): 1044–48.

Stein, Robert A. "The Colleted Poems and Epigrams of J. V. Cunningham." *Western Humanities Review* 27 (1973): 1–12.

Taylor, Henry. "The Example of J. V. Cunningham." *The Hollins Critic* 20, no. 4 (1982): 1–13.

Winters, Yvor. *The Poetry of J. V. Cunningham.* Denver: Alan Swallow, 1961.

WILLIAM EVERSON (BROTHERS ANTONINUS)

Bartlett, Lee. "Creating the Autochthon: Kenneth Rexroth, William Everson, and *The Residual Years.*" *Sagetrieb* 2, no. 3 (1983): 57–69.

———. "God's Crooked Lines: William Everson and C. G. Jung." *Centennial Review* 27 (1983): 288–303.

———. ed. *Benchmark and Blaze: The Emergence of William Everson.* Metuchen, N.J.: Scarecrow, 1979.

Carpenter, David A. "William Everson: Peacemaker with Himself." *Contemporary Poetry* 13 (1980): 19–34.

Dill, Vicky Schreiber. "The Books of William Everson." *Books at Iowa* 28 (1978): 9–24.

Williamson, Alan. "Of Sexual Metaphysics." *Parnassus* 8, no. 1 (1980): 184–91.

ROBERT HAYDEN

Crawford, John. "Irony in Hayden's 'Middle Passage.' " *Notes on Contemporary Literature* 10, no. 1 (1980): 9.

Fetrow, Fred M. " 'Middle Passage': Robert Hayden's Anti-Epic." *CLA Journal* 22 (1979): 304–18.

———. *Robert Hayden.* Boston: Twayne, 1984.

———. "Robert Hayden's 'The Rag Man' and the Metaphysics of the Mundane." *Research Studies* 47 (1979): 188–90.

Hansell, William H. "The Spiritual Unity of Robert Hayden's *Angle of Ascent.*" *Black American Literature Forum* 13 (1979): 24–31.

Lewis, Richard O. "A Literary-Psychoanalytic Interpretation of Robert Hayden's 'Market.' " *Negro American Literature Forum* 9 (1975): 21–24.

Novak, Michael P. "Meditative, Ironic, Richly Human: The Poetry of Robert Hayden." *Midwest Quarterly* 15 (1974): 276–85.

Post, Constance J. "Image and Idea in the Poetry of Robert Hayden." *CLA Journal* 2 (1976): 164–75.

Potter, Vilma Raskin. "Reconsiderations and Reviews: A Remembrance for Robert Hayden, 1913–1980." *MELUS* 81, no. 1 (1981): 51–88.

Stepto, Robert B. "After Modernism, After Hibernation: Michael Harper, Robert Hayden, and Jay Wright." In *Chant of Saints*, edited by Robert Stepto and Michael Harper. Urbana: University of Illinois Press, 1979: 470–86.

Turco, Lewis. "*Angle of Ascent:* The Poetry of Robert Hayden." *Michigan Quarterly Review* 16 (1977): 199–219.

Wright, John S. "Homage to a Mystery Boy." *Georgia Review* 36 (1982): 904–11.

DAVID SCHUBERT

Quarterly Review of Literature: David Schubert; Works and Days. Princeton, N.J.: Quarterly Review, 1983.

DELMORE SCHWARTZ

Atlas, James. *Delmore Schwartz: The Life of an American Poet.* New York: Farrar, Straus & Giroux, 1977.

Dana, Robert. "Differences of Opinion." *New Letters* 48, no. 1 (1981): 116–19.

Deutsch, Robert H. "Delmore Schwartz: Middle Poems." *Contemporary Poetry* 2 (1969): 19–28.

Dike, Donald A. "A Case for Judgement: The Literary Criticism of Delmore Schwartz." *Twentieth Century Literature* 24 (1978): 492–509.

———. "The *Poetics* and the Criticism of Delmore Schwartz." *Notes on Modern American Literature* 1 (1977): Item 27.

Fraser, Russell. "Delmore Schwartz and the Death of the Poet." *Michigan Quarterly Review* 18 (1979): 592–605.

Knapp, James E. "Delmore Schwartz: Poet of the Orphic Journey." *Sewanee Review* 78 (1970): 506–16.

Lehman, David. "Delmore, Delmore: A Mournful Cheer." *Parnassus* 7 (1979): 215–30.

Lyons, Bonnie. "Delmore Schwartz and the Whole Truth." *Studies in Short Fiction* 14 (1977): 259–64.

McDougall, Richard. *Delmore Schwartz*. New York: Twayne, 1974.

Mazzaro, Jerome. " 'Delmore, Delmore.' " *Georgia Review* 33 (1979): 712–16.

Valenti, Lila L. "The Apprenticeship of Delmore Schwartz." *Twentieth Century Literature* 20 (1974): 201–16.

Zucker, David. "Self and History in Delmore Schwartz's Poetry and Criticism." *Iowa Review* 8, no. 4 (1977): 95–103.

JOHN BERRYMAN

Bayley, John. "John Berryman: A Question of Imperial Sway." *Salmagundi* 22–23 (1973): 84–102.

Bloom, James D. *The Stock of Available Reality: R. P. Blackmur and John Berryman*. Lewisburg, Pa.: Bucknell University Press, 1984.

Conarroe, Joel. *John Berryman: An Introduction to the Poetry*. New York: Columbia University Press, 1977.

Haffenden, John. *John Berryman: A Critical Commentary*. London: Macmillan, 1980.

Hahn, Robert. "Berryman's *Dream Songs:* Missing Poet beyond the Poetry." *Missouri Review* 23, no. 1 (1982): 117–28.

Hickey, Dona. "John Berryman and the Art of *The Dream Songs*." *Chicago Review* 32, no. 4 (1981): 34–43.

Hoffman, Steven K. "Lowell, Berryman, Roethke, and Ginsberg: The Communal Function of Confessional Poetry." *The Literary Review* 22 (1979): 329–41.

Hudgins, Andrew. " 'I Am Fleeing Double: Duality and Dialectic in *The Dream Songs*." *Missouri Review* 4, no. 2 (1980–1981): 93–110.

McGuire, Jerry. "John Berryman: Making a Poet of the Self." *Modern Poetry Studies* 10, nos. 2–3 (1981): 174–89.

North, Michael. "The Public Monument and Public Poetry: Stevens, Berryman, and Lowell." *Contemporary Literature* 21 (1980): 267–85.

Siegel, Muffy E. A. " 'The Original Crime': John Berryman's Iconic Grammar." *Poetics Today* 2, no. 1a (1980): 163–88.

Simpson, Eileen B. *Poets in Their Youth*. New York: Random House, 1982.

Stitt, Peter. "John Berryman's Literary Criticism." *Southern Review* 14 (1978): 368–74.

Weiser, David K. "Berryman's *Sonnets:* In and Out of the Tradition." *American Literature* 55 (1983): 388–404.

Wyatt, David M. "Completing the Picture: Williams, Berryman, and 'Spatial Form.' " *Colby Library Quarterly* 13 (1977): 246–62.

RANDALL JARRELL

Beck, Charlotte H. "The Rilkean Spirit in the Poetry of Randall Jarrell." *Southern Literary Journal* 12, no. 1 (1979): 3–17.

———. "Randall Jarrell and Robert Penn Warren: Fugitive Fugitives." *Southern Literary Journal* 17, no. 1 (1984): 82–91.

Bottoms, David. "The Messy Humanity of Randall Jarrell: His Poetry in the Eighties." *South Carolina Review* 17, no. 1 (1984): 82–95.

Ferguson, Suzanne. "Narrative and Narrators in the Poetry of Randall Jarrell." *South Carolina Review* 17, no. 1 (1984): 72–82.

———. *Critical Essays on Randall Jarrell.* Boston: G. K. Hall, 1983.

Fowler, Russel T. "Charting the 'Lost World': Rilke's Influence on Randall Jarrell." *Twentieth Century Literature* 30 (1984): 100–122.

Funkhouser, Linda Bradley. "Acoustic Rhythm in Randall Jarrell's 'The Death of the Ball Turret Gunner.' " *Poetics* 8 (1979): 381–403.

Lensing, George. "The Modernism of Randall Jarrell." *South Carolina Review* 17, no. 1 (1984): 52–60.

Meyers, Jeffrey. "Randall Jarrell: The Paintings in the Poems." *Southern Review* 20 (1984): 300–315.

Miklitsch, Robert. "The Critic as Poet, Poet as Critic: Randall Jarrell, Deconstruction, and 'Dirty Silence.' " *American Poetry* 1, no. 2 (1984): 35–48.

Moran, Ronald. "Randall Jarrell as Critic of Criticism." *South Carolina Review* 17, no. 1 (1984): 60–65.

Quinn, Bernetta. "Randall Jarrell and the Angels: The Search for Immortality." *South Carolina Review* 17, no. 1 (1984): 65–71.

———. *Randall Jarrell.* Boston: Twayne, 1981.

WELDON KEES

Baxter, Charles. "What Ever Happened to Weldon Kees?" *Minnesota Review* 3 (1972): 122–26.

Gioia, Dana. "The Achievement of Weldon Kees." *Sequoia* 29 (1979): 25–46.

———. "Introduction." In *The Ceremony and Other Stories*. Port Washington, Wash.: Graywolf, 1984.

Justice, Donald. "Preface." In *The Collected Poems of Weldon Kees*. Lincoln: University of Nebraska Press, 1967.

Knoll, Robert E. "Weldon Kees: Solipsist as Poet." *Prairie Schooner* 35 (1961): 33–41.

Libera, Sharon Mayer. "The Disappearance of Weldon Kees." *Ploughshares* 15 (1977): 147–59.

Mangione, Jerre. *The Dream and the Deal: The Federal Writer's Project*. Boston: Little, Brown, 1972.

Nemerov, Howard. "The Poetry of Weldon Kees." In *Poetry and Fiction: Essays*. New Brunswick, N.J.: Rutgers University Press, 1963.

Rexroth, Kenneth. "Weldon Kees." In *Assays*. Norfolk, Conn.: New Directions, 1961.

Ross, William T. *Weldon Kees*. Boston: Twayne, 1985.

Sequoia 23 no. 2 (Spring 1979). "Weldon Kees special issue."

ROBERT LOWELL

Agenda 18, no. 3 "Robert Lowell special issue."

Anzilotti, Rolando. *Robert Lowell: A Tribute*. Pisa: Nistri-Lischi Editori, 1979.

Barry, Jackson G. "Robert Lowell's 'Confessional' Image of an Age: Theme and Language in Poetic Form." *Ariel* 12, no. 1 (1981): 51–57.

Bayley, John. "Moment after Moment: *Day by Day* by Robert Lowell." In *Selected Essays* by John Bayley, 45–50. Cambridge: Cambridge University Press, 1984.

———. "The Morality of Form in the Poetry of Robert Lowell." *Ariel* 9, no. 1 (1978): 3–17.

Bell, Vereen M. *Robert Lowell: Nihilist as Hero*. Cambridge: Harvard University Press, 1983.

Donoghue, Denis. *Connoisseurs of Chaos: Ideas of Order in Modern American Poetry*. New York: Columbia University Press, 1984.

Dubrow, Heather. "The Marine in the Garden: Pastoral Elements in Lowell's 'Quaker Graveyard.' " *Philological Quarterly* 62 (1983): 127–45.

Haffenden, John. "The Last Parnassian: Robert Lowell." *Agenda* 16, no. 2 (1978): 40–46.

Hamilton, Ian. *Robert Lowell: A Biography*. New York: Random House, 1982.

Kazin, Alfred. "Robert Lowell and John Ashbery: The Difference between Poets." *Esquire*, January 1978, 20–22.

Lane, Lauriate, Jr. "Robert Lowell: The Problems and Power of Allusion." *Dalhousie Review* 60 (1980–81): 697–702.

Pinsker, Sanford. "John Berryman and Robert Lowell: The Middle Generation, Reconsidered." *The Literary Review* 27 (1984): 252–61.

Procopiow, Norma. " 'Day by Day': Lowell's Poetic of Imitation." *Ariel* 14, no. 1 (1983): 5–14.

Rosenthal, M. L., and Sally M. Gall. *The Modern Poetic Sequence: The Genius of Modern Poetry*. New York: Oxford University Press, 1983.

Rudman, Mark. *Robert Lowell: An Introduction to the Poetry*. New York: Columbia University Press, 1983.

Shaw, Robert B. "Lowell in the Seventies." *Contemporary Literature* 23 (1982): 515-27.

FRANK O'HARA

Altieri, Charles. "The Significance of Frank O'Hara." *The Iowa Review* 4, no. 1 (1973): 90–104.

Blasing, Mutlu Konuk. "Frank O'Hara's Poetics of Speech: The Example of 'Biotherm.' " *Contemporary Literature* 23 (1982): 52–64.

Feldman, Alan. *Frank O'Hara*. Boston: Twayne, 1979.

Holahan, Susan. "Frank O'Hara's Poetry." In *American Poetry since 1960 — Some Critical Perspectives*, edited by Robert B. Shaw, 109–22. Chester Springs, Pa.: Dufour, 1974.

Libby, Anth. "O'Hara on the Silver Range." *Contemporary Literature* 17 (1976): 240–62.

Molesworth, Charles. " 'The Clear Architecture of the Nerves': The Poetry of Frank O'Hara." *Iowa Review* 6, nos. 3–4 (1975): 61–74.

Perloff, Marjorie G. " 'Transparent Selves': The Poetry of John Ashbery and Frank O'Hara." *Yearbook of English Studies* 8 (1978): 171–96.

———. "Frank O'Hara and the Aesthetics of Attention." *boundary 2* 4 (1976): 779–806.

———. "In Favor of One's Time (1954–1961): Frank O'Hara." *The American Poetry Review* 6, no. 3 (1977): 6–16.

———. *Frank O'Hara: A Critical Introduction*. New York: Braziller, 1977.

———. *Frank O'Hara, Poet among Painters*. New York: Braziller, 1977.

Replogle, Justin. "Vernacular Poetry: Frost to O'Hara." *Twentieth Century Literature* 24 (1978): 137–53.

Skoller, Eleanor Honig. "Franked Letters: Crossing the Bar." *Visible Language: The Research Journal Concerned with All that is Involved in Our Being Literate* 14, no. 3 (1980): 306–19.

Vendler, Helen. "The Virtues of the Alterable." *Parnassus* 1, no. 1 (1972): 5–20.

ANNE SEXTON

George, Diana Hume. "Anne Sexton's Suicide Poems." *Journal of Popular Culture* 18, no. 2 (1984): 17–31.

———. "Beyond the Pleasure Principle: Anne Sexton's 'The Death Baby.' " *University of Hartford Studies in Literature* 15, no. 2 (1983): 75–92.

Johnson, Greg. "The Achievement of Anne Sexton." *The Hollins Critic* 21, no. 3 (1984): 1–13.

Johnson, Rosemary. "The Woman of Private (but Published) Hungers." *Parnassus* 8, no. 1 (1980): 92–107.

Juhasz, Susanne. "Seeking the Exit or the Home: Poetry and Salvation in the Career of Anne Sexton." In *Shakespeare's Sister's: Feminist Essays on Women Poets*, edited by Sandra M. Gilbert and Susan Gubar, 261–68. Bloomington: Indiana University Press, 1979.

Markey, Janice. *A New Tradition?: The Poetry of Sylvia Plath, Anne Sexton, and Adrienne Rich: A Study of Feminism and Poetry.* Frankfurt am Main: P. Lang, 1985.

Middlebrook, Diane Wood. "Housewife into Poet: the Apprenticeship of Anne Sexton." *New England Quarterly* 56, no. 4 (1983): 483–503.

————. "Becoming Anne Sexton." *Denver Quarterly* 18, no. 4 (1984): 23–34.

Notes on Modern American Literature 3, no. 3 (1979). "Anne Sexton special issue."

Ostriker, Alicia. " 'What Are Patterns For': Anger and Polarization in Women's Poetry." *Feminist Studies* 10 (1984): 485–503.

————. "That Story: Anne Sexton and Her Transformations." *The American Poetry Review* 11, no. 4 (1982): 11–16.

Pritchard, William H. "The Anne Sexton Show." *Hudson Review* 31 (1978): 387–92.

Stark, Myra. "Walt Whitman and Anne Sexton: A Note on the Uses of Tradition." *Notes on Contemporary Literature* 8, no. 4 (1978): 7–8.

Tanenhaus, Beverly. "Politics of Suicide and Survival: The Poetry of Anne Sexton and Adrienne Rich." *Bucknell Review* 24, no. 1 (1978): 106–18.

Wegs, Joyce M. "Poets in Bedlam: Sexton's Use of Bishop's 'Visits to St. Elizabeths' in 'Ringing the Bells.' " *Contemporary Poetry* 15 (1982): 37–47.

SYLVIA PLATH

Alexander, Paul, ed. *Ariel Ascending: Writings about Sylvia Plath.* New York: Harper & Row, 1985.

Annas, Pamela J. "The Self in the World: The Social Context of Sylvia Plath's Late Poems." *Women's Studies* 7 (1980): 171–83.

Beirne, Daniel J. "Plath's 'Two Campers in Cloud Country.' " *Explicator* (Fall 1983): 61–62.

Broe, Mary Lynn. *Protean Poetic: The Poetry of Sylvia Plath.* Columbia: University of Missouri Press, 1980.

Bundtzen, Linda K. *Plath's Incarnations: Woman and the Creative Process.* Ann Arbor: University of Michigan Press, 1983.

Coyle, Susan. "Images of Madness and Retrieval: An Exploration of Metaphor in *The Bell Jar.*" *Studies in American Fiction* (Autumn 1984): 161–74.

Dutta, Ujjal. "Poetry as Performance: A Reading of Sylvia Plath." *Literary Criterion* 16 (1981): 1–11.

Furomoto, Atsuko. "An Approach to the World of Sylvia Plath—Through the 'Mirrors.' " *Studies in English Literature* 58 (1981): 75–88.

Gilbert, Sandra M. "Teaching Plath's 'Daddy' to Speak to Undergraduates." *ADE Bulletin* 76 (1983): 38–42.

McClave, Heather. "Sylvia Plath: Troubled Bones." *New England Review* 2 (1980): 447–65.

Moramarco, Fred. " 'Burned-up Intensity': The Suicidal Poetry of Sylvia Plath." *Mosaic* 15, no. 1 (1982): 141–51.

Morris, Christopher. "Order and Chaos in Plath's 'The Colossus.' " *Concerning Poetry* 15 (1982): 33–42.

Rosen, Lois. "Sylvia Plath's Poetry about Children: A New Perspective." *Modern Poetry Studies* 10 (1981): 98–115.

Sanazaro, Leonard. "The Transfiguring Self: Sylvia Plath, a Reconsideration." *Centennial Review* 27 (1983): 62–74.

Skei, Hans H. "Sylvia Plath's 'Lady Lazarus': An Interpretation." *Edda* 81 (1981): 233–44.

Uroff, Margaret D. "Sylvia Plath's Narrative Strategies." *Iowa Review* 13, no. 2 (1982): 1–14.

Van Dyne, Susan. "Fueling the Phoenix Fire: The Manuscripts of Plath's 'Lady Lazarus.' " *Massachusetts Review* 24 (1983): 395–410.

Wagner, Linda, ed. *Critical Essays on Sylvia Plath*. Boston: G. K. Hall, 1984.

Acknowledgments

" 'The Repressed Becomes the Poem': Landscape and Quest in Two Poems by Louise Bogan" by Sandra Cookson from *Critical Essays on Louise Bogan*, edited by Martha Collins, © 1984 by Martha Collins. Reprinted by permission of G. K. Hall & Co., Boston.

"The Literary Journey of Melvin B. Tolson" (originally entitled "Afterword") by Robert M. Farnsworth from *A Gallery of Harlem Portraits by Melvin B. Tolson*, edited by Robert M. Farnsworth, © 1979 by the Curators of the University of Missouri. Reprinted by permission of the University of Missouri Press.

"Yvor Winters: What He Did" by Robert Hass from *Twentieth Century Pleasures: Prose on Poetry* by Robert Hass, © 1984 by Robert Hass. Reprinted by permission of the publisher, Ecco Press.

"On Edwin Denby" by Lincoln Kirstein from *The Complete Poems of Edwin Denby*, edited by Ron Padgett, © 1983 by Lincoln Kirstein. Reprinted by permission of the author and Random House, Inc. This essay originally appeared in *The New York Review of Books*.

"Blackmur at Poetry" by Russell Fraser from *Salmagundi*, nos. 44–45 (Spring/Summer 1979), © 1979 by Skidmore College. Reprinted by permission.

"Richard Eberhart: Reading God's Fingerprints" by Richard K. Cross from *Concerning Poetry* 12, no. 1 (Spring 1979), © 1979 by Western Washington University. Reprinted by permission of the author and Western Washington University Press.

"Louis Zukofsky: Eiron *Eyes*" (originally entitled "Eiron *Eyes*") by William Harmon from *Parnassus: Poetry in Review* 7, no. 2 (Spring/Summer

1979), © 1980 by Poetry in Review Foundation. Reprinted by permission.

"Stanley Kunitz: The Stubborn Middle Way" by Robert Weisberg from *Modern Poetry Studies* 6 (1975), © 1975 by Robert Weisberg. Reprinted by permission.

" 'Songs of a Happy Man': The Poetry of Theodore Roethke" by Charles Molesworth from *The Fierce Embrace* by Charles Molesworth, © 1979 by the Curators of the University of Missouri. Reprinted by permission of the University of Missouri Press.

"Theodore Roethke: Death and Rebirth in a Modern Landscape" (originally entitled "Death and Rebirth in a Modern Landscape") by James Applewhite from *Seas and Inland Journeys* by James Applewhite, © 1985 by the University of Georgia Press. Reprinted by permission of the University of Georgia Press.

"Charles Olson: Violets and Bridge-Work" (originally entitled "Epilogue: Violets and Bridge-Work") by Sherman Paul from *Olson's Push: Origin, Black Mountain, and Recent American Poetry* by Sherman Paul, © 1978 by Louisiana State University Press. Reprinted by permission of Louisiana State University Press.

"Pushing Olson" by Calvin Bedient from *Parnassus: Poetry in Review* 7, no. 2 (Spring/Summer 1979), © 1980 by Poetry in Review Foundation. Reprinted by permission.

"Vision and Mastery in Elizabeth Bishop" by Bonnie Costello from *Twentieth Century Literature* 28, no. 4 (Winter 1982), © 1983 by Hofstra University Press. Reprinted by permission.

"Elizabeth Bishop's Dream Houses" by David Bromwich from *Raritan: A Quarterly Review* 4, no. 1 (1984), © 1984 by *Raritan: A Quarterly Review*, New Brunswick, New Jersey. Reprinted by permission of *Raritan: A Quarterly Review*.

"J. V. Cunningham's Roman Voices" by Jack Hill from *Modern American Poetry*, edited by R. W. (Herbie) Butterfield, © 1984 by Vision Press Ltd. Reprinted by permission of Vision Press Ltd., London and Barnes & Noble Books, Totowa, New Jersey.

"William Everson (Brother Antoninus): The Inner War" (originally entitled "The Inner War") by Paul A. Lacey from *Benchmark and Blaze: The Emergence of William Everson*, edited by Lee Bartlett, © 1979 by Lee Barlett. Reprinted by permission of the Fortress Press.

"Covenant of Timelessness and Time: Symbolism and History in Robert Hayden's *Angle of Ascent*" by Wilburn Williams, Jr. from *Chant of Saints: A Gathering of Afro-American Literature, Art, and Scholarship*, edited by

Michael S. Harper and Robert B. Stepto, © 1979 Wilburn Williams, Jr. Reprinted by permission. This essay originally appeared in *The Massachusetts Review* 18 (Winter 1977). Reprinted by permission.

"Homage to Schubert the Poet" by Irvin Ehrenpreis from *Quarterly Review of Literature: David Schubert, Works and Days* (40th Anniversary Issue), © 1983 by *Quarterly Review of Literature*. Reprinted by permission.

"Spoils of Joy: The Poetry of Delmore Schwartz" (originally entitled "The Way Out: The Poetry of Delmore Schwartz and Others") by R. K. Meiners from *The Southern Review* 7 (New Series), no. 1 (January 1971), © 1971 by R. K. Meiners. Reprinted by permission.

"How to Read Berryman's *Dream Songs*" by Edward Mendelson from *American Poetry Since 1960: Some Critical Perspectives*, edited by Robert B. Shaw, © 1973 by Edward Mendelson. Reprinted by permission.

"John Berryman: Near the Top a Bad Turn Dared" (originally entitled "Near the Top a Bad Turn Dared") by Diane Ackerman from *Parnassus: Poetry in Review* 7, no. 2 (Spring/Summer 1979), © 1980 by Poetry in Review Foundation. Reprinted by permission.

"Randall Jarrell: The Man Who Painted Bulls" (originally entitled "The Man Who Painted Bulls") by Mary Kinzie from *The Southern Review* 16, no. 4 (October 1980), © 1980, 1987 by Mary Kinzie. Reprinted by permission.

"Weldon Kees: The Ghost of American Poetry" by Charles Baxter from *A Book of Rereadings in Recent American Poetry*, edited by Greg Kuzma, © 1979 by Greg Kuzma. Reprinted by permission of the editor and the publisher, Best Cellar Press.

"Robert Lowell: The Life of Allegory" (originally entitled "Robert Lowell") by Anthony Hecht from *Obbligati: Essays in Criticism* by Anthony Hecht, © 1986 by Anthony Hecht. Reprinted by permission of the author and Atheneum Publishers.

"History's Autobiography: Robert Lowell" by Alfred Corn from *The Metamorphoses of Metaphor: Essays in Poetry and Fiction* by Alfred Corn, © 1987 by Alfred Corn. An Elizabeth Sifton Book. Reprinted by permission of Viking Penguin, Inc.

"Frank O'Hara: Glistening Torsos, Sandwiches and Coca-Cola" (originally entitled "Glistening Torsos, Sandwiches and Coca-Cola") by Thomas Meyer from *Parnassus: Poetry in Review* 6, no. 1 (Fall/Winter 1977), © 1978 by Poetry in Review Foundation. Reprinted by permission.

"Anne Sexton: 'Some Tribal Female Who Is Known But Forbidden' " by Richard Howard from *Alone With America: Essays on the Art of Poetry in the United States Since 1950* by Richard Howard, © 1980 by Richard Howard. Reprinted by permission.

"Sylvia Plath: 'And I Have No Face, I Have Wanted to Efface Myself' " by Richard Howard from *Alone with America: Essays on the Art of Poetry in the United States Since 1950* by Richard Howard, © 1980 by Richard Howard. Reprinted by permission.

Index